Petrarch in Romantic England

Also by Edoardo Zuccato

COLERIDGE IN ITALY
THE RECEPTION OF S. T. COLERIDGE IN EUROPE (co-editor with
  Elinor Shaffer)

Petrarch in Romantic England

Edoardo Zuccato

First published 2008 by
PALGRAVE MACMILLAN
Houndmills, Basingstoke, Hampshire RG21 6XS and
175 Fifth Avenue, New York, N.Y. 10010
Companies and representatives throughout the world

PALGRAVE MACMILLAN is the global academic imprint of the Palgrave
Macmillan division of St. Martin's Press, LLC and of Palgrave Macmillan Ltd.
Macmillan® is a registered trademark in the United States, United Kingdom
and other countries. Palgrave is a registered trademark in the European
Union and other countries.

ISBN-13: 978—0—230—54260—0   hardback
ISBN-10: 0—230—54260—3   hardback

This book is printed on paper suitable for recycling and made from fully
managed and sustained forest sources. Logging, pulping and manufacturing
processes are expected to conform to the environmental regulations of the
country of origin.

A catalogue record for this book is available from the British Library.

Library of Congress Cataloging-in-Publication Data

Zuccato, Edoardo.
  Petrarch in romantic England / Edoardo Zuccato.
      p. cm.
  Includes bibliographical references and index.
  ISBN 0—230—54260—3 (alk. paper)
  1. Petrarca, Francesco, 1304—1374—Influence.   2. Petrarca,
    Francesco, 1304—1374—Appreciation—England.   3. English
    literature—Italian influence.   4. English literature—18th
    century—History and criticism.   I. Title.
  PQ4537.E5Z823 2005
  851'.1—dc22   2008011822

10   9   8   7   6   5   4   3   2   1
17   16   15   14   13   12   11   10   09   08

Printed and bound in Great Britain by
CPI Antony Rowe, Chippenham and Eastbourne

Contents

Acknowledgements

A part of Chapter 1 of this book appeared in a different form in my article 'Writing Petrarch's Biography: From Susanna Dobson (1775) to Alexander Fraser Tytler (1810)', in *British Romanticism and Italian Literature*, ed. L. Bandiera and D. Saglia (Rodopi, 2005). I am grateful to the publisher for allowing me to use it. In addition, the author and publishers wish to thank the following for permission to reproduce copyright material: Oxford University Press for *The Poems of Charlotte Smith*, ed. S. Curran (1993); Harvard University Press for *Petrarch's Lyric Poems: The* Rime sparse *and Other Poems*, trans. and ed. R. M. Durling (© 1976 by R. M. Durling, rptd 2001); Mondadori for F. Petrarca, *Canzoniere*, ed. M. Santagata (2004). Every effort has been made to trace rights holders, but if any have been inadvertently overlooked the publishers would be pleased to make the necessary arrangements at the first opportunity.

This book was begun 12 years ago and has come to completion with the help of several institutions and friends, who generously made research material available or gave me useful advice. Heartfelt thanks are due to Angela Bruschi, Julia Flanders and the Women Writers' Research Project (Brown University), Roger Meyenberg, Uberto Motta, Chiara Prada, Giovanni Moscati, and all the staff of IULM University Library and the British Library. Special thanks are due to Tim Parks, Janice Giffin and Frances Hotimsky, who gave me some valuable advice, and to Jim Mays, whose generosity and learning have been as precious as ever. The project could not have been developed without the research grants of IULM University, Milan; equally important was the encouragement I received from some of its senior members, in particular Patrizia Nerozzi, Sergio Pautasso and Gianni Puglisi. Last, but not least, my gratitude is due to my family – my parents Nando and Nanda, my sister Barbara, and Rosi – and to Annalisa, who supported and encouraged me throughout.

Abbreviations

Anti-Jacobin	*Poetry of the Anti-Jacobin, 1799* (Oxford and New York: Woodstock, 1991)
AR (CC)	S. T. Coleridge, *Aids to Reflection*, ed. J. Beer (London: Routledge; Princeton: Princeton University Press, 1993)
BC	*The Browning Collections: A Reconstruction with Other Memorabilia*, compiled by P. Kelley and B. A. Coley ([Waco, TX]: Armstrong Browning Library of Baylor University; London: Mansell, 1984)
BL (CC)	S. T. Coleridge, *Biographia Literaria or Biographical Sketches of My Literary Life and Opinions*, ed. J. Engell and W. J. Bate, 2 vols (London: Routledge & Kegan Paul; Princeton: Princeton University Press, 1983)
BLJ	*Byron's Letters and Journals*, ed. L. A. Marchand, 12 vols (London: Murray, 1973–82)
CC	*The Collected Works of Samuel Taylor Coleridge*, gen. ed. K. Coburn (London: Routledge; Princeton: Princeton University Press, 1969–2001)
CL	*Collected Letters of Samuel Taylor Coleridge*, ed. E. L. Griggs, 6 vols (Oxford: Clarendon Press, 1956–71)
CLP	'Capel Lofft Page', ed. Roger Meyenberg, <www.rhone.ch/rogerm/lofft.html>
CM (CC)	S. T. Coleridge, *Marginalia*, ed. G. Whalley (vols III–VI with H. J. Jackson), 6 vols (London: Routledge; Princeton: Princeton University Press, 1980–2001)
CN	*The Notebooks of Samuel Taylor Coleridge*, ed. K. Coburn and A. J. Harding, 5 vols (Princeton: Princeton University Press, 1957–2002)
DNB	*Dictionary of National Biography*, 1885–
EB	*Encyclopædia Britannica*, 3rd edn, 18 vols (Edinburgh: Bell & MacFarquhar, 1797)
EOT (CC)	S. T. Coleridge, *Essays on his Times, in The Morning Post and The Courier*, ed. D. V. Erdman, 3 vols (London: Routledge & Kegan Paul; Princeton: Princeton University Press, 1978)
Fiori	*I Fiori del Parnasso Italiano; ovvero una Raccolta di Rime Estratta dall'Opere de' più Celebri Poeti Italiani – Extracts from the Works of the Most Celebrated Italian Poets. With Translations by Admired English Authors* (London: Rivington & Hatchard, 1798)
Florence	*The Florence Miscellany* (Florence, 1785)

Friend (CC)	S. T. Coleridge, *The Friend*, ed. B. E. Rooke, 2 vols (London: Routledge & Kegan Paul; Princeton: Princeton University Press, 1969)
Histoire	P. L. Ginguené, *Histoire littéraire d'Italie*, 9 vols (Paris: Frères, 1811–19)
Laura	C. Lofft (ed.) *Laura: or An Anthology of Sonnets (on the Petrarchan Model,) and Elegiac Quatorzains: English, Italian, Spanish, Portuguese, French, and German*, 5 vols (London: Taylor, 1813–14) (cited by volume and poem number)
Lects 1808–1819 (CC)	S. T. Coleridge, *Lectures 1818–1819: On Literature*, ed. R. A. Foakes, 2 vols (London: Routledge; Princeton: Princeton University Press, 1987)
Life	*The Life of Petrarch, Collected from Memoirs pour la vie de Petrarch*, trans. S. Dobson, 2 vols (London: Buckland, 1775)
LS (CC)	S. T. Coleridge, *Lay Sermons*, ed. R. J. White (London: Routledge & Kegan Paul; Princeton: Princeton University Press, 1972)
Mémoires	J. F. P. A. de Sade *Mémoires pour la vie de François Pétrarque, tirés de ses œuvres et des auteurs contemporains; Avec des Notes ou Dissertations, et les Pieces justificatives*, 3 vols (Amsterdam: Arskée et Mercus, 1764)
P Lects (CC)	S. T. Coleridge, *Lectures 1818–1819: On the History of Philosophy*, ed. J. R. de J. Jackson, 2 vols (Princeton: Princeton University Press, 2000)
PC	F. Petrarca, *Canzoniere*, nuova edizione aggiornata, ed. M. Santagata (Milan: Mondadori, 2004) (cited by poem number)
PEL	*Poems by Eminent Ladies*, vol. II (London: Baldwin, 1755)
Prose	F. Petrarca, *Prose*, ed. G. Martellotti, P. G. Ricci, E. Carrara and E. Bianchi (Milan and Naples: Ricciardi, 1955)
PW BLC	*The Poetical Works of Bowles, Lamb, and Hartley Coleridge*, ed. William Tirebuck (London and Newcastle: Walter Scott, 1887)
PW (CC)	S. T. Coleridge, *Poetical Works*, ed. J. C. C. Mays, 3 vols (Princeton: Princeton University Press, 2001)
Sappho	M. Robinson, *Sappho and Phaon*, in Robinson 2000a
SW&F (CC)	S. T. Coleridge, *Shorter Works and Fragments*, ed. H. J. Jackson and J. R. de J. Jackson, 2 vols (London: Routledge; Princeton: Princeton University Press, 1995)
TBC	*The Brownings' Correspondence*, ed. P. Kelley and R. Hudson (Winfield, KS: Wedgestone Press, 1984–)

Introduction

Petrarca
is again
in sight
Paul Celan

Petrarch in Romantic England? Surely that must be a misprint for Renaissance England. Few readers, or even scholars, would think of Romanticism as a Petrarchan age. And they would be right for every European country except England. The Petrarchan revival in late eighteenth-century England was a unique phenomenon which involved an impressive number of scholars, translators and poets. Its effects on poetry, fiction and scholarship were manifold and continued to make themselves felt right up to the 1830s. Though a small number of Romanticists are indeed aware of the length and depth of this fashion, a complete study of its impact on literary culture has never been attempted.

The importance of Petrarch for the Romantic age has been obscured by other writers, like Dante and Sappho, whose revivals have long been considered more relevant. So much has been written on the Romantic rediscovery of Dante that even scholars often forget that at the turn of the century he was far less popular than Petrarch. There are several reasons for this forgetfulness. In the first place, the influence of Dante was crucial for all of the Canonic Six with the exception of Wordsworth who disliked the Italian poet. The reception of Dante has been studied in several excellent essays, but his influence looks significantly less important when compared to the reception of Petrarch in the same period.

It is striking that virtually all the best women poets of the time were involved in the revival of Petrarch and the sonnet, whereas they generally disliked Dante.[1] While Dante was a territory for males only, Petrarch attracted men and women alike. A comparative analysis of the translations and imitations from Petrarch, which have so far languished in the wasteland of minor verse, will help us define the character of those versions made by women poets. The situation looks strangely similar to the sixteenth century, when both men and women were involved in a Petrarchan vogue, interpreting source texts in very different ways.

Dante and Petrarch offered not only two alternative poetics; they were two radically different types of poet and intellectual. Dante was a major model of the prophet-poet; Petrarch was a model of the scholar-poet and melancholy lover. Dante was a politician and an exile, a man of ideological certainties and unshakable principles; Petrarch was a friend of many princes, a well-to-do scholar who knew how to arrive at a reasonable compromise with political power. It is easy to understand why, after the French Revolution, many male Romantics identified with Dante and denigrated Petrarch. On the other hand, it is natural that most women poets preferred Petrarch to a masculine, muscular figure like Dante. It took almost a century before, largely thanks to the Pre-Raphaelite Brotherhood, Dante and Beatrice replaced Petrarch and Laura as the most popular couple of medieval lovers. The meaning of Rossetti's revival of *stilnovo* and pre-Petrarchan poetry cannot be fully understood if we know little or nothing – as we have done so far – about the Petrarchan fashion which preceded it.

The images of Dante as an indomitable fighter for justice and Petrarch as an erudite weakling, of Dante as emphatically masculine and Petrarch as effeminate, are inseparable from the idea that Dante had a lot to say about everything, whereas Petrarch was monotonous and limited. Hostile readers have always stressed that Petrarch was an excellent stylist who could only talk of himself, an idea repeated over the centuries by many formalist scholars of different schools. This view is quite astonishing if we consider the role of Petrarch in Italian and European culture. As Nicola Gardini points out, Petrarch and Petrarchism played the central role in establishing the norms of sexual behaviour in Italian culture. No less. Gardini recalls that Petrarch's heterosexuality was defined as 'a form of terrorism' by Pier Paolo Pasolini, a gay writer who was implicitly comparing it to the bisexuality of many Greek, Latin and Middle Eastern love poets.[2] So it was not just that the form of Petrarch's poems established a stylistic norm over several centuries; equally crucially their content fixed an influential norm which is still far from obsolete. Petrarch is not as varied a writer as Dante, but he is far from being a poet with no content.

What kind of role did Petrarch play in England? Of course, here Petrarchism was not as influential as in Italy. In England a function of the same kind was performed by the eighteenth-century novel. However, the role of the Petrarchan tradition is far from negligible. There is Renaissance Petrarchism, which was pivotal in the formation of English lyric, though it was nearly forgotten by the mid-eighteenth century; and there is the eighteenth-century revival of Petrarch, whose important role in the poetry of Sensibility and Romanticism has remained largely undefined.

Certainly, few of the eighteenth-century British Petrarchans were attracted only by Petrarch's style. They took the content of *Canzoniere* very seriously, even though they tended to concentrate on certain aspects of Petrarch's poetry at the expense of the rest. Their approach was mainly biographical and focused on a limited number of Petrarch's love poems. What they liked most of all was the romantic Petrarch, the poems where a lovelorn 'I' meditates alone while wandering in the countryside. Sonnets like 'Solo et pensoso', 'Vago augelletto', 'Quel rosignuol', and above all 'Zephiro torna' were the core of Romantic Petrarchism, even though moral meditations like 'Voi ch'ascoltate' and 'La gola e 'l somno' were also popular.

Such interest in the poems cannot be separated from an attention to Petrarch's life. The great popularity of biographies and essays like Susanna Dobson's *Life of Petrarch*, which gave momentum to the revival, confirms that the British approach was essentially biographical. The complex consequences of this attitude are examined in Chapter 1, but here it is worth pointing out that the formal difference between a novel of Sensibility and a biography like Dobson's was very small. Both told stories of melancholy love using prose interspersed with poetry. In form and content, biographies were the link between poetry and the novel of Sensibility, the genre which played the central role in the sentimental education of eighteenth-century readers.

Despite such biographical interest, few British poets and translators paid any attention to the entire *Canzoniere*. For example, there were translations of the poems that describe Petrarch's religious repentance of his sentimental obsession, but they were neither admired nor discussed nor imitated. The same happened with many of the sonnets that are rich in conceits and mythological references. In other words, the British readers of the Romantic age treated *Canzoniere* as though it were a collection of 'scattered rhymes'. None of them understood the impressive structure of *Canzoniere* as an exemplary autobiography. It had taken Petrarch the work of a lifetime, not to mention a good deal of fabrication, to construct a Stoic and Augustinian progress that went from the scattered rhymes of his early, fragmented self and his love for Laura, to his later ego, whose regained unity was represented by the harmonious construction of a book where everything is in its right place, including the final, religious recantation of his juvenile errors. This construction went unnoticed in Romantic England, although readers of the time should not be treated too harshly. The structure of *Canzoniere* had already been lost to sight in the Renaissance, which was as blinkered as the Romantic age in its imitation of Petrarch.

However limited, the Romantic Petrarch is nevertheless liberating for an Italian reader. Petrarch's style was not the only interest of British writers, and even the traditional opposition with Dante – a tedious obsession of Italian culture – was given a different, political meaning. One of the most surprising things is that Petrarch, who in Italian literature is the emblem of the arch-canonical, conservative writer, mainly attracted various types of marginal poets in Romantic England: women poets, like Mary Monk early in the eighteenth century and Mary Robinson; sexually eccentric poets like Gray and Nott; and poets of the radical circles later in the century. Of course, this is an artificial division, as these categories often overlap. For instance, several women poets were considered as sexually eccentric in comparison to the accepted norms of the age, and more often than not they were involved in political radicalism. Foscolo's observation that Petrarch was a model used by the clergy to teach the Italian youth political quietism sounded quite out of place in England, where Petrarch was really only admired outside the establishment. However strange it may sound, Capel Lofft, a Unitarian radical, was simultaneously the most ardent champion of both Petrarch and Napoleon at the turn of the century.

Though Gothic romances and novels of Sensibility were the main forms where amorous discourse was developed in the late eighteenth century, poetry also played an important role in the process. Poetry was not as popular as the novel, but it was attributed greater intellectual prestige. It is important, then, to find out how the ideas of love and desire were developed in verse, in order to define, among other things, how women poets acquired a space of their own in this most prestigious literary genre, a genre whose tradition was predominantly male.

The social prestige of poetry and the increasing presence of women on the literary scene are unquestionable facts of Romantic culture. One need only recall, for example, that Charlotte Smith's son asked her to send him some copies of her collections of sonnets, rather than any of her novels, since her poems had been the most effective means of introducing him to the best society in Quebec. Charlotte Smith's literary career was proverbially arduous but, as Judith Phillips Stanton has noted, the interesting point is that, despite her difficulties, her life demonstrates that 'it was possible for a woman of her class to write from the provinces with the most irregular support and patronage, to achieve a measure of respectability, to gain a reputation, and to earn a living, however modest.'[3] Statistically, the number of books published by women poets increased constantly from 1770 and peaked with nearly 80 collections in 1808.[4] This certainly deserves critical attention, though we should never forget that in poetry the most relevant element is not quantity, but quality. Large numbers are sociologically interesting, but they need not be aesthetically interesting.

Women writers, as Stuart Curran has noted, were active in all literary genres, but they were most closely associated with the revival of the sonnet and the metrical tale.[5] The sonnet and Petrarch were synonyms at that time, and they were inseparably linked to love poetry. In fact, Petrarch was one of the three figures – the other two being Sappho and Werther – around whom love poetry revolved in the late eighteenth century. Sappho's and Werther's roles, of course, have received far more attention than Petrarch's.[6] In particular, in recent years there has been a tremendous surge of interest in Sappho, and the study of her works has turned into a sort of industry. It's hardly surprising that women's studies and feminist criticism have concentrated on the revival of Sappho, a subject which lends itself to their interests and ideology. Statistics that feminist scholars brought forward as evidence of the importance of women in Romantic writing have been quickly laid aside in this case. It would be difficult to deny that there were many more translations, imitations, adaptations and re-writings of Petrarch than Sappho. Most women writers had some knowledge of the Italian language, which was part of a girl's education at the time, whereas hardly any of them knew Greek. Besides, Petrarch's texts were easily available, whereas only a few fragments of Sappho – far fewer than at present – were known at that time. It might be argued that this ignorance of Sappho's texts was actually an advantage, since it was easier to reinvent her character at will in what have come to be called 'fictions of Sappho'. As it turned out, the wealth of material both by and about Petrarch was no obstacle to people's imagination, not only in poetry, but in scholarship too. Fictions of Petrarch, in prose and verse, were so numerous that despite all the many essays being written about him, Foscolo was able to complain that there were no biographies of Petrarch's life, only romances.[7]

As might be expected, the relation women had with Petrarch was more complex than their relation with Sappho, and feminists today find it more difficult to absorb it into their view of literary history. In most cases, women writers both identified with and distanced themselves from Petrarch. Their attitude to Laura was equally important and contained a similar mixture of identification and distancing. It was a complicated reception, more nuanced and problematic than their response to Sappho – which may explain why feminist scholars have so far ignored it.

But did Sappho and Laura ever meet in Romantic England? Before Mary Robinson's *Sappho and Phaon*, Sappho and Laura appeared together in two dialogues, published anonymously in 1773, which are free translations from Fontenelle's *Nouveaux dialogues des morts*. In this text, Laura represents the cautious though determined lover, while Sappho is the incontinent, aggressive partner overwhelmed by a passion that disrupts normal social relations.[8] The dialogue opens with Laura, who notes that their amours have been accompanied by the muses but that, while Sappho sang her own love, Laura had verses made about hers. Sappho agrees and adds that she was a violent lover, whereas Laura was violently loved.[9] Laura tells Sappho that she was too aggressive and spoke out her passion explicitly, whereas 'it is the woman's province, to act out upon the defensive.' Sappho replies that she was provoked by that 'impertinent custom' which restrains women's 'natural liberty' – a concept added by the English translator. Men left women 'the hardest part; for it is much easier to attack, than defend'. Laura replies that a woman's part has its advantages, as the besieged 'may surrender at discretion, but the besiegers cannot carry the fort when they please'. Sappho argues that men attack women because they have an inclination to behave like that, whereas women's modesty is not natural behaviour but, as the English translator added, the product of custom. Laura notes that compliments paid to women show how highly men value 'a hard-won heart'. Sappho answers that being obliged to resist 'soft addresses' for a long time is a torture. Men's pleasure in being loved 'is their triumph over the person that loves them'. Laura concludes the first part of the dialogue by noting that Sappho 'would have a law made' that women should attack men so as to add, as the translator specified, the pride of conquest to the pleasure of love.[10]

Sappho opens the second part of the dialogue with a reasonable remark: why cannot men and women, rather than behaving as though involved in siege warfare, 'meet one another half way, and love upon the square?'. Laura answers that love would be impoverished by such behaviour: 'courtship is so agreeable a commerce, that we should spin it out as long as we can.' Saying yes immediately would destroy all the polite attention, the 'inexpressibly delightful mixture of pleasure and pain, which is the soul of an amour', for, as the translator added, 'there is nothing more insipid than plain love for love.'[11]

In short, Laura's point of view is that sex devoid of courtship and emotion is tedious. Sappho's reply is sarcastic. In a passage entirely added to the French original, she cries that Laura's story is 'excellently adapted to the Platonic ideas of your poetical lover, the harmoniously insipid Petrarch'. Her own lover, the 'voluptuous Alcæus', was completely different. He was a sort of hog, who, 'while devouring an acorn, is eying another'.[12] Going back to the original text, Sappho notes that if love is a battle, it is better to attack than defend all the time.[13] Laura specifies that resistance must not be absolute, and this time Sappho agrees with her. As the translator added, resistance must be used only to whet 'the appetites of the men'. Laura agrees cautiously: 'Perhaps it may; but it is likewise a salvo to our pride, and the foundation of our self-esteem. One would not be so weak as to surrender at first sight, nor so stout as not to surrender at all.'[14] However much we speculate on love, 'we shall find, at the foot of the account, that things are much better as they are; and that, in attempting to mend them, we should spoil them entirely.'

In the English text, the last word is left to Sappho the Amazon, who agrees with Laura and adds: 'I had always such a violent inclination to attack, and so little will to resist, that I would gladly have custom on my side.' Men, however, would defend too well and the love game would be impossible. Let men remain 'in possession of their proud prerogative, since we should have been losers by the alteration. They conquer,—only to be vanquished!'[15]

This dialogue shows clearly how Laura and Sappho were perceived before the Petrarchan revival. Sappho was the oversexed, aggressive woman at odds with eighteenth-century morals; Laura stood for a conventional lady who accepted the dominant morality, even though she clearly saw its limitations and its artificial nature. Within a few years the Petrarchan revival changed such neat opposition, making the figures of Laura and Petrarch as problematic as that of Sappho.

1
Writing the Biography of Petrarch: From Susanna Dobson (1775) to the Romantics

1.1 Sade and Dobson

In 1820 Ugo Foscolo complained that 'We write romances instead of biography, which from being under the masque of history, mislead inexperienced readers and prove unsatisfactory to those of more sagacity, who can know Petrarch in biography only.' These 'biographies' reflect the views of their authors and times rather than those of Petrarch.[1] Foscolo's words may sound strange, because Petrarch's life is much better known than that of any other ancient poet. None the less, Foscolo's remark was not gratuitous. The numerous studies and biographies of Petrarch which were published in his time are as fictional as those of Sappho, though her fictions have received much greater critical attention in recent years. In fact, though it is well known that Petrarch's poetry played a relevant role in the revival of the sonnet that took place in England in the late eighteenth century, no one has ever studied it in detail. Since poetry was never a merely technical enterprise, especially in an age when art and life were often mixed up, British attention to Petrarch was not confined to his verse. That is why an interest in the life of the poet preceded and fostered the enthusiasm for his poetry, which is autobiographical and lends itself to a mixed interest of that sort.

If we look at chronology, the date that marks the real beginning of the eighteenth-century British revival of interest in Petrarch is 1775, the year of publication of *The Life of Petrarch. Collected from Memoires pour la vie de Petrarch*. It is a biography in two bulky volumes that Susanna Dobson abridged and translated from the most important Petrarch biography of the time, the Abbé de Sade's *Mémoires pour la vie de François Pétrarque* (1764).[2] The main aim of Sade's monumental study – three huge quarto volumes – was to correct some biographical conjectures that had long been taken as facts in Petrarch criticism. In particular, he did his best to find out the real identity of Laura and the main events of her life. Sade argued that she was a Laura de Noves who got married to an ancestor of his, Hugues de Sade, bore him 11 children and died of the Black Death in 1348.[3] The views he wanted to refute were that she was a member of the Sade family, as some French scholars believed, or a Laura de Cabriers born at Avignon in 1314 and unmarried, a view introduced by Alessandro Vellutello in the sixteenth century.[4] Of course, one of the archetypal love stories of Western literature was made inappropriate by Sade's study, which met considerable critical opposition for some time after its publication.

Such an alarmed response was due to the fact that, as Sade emphasised, Petrarch was commonly regarded as a poet for women or for effeminate men who spent their time with them.[5] Like Dante, Petrarch decided to write in the vernacular because he wanted to be understood by women too, and he always remained their favourite poet.[6] Though these explicit sentences were omitted by Dobson, it was undeniable that her English edition contained many a point of extreme interest for women. She accepted Sade's main theses and reproduced most of the biographical events contained in his essay; the tone of her edition, however, belonged to another intellectual climate.[7] Sade believed that love stories were monotonous; moreover, Petrarch's *Canzoniere* was a melancholy story, which the French generally disliked.[8] It was probably for that reason that he gave little space to the *in morte* poems of *Canzoniere*.[9] Significantly, these statements were not included by Dobson, who, on the contrary, affirmed in the first pages of her edition that only a mind which has something profound in common with those of Petrarch and Laura can understand and justify them. Petrarch will be cherished only by 'susceptible and feeling minds'. In other words, Dobson made Petrarch and Laura heroes of sensibility.[10] In the conclusion to her translation, where she expressed her opinions openly, she argued that Petrarch 'was a prey to the keenest sensibility' in his youth and early maturity. Thereafter he failed to recover peace. His story was a great lesson for everybody, because it showed the wonderful power of love, which was not something vain that ought to be avoided.[11] Her last paragraph solemnly declares: 'Those Readers who have been interested in the fortune of Petrarch, will pity his fate, admire his sublime and exalted genius, and revere his humble piety, which their candour, penetration and sensibility will draw out to life from this faint and imperfect representation.'[12]

Dobson believed that Petrarch's private character was the most interesting part of his life. She concentrated on it and left out many erudite details of the French original.[13] Her Petrarch was a lover and a poet more than a scholar and a politician. However, despite her perspective and despite the fact that she reproduced the essential points of the original, she toned down Sade and made several additions to render the protagonists of the story more respectable. After all, if Sade was right, this was an adulterous relationship, however noble and dignified. In her introduction Dobson stated that, even though Petrarch and Laura were not guilty of anything, she was a married woman, and therefore their behaviour could not be wholly justified.[14] It was presumably for this reason that, despite her sincere admiration for Petrarch's poetry, Dobson did not follow Sade's view that the great advantage of Petrarch over the classical love poets was that even a virgin could read him without blushing.[15] However, Dobson's reservations may well be only inevitable, preliminary lip-service paid to the mentality of her country and age, since the story she told with enthusiasm pointed to a very different direction.

What is the image of the protagonists that Sade and Dobson created for their readers? As a young man, Petrarch was handsome, impulsive and sometimes even violent. At that time he had some illicit affairs, of which he repented later in life.[16] On the contrary, Laura looked extremely delicate and beautiful and was naturally elegant in her behaviour.[17] Sade pointed out how Petrarch's initial shyness was gradually replaced by outbursts of passion that alarmed Laura, who ran away and left him in despair. Dobson translated most of the French text in this section, but she toned down the intensity of Petrarch's passion, adding that 'he behaved with tenderness and esteem, and she enjoyed at ease the pleasures of his conversation.'[18]

As Sade and Dobson described it, the relationship between Petrarch and Laura was an extenuating sequence of meaning smiles and severe frowning, of vague hope and bitter disappointment, of expectation and dejection. They pointed out on several occasions how Laura was displeased with both Petrarch's boldness when he wooed her openly, and his indifference to her when she withdrew from him. The morality of her behaviour was, of course, dubious and needed to be defended.

Dobson affirmed that Laura's love was constant and undivided, that is, the opposite of coquetry.[19] Evidence for this could be found in an episode when there were rumours that Petrarch was wooing another woman under Laura's name. Laura was indignant and disappeared, which, in Dobson's mind, showed her love for Petrarch.[20] Unlike Sade, Dobson believed that the Middle Ages were times of great moral corruption and widespread debauchery.[21] The 'declining age of Chivalry' bore 'a strong resemblance to that of the present times', and she hoped that especially the young would revive the pristine spirit of that age to 'check the progress of dissipation'.[22] Laura was very reserved, and though she lived in a corrupt age, she (Dobson's addition) always put honour before life.[23] However narcissistic and questionable it might appear, Laura's behaviour was the only way she had of preserving her honour and, at the same time, keeping alive a genuine sentiment for 20 years.[24] Dobson even affirmed that Petrarch and Laura would have been a happy couple if they had got married. Unfortunately, Petrarch was compelled to wander and agonise throughout his life.[25] Laura's lot was equally woeful: her married life was unhappy, her husband jealous, and her 11 deliveries quickly impaired her health and spoiled her beauty.[26] In spite of the moral reservations put forward in her introduction, Dobson was at pains to highlight how true and mutual the relationship between Laura and Petrarch was, so that, for instance, she added Laura's anxiety for Petrarch's absence as a cause of her early decay.[27]

If Dobson envisaged a happy married life for Petrarch and Laura, Sade was more ambiguous towards the nature of their relationship. In two passages omitted in the English edition, he rejected indignantly Ercole Giovannini's insinuation that there was an affair between Petrarch and Laura.[28] At the same time, he reported Benedetto Varchi's opinion that there is a mixture of sublime and gross sentiments in any kind of love, including that which Petrarch felt for Laura. Sappho meant this when she argued that Love was born from heaven and earth. Sade said he could not make up his mind because he had not read enough about this. Was it a subtle way of agreeing without compromising himself as a clergyman? In any case, he disagreed with two other views: that Petrarch never desired Laura's favour, and that he obtained it. He believed that both were offensive to Laura.[29] At the same time, Sade defended Petrarch's poems, which had unjustly been censured for their immorality by many ecclesiastic scholars.[30]

The poems were, obviously, an element of immense attraction for the readers of Dobson's biography, all the more so as English translations of Petrarch were rare at that time. However, Dobson gave readers only a vague idea of them. In her introduction, she said she did not dare to translate the sonnets; she just preserved some lines to illustrate Petrarch's life.[31] Dobson translated Sade's translations rather than Petrarch's original poems, which are included in Sade's book. Against the advice of many French scholars, who argued that poetry translates better in prose than in verse, Sade translated freely and took the liberty of improving and amending the original when necessary. He left out the obscurest texts, such as some *canzoni* and sonnets, and he suppressed some quatrains and single lines here and there.[32] Sade's taste was that of eighteenth-century French classicism and, in most cases, his versions are a sort of paraphrase of the original.[33] He disliked the 'Metaphysical' elements in Petrarch, such as puns, antitheses and hyperboles, and he omitted most of them. Dobson carried such attitude a step further and left out some physical details of the French versions, which were made even more abstract than they already were. A clear example of her method is 'Zephyrus returns', which became the most popular of Petrarch's sonnets in Romantic Britain.[34] Dobson translated Sade's prose translation making some typical changes.[35] After the second sentence, 'Jupiter regarde Venus avec complaisance' was omitted, probably both as neoclassical ornament and an erotic allusion; 'les animaux recommencent à aimer' ('animals begin to love again') was rendered as 'all creatures feel his [Love's] sovereign power', which implies a passive rather than an active attitude; 'the charms of beauty' is more abstract than the charms of 'les plus belles Dames' of the French version; in the conclusion, Dobson did not specify that 'the most gloomy desarts' were 'abité par des bêtes féroces' ('populated by wild animals'), whereas she added, 'for Laura is no more!'

However, Dobson could be literal in her translation, presumably in those sections she considered as crucial. One of these moments, in particular, is worthy of attention. Dealing with Petrarch's early fame, Sade wrote that a lady called on him 'comme un oracle'. She was Giustina Levi-Perotti and belonged to the Levis, one of the noblest French families, who had married into the Perottis of Sassoferrato, an important family of the Italian aristocracy. Her father was a learned and sensible man who gave her an unusual education. 'From her earliest years she was inspired by the Muses' and wrote poems; however, 'the people of the world' teased her and advised her to ' "cease to aspire to the poetic laurel; lay down your pen, and take up the needle and distaff." '[36] At this point, Giustina asked Petrarch's advice in a sonnet she sent him, which Sade gave in the original in a note:

> *Io vorrei pur drizzar queste mie piume*
> > *Colà, signor, dove il desio n'invita*
> > *E dopo morte rimaner' in vita,*
> > *Col chiaro di virtute inclyto lume.*
> *Ma 'l volgo inerte, che dal rio costume*
> > *Vinto, ha d'ogni suo ben la via smarita,*
> > *Come degna di biasmo ogn' hor' m'addita*
> > *Ch'ir tenti d'elicona al sacro fiume.*
> *All'ago, al fuso, più ch'al lauro, o al mirto,*
> > *Come che qui non sia la gloria mia,*
> > *Vuol c'habbia sempre questa mente intesa.*
> *Dimmi tu hormai, che per più dritta via*
> > *A parnasso t'en vai, nobile spirto,*
> > *Dovrò dunque lasciar sì degna impresa?*[37]

Dobson translated the French prose translation:

> O Thou! who by a noble flight hath arrived at the summit of Parnassus, tell me what part ought I to act? I would fain live after I am dead: and the Muses can alone give me the life I desire. Do you advise me to devote myself to them, or to resume my domestic employments, and shield myself from the censure of vulgar minds, who permit not our sex to aspire after the crowns of laurel or of myrtle?[38]

Here too Dobson simplified the French, though she did not weaken the claims of the text.[39]

Petrarch's reply to this sonnet was 'La gola e 'l somno', a frequently anthologised poem, which in the context reads like a defence of the right women have to poetry, writing and education:

> Idleness and the pleasures of the table have banished all the virtues; the whole world is changed; we have now no light to direct our way; the man inspired by the Muses is pointed at; the vile populace who think of nothing

but advancing their interest say, Of what use are crowns of laurel or myrtle? Philosophy is abandoned, and goes quite naked. O thou! whom Heaven has endued with an amiable soul, be not disheartened by such advice! Follow the path you have entered, though it is but little frequented.[40]

This, again, is a translation of Sade's prose version with a few minor changes, the most relevant being the vaguer 'who think of nothing but advancing their interest' for the more specific 'ne songe qu'à gagner de l'argent'.[41] After this poem, Dobson moved on to narrate some political events, omitting a philological discussion which gives the French reader a different sense of Giustina's sonnet.

Sade specified that some Italian critics argued that Giustina's poem was in fact written in the sixteenth century using the rhymes of Petrarch's 'La gola e 'l somno'. They believed no woman could have written such a good sonnet at so early a date. Though Sade defended the sonnet against these strictures, his section does not read as boldly feminist as it does in Dobson, who omitted the philological debate completely.[42] What the English text presents is a young noblewoman with a literary talent who, ridiculed by common people for her poetic interests, claims her intellectual rights and is supported by Petrarch in her battle. The impact of this section is not weakened by another one several hundred pages below, where Sade and Dobson argued, against Nostradamus, that Laura was not interested in poetry and probably received the same education as the other girls of her time.[43]

1.2   T. Warton, Gibbon, Tytler

Sade's and Dobson's celebration of women's rights, intellectual claims and adulterous love could not go unnoticed, especially because Dobson's biography ran through six editions and Petrarch's poems became more and more popular in the later eighteenth century.[44] In fact, the impact of Dobson's translation was not only that of a scholarly work. Her biography of Petrarch was received by British readers like a novel of Sensibility, which told a pathetic love story using prose interspersed with poems. The difference between the fictional biography of historical figures, such as Dobson's *Petrarch* or Nott's *Sappho*, and the biographical fictions of invented characters we find in innumerable novels of Sensibility was very slight at the time – if there was a difference at all in the readers' minds.

Critical reactions to Sade and Dobson followed two main strategies: they either undermined Petrarch's poems and highlighted his scholarly and political life, or they tried to refute Sade's arguments directly. For instance, two of the foremost historians of the time, Thomas Warton and Edward Gibbon, drew on Sade's essay and accepted his theses, but both of them showed a limited interest in Petrarch's poetry. Despite some reservations, Warton admired

Dante much more than he did Petrarch, to whom he paid only marginal attention in his *History of Poetry*.[45] Gibbon gave Petrarch more space but, unlike Sade and Dobson, he was not thrilled with his amorous torments.[46] Petrarch appears in the last sections of *The Decline and Fall of the Roman Empire* first as a politician, then as a scholar, and only finally as a poet.[47] Gibbon celebrated the political skill of Petrarch, his enthusiastic support of Cola di Rienzo, and his pleas to the popes that they return from Avignon to Rome. However, Gibbon also noted how easily Petrarch could turn his coat, as when he flattered Charles IV immediately after Cola di Rienzo's death.[48] Like other eighteenth-century scholars, Gibbon seems to have found Petrarch's poetical talent unimpressive. It was only modern readers, he argued, that celebrated Petrarch as 'the Italian songster of Laura and love'. Gibbon did not know enough about Italian poetry to contradict the prevailing opinion on Petrarch's poems, but he hoped that Italians did not compare 'the tedious uniformity of sonnets and elegies' with the sublimity of Dante, the variety of Ariosto and the regular beauties of Tasso. Gibbon found the morality of Petrarch's poems even more puzzling. Drawing on Sade, he noted the oddity of Petrarch's metaphysical passion for 'a shadowy nymph' who was, at the same time, 'a matron so prolific who was delivered of eleven legitimate children, while her amorous swain sighed and sung at the fountain of Vaucluse'.[49] Though Gibbon never questioned Laura's virtue, he noted that Petrarch's sonnets and love were adjudged frivolous in their time. It was Petrarch's scholarly work that earned him fame with his contemporaries and the gratitude of posterity.[50] Gibbon was more excited by Petrarch's coronation on the Capitol in Rome, which he described lavishly.[51] In short, though Gibbon was intrigued above all by Petrarch's political and scholarly life, none the less he gave his prestigious consent to Sade's version of the relationship between Petrarch and Laura.[52]

The most direct riposte to Sade and Dobson came from Alexander Fraser Tytler, the author of the *Essay on the Principles of Translation*, who in 1784 published an *Essay on the Life and Character of Petrarch* to refute their view of Petrarch's and Laura's lives. In 1810 he brought out an expanded version, which included the former pamphlet as part I of the book.[53]

Tytler took its start from Sade's *Mémoires*, which shed light on several aspects of Petrarch's life, but impaired the general esteem for his morality, 'the most important point of his character'.[54] Tytler could not believe that Laura was a married woman and, consequently, that Petrarch was a rake, almost as though she was an eighteenth-century coquette 'sensible to the passion of her *Cicisbeo*', albeit 'without a direct breach of her matrimonial vow'.[55] Although he acknowledged that the view of Laura's identity introduced by Vellutello was unfounded, the only way of restoring the older, more respectable image of Petrarch was to refute, point by point, the evidence Sade had brought forward.[56] In particular, Sections II, III and IV of the 1810 essay, which considerably enlarged the 1784 version, were devoted to confuting

Sade's argument that Laura was Laura de Noves, born at Avignon in 1307 or 1308, who married Hugh de Sade in 1325 and died in 1348.

Tytler tried to demonstrate that she was neither born nor married nor buried in Avignon.[57] He returned to the traditional view that Laura was a descendant of the Sade family rather than a woman married into it.[58] He wondered how Sade could support the view that an ancestor of his was a potential adulteress. The answer was that Sade and his countrymen were 'but very little acquainted' with the morals Tytler was referring to. For them, coquetry and extra-marital relationships, albeit only potential, were acceptable.[59] Laura was not insensible to Petrarch's love; she only pretended she was indifferent. Tytler reported some passages from Sade which describe Laura as a coquette kindling Petrarch's love with 'doux regards' and 'petits mots'. He was flabbergasted that Sade could describe her as 'une femme tendre et sage' who kept alive Petrarch's passion for 21 years, 'and all this *sans faire la moindre breche à son honneur*'.[60] She bore 11 children and died of consumption at about 40, and yet

> all the while, this hackneyed and antiquated coquette, regardless of the character of a wife and a mother, is practising her *petit manege* of alternate favours and rigours, to turn the head of an infatuated *inamorato* [*sic*], whose passion was in itself an affront to virtue and morality, and amuse him for a lifetime with the expectation of favours which she is determined never to grant. Such, in the system of the Abbé de Sade, is the all-accomplished Laura, and such the respectable and virtuous Petrarch. How absurd, how disgusting, how contemptible the one; how weak, how culpable, how dishonourable the other![61]

Despite the touch of francophobia, Tytler did not dismiss Sade's essay as drastically as Beattie, who called it a romance concocted for commercial purposes. However inaccurate, it was 'a most instructive as well as a most amusing work'.[62] Though Tytler found Sade's libertine Petrarch unpalatable, he was not persuaded by the opposite view either. Tytler rejected the idea that Petrarch's love was Platonic. As evidence, he quoted some passages of Petrarch where the poet seems to be longing to possess Laura physically.[63] In other words, Tytler did not believe that Petrarch's passion was merely literary and fictional, and he looked for a middle course between real adultery and fiction.[64]

Tytler even wondered why the story between Laura and Petrarch did not end up in marriage, which he could not explain, even though he hinted at 'a temporary indiscretion' of Petrarch's which irritated Laura.[65] She was coy in order to put Petrarch to trial, but she 'gave him at times abundant testimony of a reciprocal affection.' Such favours were 'small indeed, and unimportant expressions to insensible and vulgar minds', but they made Petrarch momentarily happy.[66] Whatever may have happened, there was no doubt that their relationship remained virtuous. Had Laura conceded herself to Petrarch, he would not have written his *Canzoniere*, 'for it is not to be denied that Petrarch cherished his sorrows', as many a sonnet shows.[67] Tytler believed that Sade's view was not only unsupported by historical evidence but, also, that it went against the grain of the love expressed in Petrarch's sonnets.

The enthusiasm Tytler put into his argument was due, besides moral reasons, to the fact that he admired Petrarch's poems greatly. To enjoy them, one needed not only 'congeniality of feeling, but a similarity of circumstance', which, of course, would have been embarrassing in case of adultery.[68] Though a conservative in his translation theory, Tytler was more of a Romantic in his poetic taste, as his influential version from Schiller's *Räuber* shows.

Tytler's translations from Petrarch were mainly meant to illustrate some significant points of his argument and, in particular, his view of the pure and honest character of Petrarch's love.[69] First published in 1784, the same year as Charlotte Smith's *Elegiac Sonnets*, they stemmed from a different and more traditional sensibility. Smith's selection was more personal: she chose sonnets which fitted her project in *Elegiac Sonnets*, that is, melancholy reflections of a solitary figure in a landscape. This romantic Petrarch was only a part of Tytler's choice; the rest was meant to show the idealism of Petrarch's passion, his torments, and their vanity – the last sonnet included in his selection is the first in *Canzoniere*. It is noteworthy, however, that most of them belong to the second section of *Canzoniere*, that *in morte* of Laura, which he considered 'by far the most beautiful'. These poems are so deep that they 'have exhausted the whole powers of pathetic expression'.[70] Sometimes a Gothic vein for the macabre seemed to emerge in his taste. He affirmed, for example, that it was impossible not to sympathise with Petrarch's pain when the poet described Laura's fine eyes and body 'mouldering in the earth'.[71]

Though not as free as those of Sade's, Tytler's versions are for the most part imitations rather than translations.[72] He added in phrases, paraphrased original lines and rearranged their position for metrical and ideological reasons.[73] The most interesting example for our discussion is his version of 'Voi ch'ascoltate' (*PC*, 1):

> Ye, that with favouring ear, and feeling heart,
>   'Sdeign not to list to these disorder'd rhimes,
> Which the full sorrows of my soul impart,
>   Whilst, error-led, in those past early times,
> I cherish'd in my breast th' impoison'd dart:
>
> For these poor trifles which the Muse inspir'd,
>   Alternate birth of fleeting hope, and pain,
> From you, whose hearts a kindred flame has fir'd,
>   Should pardon be denied, I trust to gain

> At least compassion.—Late, at length I know,
>   That, as, through many a year, the bitter scorn
>   And taunting speech of men I've meanly borne,
> And reap'd alone the fruits of shame and woe;
> So this said truth remains,—that all is vain below![74]

> *Voi ch'ascoltate in rime sparse il suono*
> *di quei sospiri ond'io nudriva il core*
> *in sul mio primo giovanile errore*
> *quand'era in parte altr'uom da quel ch'i' sono,*

> *del vario stile in ch'io piango et ragiono*
> *fra le vane speranze e 'l van dolore,*
> *ove sia chi per prova intenda amore,*
> *spero trovar pietà, nonché perdono.*

> *Ma ben veggio or sí come al popol tutto*
> *favola fui gran tempo, onde sovente*
> *di me medesmo meco mi vergogno;*

> *et del mio vaneggiar vergogna è 'l frutto,*
> *e 'l pentersi, e 'l conoscer chiaramente*
> *che quanto piace al mondo è breve sogno.*[75]

Some of Tytler's choices modify the sense of the original sonnet considerably.[76] 'Whilst, error-led, in those past early times, / I cherish'd in my breast th' impoison'd dart' leaves out the partial change in character over the years of 'quand'era in parte altr'uom da quel ch'i' sono'. The 'poor trifles which the Muse inspir'd' are not only different from 'del vario stile in ch'io piango et ragiono', but also self-derogatory. The crucial term 'vain' in 'fra le vane speranze e 'l van dolore' does not appear in 'alternate birth of fleeting hope, and pain'. Above all, the last part of the translation is morally more severe than the original, as in 'the bitter scorn / And taunting speech of men I've meanly borne' for 'Ma ben veggio or sí come al popol tutto / favola fui gran tempo', which mentions neither 'bitter scorn', nor 'taunting speech', nor meanness. Lines 11–12, 'di me medesmo meco mi vergogno; / et del mio vaneggiar vergogna è 'l frutto, / e 'l pentersi', an essential passage which includes raving, shame with himself and the others, and repentance, are not justly reproduced by 'And reap'd alone the fruits of shame and woe'.[77] Petrarch's explicit repentance was made implicit only in Tytler's line, where Petrarch sounds worried more about his reputation than his morals. 'That all is vain below' is, again, an exaggerated version of line 14, which says that 'whatever pleases in the world is a brief dream'. The most relevant changes, however, are those in line 8: 'spero trovar pietà, nonché perdono' became

'Should pardon be denied, I trust to gain / At least compassion', whose liberty Tytler himself pointed out in a footnote.[78] Calvinistically, Tytler's Petrarch did not seem to expect forgiveness but only compassion, which is the opposite of Sade, Dobson, and some women poets of the time, who ultimately justified the two lovers.

1.3   The 1810s: Ginguené, Sismondi, H. Hallam

In the 1810s several essays on Petrarch and Laura appeared in Great Britain and France, which shows how live the issue still was and how open the result of the debate remained. Historians like Henry Hallam, Pierre Louis Ginguené and Simonde de Sismondi, and figures of the literary establishment such as Coleridge, Hazlitt, Landor and Foscolo intervened in the discussion, not to mention the fact that Petrarch was a significant source of inspiration for Shelley, Hunt, Keats, L.E.L., Hemans and a spate of other poets.

Though most scholars were in part uneasy about the morality of Sade's Petrarch, few of them took sides with Tytler. One of these was Romualdo Zotti, an Italian emigrant whose mediocre edition of Petrarch's poems was published in London in 1811. It was dedicated to several noblewomen and, significantly, it included Tytler's essay in an Italian translation. To respect the moral norms of the age and please his aristocratic patronesses, Zotti rejected Sade's view of Laura and turned Petrarch into her potential husband.[79] Plagiarised from a number of sources, Zotti's edition was hardly noticed and ultimately showed that Tytler's argument was a blind alley. Other scholars tackled the issue in subtler ways.

Ginguené's *Histoire littéraire d'Italie* (1811–19) and Sismondi's *De la littérature du Midi de l'Europe* (1813) were widely read on the Continent and in England and popularised in condensed form the erudite essays of scholars like Tiraboschi, Baldelli and Sade.[80] Though the historical data of Ginguené's and Sismondi's biographies were drawn from those sources, their essays gave readers a different image of Petrarch. Ginguené accepted Sade's thesis about Laura and found his work excellent. He believed, none the less, that it contained several mistakes, and he decided to write a more correct life of Petrarch in French.[81] Ginguené's biography is a balanced mixture of news on Petrarch's passion for Laura and his political, scholarly and social life. Like other readers of Sensibility, Ginguené thought that Petrarch required empathy to be understood properly. Petrarch could be enjoyed only by those who were aware of his life and the occasions on which his poems were written.[82]

Ginguené admired Petrarch's love for Laura. He emphasised its nearly religious quality rather than pointing out its moral and psychological dubiousness, which he hardly mentioned. Laura's marriage was arranged and worked well; however, it was devoid of love, which she found in Petrarch instead.[83] His passion was only in part Platonic, because the grief he felt was all too real. He had two illegitimate children, a fact that Ginguené refused to judge.[84] It was his love for Laura that kept him virtuous despite diversions.[85] Ginguené believed that in the Middle Ages social customs were corrupt, but private life was virtuous.[86] Thanks to Christianity and the revival of Platonism, a new conception replaced the classical view of love, which consisted either in sensual delirium and witty, physical pleasure, as in Sappho and Anacreon, or in sex, betrayal, envy and jealousy, as in Ovid, Tibullus and Propertius.[87]

Ginguené's taste, as his view of love, was a mixture of neoclassical and romantic attitudes. Sonnets were a sort of Horatian ode and *canzoni* were like classical odes, though, in fact, they were an evolution of the Provençal *chansons*.[88] He disliked conceits, personifications and sestinas, but he found it pointless to spend time on them when in Petrarch there was so much to admire.[89] A most attractive feature of Petrarch's poetry was the landscape where his melancholy reflections often took place.[90] Typically, Ginguené referred to 'Chiare, fresche et dolci acque' as one of the most beautiful *canzoni* and he included Voltaire's version but, also, a literal translation so as not to mislead readers.[91] Though full of real suffering and spontaneous feeling, Part II of *Canzoniere* was not necessarily better than Part I.[92] Ginguené admired even Petrarch's political poems, as he found them full of patriotism and resentment towards the Pope's court at Avignon.[93]

Sismondi disagreed on this point radically. Like Foscolo, Byron and other liberals of the time, he found Petrarch unmanly, self-complacent and all too ready to compromise with political power. The model they held up was Dante, the indomitable champion of political liberty who preferred to be exiled rather than compromising with oppression. Sismondi argued that Petrarch made no bones about making friends with mean tyrants, who flattered his vanity and obtained his 'basse adulation' in return. However, Sismondi honestly recalled that Petrarch backed up the Roman republic of Cola di Rienzo, and that his behaviour often depended on his overwhelming passion for learning and poetry.[94]

Sismondi's judgement wavered between admiration and blame owing to his uneasiness about Petrarch's politics. For example, he argued that Petrarch was a genuine poet and had great merits as a scholar; his writings, however, were artificial, affected and conceited and, according to some critics, they even perverted Italian taste.[95] With Petrarch, Italian poetry gained clearer rules, a melodious language, a refined vocabulary and elegant taste, but it lost truth in comparison to Dante.[96] Petrarch failed when in his *Triumphs* he imitated Dante, because he could never forget his allegories and didacticism, whereas Dante took a genuine interest in the lives of his characters.[97] Even Petrarch's sonnets were not impeccable. Lyric poetry was the most intrinsically poetic of all genres and the sonnet was the best lyric form, owing its effect to sound as much as to meaning, but it was also a kind of Procrustean bed.[98] *Canzoni* were ultimately better because they were freer in sound and structure.[99]

As far as Petrarch's love story was concerned, Sismondi generally followed Sade though with personal additions. He noted that though none of Petrarch's models – the troubadours, the Avignon court and even Petrarch himself with other women – behaved morally, his love for Laura was pure, blameless and almost mystical.[100] Sismondi was not disturbed by the fact that Laura was married; rather, he found that Petrarch's love was not as passionate as most readers believed. He would have liked to read something more about Laura's thoughts and desires rather than repetitive puns on Laura/laurel, apostrophes to his heart and other cold personifications.[101] This was an unusual request at a time when few male critics complained about women's silence. Petrarch's Latin works were equally marred by their coldness and artificiality. *Africa* was a tedious poem. His treatises were rhetorical exercises devoid of truth and passion. His epistles were public rather than private writings; they were extremely artificial and revealed nothing about his feelings.[102]

The section on Petrarch in Henry Hallam's *View of the State of Europe during the Middle Ages* sounds like a vindication of the poet against Sismondi's political strictures and Tytler's moral reservations. Hallam noted that as a poet, Petrarch was supported by lords and princes more than any other writer, especially in comparison to Dante. However, Petrarch was not a mere flatterer; he praised his powerful friends because he loved them, and he was extremely sensitive to blame and criticism.[103] Like Sismondi, Hallam noted that, though Petrarch was offered prestigious posts by Popes and princes, he supported Cola di Rienzo's *coup* in Rome. His fame was so great that he was crowned poet laureate in Rome in 1341 before writing anything of any relevance, which means that politicians were aware of his influence. Essentially, his character was that of a poet, full of passion for women, friendship, the arts, learning, religion and his country. His dominant passion was that for Laura.[104]

Hallam concurred with Sade that Laura was married when she met Petrarch, 'a fact, which, besides some more particular evidence, appears to me deducible from the whole tenor of his poetry'. Here Hallam appended a long note where he mentioned Sade's genealogical researches, Tiraboschi's reluctant approval and Tytler's criticism of Sade.[105] Hallam tried to refute Tytler's argument, noting that nowhere did Petrarch call Laura 'a virgin'. Petrarch's love seemed ridiculous if Laura was unmarried – and that was why most Italian critics found his passion affected and fictional. But if she was married, the whole story was more compelling and convincing: on the one side, a passionate lover; on the other, a married lady who could not fulfil her lover's desire but who, at the same time, was flattered by fame and courtship, which she kept alive by a cunning 'mixture of prudence and coquetry':

Unquestionably, such a passion is not innocent. But Lord Woodhouselee, who is so much scandalized, knew little, one would think of the fourteenth century. His standard is taken not from Avignon, but from Edinburgh, a much better place, no doubt, and where the moral barometer stands at a very different altitude.

Tytler had carried his severity to an excess of prudery, especially in some parts of his essay. The only surprising thing in Petrarch's story was Laura's persever-ance in virtue, which was extremely rare at the time, as the troubadours show. Finally, Hallam quoted a passage of *Secretum* which showed that Petrarch's passion could not have been satisfied without dishonourable behaviour.[106] Whereas in this note Hallam was very cautious, in the text he stated that Petrarch's love was morally indefensible, even keeping in mind the stand-ards of his time.[107] Laura was not blameless either. Though Hallam did not question her morality, he thought that she sadistically prolonged Petrarch's suffering as much as possible for her own narcissistic pleasure.[108]

Petrarch's main poetic merit was that he purified his native tongue. His mixture of melancholy and passion was ethereal and touching, far more than any classical lyric poet. Catullus, who was a more talented mind, blended fine thoughts with the most degrading grossness. On the contrary, Petrarch's poetry could elevate and refine the imagination of the young. His major defect was his lack of originality. Hallam liked the *Triumphs* better than the *canzoni*, and these better than the sonnets, which is the opposite of the com-mon view in his time. He agreed with it, however, when he found the *in morte* sonnets superior to the others.[109]

However second-hand were their materials, the importance of these histor-ians in establishing an 'average' interpretation of Petrarch with the reading public cannot be underrated. Hallam's was one of the most widely read and influential books on its subject, whereas Ginguené's and Sismondi's essays were quarried by all the writers of the age. It is no coincidence, for example, that the occasion for Hazlitt's 1815 essay on Petrarch and other Italian poets was his review of Sismondi's *De la littérature du Midi de l'Europe*.

1.4   Hazlitt and Foscolo

In comparison to many of his colleagues, Hazlitt's knowledge of Italian was limited; but, though he began learning the language only in his late maturity, his critical opinions on Petrarch were personal and worthy of attention.[110] Though he never mentioned a specific edition, it is reasonable to assume that he read Petrarch in English and, perhaps, French translation. Dobson and Sismondi, together with Gibbon and Roscoe, seem to have been his major sources. Besides, he was certainly aware of the Petrarchan strain in recent British poetry.

Hazlitt found Sismondi's *De la littérature* colder than his *Histoire*. Hazlitt's ideas on Provençal literature, which was discussed in the first part of the review, were vaguer than those on Italian poetry. One of the long passages he cited concerned the nature of love at the time of the troubadours, when profligacy was the norm.[111] He agreed with Sismondi that Provençal poetry was mediocre.[112] Before coming to Petrarch, Hazlitt touched on Dante, who was 'nothing but power, passion, self-will'. His passion lent interest to the objects he described, which were nothing in themselves. Dante combined powerful feeling with familiar objects, the absolutely local with the wildest mysticism.[113]

If Hazlitt's admiration of Dante was predictable, his enthusiasm for Petrarch was surprising. Hazlitt began his analysis from one of the most controversial points in the British debate on Petrarch: the meaning of his style and, more specifically, the value of his conceits. Petrarch posed a major problem to the Wordsworthian rhetoric of sincerity which was gradually becoming an undisputable truth in Romantic England. Petrarch was recognised simultaneously as one of the masters of love poetry and an extremely skilled rhetorician who exhibited his technical devices with unashamed pride. How could exalted passion and extreme artificiality coexist? Like many other poets and critics from the mid-eighteenth century onwards, Sismondi believed that they could not, and he argued that Petrarch's conceits showed how artificial his feelings were. Hazlitt refuted this view drastically.

Petrarch's conceits were a technical jargon that had become natural to him. It was the language in which love was described and discussed in his time, as well as later in masterpieces of love poetry such as *Romeo and Juliet*. There was 'more truth and feeling' in Cowley and Sidney than in many 'insipid and merely natural writers', by which Hazlitt probably meant many sonneteers of the later eighteenth century.[114] Had Shakespeare written only his sonnets, he would be wrongly classified as a cold, artificial writer. Hazlitt even drew a surprising comparison between Petrarch and Burke, whose style and imagination led many people to believe that they were mere rhetoricians with neither feeling nor thought.[115]

The scholastic style was a mental habit to Petrarch, who found it natural to express his most intense feelings in that language. The same happened to Milton, whose erudite language was the vehicle for his moral and political passions. Strong passions are best expressed in exaggerations, which are usually emphatic rather than simple. The sonnet 'Gli occhi di ch'io parlai sì caldamente' was not a display of cold wit, as Sismondi argued, but a specimen of Petrarch's passionate feelings.[116]

Hazlitt was aware that the poets of the English Renaissance imitated Petrarch, and his reading of Petrarch must also be understood as a defence of them.[117] He cited Raleigh's 'Methought I saw the grave where Laura lay', and he commented that only Spenser was able to divert Raleigh from his fanatic enthusiasm for Petrarch and Laura.[118] Some of Drummond of Hawthornden's sonnets were 'more in the manner of Petrarch than any others that we have, with a certain intenseness in the sentiment, an occasional glitter of thought, and uniform terseness of expression', a definition which caught the main characters of Petrarch's poetry with admirable conciseness.[119] More-over, Hazlitt saw that there was a specific kinship between Renaissance and Romantic Petrarchism. Discussing Drummond's sonnet 'Slide soft, fair Forth', he noted: 'if a mixture of the Della Cruscan style be allowed to enshrine the true spirit of love and poetry, we have it in the following address to the River Forth, on which his mistress had embarked.' In this context, the reference was not meant to debunk the Della Cruscans, whose reputation was at its low-est point in the late 1810s, but to reassess the value of a noble tradition which had unjustly been ridiculed by British criticism. The sonnet to the River Forth 'to the English reader will express the very soul of Petrarch, the molten breath of sentiment converted into the glassy essence of a set of glittering but still graceful conceits.'[120]

The eccentricity of Hazlitt went beyond this. Though he admired Petrarch's style, he did not partake of the Romantic enthusiasm for the sonnet, a form inseparably associated with Petrarch. He shared the common view that the sonnet was the expression of 'some occasional thought or personal feeling' – especially melancholy ones – uttered 'with undivided breath'. The sonnet form was suited to the lowly incidents and feelings of common life. After the sublimity of *Paradise Lost*, Milton let 'fall some drops of "natural pity" over hapless infirmity, mingling strains with the nightingale's "most musical, most melancholy"'.[121] Though Hazlitt was no enthusiast of the sonnet, his ideas depended on the prevailing taste of his time. Not even Milton, whom he admired immensely, could convince him that the sonnet was not primar-ily a vehicle for personal, melancholy musings. In his essay, he significantly ignored the sonnets of Milton which were 'of a more quaint and humor-ous character' and concentrated on those 'serious and pathetic', 'the first effusions of this sort of natural and personal sentiment in the language'. Drummond's sonnets might well have been an alternative, 'were they formed less closely on the model of Petrarch, so as to be often little more than translations of the Italian poet'. Sidney's sonnets were personal but they were over-elaborate and quaint, 'more like riddles than sonnets'. Though some critics believed that Shakespeare's sonnets were excellent, Hazlitt found them devoid of structuring ideas, 'overcharged and monotonous', and ulti-mately with 'neither head nor tail', a severe judgement which is curiously at odds with the opinions mentioned before.[122] Hazlitt held most Romantic sonneteers in low regard. He maintained that after Milton, the only son-neteer worth discussing was Thomas Warton, whose sonnets were exquisitely musical though poor in ideas. Hazlitt admired Wordsworth's sonnets, even though he found them and their author wanting in morality and political credibility in comparison to Milton.[123]

These sceptical judgements on the sonnet, however, were not Hazlitt's last word on the relation between artificiality and passion, rhetorical devices and spontaneity. His prevailing opinion seems to have been the opposite, as other observations show. In 'On Reading New Books', he affirmed that stories set in a remote time 'require to be bolstered up in some measure by the embellishments of modern style and criticism'. Two such stories were those of Abelard and Eloisa and Petrarch and Laura, whose passionate character 'contrasts quaintly and pointedly with the coldness of the grave'. Hazlitt believed that Pope's version of Abelard and Eloisa was more moving than the original letters. He did not mention any specific work on Petrarch, but he may have been implicitly referring to the biographies, the imitations and the fictions of their lives.[124] Besides, in a letter to his son written when he was composing his *Liber Amoris*, Hazlitt argued that authors

> feel nothing spontaneously. [. . .] Instead of yielding to the first natural and lively impulses of things, they screw themselves up to some farfetched view of the subject in order to be unintelligible. Realities are not good enough for them. [. . .] They are intellectual dram-drinkers; and without their necessary stimulus, are torpid, dead, insensible to every thing. [. . .] Their minds are a sort of Herculaneum, full of petrified images; – are set in stereotype, and little fitted to the ordinary occasions of life.

The letter includes a barbed judgement on scholars, who are defined as sad, impotent beings without 'a mate or fellow'. Women are not attracted by learned men, and learning is a vicious hindrance to sentimental happiness.[125] It is not surprising that, unlike Coleridge, Hazlitt took no interest in Petrarch's scholarly works in Latin; on the contrary, he recalled Petrarch's complaint that ' "Nature had made him different from other people" – *singular d'altra genti.*'[126]

Going back to the review of Sismondi, after Petrarch's style Hazlitt defended his view of love. Among other things, Hazlitt's review is a sort of vindication of the rights of passion in its variety, since he emphasised its meaning and crucial importance in Dante, Petrarch and Boccaccio, whose genuine feelings he defended against the common charges of immorality. Hazlitt was open-minded: he did not extol the type of sentiment he preferred while condemning all the others, but he understood and justified even Petrarch's love, which was remote from his frame of mind. Whereas Sismondi affirmed that Petrarch's love was too abstract, Hazlitt, on the contrary, argued that such a form of love was not a literary pose. Hazlitt specified that he did not want to defend Platonic love, but only clarify the way in which passion operated on contemplative minds.[127] Hazlitt's open-mindedness was a reaction to an attitude which belonged to Sismondi as well as other British writers of the time, who deplored both Petrarch's platonism and Boccaccio's sensuousness.

Hazlitt's visual talent even led him to speculate on Laura's physical appearance. He believed that her grace and beauty were typically Italian:

> Grace in women has more effect than beauty. We sometimes see a certain fine self-possession, an habitual voluptuousness of character, which

reposes on its own sensations, and derives pleasure from all around it, that is more irresistible than any other attraction. There is an air of languid enjoyment in such persons, 'in their eyes, in their arms, and their hands and their faces', which robs us of ourselves, and draws us by a secret sympathy towards them. Their minds are a shrine where pleasure reposes. Their smile diffuses a sensation like the breath of spring. Petrarch's description of Laura answers exactly to his character, which is indeed the Italian character.

This idea of Laura's grace as a product of sensuous languor recalls the 'Oriental' view of Petrarch's poetry which first emerged in Voltaire and Sir William Jones. Hazlitt found that element a permanent feature of Italian culture, as was also evident in the fine arts. Titian's portraits were full of that type of grace, which, combined with an 'infinite activity of the mind', helped 'the greatest men' to bear serenely the loss of empires or the main tragedies in their lives. Such grace belonged to the Southern and Eastern races more than the Northern peoples. In the South there was a stronger link between physical motion and feeling. Grace was connected with indolence, so much so that Hazlitt blamed Wordsworth's sonnet against gypsy inertia as philistine and hypocritical, as it came from the pen of a poet who once celebrated contemplative passiveness.[128] In other words, grace was both a moral and an aesthetic quality, which stemmed from a relaxed way of life belonging to Southerners – seen as Schiller's *schöne Seelen* – rather than Northerners.

Of course, it is difficult to discuss Hazlitt's view of ideal passion and beauty without thinking of his unusual love story with Sarah Walker. Recent scholarship has taught us to read the *Liber Amoris* as a deconstruction of the Wordsworthian ego whose harmonious growth can be told in an organic autobiography.[129] Seen in the context of the Petrarchan tradition, the *Liber Amoris* looks at the same time like a parody of *Canzoniere* and a confirmation of it. Sarah was only initially Hazlitt's Laura, as he later saw her as a cold and unfeeling Lolita duping the men who wooed her.[130] Still, despite its immense differences, the *Liber Amoris* remains an odd sort of Petrarchan rather than Wordsworthian autobiography, hinging on irrational passion which made a fool of his protagonist, and yet it forced him to tell everyone his tale. 'But now I see well how for a long time I was the talk of the crowd, for which often I am ashamed of myself within, and yet I write my story': these words from the opening sonnet of *Canzoniere* apply to Hazlitt's *Liber Amoris* more than any other British book of the age.

A secret autobiographical element can also be traced in Ugo Foscolo's *Essays on Petrarch*, the last stage of our enquiry. Foscolo's essays have a complicated editorial and biographical history which, however, sheds light on his interpretation of Petrarch. An exile in London with unresolved financial problems since 1816, Foscolo began to contribute to some of the major periodicals of the time. The literary occasion for the first, shorter draft of his essay was a review of two French books on Petrarch, a biography by the Abbé de Roman and a novel, *Pétrarque et Laure*, by the Comtesse de Genlis. Besides, there was a personal reason for writing about Petrarch rather than any other Italian poet. As Cesare Foligno emphasised, Foscolo's project was due to his passion for Caroline Russell, with whom he read Petrarch's poems in the summer of 1818.[131] Foscolo's review should have appeared in the *Edinburgh Review* but, since Francis Jeffrey delayed publication, Foscolo printed it in only eight copies, one of which was sent to Caroline as a sort of love letter.[132] Foscolo then arranged to have the article published in the *Quarterly Review*; but, as in March 1820 it became clear that Caroline would never return his love for her, he decided to revise and expand his thoughts on Petrarch. When the article appeared in April 1821, Foscolo complained about William Gifford's editorial revision, which was significant though not heavy.[133] Foscolo himself omitted the initial pages of the first draft, which contained his views on Genlis, Roman, Sade and Dobson, who were his main sources together with two Italian scholars, Beccadelli and Tiraboschi.[134] In 1821 Foscolo collected his essays in a book, an expensive imprint which was followed by the expanded, definitive version in 1823, whose main addition was the Appendix containing Lady Dacre's translations from Petrarch.

Though Foscolo's familiarity with Petrarch was much greater than that of the English admirers of *Canzoniere*, it is worth emphasising that his starting point was the same one. In the first draft of his essay, Foscolo expressed his dissatisfaction with the contemporary biographies of Petrarch, as we saw at the beginning of this chapter. An example of fictional biographer was the Abbé de Roman, who debased Petrarch's love into that of a provincial Frenchman. Even Sade, whose work was valuable for scholars, was no exception: 'a great many editors and commentators on the works of Petrarch have published each a romance.' On the other hand, some scholars, like Sade, lost themselves in innumerable minutiae or focused too much on the historical background to the disadvantage of their true topic, that is, the author's life.[135] However critical, Foscolo could not help taking sides in the debate on Sade's theses, which he found convincing. Tytler's dissertation, which he also knew, only confirmed Sade's ideas. Foscolo was aware that many women had written about Petrarch. He chose to discuss only Dobson, on account of her popularity, and Madame de Genlis.[136] Dobson was more concise than Sade, which was a great merit, but she was colder and often added comments that most readers were able to make on their own. She left out the evidence of Sade's arguments, so that English readers were not able to judge properly. In the plates included in her edition, Petrarch had unjustly been portrayed as a troubadour. Her Latin and her Italian were not good enough to understand Petrarch as he really was and not as the 'female world' always pictured him, that is, only as a tormented lover, forgetting his scholarly and political life.[137] Madame de Genlis was another example. She affirmed she had written a book which was at the same time a history, a romance and a poem.[138] In other words, though Foscolo was annoyed with the male pedantry of scholars like Sade, he was also critical of the female vision of Petrarch's story as a romance of Sensibility.[139] Tradition taught readers to believe that the 'object of romance is to insinuate that the more vehement passions are consistent with the purest virtue; and that it is possible to loose the imagination, without leading the mind into dangerous excesses and sensual indulgencies.' For centuries Petrarch's poetry had been brought out as evidence for this, which, in Foscolo's mind, was a mistake. The form of love celebrated in Petrarch's poetry was another.[140]

Foscolo divided his study of Petrarch into four essays, on 'the Love of Petrarch' (Essay 1), 'the Poetry of Petrarch' (Essay 2), 'the Character of Petrarch' (Essay 3), and 'A Parallel between Dante and Petrarch' (Essay 4). The very order of his argument shows that his perspective on Petrarch was the same one for which he had before blamed the other critics. He read Petrarch's poetry as part of his life, as most scholars did, and he started from Petrarch's love, as did most common readers – especially women. Foscolo's ideas on Petrarch's love, however, were unconventional. He believed that, though Petrarch had thrown a thin veil over the figure of Love, this god was still the same as that of the classics, who distinguished between a celestial and a terrestrial Venus. In ancient times, women lived separately from men. Artists and the fashionable world, however, met in the houses of ladies, who 'made an avowed traffic of their charms' and were the models for their works. Foscolo described the view of love in Plato's *Symposium*, part of which furnished the basis for Petrarch's philosophy of love, which reflected common medieval ideas. Each soul had only one true lover, who was the means by which both were lifted towards God, whence they had come.[141] To demonstrate the continuity of the tradition, Foscolo included in the Appendixes a generous selection of Greek, Latin, Italian, and English love poems in French, English, and Italian translation. The comparison with Sappho is especially noteworthy, as she was the other great model for the love poets of the time. Foscolo read Sappho in a Petrarchan way, since he stated that the 'Blest as the immortal God' ode, of which he gave a masterly translation, undoubtedly must have ended in the last, missing section with 'profound reflections upon the misery of desperate love'.[142] It is not surprising that Foscolo's parallel between classical and Petrarchan love was omitted by Gifford, who evidently could not accept the idea that they were ultimately the same thing, and that *Canzoniere* was a celebration, behind a Christian mask of moderation, of erotic desire.

In Foscolo's account, Petrarch's story sounded less recommendable to young ladies than English readers believed. After his introduction, Foscolo mentioned his sources (Sade, Dobson and Tytler) to point out that Petrarch's love was adulterous, as Laura was a married woman. Like Hazlitt, Foscolo reflected on the physical appearance of Petrarch and Laura, whose early portraits gave but a vague idea of her countenance. They were French works and had neither the warmth of the Italian nor the cheerful serenity of the English beauties.[143] Foscolo, then, reported the usual development of the relationship between the two lovers, with Laura's unhappy marriage, her tricky coyness and Petrarch's anxieties, up to Section XVI, where he commented on Laura's attitude. This significant passage was added in the volume edition and was tinged with the consequences of his recent, unhappy love story. In February 1821 he told Mary Graham that, for women, the most interesting part of his essay would be that it revealed something of the heart of the ' "*Civettissima Santissima Madonna Laura*" ' ('holiest arch-coquette, Madonna Laura'), a sour definition which most probably reflected his resentment towards Caroline Russell.[144]

What did Foscolo see in Laura's heart? He argued that her attitude was typical of many beautiful women, who take a narcissistic pleasure in being adored and giving nothing in return. Like Eve in Milton's paradise, they 'delight to search in the heart of their lover for the reflection of their own image only'. Foscolo did not forget that Laura, a married woman, may have been forced to behave like that to save her honour. This, however, was no sufficient excuse, because in Avignon sexual morality was not strict. Viciously, she justified her behaviour saying that her refusal could guide Petrarch to heaven, a view that, eventually, he made his own. Foscolo was surprised that such a situation could last for 20 years. The doubt whether he had been loved or deluded by Laura continued to corrode Petrarch's mind even after her death.[145] In short, Foscolo found nothing admirable in Laura's virtue, which was to him a subtle sadistic perversion; he highlighted Petrarch's torments and was not impressed by the transcendental consolations of the final section of *Canzoniere*, which were summarised in the last pages of his essay.

The following essay, 'on the Poetry of Petrarch', contains perhaps Foscolo's most original contributions. His subtle observations on Petrarch's style stemmed from a familiarity with the Italian tradition that no English or French writer could equal. To the surprise of many naive Romantics, Foscolo stressed that Petrarch's wonderfully melodious poetry, whose language was renowned for purity and naturalness, was the result of a painstaking labour of correction which ended only with his death.[146] This fact gave rise to the idea that Petrarch was more a poet than a genuine lover. Foscolo resolved the dilemma with a Wordsworthian move: he argued that the effects of passion last longer in men of genius, and what we call imagination is, in fact, a 'combination of strong feelings and recollections'.[147] In this way, his Petrarch could be presented as both a warm-hearted, romantic lover and a meticulous classicist, a feature which often remained in the background of the British views of Petrarch. Provençal or Spanish poetry may well have been the sources of Petrarch's notorious conceits, which did not harmonise with the solemn, meditative character of his poetry.[148]

Petrarch restored 'the glow and the warmth' of Sappho, which Horace had converted into mere gaiety and gallantry. Moreover, Petrarch added in a delicacy, drawn from the Bible, that no classical poet possessed. An example was his comparison between Laura and the Virgin Mary, which David Hume had blamed as absurd.[149] The genius of giving universal value to one's passions belonged to very few poets, like Sappho and Petrarch; a 'modern Sappho', that is, Madame de Staël, was more skilled in displaying the interior anatomy of her feelings 'to the understanding, than to the eyes and hearts of her readers'.[150] The representation of love 'had the greatest influence upon mankind', because anyone could understand it. Novels, however, 'seldom please the next generation', because they represent external accidents rather than the inward nature of love. Petrarch's portrait of his heart made readers see through the metaphysical and technical paraphernalia by which he painted it. At this point, Foscolo's Petrarch became quintessentially Romantic: 'It is chiefly in the expression of grief that Petrarch enters into every heart.'[151]

Petrarch sang his poems to the sound of his lute, but whereas Metastasio, another great melodist, emptied his language of meaning to favour sound, Petrarch created a language which was full of meaning and still entirely in use, which was amazing considering that he rarely spoke Italian, as he spent most of his life far from Tuscany.[152] The last section of the essay describes Petrarch as a scholar and an indefatigable, proto-romantic traveller wandering through Europe in search of manuscripts of classical authors.

The 'Essay on the Character of Petrarch' goes back to a perspective by now familiar to us. Foscolo described Petrarch's powerful friends; his anti-clericalism, which Foscolo grossly exaggerated; his fame, which made him a respected man everywhere; and his political career, which Foscolo defended against his critics. Foscolo responded to Sismondi, who, typically, held that Petrarch flattered all the tyrants of his age. Foscolo pointed out that Petrarch's family was exiled from Florence, and that Petrarch spent most of his life away from his town. He was a friend of princes and cardinals, but he always kept them at some distance. His political *canzoni*, which Foscolo read in a nationalist perspective, were among the best of their genre. With nationalist effrontery, which was also a way of winning the favour of the British public, Foscolo affirmed that Petrarch hated the French and the Germans.[153] In the final part of the essay, Foscolo focused on those aspects of Petrarch's personality which often went unmentioned in shorter biographies which described only Petrarch the lover: his surprising influence on the powerful men of his time; his lack of humour; his attachment to money in old age; his disturbing coldness towards his natural children; his sober lifestyle; his pleasure for solitude and his modern restlessness.

In the last essay, 'A Parallel between Dante and Petrarch', Foscolo elucidated the main characteristics of the founders of Italian poetry, with a view to telling the English public, whose attention concentrated only on some aspects of their works, what they represented in Italian culture. Foscolo recalled that Petrarch's poetics had been the most influential of the two, as it had been normative up to Romantic times. Foscolo focused on their styles from the start. He contrasted the variety and 'impurity' of Dante's language with Petrarch's elegance, and Petrarch's melodiousness with Dante's more sober and powerful music. The reader's response to them was very different: Petrarch 'awaked the heart to a deep feeling of its existence'; Dante led the imagination 'to add to the interest and novelty of nature'.[154] Petrarch was only interested in himself, and his morbidity paralysed readers; Dante was the historian of his time and rendered everything interesting.

At this point, Foscolo found a precise political reason for Petrarch's prevalence over Dante in Italian culture. Churchmen and courtiers chose Petrarch's Platonic language to justify their commerce with the fair sex. That language was also 'admirably calculated for a Jesuits' college, since it inspires devotion, mysticism, and retirement, and enervates the minds of youth'. After the French Revolution and the introduction of a new system of education, however, 'Petrarch's followers have rapidly diminished; and those of Dante have written poems' to stir Italian nationalism. Dante's poetry was linked to his time, 'when liberty was making her dying struggle against tyranny'; on the contrary, Petrarch 'lived amongst those who prepared the inglorious heritage of servitude for the next fifteen generations.'[155] Though Foscolo had been more balanced in the previous essays, here he let the exiled romantic nationalist take the upper hand. These views were common in liberal and nationalist circles, and Foscolo himself answered them, as we saw before, when he criticised Sismondi's ideological opinions on Petrarch, whose politics could not be reduced to a form of enervated servilism. Of course, there may well be an element of sympathetic identification between Dante and Foscolo, both of whom were exiles, and a form of envy towards Petrarch, who was able to preserve his independence while, simultaneously, being listened to with reverence by the most powerful politicians of his time. Petrarch was born in exile and died a wealthy and respected man; Dante was born an aristocrat and died in exile and misery. None the less, Petrarch was the most unhappy of them owing to his anxious restlessness and his contempt of the world.[156]

Foscolo wrote with great insight on Petrarch even though his sympathies lay with Dante. His preference re-emerged forcefully after Caroline's rejection and led him to his essay on Dante and Petrarch. Thomas Campbell, who was a good friend of Foscolo's, remembered that he always thought Dante the greatest writer. However, he could recite by heart many of Petrarch's sonnets, which he read with the deepest tones of admiration.[157] It is significant that even a convinced Dantist like him turned Petrarchan during a love story. Foscolo's essays contain a biographical element of identification – sentimental frustration – which intermingles with their subject. This was not an exception but the rule with all the critics and poets who were involved with Petrarch in the Romantic age. Biographical empathy played an essential role in the Romantic fashion for Petrarch. Moreover, Foscolo's essays, which in Italian literature have the same place as Coleridge's lectures on Shakespeare in English literature, are significantly indebted to British culture. I doubt that Foscolo would have written such an extensive book on Petrarch, had he not lived in England in the early nineteenth century. Certainly, Italy would have been a far less favourable place for it, as Italian writers were concentrating their attention on Dante and modern foreign poetry. The numerous British translators, imitators and critics of Petrarch, together with a coincidental disgrace in Foscolo's sentimental life, gave him the chance to raise one of the monuments of Italian Romantic criticism.

2
'Englishing' Petrarch: The Translators' Role

2.1 Beginnings

As François Mouret has pointed out, British Petrarchism was a unique phenomenon in late eighteenth-century Europe. It had no counterpart in Italy, France, Germany, Spain or other European nations. In those countries, exactly as in England, there was a revival of Dante which continued throughout the nineteenth century, and is well documented in recent criticism. Conversely, the revival of Petrarch was much more limited on the Continent and has never received the scholarly attention it deserves. According to Mouret's bibliography, in late eighteenth-century Britain there were 51 translators who wrote 398 versions from Petrarch – remarkable numbers by any standard.[1] The innovating power of these writers can be understood only against the critical views of Petrarch which prevailed earlier in the century, at least up to the publication of Dobson's biography.

A champion of Italian literature like Giuseppe Baretti, who did more than anyone else to popularise it at mid-century, was a tepid supporter of Petrarch. Italian lyric poetry was considered effeminate, and this opinion was reinforced even by those critics who might be expected to defend it.[2] Baretti, a friend of Samuel Johnson's, disliked Petrarch precisely for his effeminacy, whereas he extolled Dante, Ariosto and Tasso for their manly power and greatness.[3] On the contrary, Petrarch was a kind of minimalist, full of 'trifles and little thoughts', of 'little sentiments and little images', which fitted the mediocre skills of most writers better than Dante's sublime inventions.[4] The difference between the genius of Dante and that of Petrarch was the same 'as between the size of an elephant and a fly'.[5] Baretti believed that even in sweetness Petrarch was inferior to Dante.[6] In addition, English poets such as Young, Tillotson and Johnson made him reconsider 'tutto il *nonsenso* del Petrarca' ('all the *nonsense* of Petrarch'), whose only merits were the creation of a pure language and a harmonious poetic style.[7] Such opinions are common in the history of Petrarchan criticism. They stem from the idea that Petrarch's poetry has no content. In such formalistic views, which have dominated a large part of twentieth-century scholarship, Petrarch was a great stylist who had little to say but said it very well. Obviously, a kind of poetry in which form is paramount and content irrelevant translates with great difficulty. It is not surprising that Baretti wondered who could translate a single sonnet by Petrarch into French or English.[8] However, is it true that Petrarch's poetry has no important message for its readers? That it is good form without content? The eighteenth-century British translators and imitators of Petrarch had a totally different opinion.

Another critic who might be expected to have an interest in Petrarch was Joseph Warton. However, he extolled epic poetry and shared Baretti's judgement on Petrarch, whose stanza, in comparison to those of Greek odes, displeased 'the ear, by its tedious uniformity, and by the number of identical cadences'. There was 'little valuable in Petrarch', whose 'sentiments, even of love, are metaphysical and far fetched'.[9] In other words, even the champions of medieval culture were in some cases against Petrarch. In fact, several protagonists of the revival of Dante and epic poetry were overtly hostile to Petrarch, who was in their opinion weakly, effeminate, repetitive in his subjects, limited in his stylistic range, abstract in his feelings.

Petrarch fared no better with philosophers. For example, David Hume mentioned him briefly in the conclusion to his *Of the Standard of Taste* (1757). According to Hume, religious errors were 'the most excusable in compositions of genius', provided that religious principles did not become superstition intruding 'into every sentiment'. In this case, they were 'a blemish in any polite composition'. Therefore, it 'must for ever be ridiculous in PETRARCH to compare his mistress LAURA, to JESUS CHRIST'.[10] Though the sonnet Hume had in mind had been considered as near blasphemous even in Italy, it is clear that he was uneasy with that mixture of religious and amorous feelings which is a prominent feature of the poetry of Petrarch's time.

Another guru of eighteenth-century thought like Voltaire dealt with Petrarch briefly in his *Essai sur les mœurs*. He translated the beginning of the *canzone* 'Chiare, fresche et dolci acque' even though he did not admire its author.[11] Petrarch was the greatest European poet of his century, but he only wrote elegant trifles that enjoyed great popularity in their time because they were a rare form of writing.[12] Petrarch was the greatest genius in the art of saying always the same thing.[13] His main merit was that he had purified the tongue of his tribe. Voltaire noted, with witty malice, that Petrarch's universal fame was due to his amorous troubles rather than his scholarly labours.[14] To his dismay, English sonneteers would later consider this fact as a virtue rather than a defect. Like other scholars, Voltaire was sceptical about Petrarch's love. After receiving volume I of Sade's biography, he wrote that the Abbé was an ally of Petrarch because he supported not only Petrarch's grace and taste, but also his lifelong passion for an ungrateful woman, which Voltaire found foolish and unbelievable.[15]

Predictably, Rousseau's attitude to Petrarch was the opposite of Hume's and Voltaire's. The passionate letters of the protagonists of *La Nouvelle Héloïse* contain several quotations from Petrarch, an example which was followed by many novels of Sensibility in the subsequent decades.[16] As in *La Nouvelle Héloïse*, the characters of the English epistolary novels often used sonnets to express their most intimate feelings. However, not just any poet would do. Petrarch was one of the very few authors that Rousseau recommended. The protagonist couple of *La Nouvelle Héloïse* planned to lay aside most subjects normally taught at school in order to learn from nature alone. All languages will be dismissed 'except the Italian, which you understand and admire'.[17] The same happened to most writers: 'Except Petrarch, Tasso, Metastasio, and the best French theatrical authors, I leave you none of those amorous poets, which are the common amusement of your sex. The most inspired of them cannot teach us to love. Ah, Eloisa, we are better instructed by our own hearts.' Borrowed phrases were insipid, cramped the imagination and enervated the mind.[18] Therefore, the few, chosen quotations from Petrarch that Rousseau included in his novel were all the more significant and had a greater echo among his innumerable admirers.[19]

2.2   Early translators and imitators

Before the publication of Sade's biography and, above all, Dobson's abridged version in 1775, English translations from Petrarch were only occasional. In most cases, as we just saw, they appeared as citations in essays which were often translations of works of foreign scholars.[20] In the first half of the century there was only a handful of British translations from Petrarch, which are worth mentioning because, in hindsight, they look almost prophetic.[21] Among them, there are three versions, made by Mary Monk in 1716 and reprinted in several anthologies, of the famous *canzone* 'Chiare, fresche et dolci acque', the sonnet 'Stiamo, Amor, a veder la gloria nostra', a eulogy of Laura's beauty which illuminates everything around her, and the sonnet 'Solo et pensoso', later one of the great favourites with the British Petrarchists.[22] A woman poet who translated a poem on a melancholy lover wandering alone in a landscape to keep away from common folk, who would make a laughing stock of her: this became a central trend in British Petrarchism later in the century.[23]

The other, more relevant contribution of the early eighteenth century was Thomas Gray's only sonnet, 'on the Death of Mr. Richard West', which was composed in 1742 and published posthumously in 1775. Its seminal influence on the revival of the sonnet has been known for a long time.[24] Its kinship with Petrarch's 'Zephiro torna, e 'l bel tempo rimena', one of Petrarch's masterpieces and his most frequently translated sonnet in Romantic England, has been noticed at least since the early nineteenth century, but it has never been paid much attention by British critics. Other sources, from classical poetry to

Milton, have been considered more relevant, though all of them are vaguer than 'Zephiro torna'.[25] My intention is to follow the tracks of the Petrarchan influence as far as possible.

I suspect that the popularity of 'Zephiro torna' with the British translators owed something to Gray's sonnet, which, in its turn, owed more than a suggestion to Petrarch's poem. The subject of the two sonnets is the same: the dramatic opposition between the cyclical rebirth of natural life and the melancholy of the protagonist, who is excluded from the happiness of the other living beings because he is mourning in vain a person he loved:

> In vain to me the smiling mornings shine,
> And reddening Phoebus lifts his golden fire:
> The birds in vain their amorous descant join;
> Or cheerful fields resume their green attire:
> These ears, alas! for other notes repine,
> A different object do these eyes require.
> My lonely anguish melts no heart but mine;
> And in my breast the imperfect joys expire.
> Yet morning smiles the busy race to cheer,
> And new-born pleasure brings to happier men:
> The fields to all their wonted tribute bear:
> To warm their little loves the birds complain:
> I fruitless mourn to him that cannot hear,
> And weep the more because I weep in vain.

> *Zephiro torna, e 'l bel tempo rimena*
> *e i fiori et l'erbe, sua dolce famiglia,*
> *et garrir Progne et pianger Philomena,*
> *et primavera candida et vermiglia.*

> *Ridono i prati, e 'l ciel si rasserena;*
> *Giove s'allegra di mirar sua figlia;*
> *l'aria et l'acqua et la terra è d'amor piena;*
> *ogni animal d'amar si riconsiglia.*

> *Ma per me, lasso, tornano i più gravi*
> *sospiri, che del cor profondo tragge*
> *quella ch'al ciel se ne portò le chiavi;*

> *et cantar augelletti et fiorir piagge,*
> *e 'n belle donne honeste atti soavi*
> *sono un deserto, et fere aspre et selvagge.*[26]

As Contini and other scholars have noted, the celebration of the resurrection of life in spring can be found in Lucretius and Virgil, and it is commonplace in Provençal lyric poetry. Other authors well-known to Gray used the same *topos*, as Lonsdale pointed out in his edition of the poems. Besides, in their intense correspondence Gray and West exchanged poems and translations, in Latin and English, in which images of reawakening life in spring and puns on Zephyrus, West's nickname from the time of their Eton school-days, loom large, as they appear, for example, in West's 'Ad Amicos' (1737) and 'Ode to May' (1742), and in Gray's 'Ad C: Favonium Aristium' (1738), 'Ad C: Favonium Zephyrinum' (1740), 'De Principiis Cogitandi' (1740–42) and 'Ode on the Spring' (1742, which he sent to West not knowing he was already dead).[27] Finally, in the weeks preceding West's death Gray was reading Petrarch, whom he found 'sometimes very tender and natural'.[28] It not surprising, then, that in the poetic outburst following the shocking news of the death of his friend, Gray turned to Petrarch's sonnet, in which many of his recent experiences seemed to be condensed.

Though the theme of 'Zephiro torna' appears in other authors, it was Petrarch who used it specifically to create friction between the joy of nature reawakened by eros and the sadness of a lyrical 'I' deprived of his lover. In fact, the number of common elements in Petrarch's and Gray's texts cannot be mere coincidence. Gray chose to treat this exquisitely Petrarchan theme in a sonnet at a time when this form was extremely rare. It is worth remembering that the first sonnets by Thomas Edwards, who is usually considered as the initiator of the eighteenth-century revival, were published in 1748. Moreover, it has never been noted that the rhyme schemes of Petrarch's and Gray's texts are identical (abab abab cdc dcd), and that both of them have a syntactic turning-point in the 'Yet' in line 9. This is not mere accident, as the notes in Gray's *Common-place Book* show. In the entry 'Metrum' he described different rhyme schemes for the sonnet, identifying only two of them as genuinely Italian and Petrarchan. He chose one of these for his sonnet.[29] Gray's intentional choice of the Petrarchan rather than the Miltonic sonnet is extremely significant, since Petrarch's sonnets, however unpopular at this date, were synonymous with love poetry.

The imagery of the two sonnets, also, is the same, though Gray gave the single images a different emphasis and a different order. One obvious difference is that there is no 'Zephiro' at the beginning of Gray's sonnet, but the reason for it is elementary. A literal translation of this point was impossible, because in the original text Zephyrus returns, whereas Gray's Zephyrus had gone for ever. However, the presence of West's nickname in Petrarch's sonnet must have been one more element of attraction for Gray, when he began to conceive a poetic homage to his unlucky friend. It was a way of continuing and concluding a game they had played in their poems with the name 'Zephyrus' for a long time. The crucial difference was that in Gray's sonnet the joy of spring was not brought along by Zephyrus, whereas in the earlier poems it was the presence of his friend which vivified and gave sense to natural life.

Despite the absence of the word 'Zephyrus' in Gray's sonnet, Petrarch's description of the return of spring is only postponed to Gray's lines 3–4, which correspond exactly to the original. Petrarch's 'fine weather' (l. 1), on the contrary, is spread over Gray's lines 1–2. The main difference between the two poems is that Gray is openly pessimistic from the beginning, considering the 'in vain' which opens and closes his sonnet. In the eternal cycle of life, the only cyclicity granted to Gray was the vanity of his sorrow, for which he, in this text, could find no otherworldly consolation. An ultramundane perspective is usually present in Petrarch, though 'Zephiro torna' is devoid of it and only concentrates on his worldly grief, which could be consoled by neither fine women nor cheerful nature.[30]

If Petrarch separated neatly the portrait of joyful nature (ll. 1–8) from his hopeless melancholy (ll. 9–14), Gray redoubled the conflict: cheerful nature is celebrated in Gray's quatrain I, whereas quatrain II describes his anguish; lines 9–12 describe once again the amorous pleasures of animals and 'happier men', while his despondency was condensed in the final couplet. To make the second part more dramatic, Gray created a sort of discrepancy between syntax and metrics, that is, between the form of the argument (ll. 9–12 and their answer in ll. 13–14) and the metrical scheme of the two tercets. This structural dissonance was anticipated in line 10 in the sonnet's only imperfect rhyme, whose effect is to highlight the rhyme word 'men'. This offers another important clue to our interpretation. The main difference between the two sonnets would seem to be that Petrarch was mourning his departed lover, and Gray a dead friend. However, as a repressed homosexual, Gray probably used Petrarch's sonnet as a subtext to encrypt his otherwise unspeakable feelings: 'My lonely anguish melts no heart but mine; / And in my breast the imperfect joys expire.' Rewriting what was then the obscure sonnet of a half-forgotten Italian poet, Gray was able to give vent to his twofold anguish, for the loss of a beloved friend and for the impossibility of expressing it fully. It is now clear, also, why the name 'Zephyrus' could not appear in the sonnet to West. Gray rewrote Petrarch in the same way as he and West had rewritten Propertius and Tibullus to encode the obscure amorous feelings they had for each other. However, the source and the addressee of Gray's imitation – Petrarch and 'Zephyrus' – needed to be concealed, as they would have made its dangerous meaning apparent.[31] Still, as Esther Schor argued, it was so difficult not to read the poem as a lover's complaint that in Mason's edition the original title, 'Sonnet', was changed into 'Sonnet on the Death of Mr. Richard West'.[32]

Further evidence for our interpretation can be found in Gray's Latin translation of Petrarch's 'Lasso, ch'i ardo, et altri non me 'l crede', made in 1736–37.[33] Whereas Gray's other versions from Latin have received greater critical attention, this translation has been generally considered as a technical exercise from an author with whom Gray had little in common.[34]

Lasso, ch'i' ardo, et altri non me 'l crede;
sì crede ogni uom, se non sola colei
che sovr'ogni altra, et ch'i' sola, vorrei:
ella non par che 'l creda, e sì sel vede.

Infinita bellezza et poca fede,
non vedete voi 'l cor nelli occhi mei?
Se non fusse mia stella, i' pur devrei
al fonte di pietà trovar mercede.

Quest'arder mio, di che vi cal sì poco,
e i vostri honori, in mie rime diffusi,
ne porian infiammar fors'anchor mille:

ch'i' veggio nel penser, dolce mio foco,
fredda una lingua et duo belli occhi chiusi
rimaner, dopo noi, pien' di faville.[35]

Uror io! veros at nemo credidit ignes:
*   quin credunt omnes; dura sed illa negat.*
Illa negat, soli volumus cui posse probare:
*   quin videt, et visos improba dissimulat.*
Ah durissima mi, sed et ah pulcherrima rerum!
*   nonne animam in misera, Cynthia, fronte vides?*
Omnibus illa pia est, et, si non fata vetassent,
*   tam longas mentem flecteret ad lacrimas.*
Sed tamen has lacrimas, hunc tu, quem spreveris, ignem,
*   carminaque auctori non bene culta suo*
Turba futurorum non ignorabit amantum:
*   nos duo, cumque erimus parvus uterque cinis,*
Iamque faces, eheu! oculorum, et frigida lingua
*   hac sine luce iacent, immemor illa loqui:*
Infelix Musa aeternos spirabit amores,
*   ardebitque urna multa favilla mea.*

Alas, I am on fire; but no one believed that the fires are real: or rather, they all believe – it is just she, hard as she is, that denies it. She denies it, whom alone I long to convince. In fact, she sees them, and, wicked woman, pretends that she has not. Ah, most cruel to me! but also, alas, the most beautiful of creatures! Do you not see my soul in my wretched face, Cynthia? She is gracious to all, and if the fates had not forbidden it, she would have softened her heart in the face of such prolonged weeping. But yet the throng of future lovers will not be ignorant of these tears, the fire which you disdain, and the songs that have brought no profit their poet; even when we two will each be no more than a handful of ashes, then alas, the flames of my eyes will lie deprived of light, and my cold tongue forget how to speak: but the ill-starred Muse will breathe out eternal love and many a spark will glow in my urn.[36]

The sonnet is a complaint that everyone but Laura believed that Petrarch was in love with her. The passion embodied in his verse would kindle the passion of many readers and it would survive, in a sort of surrealist vision, even in Laura's eyes and on Petrarch's tongue after death thanks to his poetry. Gray's lament over unrequited love must have had a different meaning, which he concealed, to use Gibbon's charming phrase, 'in the decent obscurity of a learned language'. It is naive to believe, as, for example, Robert Mack does, that a translation into Latin signals a detached, merely erudite interest in the original. The truth is the exact opposite. As Walter Ong has pointed out, until the nineteenth century Latin was a sexually specialised language used almost exclusively among males.[37] W. Hutchings and other scholars have noted that Gray's Latin poems to West, far from being inert exercises in a dead language, embody his most intimate feelings for his friend and include several daring expressions of them.[38] Petrarch's love poetry touched Gray to the quick and Latin, a familiar though not an everyday language, furnished the necessary distance to deal with a problematic topic.[39]

Petrarch's sonnet and its Latin version were important, since the last tercet, which Gray found particularly intriguing, furnished the turning-point in his 'Elegy Written in a Country Churchyard', lines 89–92: 'On some fond breast the parting soul relies, / Some pious drops the closing eyes requires; / Ev'n from the tomb the voice of nature cries, / Ev'n in our ashes live their wonted fires.'[40] This paradoxical statement, that passion does not die out with physical death thanks to poetry, concludes the first part of the 'Elegy' and immediately precedes the introduction of a new figure, a 'thee' (l. 93) whose identity has been widely debated.[41] Whoever that figure may be, it is clear that his 'wonted fires', primarily, are those of a frustrated lover, since the conclusion of the poem describes him as a melancholy swain musing alone in the countryside, a figure of the pastoral but also the Petrarchan tradition.

Petrarch turns up at another delicate point of the 'Elegy' (ll. 125–8): '*No farther seek his merits to disclose, / Or draw his frailties from their dread abode, / (There they alike in trembling hope repose) / The bosom of his Father and his God.*' Petrarch was the source of 'trembling hope' in the penultimate line, as Gray pointed out in a note – which means that he must have considered the intertextual link as particularly noteworthy. Petrarch's phrase 'paventosa speme' ('trembling hopes') comes from Sonnet 147, 'Quando 'l voler che con duo sproni ardenti', which does not deal with otherworldly expectations, as the context of Gray's 'Elegy' might lead one to think, but with frustrated sexual desire. In fact, it is one of the sonnets where Petrarch's physical desire is expressed most powerfully. Irrational passion moved him ardently with two spurs, desire and hope, but also halted him with great fear, raised by Laura's stern frowning at the desire she could see in his face. At that point he withdrew, 'Ma freddo foco et paventosa speme / de l'alma che traluce come un vetro / talor sua dolce vista rasserena' ('but cooling fires and trembling hopes in my soul, which is transparent as glass, sometimes make clear again her sweet countenance', Petrarca 2001, 147). As Marco Santagata has pointed out, the tercet can be read in two different ways: either, cooled desire and fearful hope, which show in my soul as through a glass, make her look more tender and serene; or, Laura regains her habitual serenity when she sees that my desire has cooled down.[42] Gray used Petrarch's phrase in a metaphysical sense: his merits and frailties are reposing in God in 'trembling hope'. However, in the Eton manuscript version of the 'Elegy' the last quatrain runs as follows: 'No farther seek his Merits to disclose, / Nor seek to draw them from their dread Abode / (His Frailties there in trembling Hope repose) / The Bosom of his Father & his God.'[43] Here 'trembling hope' is used much more literally in the original sense, since it refers only to his frailties, that is, his moral weakness. The intertextual link clarifies their nature: they have specifically to do with erotic desire rather than generically, as the last version of the 'Elegy' seems to suggest, with some moral shortcoming.[44]

After Mary Monk, Gray anticipated other major strains of the revival of Petrarch. His sonnet on the death of West is an early example of the commemoration of a departed lover, for whom no consolation could be found in the cyclical life of nature. Later in the century, the *in morte* section of *Canzoniere* was ransacked by many poets to mourn the loss of their beloved. Besides, Gray's explicit references to Petrarch in two key points of his 'Elegy' established a permanent link between elegiac poetry and Petrarch, which in the following decades, with Charlotte Smith and many others, became the quintessentially Romantic approach to the *Canzoniere*.

There was a third, obvious possibility for translators and imitators: using Petrarch to create intimacy between two lovers, as Rousseau had done in *La Nouvelle Heloïse*. The earliest of these figures was John Langhorne (1735–1779), who in 1762 complained about the fashion for elegiacs and the mournful poses of poets.[45] His critical opinions on Petrarch were in part like those of Baretti, Voltaire and Hume. He did not read Sade and doubted the sincerity of Petrarch's love for Laura. He argued that Petrarch would have married Laura, if he had really loved her.[46] He partly shared the view of Petrarch's love as unmanly and he even specified that 'Petrarchal and Platonic love are [...] very foolish things.'[47] Despite such reservations, in 1765 he translated Petrarch and in 1770 he referred to him several times in his *Letters to Eleonora*, an epistolary novel where he collected the correspondence with his wife, Ann Cracroft, before marriage.[48] Langhorne could not be completely satisfied with Petrarch because his ideal was marital love, which he celebrated in *Letters to Eleonora*. Though he had criticised the elegiac element in Petrarch, the story he told in *Letters to Eleonora* was not a cheerful one, as the novel was published after his wife's death in 1768.[49] Petrarch was mentioned again in *Letters between Theodosius and Constantia*, the correspondence of another tragic couple which resembles Eloisa and Abelard: two fine young people whose families were hostile to their love and forced her to retire to a convent. They both died a short time later and were buried together.[50] Though these two novels are now forgotten, they went through several editions in the Romantic age and, despite Langhorne's reservations, they reinforced the ties between Petrarch and the rising culture of Sensibility – including its morbid side. Langhorne's poems, which took issue with Petrarch for his languid melancholy, were also popular, and his versions from Petrarch were reprinted in several anthologies.[51] Though the aesthetic value of Langhorne's writings is limited, their mixture of attraction and revulsion illustrates in the best way the transition from Augustan to Romantic attitudes towards Petrarch.

2.3 Sir William Jones and Charles Burney

Langhorne's complaint in *Letters to Eleonora* that there were no English translations of Petrarch was met in the following years by Dobson and some important translators.[52] The first of these was Sir William Jones, whose role in the Romantic revival of Petrarch has not yet been given the importance it deserves. Jones was from the beginning an enthusiastic admirer of Petrarch, and his admiration never wavered. In India in 1787 he used to read Italian literature with his wife in their garden in the evening. He wrote that they finished Ariosto, Tasso, Metastasio and wanted to begin Dante, but he specified, 'Petrarca's Odes I read again and again, and shall never be tired of them', and even, 'Petrarca I have almost by heart'.[53] Though by 1787 British interest in Petrarch had grown considerably, after receiving Charlotte Smith's sonnets Jones wrote: 'Petrarca is little known; his sonnets, especially the first book, are the least valuable of his works, and contain less natural sentiments than those of the swan of Avon; but his odes which are political, are equal to the lyric poems of the Greeks; and his triumphs are in a triumphant strain of sublimity and magnificence.'[54] This passage contains three intriguing critical views: firstly, Jones preferred Petrarch's heroic *canzoni* to the sonnets, though he disliked above all the *in vita* ones; secondly, he believed that Shakespeare's sonnets contained more natural sentiments than those of Petrarch's, which was a very unusual opinion at this date; thirdly, he admired the magnificence of Petrarch's *Triumphs*, which were rare reading at this time.

Unlike many literati, who knew politics only second-hand and blamed Petrarch for compromising too easily, Jones, who had a direct experience of power, admired Petrarch's political wisdom. Jones argued with Plato that a good nation should be like a great orchestra, where harmony rules. Unfortunately, in real life he only found conflict and dissonance. He wished with Petrarch he could spend his time among those, like a couple of his friends, who loved goodness, as his 'favourite Petrarch' said in the *canzone* 'Italia mia'.[55] He cited some lines from this poem again to support his view that a good officer abroad needed to have cultural interests.[56] Clearly, Jones adhered to the humanistic ideal founded by Petrarch, with whom he shared another tenet: the aspiration towards a quiet, retired life of study. If he could lay aside the thorns without the roses of his life as a lawyer, he would enjoy the *'vita serena'* ('serene life') Petrarch described in 'Italia mia' and *De vita solitaria*, which would allow him to gather more frequently the roses without thorns of poetry.[57]

Jones's enthusiasm for Petrarch was not confined to these late remarks; in fact, his interest goes back to his youth. On the occasion of his first visit to Vaucluse in 1769, he gave his 'favourite Petrarch' a second reading and liked 'his lamentations over Laura' so much that he selected 'the most beautiful passages, and threw them altogether in the form of an Elegy'. He was so impressed by Vaucluse that he immediately composed a description of it, which he added to his 'Elegy'.[58] *Laura, an Elegy from Petrarch* was the title Jones gave to a group of Petrarch's sonnets he translated and gathered as sections of one poem in his *Poems Consisting Chiefly of Translations from the Asiatick Languages* (1772). The context in which they appeared is of extreme interest.

In the Preface, after introducing his versions from the Eastern literatures, which are imitations rather than close versions, Jones said that 'The ode of *Petrarch* was added, that the reader might compare the manner of the *Asiatick* poets with that of the *Italians*, many of whom have written in the true spirit of the *Easterns*: some of the *Persian* songs have a striking resemblance to the sonnets of *Petrarch*; and even the form of those little amatory poems was, I believe, brought into *Europe* by the *Arabians*.' In particular, the images of the breeze playing with Laura's hair in a sonnet like 'Aura che quelle chiome bionde et crespe' (*PC*, 227) could have been written by Hafiz or Jami, who often used the same images. Jones's elegy on the death of Laura was inserted precisely to allow readers to draw 'a comparison between the *Oriental* and the *Italian* poetry'.[59] The idea of these comparisons can partly be traced to Voltaire, who in his *Essai sur les mœurs* said that Sa'di was a contemporary of Petrarch and enjoyed the same popularity. Jones took up this hint, reversing its original value which was not that of a compliment.[60] Unlike Voltaire, Jones was endeavouring to promote Eastern poetry, as he believed that it could be translated and adapted with great profit to European languages, even though he affirmed that his ultimate aim was to stimulate the study of the original languages.[61] It may seem strange that a pillar of Western literature like Petrarch should be used as a term of comparison for Eastern poetry. Jones's aim was probably twofold: on the one hand, he was suggesting that, however remote, the Eastern literatures did have something profound in common with a significant part of the European tradition, which was only waiting to be unearthed; on the other, he was trying to point out that there might be a deep unity, or at least significant links that needed researching, between the Eastern and Western poetry of the late Middle Ages. It was an intelligent way of bringing to public attention and legitimating some forgotten poetic traditions. However, criticism alone could not achieve this result; translation was indispensable.[62]

As we said before, Jones included in his book 13 of Petrarch's poems in translation, preceded by his version of 'Chiare, fresche et dolci acque'. His translations show how difficult it was, even for an enthusiast, to retrieve a poetic style as out of fashion as that of Petrarch in the mid-eighteenth century. Though Jones pointed out in a note that Voltaire's partial version of the same *canzone* was a free rewriting that had little in common with the original, the principles on which he composed his translations were akin to those of Voltaire.[63] Jones gave an extremely free version of the *canzone* and even more freely imitated Petrarch's sonnets in his 'Elegy'.[64] As was common with imitations at that time, Jones reproduced the original Italian on the page bottom and elaborated on it freely. 'Laura, an Elegy from Petrarch' is a patchwork of imitations of *in morte* sonnets – or part of sonnets – and connecting sections added by Jones. He preserved neither the original form nor the original type of language; he turned for both to the poetic models his age provided for the lament for a distant or dead lover: the Ovidian elegy, particularly in Pope's interpretation. The result is a curious elegy in heroic couplets which, in a rather random order, presents Petrarch's anguished reminiscences of Laura, his despondency even in the middle of joyful nature ('Zephiro torna', which opens the 'Elegy'), his meditations on the brevity and vanity of human happiness, and several landscape beauties. Jones left out most mythological references and expanded freely on both Petrarch's sententious passages and landscape descriptions.[65] His insistence on landscape and a tragic love story ring a Romantic bell; the language and the form in which they were expressed remain those of the eighteenth-century Ovidian verse epistle. Jones made an important step forward in the revival of Petrarch: he read him in the context of medieval poetry, Eastern and Western, and he circulated some poems which soon became Romantic favourites. Petrarch's language and poetic forms, however, remained to be uncovered.

Another major scholar who dealt with Petrarch and translated some of his sonnets was Charles Burney. Like many others, he was drawn to *Canzoniere* at a critical time of his life: he began translating it when his wife Esther died in 1762 and, predictably, he focused on the *in morte* poems.[66] However, his main interests lay in the musical element in Petrarch, which was discussed in his *General History of Music*. Once again, his sources were Sade and Dobson, for whom he expressed admiration.[67] Burney described at some length one of the favourite Romantic episodes in Petrarch's life, his crowning on the Capitol in Rome in 1340, where secular music was employed. However, unlike his contemporaries, Burney was sceptical about the ceremony. All the wisdom and delicacy of Petrarch 'seem on this occasion to have been wholly laid aside and forgotten. To become a public spectacle, and exhibit his person for the gratification of his own vanity, and the idle curiosity of an ignorant multitude, in these days would rather qualify a man for Bedlam, than for the sovereignty of Parnassus.'[68] The pleasure of showing oneself in elaborate pageants to be adulated by a mass of ignorant people could be found in other medieval customs, like tournaments. Burney added that in his later years Petrarch himself blamed the vanity and uselessness of that ceremony, though he had basked in the celebration. One reason for the crowning, however, was Petrarch's great superiority over any other writer of his age and time. Only Shakespeare was a better writer.[69]

After this long preamble, Burney came to the theme of music in Petrarch. He noted that in his sonnets there were many references to it, especially to Laura's voice, of which he gave two examples, 'I' vidi in terra angelici costumi' and 'Quando Amor i belli occhi a terra inchina'.[70] The translations are literal enough, especially the first, and their style still depends on eighteenth-century poetic diction. They seem to have been made more with an eye to the musical references in the texts than to the poetic quality of the English. At the end of this section, Burney pointed out that the music to which Petrarch set his sonnets did not survive. However, Burney was not certain that it was as good as the poems, because he noted that everywhere in Europe music developed well after poetry.

The relevance of Burney's pages on Petrarch does not lie in his versions alone, which were very few. Since his *History of Music* was widely used for decades, he certainly stirred further curiosity about Petrarch. The Romantic image of Petrarch singing his poems to the music of his lute, which, enthusiastically or critically, was often evoked in the succeeding years, had its main source in Burney, who certified its historical basis. One can never overemphasise the importance of scholars such as Burney in the Romantic revival of Petrarch or, indeed, in any revival. Whenever an author is considered silly or unfashionable, a respected scholar's reassessment is in most cases a necessary stage to render that author once more valuable or, at least, legitimate reading. That is why Capel Lofft's *Laura*, an anthology which is a sort of summa of the Romantic taste for the sonnet, included Burney's version of 'I' vidi in terra' and 'To Charles Burney, M.D. On the Sonnets in His History of Music', where Lofft eulogised Burney's love of the sonnet, the poetic form which best united music and poetry (ll. 9–14).[71]

2.4   John Nott

John Nott (1751–1825) was the first significant translator to be fascinated by Jones's ideas. Over a period of 30 years from 1775, Nott edited substantial translations of classical, European and Eastern poetry, which, as Lawrence Venuti has noticed, were the most innovative attempt of reform of the British canon of foreign literatures.[72] Nott translated only love lyric, which he presented as the centre of the poetic canon instead of epics and satire, the dominant genres in the Augustan age. His versions from Johannes Secundus Nicolaius (1775), Petrarch (1777 and 1808), Propertius (1782), Hafiz (1787), Catullus (1795), Horace (1803) and his fiction of Sappho (1803) were not only aesthetic novelties. They contained remote views of love which radically questioned the relation to sex and the relations between the sexes. The moral, social and political implications of the texts he 'Englished' were far-reaching and often met the hostility of reviewers. Obviously, his versions from Petrarch were not as disturbing as those from Hafiz and Catullus, which contained sexually explicit passages and have recently received more critical attention.[73]

The 'Advertisement' to Nott's 1777 edition pointed out that in Britain Petrarch was often discussed and quoted, though translations were infrequent. He believed the best one was 'the Ode translated by Jones'.[74] Jones influenced Nott's project in many ways, in the choice of some authors and the light in which he saw them. Like Jones, Nott found many similarities between Petrarch and Hafiz. For example, Nott wrote that the *gazel* was the Persian ode, whose stanza ended with a 'royal distich' in which the poet introduced himself. 'The Italians, who have a strange mixture of ancient literature with modern tinsel and conceit, do also conclude most of their amatory verses in a similar manner. I need but mention the Canzoni of Petrarch; which, in this instance at least, is an exact imitation of the Persian *Gazel*.'[75] Like Petrarch after his death, Hafiz came to be considered as a sort of prophet, whose works were sometimes opened randomly for divination.[76] Nott included in his edition of Petrarch the sonnet 'Aura che quelle chiome bionde et crespe' and a footnote with Jones's observation that the love sonnet had been 'brought into Italy by the Arabians', because the initial image of the wind playing in the lady's hair was very common in that tradition.[77]

In 1777 Nott pointed out that he selected only some sonnets for his edition because few people would read the entire *Canzoniere*. Later he changed his mind, as in 1808 he edited a second, larger anthology and announced the publication of a complete English edition of Petrarch's poems, which unfortunately remained in manuscript.[78] Translating Petrarch was difficult, and he included in his edition the original texts to show the origin of their oddities – conceits especially. If his versions sometimes lacked poetic harmony, it was due to his 'endeavour of strictly copying Petrarch's singular style, where he often sacrifices harmony to quaint conceit.'[79] Literalism was Nott's usual translating method, which he applied in part to Petrarch. Though his method has been praised by Venuti for its foreignising effect, in Petrarch's case its results were less extreme than with other poets.[80] None the less, some reviewers found his versions inelegant and too literal, especially in their syntax.

Nott's translations from *Canzoniere* are devoid of misinterpretations and, for the most part, close to the original. One significant point is that he adopted the Italian sonnet form, though he often modified the rhyme scheme, above all in the tercets. Also, his respect of the original formal grid obliged him to introduce frequent changes in the line endings for the sake of rhyme.[81] Together with the habits of the eighteenth-century poetic diction, this accounts for the frequent use of paraphrase in his language, which departed significantly from the terseness of the original.[82] Though Nott's sonnets were not as literal as one might have expected from him, he was even freer in his versions of Petrarch's *canzoni*, which he read against the tradition of the seventeenth- and eighteenth-century English ode. Though his versions approximately follow the original, they are paraphrases rather than translations. Like Jones, he did not reproduce Petrarch's form, which was replaced by shorter and metrically simpler stanzas.[83]

Nott's versions are correct and sometimes even elegant, but they do not display an original view of Petrarch. Their interest lies in the selection he made from *Canzoniere* rather than in the interpretation of the single poems. Though Nott's language was Augustan, he showed a pre-Romantic taste in his selection of Petrarch's sonnets. More than half of them are meditations in a landscape or contain natural descriptions, whereas the rest is divided between amorous obsessions (six sonnets), descriptions of Laura and pleas to her (seven), and moral meditations (two).[84] Nott showed impatience with conceits, which was typical of the eighteenth-century and Romantic responses to Petrarch; none the less, he translated some archetypes of concettism like 'Pace non trovo, et non ò da far guerra'. In line with his poetic project, he selected above all *in vita* sonnets, as his interests lay in the phenomenology of love rather than the elegiac lament for past life.[85]

In his view of Petrarch's love, Nott followed Sade and Dobson.[86] Though he pointed out that Petrarch's youth was dissolute, he believed that Petrarch's relationship with Laura was only platonic.[87] Nott compared Petrarch with some passages of Johannes Secundus's poems, which are extremely physical and almost pornographic in their anatomical description of sensual pleasure.[88] But these were isolated cases, since Nott did not insist on the point. He discreetly pointed out that Petrarch was left with 'nought but unsubdued desires', a free rendering of 'né di sé m'à lasciato altro che 'l nome' which made the cause of Petrarch's torments more explicit and bodily.[89] Otherwise, Nott toned down the occasional physical details of Petrarch's passion, as for instance in the sonnet 'Per mezz'i boschi inhospiti et selvaggi', where he paraphrased Petrarch's hallucination (ll. 7–8), and in the sonnet 'Aura che quelle chiome bionde et crespe', where Nott omitted the animal comparison Petrarch used to describe his upset mind.[90] The only signs of Nott's opinion of Laura are some minor changes which indicate that he found her cold and distant. In his version, Laura's bosom was not 'pacifico et sereno' ('peaceful and bright'), but 'froze, estrang'd to am'rous care'.[91] Love did not make her face pale, as Petrarch had it in 'Sennuccio, i' vo' che sapi in qual manera'; for Nott, she would 'frown contempt'.[92]

Nott's edition remains an important stage in the history of Romantic Petrarchism. It was the first and only bilingual anthology available in England for a long time and it was probably used by other translators later in the century. However, Nott's attention to the *in vita* section of *Canzoniere* did not coincide with the main Romantic interest in Petrarch. This may account for the limited impact of his versions in comparison, for example, with those of Charlotte Smith, who in this sense was the best interpreter of the spirit of the age. Significantly, when Nott edited his 1808 translation of Petrarch, which was meant as a preliminary stage for a complete edition, the ratio between *in vita* and *in morte* texts was drastically changed.[93] Also, the 1808 edition shows that Nott, though seemingly more attracted by love poets of open sensuousness, must have found Petrarch a congenial author, the only one he took up twice and retranslated.[94] In the 1808 versions, Nott became more literal, as a comparison with some of the passages mentioned before illustrates.[95] A good example of his style is 'Se lamentar augelli', a free version in 1777 and a literal one in 1808, when he decided to preserve direct speech in the tercets and the final antithesis:

> If in sweet accent moans the plaintive bird,
> > Or green groves whisper soft in summer air
> > Or from the fresh and flowery shore is heard
> > Down the rock's side the falls of water fair,
> There where I sit, enditing midst fond care;
> > Then she, whom heav'n just shew'd us, now interred,
> > Whom my fond senses living yet declare,
> > Answers from skies above each sigh preferr'd.
> "Ah why to waste thy life untimely seek?"
> > With pity she exclaims: "And wherefore flows
> > "That flood of sorrow down thy faded cheek?
> "Weep not for me; death made for ever bright
> > "My days; and, when these eyes appear'd to close,
> > "Then were they open'd in eternal light."[96]

Nott's literalism was probably a reaction to the approach to Petrarch of Charlotte Smith and many other British poets, who made free use of the original. Nott tried to draw their attention to the formal values of Petrarch's texts, but his endeavour did not have a significant impact. His contemporaries continued using Petrarch freely for their own purposes, as poets typically do.

2.5   Three anthologies

At the turn of the century, the popularity of Italian created a space in the book market for anthologies of poetry.[97] Though none of them was specifically devoted to Petrarch, they show the average way in which he was seen after a

30-year vogue. Besides, anthologies possess not only commercial value; they are part of the process of canonisation, which is all the more significant with foreign authors like Petrarch. The first anthology, *I Fiori del Parnasso Italiano*, appeared in 1798. In the 'Advertisement', the anonymous editor emphasised its novelty, which would hopefully meet the taste of those who loved Italian poetry.[98] The volume included parts of Boyd's and Hayley's Dante, Hoole's Ariosto, poems by Boiardo, Guarini and Tasso, a generous selection of Metastasio, a great favourite at the time, and a dozen of Petrarch's poems. The editor pointed out that he used good existing translations when possible; in Petrarch's case, he chose Susanna Dobson and John Langhorne – whom we have already met, William Hayley, William Collier and Thomas Le Mesurier. The selection of the texts was equally intriguing.

The first sonnet in *I Fiori del Parnasso Italiano* was not, as might be expected, a favourite masterpiece by Dante, Petrarch or Tasso, but Giustina Levi-Perotti's sonnet to Petrarch followed by his answer, both translated by William Hayley. This is extremely surprising, considering that Levi-Perotti was and remains an absolutely obscure figure. There is no doubt that the unexpected popularity she won was due to Sade and Dobson. Added to this, I suspect that *I Fiori del Parnasso Italiano* may have been compiled in some radical circle with which Hayley was in contact, or it might even have been sponsored by him directly. This could explain the space and the place his versions were given. Also, Hayley paid special attention to poetic exchange, since, as Reggie Allen pointed out, much of his 'literary career had its foundation in the simple exchange of favors and sonnets'.[99] Whatever the ultimate reasons may have been, the result deserves discussing. Hayley's version of the first two lines is a paraphrase which renders the original message more explicit: 'Gladly would I exchange inglorious ease / For future fame, the Poet's fond desire!'[100] In line 6, he translated 'ha d'ogni suo ben la via smarrita' ('has lost the way of all his good', Petrarca 2001, 7) with 'void of liberal fire', which had a political meaning no one could miss in 1798. The change of 'gloria mia' ('my glory') into 'our view' in line 10 turned Giustina's individual request into a political battlecry for women at large.[101] In short, Hayley politicised Levi-Perotti's sonnet and made it a more explicit message in support of women's rights to poetry.

'Petrarch's Answer to Signora Giustina' is equally interesting. Hayley opposed the 'bright desire' (for 'ogni vertù', 'every virtue', l. 2) to 'Custom's cold powers' (for 'costume'), which seize 'drooping fancy' (for 'nostra natura', 'our nature', l. 4). Those who feel the fire of inspiration (l. 6) 'Are frantic deem'd, by Folly's dull decrees', which is a harsh version of 'che per cosa mirabile s'addita' ('is pointed at as a strange thing', l. 7). Hayley's last couplet addressed Giustina directly: 'The more I pray thee, Nymph of graceful song, / Indulge thy spirit in its noble bent!' Hayley's version made the question a problem of morality as much as one of sensibility. He eroticised it by opposing 'bright desire' to 'Custom's cold powers' which made fancy droop, by mentioning the heavenly fire of inspiration, and by turning the neutral 'gentile spirto' ('noble spirit') into a 'Nymph of graceful song'.[102]

Hayley's versions first appeared in his *Essay on Epic Poetry* (1782) in an interesting context. His work was modelled on Pope's *Essay on Criticism* and consisted of several critical epistles. As far as Petrarch is concerned, Hayley defended his *Africa* against Sade's strictures, which he found too severe.[103] In the Fourth Epistle he recalled the episode of Giustina Levi-Perotti's sonnet to Petrarch and included 'an imitation of each', as he called his versions.[104] 'Remarks on the supposed Parsimony of Nature in bestowing Poetic Genius' is the subject of the Epistle, which contains more than a passage in defence of women writers. The voice of 'Prejudice', that 'bane of Arts', has often 'with brutal fire / Forbidding Female hands to touch the lyre, / Deny'd to Woman, Nature's fav'rite child, / The right to enter Fancy's opening wild!' He praised his time as a blessed hour when 'Fair-ones cancel such absurd decrees'. As a 'leader of the lovely train' he addressed his friend Anna Seward, 'potent thro' spirits masculine to spread / Poetic jealousy and envious dread.' However, 'If Love and Envy could in union rest', male poets 'Will glory to behold such rivals rise', to 'bless the earth, and humanize mankind'.[105]

After Sade and Dobson, Hayley played an important role in giving the poetic exchange between Levi-Perotti and Petrarch a relevance which had no counterpart elsewhere. This significance was reaffirmed in the most comprehensive sonnet anthology of the age, Capel Lofft's *Laura*, which included one version of Giustina's sonnet and three of Petrarch's answer to her. Lofft's 'Giustina Lievi Perotti al Petrarca', one of his best versions, is more literal and politically moderate than Hayley's, though he made the message clear with an addition to line 11, 'The Spinning wheel, not Lyre, they bid me take', which reiterated the concept expressed in line 9.[106] Lofft included his own literal version of Petrarch's answer before two progressively free translations, so that no one could overlook their meaning. The author of the first, William Preston, was more contemptuous than Lofft of the 'sordid throng', but he did not mention money and politics as the chief causes of contemporary decadence, which was due, rather, to the 'tyrant fashion' of moral looseness.[107] However, Lofft politicised Preston's original conclusion, replacing it with a tercet which reintroduced the theme of money.[108]

Thomas Rickman, a friend of Thomas Paine, was the author of the second version, an imitation which, as might be expected, took Hayley's sharp criticism of society a step further.

1

Banisht from Earth was Virtue long ago
By foul Corruption: Tyranny and Pride
And Sloth, Intemperance, Vanity, and Woe,
Baneful, among the Sons of Men reside.

2

Intent on Wealth, on sordid gain alone,
Each light celestial driven far away,
The World will only error, falsehood, own
And mock the Poet and his heavenly lay.

Rickman paraphrased most of Petrarch's lines 1–8. He attacked contemporary decadence directly, talking of 'foul Corruption: Tyranny and Pride' (l. 2) and 'Vanity' (l. 3). Lines 7–8 also made Petrarch's invective more explicit.[109] The same happens in lines 11–12, which expand the original line 11: 'The sordid and ignoble crowd exclaim: / We seek alone for riches, rank, and state'. Rickman's critique of the modern obsession with money had already been expressed in his line 5, which corresponds to the original line 10. His conclusion emphasises the virtues of poetic achievement, as he advises his 'fair Friend' to pursue the path of poetry 'Which leads to Happiness and Glory too' (l. 14), whereas Petrarch only said, 'non lassar la magnanima tua Impresa' ('your magnanimous undertaking'). If Hayley's version made Petrarch a champion of specifically women's rights to literature, Rickman turned him into a supporter of the rights of man, an enemy of wealth, privilege and base materialism.

In our time, Hayley is mainly remembered as a friend of Cowper and Blake, and, as an Italophile, for his translations of Dante.[110] However, his interest in Petrarch was not transitory, as his most successful poems were *The Triumphs of Temper* (1781) and *The Triumphs of Music* (1804), which are usually known today because they were ridiculed in Byron's *English Bards and Scotch Reviewers* but, from our perspective, deserve mentioning for their debt to Petrarch's *Triumphs*.[111] Also, Hayley published *The Young Widow*, one of those epistolary novels whose characters quote Petrarch adapting him to their troubled passions.[112] This is especially the case with Giuliana, an Italian woman, whose passionate readings made Seymour, one of the main characters, feel the beauty of Petrarch, 'that insipid and wearisome sonneteer in the estimation of ordinary readers, that most exquisite and enchanting of all poets to every refined spirit under the immediate influence of sorrow or of love'.[113] This is a summary of the main attitudes to Petrarch at the turn of the century. Hayley's versions from Petrarch highlight how deeply political the view of sentiment and love was. Hayley's role in the Petrarchan revival was an important one and it went beyond the relatively few translations he did. It is not a coincidence that in 1784 Charlotte Smith dedicated her *Elegiac Sonnets* to him; and equally significant is the fact that William Gifford delayed as long as possible the publication of an article by Southey on Hayley because Gifford '"could not bear to see Hayley spoken of with decent respect"'.[114]

The two remaining translators of Petrarch included in *I Fiori del Parnasso Italiano* were more moderate than Hayley. William Collier (1743–1803),

Professor of Hebrew and Fellow of Trinity College, Cambridge, and Thomas Le Mesurier (1757–1822), an Anglican Rector of two parishes, are minor figures whose translations from Petrarch were popular enough to be included in other anthologies.[115] Their views of Petrarch are not particularly original; the interest of their work lies in the way they chose to translate.[116] Theirs are good literal versions, which show that the changes of the other translators were mainly intentional. Translating Italian sonnets into English does not require significant omissions, since the English language is richer in monosyllables and more compact than the Italian. Their literalness, however, was not identical. Collier even supported it theoretically in the notes to his versions, but he always respected the natural word order of the English language, albeit a poetic one.[117] Sometimes he was more emphatic than Petrarch and made him more socially respectable.[118] The first point is strange, because he said he preferred the simple writing of Charlotte Smith to the elaborate styles of Milton and Petrarch.[119]

Thomas Le Mesurier published his versions anonymously probably because he wanted to safeguard his reputation as a priest. There is nothing improper in them, but he specified in the 'Advertisement' that they were made in his youth, 'when the mind is particularly alive to the sensations described by Petrarch, Metastasio, and Zappi.'[120] Le Mesurier translated 24 of Petrarch's sonnets, which were well received and sometimes, as in Henderson's *Petrarca*, were included among the best amatory sonnets in English.[121] Unlike other poets, Le Mesurier wrote that he aimed at literal translation, which, however, must preserve something of the original style and manner.[122] Consequently, his literalism was more radical than Collier's. He tried to preserve all the words and sometimes even the word order of the original, with relatively successful results in some cases, as, for example, in 'Vago augelletto che cantando vai' ('If, as thou know'st the cause that makes thee groan, / Thou knew'st alike my woes to thine allied, / Thou'd'st come in this ill fated breast to hide, / And mix with mine thy melancholy moan').[123] Elsewhere, however, the lines are strained, as in the opening of 'Solo et pensoso' ('Alone, and lost in thought, in desert glade / Measuring I roam with ling'ring steps and slow') or in 'Voi ch'ascoltate' ('And late I feel how to the country round / A common tale I grew, in memory / of which full oft asham'd I bow my head').[124] Though this type of translation has recently been praised in translation studies for its respect of the foreigness of the original, it actually gives a distorted image of what Petrarch sounds like in Italian. Petrarch's prominent characteristic to a native Italian ear is his melodiousness. His syntax may be difficult, but it is never crabbed or unnatural, which is exactly what happens to an extremely literal English translation. Le Mesurier's versions are pleasant, perhaps as good as a literal translation of Petrarch into English verse can be; however, some of his most literal passages fail to suggest the harmonious fluency of the original turns of phrase. To achieve fluent English poetry, in many points he was compelled to add in words or to paraphrase the original, as other translators usually did.[125] However, he did not insert anything compromising into his version of 'La gola e 'l somno', of which, unlike Hayley and Rickman, he gave a depoliticised interpretation.[126] This probably helped the favourable reception of his volume.

These were the translators of *I Fiori del Parnasso Italiano*. Though the number of Petrarch's poems the editor included was limited, the selection was representative, both in terms of subjects and translation modes (from literal versions to freer adaptations to the British society of that time). Though no *canzone* was included, there was a rare text like the 'Triumph of Death', sonnets on morals and politics, on unfulfilled desire and, above all, several *in morte* poems on Petrarch's despair after Laura's death.[127]

Whereas in *I Fiori del Parnasso italiano* Petrarch was seen in the context of Italian poetry, the other two anthologies placed him in a different tradition. George Henderson's *Petrarca* and Capel Lofft's *Laura* are the result of four decades of interest in the sonnet, which both made possible and required some selection. Their titles are extremely significant, because they show that in early nineteenth-century England the sonnet tradition was identified with Petrarch more than any other poet. Petrarch's and Laura's names were popular enough to work on the book market as watchwords for the sonnet. After the Renaissance, the Romantic age was the only time when this could happen. If in *I Fiori del Parnasso Italiano* Petrarch was only a *primus inter pares*, in the sonnet tradition illustrated by those later anthologies he stood out as the fountainhead and the term of comparison for all sonneteers. Sometimes the admiration he enjoyed came close to idolatry, which made his adversaries more hostile than ever.

Petrarca is an elegant little volume edited by George Henderson, an enigmatic figure about whom hardly anything is known besides this work.[128] In his Preface, he pointed out that he chose that title because Petrarch wrote the best sonnets, and admiration for him favoured the sonnet revival. English poets would have never written sonnets if they had not known him.[129] Henderson's selection was preceded by an 'Introductory Dissertation', whose historical section was mainly based on Roscoe's *Life of Lorenzo de' Medici*. Henderson believed that the sonneteers of the English Renaissance were too hyperbolic; only Drummond and Milton were really excellent.[130] English sonneteers could be divided into two main groups: those who wrote sonnets on the Italian model, like Seward and Warton; and those who wrote in a freer form, which sometimes led to 'a much softer and more agreeable harmony of versification'.[131] Though Seward argued that little elegies with a couplet at the end were not sonnets – she was referring to Charlotte Smith – Henderson remarked that almost all the sonnets which attained popularity in England 'have assumed the Elegiac measure'.[132] Like Thomas J. Mathias, Henderson believed that Gray's sonnet to West was the best English example in the Petrarchan style.[133]

Henderson divided his anthology into three thematic sections of equal length: 'Sonnets Amatory', 'Sonnets Elegiac', and 'Sonnets Descriptive'. In his Introduction, he expressed his preferences for each group. Warton, Bowles, Sotheby and Polwhele were the best authors of sonnets of 'scenes of rural or domestic life' portrayed with the rich simplicity of nature. In the amatory sonnets, the best examples were those of Mary Robinson, Roscoe's translations in *Life of Lorenzo*, Le Mesurier's translations from Petrarch (which Henderson labelled as anonymous), and Hoole's versions from Ariosto and Tasso. In the pathetic genre, Henderson preferred Gray, Sir Brooke Boothby, Charlotte Smith and Anna Seward.[134] His selection reflects these ideas, and it looks unusual to us. With the exception of Petrarch, no pre-eighteenth-century poet is given substantial space. Henderson even specified that some sonnets – probably the few Renaissance texts included – were selected not for their intrinsic merit, but only to illustrate the development of versification in this form.[135] That is why in Section I, 'Sonnets Amatory', there are two sonnets by Surrey, four by Spenser, two by Shakespeare and Drummond, six by Milton (one English and five Italian sonnets in Langhorne's translation) against 12 of Petrarch's, translated by Le Mesurier and Penn.[136] The only well-represented English poet was Mary Robinson with 7 sonnets, from both *Sappho and Phaon* and *Poems 1791*.

Henderson included in the 'Sonnets Amatory' only texts from the *in vita* part of *Canzoniere*, whereas he collected a few *in morte* poems in the following section, 'Sonnets Elegiac'. Thus, Petrarch was recognised as the model for two of the main modes of the Romantic sonnet. His translators in this section were Le Mesurier once again (four texts) and Langhorne (three).[137] It is noteworthy that the only other ancient sonnet included was one by Drummond; all the others were eighteenth-century texts, from Gray (one sonnet), to Bowles (six), C. Smith (seven), Boothby (ten), Seward (three), Robinson (two) and a few other authors with one or two poems each. Petrarch does not feature in Section III of the anthology, 'Sonnets Descriptive'; other Italian poets appear in translation as the only authors from the preceding centuries.[138] The British poets were all recent, ranging from Thomas Warton (nine sonnets), to Hayley (three), Cowper (two), Robinson (four), Sotheby (six), Seward (four) and others with fewer sonnets. Bowles is strangely missing from the list, though the strangest thing remains the total absence of ancient British poets. This anthology, the first of this kind, shows that to early nineteenth-century British readers the sonnet tradition went no farther back than half a century. Before then, that tradition was much more Italian than English. The exceptions of Milton and Drummond confirmed the rule, as they were the most Italianate British sonneteers.

The climax of such identification of the sonnet tradition with Italy was Capel Lofft's *Laura*. Lofft was a poet and a Unitarian radical actively engaged in the hottest debates of his time, that is, the abolition of slavery, the French Revolution, the war with France and Napoleon. Born into a well-to-do middle-class family and educated at Cambridge, he began the study of Italian in Bath in 1777. Roger Meyenberg, the author of the only substantial study on Lofft, points out that it was a lifelong passion which even led Lofft to sign his own copy of *Laura* with the Italianised form of his name, 'Capello Lofft di Trostuna'. In his time, Lofft was known to the public above all as an activist who fought relentlessly for the extension of social and political rights. For this reason, though he was a dissenter, he strongly disapproved of the anti-Catholic Gordon riots in 1780. He was an advocate of the French Revolution and published an answer to Burke's *Reflections* with Joseph Johnson. Later, Lofft became the most ardent champion of Napoleon in Great Britain and he even tried to have him released from St Helena.[139] In 1818, when all his political efforts seemed to have hopelessly failed, he left England with his family. After a year near Lausanne, in 1822 he settled in Italy, where he died in 1824.[140]

As Lofft himself acknowledged, *Laura* was inspired by Henderson's *Petrarca*.[141] Lofft began collecting material for it in the early 1800s. In 1809 the publication was delayed after a quarrel with the publisher over the growing size of the anthology, which finally appeared in five octavo volumes in 1814.[142] Lofft put the anthology together as he received the material; the result was a rich and chaotic work or, at least, a work in which the order of the poems looks random. The only clear thing is the general structure: Volumes II–V contain 250 sonnets each, whereas Volume I is entirely filled by the editor's 'Preface'. This was the longest discussion on the sonnet in a time when many poets and critics published essays on the subject, both in journals and poetry volumes. Though Lofft expressed his own opinions, his detailed 'Preface' is a helpful introduction to a debate otherwise known above all through dismissing statements like Coleridge's editorial preface to his *Sonnets from Various Authors*.

First of all, Lofft tried to define the subject of his anthology. Before him, the debate on the sonnet revolved round the distinction between legitimate and illegitimate form. Lofft laid aside the term 'illegitimate', which had an obvious negative resonance, and he distinguished between sonnets and quatorzains: the former were only regular sonnets; the latter were all the other poems of 14 lines. The regular sonnet in its strict form usually consisted of two quatrains and two tercets, and it had been used by most Italian poets from Guittone d'Arezzo to Michelangelo. Sidney, Spenser and Milton introduced it into England. Shakespeare's were quatorzains rather than sonnets, and even Spenser's were sonnets of the '2nd or *imperfect* Order'.[143]

In origin, the sonnet had a close affinity with the Greek ode. In addition, there was an even more interesting analogy with music, which consisted in this: the sonnet's 'major system' was divided into 'a double TETRACHORD', its minor into a 'double *Trichordon*.'[144] Though Lofft's explanation of the structural analogies between music and the sonnet are sometimes cryptic, he wanted to demonstrate that the 14-line structure is not arbitrary, but possesses an intimate harmony which can be evoked only by those poets who use it in its strict form.[145] The two quatrains usually contain the main argumentation of a sonnet; the two tercets provide the solution to it. The two parts of a Petrarchan sonnet are like two movements of a musical composition and constitute 'a perfect *rhythmical* WHOLE'.[146] Unity of design is perhaps the sonnet's greatest virtue. The sonnet is a miracle of concentration and there is no space in it for repetition.[147] In art, as in morals, excellence is seldom easy to attain. Here Lofft went so far as to suggest that there is an inherent morality in formal difficulty.[148]

The sonnet had a long history and was not a product of modern fashion or caprice. Unlike Crescimbeni, who thought that the sonnet had a Latin origin, Lofft argued that the Greek ode had been its main classical model.[149] Guittone d'Arezzo gave the sonnet its structure and later writers, from Petrarch onwards, brought it to a perfection that remained unsurpassed.[150] Lofft's insistence on the classical origin and the rigorous structure of the sonnet might seem exaggerated. In fact, it was a way of opposing the widespread idea that the sonnet was a minor, sloppy, feminine form, which, however good, could not vie with sublime, masculine forms like the ode.[151]

As far as the content was concerned, Lofft was convinced that no kind of poetry was 'so pure' as the sonnet, and 'the exceptions are indeed rare'. There were burlesque sonnets, but a true sonnet should never become coarse.[152] This was clearly false. Lofft, who was well-read in Italian poetry, knew that there was an anti-Petrarchist tradition whose subjects and language could be salacious and outspoken in their physicality. Grossness and even pornography are major features of that tradition, in which satire is central. However radical in his politics and open-minded in his approach to the sonnet, Lofft excluded from his anthology a large portion of that tradition, which in his time was flourishing anew thanks to the Milanese poet Carlo Porta. Lofft argued, in fact, that there were no proper subjects for the sonnet; any subject could do – excluding sanguine ones, as we have just seen. But, despite such flexibility, the sonnet was particularly suited to themes like love, friendship, public and private affections, natural and moral philosophy, and piety. Of course, these were the characteristic themes of most Romantic sonneteers.[153] Ultimately, the sonnet was the best form for pure lyrical poetry, as 'no species of Poetry contains so much of GOOD and little of BAD in equal Quantity as the genuine SONNET.'[154]

The next section of Lofft's 'Preface' is a long history of the sonnet, from its origin to his time. The list of authors begins with a long series of early Italian poets, which includes no Sicilian and only a few *stilnovo* poets. Though Lofft called Dante great, he gave him a mere half-page against Petrarch's six.[155] In spite of so much space, the greatest given to any poet in Lofft's 'Preface', he apologised for his discussion, which could never do justice to Petrarch's immense merits. Lofft talked about his birthplace, his role as a scholar, and his Platonism. He was a comet that enlightened the darkness of his age, whose taste was still coarse. It was totally false that there were but few excellencies in Petrarch's poetry. The truth was to be found in the opposite: there were but few sonnets which were not extraordinary.[156] Lofft did not know whether Petrarch's love affair with Laura was successful or not. He recalled the opinion that Laura was not married, though most scholars in his time believed in the opposite thesis.[157]

After some other poets, Lofft discussed Giustina Levi-Perotti. On the basis of the 'nobly spirited Remains of her *Poetry*', he was tempted to wish she had been Petrarch's Laura. Yet the portrait of the real Laura showed a woman of such modesty, grace and sweetness that she alone could be the object of Petrarch's passion. In a note, Lofft said that Tiraboschi questioned the existence of 'both these Poetesses' – evidently, he considered Laura a poet too.[158] Next, Lofft celebrated Lorenzo de' Medici, who was the initiator of the third era of Italian poetry.[159] He described him as a great man and praised Roscoe's biography. Lofft highlighted that Charles VIII – a French king – sacked art works and books in Florence. Despite his admiration for Napoleon and his radicalism, it is noteworthy that Lofft celebrated Lorenzo de' Medici, who at this time had become a synonym for tyranny in British liberal and radical circles.

A long discussion of the Italian *Cinquecento* preceded a section on Milton, who was analysed among seventeenth-century Italian poets. Lofft emphasised that Milton loved the Petrarchan sonnet form, and those who despised the sonnet should have taken this into due consideration. Charlotte Smith, Seward and other women poets were introduced as Milton's followers.[160] Earlier in his 'Preface', Lofft pointed out that the title of the anthology was chosen in honour of Petrarch and as a homage to 'many FEMALE POETS' who 'have graced this elegant Department of Poetry'.[161] His history of the sonnet, which ended with eighteenth-century Italian poets such as Alfieri, was composed to refute those who believed that Italian poetry was effeminate, and that Italian sonnets contained only quibbles and conceits. Conceits were not more frequent in Italian poetry than elsewhere.[162] The 'Preface' ends with an Appendix which contains an anthology of the historical development of the sonnet from its origin in the Italian Middle Ages to the eighteenth century.[163] On the very last page of his interminable introduction, Lofft defended the value of his selection, which he dedicated 'to the genius of Petrarch and Italy'.

As might be expected, Petrarch appears in the first text of the anthology (vol. II), 'On the Peculiar Character of the Sonnet', which stresses the difficulty of the form if used properly. The sonnet derives 'From HIM [...] who shunn'd the city throng, / And warbled sweet thy rocks and streams among, / Lonely Valclusa!', a picture of Petrarch as a proto-Romantic poet. In the two tercets, the other model evoked by Lofft was Milton, who showed that the English language was perfectly suited for the sonnet. Laura is not far away, as Number V is the sonnet supposedly found in her tomb in Avignon. This legendary though fake sonnet is placed at the beginning of the collection without a translation, as biographical interest in Petrarch's life was so strong that Lofft could never have excluded it. At Sonnet VII, 'Quel rosignuol, che sì soave piagne', we meet Lofft the translator. In fact, besides editing the anthology, he translated a remarkable number of sonnets.

Lofft's principles of translation were set out in his 'Preface'. He supported literal translation whenever possible, but he always tried to preserve the imagery and the original order of thought: '*Fidelity* itself in *Translation* demands a certain degree of *Freedom*.'[164] In his practice, Lofft was mainly literal owing to his admiration for the sonnet form, especially in those texts which were already well known.[165] He often accompanied the freer versions other poets made from Petrarch with his own, more literal translations on behalf of readers. Some spirit of poetic competition seems also to have been at work, as his versions were not always as literal as they might have been.[166] This is confirmed by the fact that, when he translated rarer texts, he felt free to omit, add and paraphrase generously, as for example in 'Onde tolse Amor l'oro, et di qual vena'.[167] Lofft could even be extremely free when necessary, as in 'Di Petrarca. Canzone', 'Libertà, dolce & desiato Bene!' (*Laura* CCXXIV), a hymn to liberty whose translation was strongly marked by the atmosphere of the French revolution. The original was a part of stanza III of 'Quel ch'à nostra natura in sé più degno', a *canzone* not included in *Canzoniere*, which Lofft turned into a sonnet.[168] Petrarch wrote the poem to celebrate the liberation of Parma from the tyranny of the Della Scala brothers. Lofft's additions stress the nearly divine nature of liberty, which alone can render human life valuable and joyful, regardless of wealth. Though Lofft did not add much, he added enough to make Petrarch sound like a Jacobin.[169]

Lofft was certainly aware that the sonnets of women poets had a political as well as an aesthetic meaning. He included many of them, beginning from his second wife, the poetess Sarah Watson Finch (1780?–1855), who translated some of Petrarch's sonnets and was addressed compliments in verse by her husband.[170] Besides her, Lofft included sonnets, both original and translated, by Mary Robinson, Charlotte Smith, Anne Bannerman, Mary Monk and Anna Seward, often accompanying them with eulogies of their works and personalities, even those who had fallen into disgrace like Robinson.[171] The number of sonnets by Italian women poets included in the anthology is even more impressive and covers a much longer time span, from the Middle Ages to the nineteenth century. Lofft summarised his feelings in 'On Sonnets by Female Authors' (*Laura* III, CCCXVIII). Poetry was 'The Work and Triumph of mysterious LOVE' (l. 5), which survived and became more and more charming over the years. Lofft was inspired not only by the sighs the shade of LAURA breathed from her tomb (l. 9), though it possessed a heavenly harmony; future readers would hear not only Petrarch but also his female followers (ll. 13–14): '"His Praise of LAURA shall her Sex inspire; / They emulative wake the' immortal TUSCAN LYRE."'[172]

Certainly, in Lofft the Tuscan lyre fared better than that of Renaissance England, which appears sparingly in *Laura*. The only translation included is one of Wyatt from Petrarch. There are sonnets, though not many, of the major Renaissance authors including, interestingly, three 'elegiac sonnets' from Shakespeare which are not taken from his sonnets, but from passages of his plays turned into sonnets.[173] This is all the more impressive as Lofft's pan-sonnetism could find sonnets and quatorzains everywhere. In *Laura* he made room for some French translations from Petrarch, and he turned into sonnets two stanzas by Pindar, a little fable by La Fontaine, two psalms (Collier's versions), a passage from Racine's *Esther*, and even Petrarch's 'Madriale' 'Lassare il velo', which was presented by Lofft as an irregular sonnet (4 + 7 + 3 lines).[174] Though Lofft was above all interested in celebrating the virtues of the sonnet in all its facets, in comparison to Henderson he gave more space to the poets of the British Renaissance. However, the impression his anthology leaves in the reader is that in Great Britain there was neither a strong sonnet tradition nor a significant interest in Petrarch before the late eighteenth century. It is time to see who the protagonists of this sonnet revival were.

3
Charlotte Smith and Anna Seward

After a century and a half of oblivion, Charlotte Smith's reputation, at least in academia, stands as high today as it did in her time. Whereas her central role in the eighteenth-century revival of the sonnet has been firmly reassessed, her role in the Petrarchan revival has remained vague. Daniel Robinson, the author of the best recent studies on the sonnet revival, wrote that 'a comprehensive study of Petrarch's influence on the Romantic period [...] would have to begin with Charlotte Smith.'[1] Though her contribution was essential, she was clearly not the first to consider Petrarch as a model for elegiac poetry, since she was anticipated by the biographers and the translators discussed in the previous chapters.[2] More precisely, her reading of Petrarch can be fully understood only in a threefold relation, which can be pictured as three concentric circles: her translations and imitations from Petrarch; the relation of her translations of Petrarch with the rest of her poems; and her use of Petrarch in the context of the eighteenth-century Petrarchan revival.

Petrarch is a central component of the book which established Smith's fame, *Elegiac Sonnets*, which includes four translations and one imitation from *Canzoniere*. Petrarch's importance was even more evident in the first three editions of the collection (1784 and 1786), slim quarto volumes which for the most part consisted of translations and imitations.[3] This shows that Smith's sonnets grew in the same soil of the other English Petrarchans of the time, who, as we have seen before, found in translation and imitation their essential tools.

Petrarch appears at the very beginning of *Elegiac Sonnets*. Smith's footnote to Sonnet 3, 'To a nightingale', says that the idea was taken from Petrarch's 'Quel rosignuol, che sì soave piagne', one of those 'bird poems' the Romantics particularly liked:

> Poor melancholy bird—that all night long
>> Tell'st to the Moon thy tale of tender woe;
>> From what sad cause can such sweet sorrow flow,
> And whence this mournful melody of song?

Thy poet's musing fancy would translate
   What mean the sounds that swell thy little breast,
   When still at dewy eve thou leavest thy nest,
Thus to the listening night to sing thy fate.

Pale Sorrow's victims wert thou once among,
   Tho' now releas'd in woodlands wild to rove?
   Say—hast thou felt from friends some cruel wrong,
Or died'st thou—martyr of disastrous love?
Ah! songstress sad! that such my lot might be,
To sigh, and sing at liberty—like thee!

Quel rosignuol, che sì soave piagne
forse suoi figli o sua cara consorte,
di dolcezza empie il cielo et le campagne
con tante note sì pietose et scorte,

e tutta notte par che m'accompagne,
e mi rammente la mia dura sorte:
ch'altri che me non ò di ch'i' mi lagne,
ché 'n dee non credev'io regnasse Morte.

O che lieve è inganar chi s'assecura!
Que' duo bei lumi, assai più che 'l sol chiari,
chi pensò mai veder far terra oscura?

Or cognosco io che mia fera ventura
vuol che vivendo et lagrimando impari
come nulla qua giù diletta et dura.[4]

Smith's text is an imitation of Petrarch's sonnet, which she adapted to her situation. A more literal translation would not have made sense, as the main theme of Smith's collection was not the complaint over a deceased lover. If Petrarch wondered whether the nightingale was weeping 'perhaps for his children or for his dear consort', Smith asked what her bird, which also sang sweetly at night, was lamenting. Her answer was delayed till lines 11–12 ('Say—hast thou felt from friends some cruel wrong, / Or died'st thou—martyr of disastrous love?'), whose position made the response more emphatic. At this point, Smith's adaptation of Petrarch to her life was clear. Whereas Petrarch was blaming his younger self for ignoring that everything on earth, including Laura, was transitory, Smith pointed out that the sources of her sorrow lay in betrayed friendship and disastrous love, as she had already done in sonnet 1.[5]

The other main element of Sonnet 3, the comparison between the nightingale and the poet, also took a different form in Smith. Daniel Robinson has rightly noted that, in comparison to Petrarch, who dismissed the bird in the tercets to concentrate only on himself, Smith stuck to the simile and developed it in a different way.[6] Smith's first, significant change appears at lines 5–6, 'Thy poet's musing fancy would translate / What mean the sounds that swell thy little breast'. In that context, her use of 'translate' (rhyming with 'fate', to boot) is a powerful pun: it alludes to the fact that she is translating those sorrows from Petrarch; that the nightingale is 'translating' them from her breast, as Smith herself, whom the bird represents, is also doing; that she, as a poet, is 'translating' the voices of nature by giving them meaning. The sense of this phrase is even more prysmatic if we note that 'Thy poet's musing fancy' can refer syntactically to both the bird and Smith, who, in this case, is 'thy poet' because she is transcribing the nightingale's song into words. This reading is reinforced by Smith's suppression of a question mark at the end of the quatrain from the fifth edition of *Elegiac Sonnets* onwards. In the first version, the quatrain was one more question in a series of uncertainties; in the second version, after four editions and popular success, Smith felt confident enough to replace the question mark with a full-stop, which turned the quatrain into an assertion of the poet's capability to 'translate', that is, to write out her feelings and thoughts.

Smith's identification with the nightingale is completed in the final couplet, after another quatrain that, like the first, asks whether the bird is among 'Pale Sorrow's victims': 'Ah! songstress sad! that such my lot might be, / To sigh, and sing at liberty—like thee!' Stella Brooks affirms that Smith's nightingale is a 'songstress sad' rather than the image of 'poetic inspiration' and 'joy or love' of many male poets because a woman poet cannot celebrate a myth of rape and mutilation like that of Philomel, but 'she can only mourn with her'.[7] This interpretation is not wrong but, in my opinion, it is not particularly relevant to this sonnet. The final couplet makes explicit the comparison between Smith and the bird, which so far had remained only implicit. However, the comparison serves to emphasise that Smith's condition is the worse: like the bird, she is singing out of suffering but, unlike the bird, she is not free. This lack of freedom certainly refers to her disastrous marriage, whose story is too well known to need repeating here. Moreover, one should not forget that Smith composed the 1784 *Elegiac Sonnets* in gaol, where she ended up with her children and her reckless husband for debts he had not paid. Therefore, liberty has a double meaning here: specifically, liberty from prison; in general, from the cage of her husband and, perhaps, their family.

This desire is satisfied, at least literarily, in the next two sonnets, which portray the poet wandering in the countryside. Interestingly, Petrarch is there again. In fact, Sonnet 3, 'To a nightingale', is placed between two Petrarchan texts, as *Canzoniere* has a specific bearing also on Sonnet 2. Sonnet 4, 'To the moon', runs as follows:

> Queen of the silver bow!—by thy pale beam,
>   Alone and pensive, I delight to stray,

> And watch thy shadow trembling in the stream,
>   Or mark the floating clouds that cross thy way.
> And while I gaze, thy mild and placid light
>   Sheds a soft calm upon my troubled breast;
> And oft I think—fair planet of the night,
>   That in thy orb, the wretched may have rest:
> The sufferers of the earth perhaps may go,
>   Released by death—to thy benignant sphere;
> And the sad children of Despair and Woe
>   Forget, in thee, their cup of sorrow here.
> Oh! that I soon may reach thy world serene,
> Poor wearied pilgrim—in this toiling scene!

Line 2 is an unmistakable quotation from the beginning of Petrarch's 'Solo et pensoso', a favourite Romantic sonnet:

> *Solo et pensoso i più deserti campi*
> *vo mesurando a passi tardi et lenti,*
> *et gli occhi porto per fuggire intenti*
> *ove vestigio human la rena stampi.*
>
> *Altro schermo non trovo che mi scampi*
> *dal manifesto accorger de le genti,*
> *perché ne gli atti d'alegrezza spenti*
> *di fuor si legge com'io dentro avampi:*
>
> *sì ch'io mi credo omai che monti et piagge*
> *et fiumi et selve sappian di che tempre*
> *sia la mia vita, ch'è celata altrui.*
>
> *Ma pur sì aspre vie né sì selvagge*
> *cercar non so, ch'Amor non venga sempre*
> *ragionando con meco, et io co·llui.*[8]

   Smith created a complex intertextual net which is not easy to disentangle. Her sonnet is addressed to the moon, which has just listened to the nightingale's 'tender tale of woe' of the preceding sonnet (l. 2). The moon is defined as 'Queen of the silver bow' (l. 1), a classical epithet of Diana, as Curran pointed out in the footnote. Diana, or Artemis to whom she was quickly assimilated, was the goddess of woods and hunting but, also and more importantly, the virgin goddess of natural fertility and, specifically, of feminine fertility, the protectress of childbirth but, also, the source of labour pains and mortal danger in childbearing. Thanks to these attributes, she was the most popular goddess in ancient Greece. It is absolutely reasonable for Smith, who was pregnant for most of her married life and bore 12 children, to have asked protection from such a deity. Smith's hope to rest in the moon's 'benignant sphere' (l. 10) can be read as a sinister desire of death, which was expressed in other sonnets too, but also, more practically, as a wish to interrupt her almost constant state of pregnancy or, at least, as a prayer to be protected during childbirth. What has Petrarch's sonnet got to do with this?

'Solo et pensoso' has a completely different theme, the effects of maddening love, condemned by Augustine and read by the Romantics as the bittersweet solitude of the melancholy lover. Petrarch wandered alone because he was worried that other people would make fun of the passion they read on his face. The last tercet, however, specifies that nowhere could he forget the cause of his trouble, as Love always remained with him. Clearly, Love could not be Smith's companion, since it was not the cause of her trouble. She addressed the moon which, as we have just seen, was the proper interlocutor for her. However, the presence of Petrarch's hidden subtext generates an inevitable resonance in Smith's sonnet. Like him, Smith wished she were alone, far from common people and false friends who were bound to be gossiping about her shameful condition, that of a decayed aristocrat innocently in gaol for her husband's debts. However, Smith's hope for serenity, expressed in her last couplet, is in fact crossed out from the start. Her subtext, 'Solo et pensoso', affirms that there is no place where one can get rid of one's obsessions, just as, in the same way, the conclusion to Petrarch's 'Quel rosignuol, che sì soave piagne', which states that nothing on earth lasts for long, undermines Smith's wish for permanent liberty in the last couplet of her imitation, 'To a nightingale'.[9]

I am aware that my reading greatly differs from the one put forward by scholars such as Robinson, Brooks and others. However, I think that it is simplistic to believe that the later text always has the last word, as their interpretations assume. Rewritings do not blot out or manipulate the original text like a dead thing which cannot react. It might have been so in the author's mind; it cannot be like that in our minds, as for us both texts are equally dead and alive, mirroring themselves mutually. In many cases, the older authors are so alive that, as time goes by, they turn the younger ones into mere followers. In these cases, which are very common, it is the older text that reads and changes the later one. But even in successful rewritings, an imitation or a translation often keeps the original meaning alive, not merely as something to be distorted, changed or denied, but as a second, more secret layer of meaning to be played against the surface of the text, as for instance in Gray's sonnet to West.[10] One can never be completely certain whether a text 'simply' denies its source, or whether it denies it and, at the same time, preserves its meaning in a sort of semantic counterpoint.

As I was saying before, Petrarch appears as a kind of shadow also in Smith's Sonnet 2, 'Written at the close of spring'. If Smith's Sonnet 3 was an adaptation of 'Quel rosignuol' (*PC*, 311), Sonnet 2 corresponds to 'Zephiro torna' (*PC*, 310). Petrarch's are a couple of closely linked sonnets which often appear together in anthologies.[11] Smith's approach to 'Zephiro torna' was exactly the same as the one she had to 'Quel rosignuol': she rewrote the idea of Petrarch's sonnet and adapted it to her life:

> The garlands fade that Spring so lately wove,
>   Each simple flower, which she had nursed in dew,
> Anemonies, that spangled every grove,
>   The primrose wan, the hare-bell, mildly blue.
> No more shall violets linger in the dell,
>   Or purple orchis variegate the plain,
> Till Spring again shall call forth every bell,
>   And dress with humid hands her wreaths again.—
> Ah! poor Humanity! so frail, so fair,
>   Are the fond visions of thy early day,
> Till tyrant Passion, and corrosive Care,
>   Bid all thy fairy colours fade away!
> Another May new buds and flowers shall bring;
> Ah! why has happiness—no second Spring?[12]

Petrarch contrasted the joy of blossoming life in spring with his incurable despondency due to Laura's death. Smith also cried over past happiness, the illusions of youth destroyed by 'tyrant Passion, and corrosive Care'. Her conclusion was the same as Petrarch's: spring forever returns, whereas happiness has 'no second Spring', whatever the reason for it may be. It is no coincidence that this theme appears in the first sonnet after the introductory one, as it is the basic theme of her collection. Smith repeated it in an impressive number of sonnets, including, significantly, the last of her book.[13]

Scholars have noted that Smith's sonnets are not typically elegiac because they do not mourn a specific death, as elegies usually do. The sonnets that commemorate particular deaths, like those for her daughter Augusta or Robert Burns, were later additions which, according to Daniel Robinson, 'are uncharacteristic of [her] sonnets as a whole'.[14] In fact, as other scholars have noted, *Elegiac Sonnets* is a legitimate title because there is one person whose death they incessantly mourn: Smith's own young self.[15] Unlike Blake, Smith could never have written that she died and was born again many times. She died only twice, and in-between she could only mourn the happy life of a privileged little girl which was followed by an adult death-in-life of betrayed friendship, family bereavement, Kafkaesque litigations, sexist injustice, hard work and constant shortage of money. Stuart Curran has justly claimed that Smith can be considered the first Romantic; as such, she had mainly one theme: herself, or, more precisely, the contrast between her two selves in two opposite conditions, material and psychological. This does not mean that she did not deal with subjects of public interest, but that the pivot of her writing remained her self, as it ought to be for a lyric poet.

Petrarch, then, was an ideal model for a personality like Smith's. Of course, instead of a dead Laura, there was a young Charlotte to commemorate. 'Zephiro torna' condensed in 14 lines Smith's obsession, and it is not a coincidence that the sonnet stayed in her mind. Its underground presence in her Sonnet 2 is confirmed by other poems on the same topic. 'April' is an elegy in quatrains that pulls together the themes of greatest emotional importance to her: the opposition between the illusions of youth and the hard reality of adult life, expressed through the metaphor of spring; the melancholy, hopeless wanderer; and the death of her daughter. In a footnote to the poem she pointed out: 'The return of the Spring, which awakens many to new sentiments of pleasure, now serves only to remind *me* of past misery.' She added that the force of these sensations, common to the wretched, had been felt by many poets, but, as an example, she quoted the first two lines of 'Zephiro torna' and a passage from Guarini's *Pastor fido*.[16] Evidently, Petrarch was in her mind a poetic archetype for this theme, as she also mentioned a phrase from 'Zephiro torna' in a footnote to *Beachy Head*.[17] The place of 'April' in the collection is also noteworthy: it is the penultimate poem of the first edition of Volume II, and it corresponds symmetrically, in theme and position, to Sonnet 2 of Volume I, 'Written at the close of spring'.[18]

Besides the introductory sonnets, Petrarch played an important role in the original final section of *Elegiac Sonnets*, which consisted of translations from *Canzoniere* and adaptations from Goethe's *Werther*. What at first sight seems strange about these translations is that Smith selected, besides two of Petrarch's elegiac lamentations over Laura's death from the second part of *Canzoniere*, two *in vita* sonnets in praise of her beauty. In the early editions of *Elegiac Sonnets*, the Petrarch versions are preceded by a couple of poems which gradually introduce the theme of maddening love.[19] The poem immediately before the Petrarch versions was 'The origin of flattery', a significant signal of Smith's attitude.[20]

Though Smith mentioned love several times, starting from Sonnet 1, as a major cause of unhappiness, she attempted to define its role only in the last part of her collection. As it stands in the definitive edition, her analysis of amorous passion begins with Sonnet 13, the first of her versions from Petrarch. The elated tone of her translation of Petrarch's 'Ponmi ove 'l sole occide i fiori et l'erba' creates a sharp break from the previous sonnets, which are mournful in tone and subject:

> Oh! place me where the burning noon
>   Forbids the wither'd flower to blow;
> Or place me in the frigid zone,
>   On mountains of eternal snow:
> Let me pursue the steps of Fame,
>   Or Poverty's more tranquil road;

> Let youth's warm tide my veins inflame,
>   Or sixty winters chill my blood:
> Tho' my fond soul to heaven were flown,
>   Or tho' on earth 'tis doom'd to pine,
> Prisoner or free—obscure or known,
>   My heart, O Laura, still is thine.
> Whate'er my destiny may be,
> That faithful heart still burns for thee!

Petrarch's original runs:

> *Ponmi ove 'l sole occide i fiori et l'erba,*
> *o dove vince lui il ghiaccio et la neve;*
> *ponmi ov'è 'l carro suo temprato et leve,*
> *et ov'è chi ce 'l rende, o chi ce 'l serba;*
>
> *ponmi in humil fortuna, od in superba,*
> *al dolce aere sereno, al fosco et greve;*
> *ponmi a la notte, al dì lungo ed al breve,*
> *a la matura etate od a l'acerba;*
>
> *ponmi in cielo, od in terra, od in abisso,*
> *in alto poggio, in valle ima et palustre,*
> *libero spirto, od a' suoi membri affisso;*
>
> *ponmi con fama oscura, o con ilustre:*
> *sarò qual fui, vivrò com'io son visso,*
> *continuando il mio sospir trilustre.*[21]

Though Smith's translation is not literal and rearranges the original in a different way, it preserves most of Petrarch's sonnet with few, significant changes and one important omission. Petrarch is saying that whatever may happen to him, and wherever he may end up, his life cannot change: he will go on loving Laura hopelessly. Smith left out some of the places and situations mentioned by Petrarch and emphasised others, which were of greater relevance to her: after climate and geography in the first lines, she mentioned 'Fame' (l. 5, from the original l. 12) and 'Poverty' (l. 6, from the original l. 5), the passion of youth (l. 7) and the chill of old age (l. 8), death and life (ll. 9–10), imprisonment or freedom (l. 10), obscurity or fame (again, l. 11).[22] The changes in these lines are marginal in comparison with the conclusion, where Smith, in a rather un-Petrarchan way, tells Laura directly that (l. 12) 'My heart [...] still is thine.' Petrarch's anaphoric list encompasses line 12, and his final couplet does not correspond exactly to Smith's. Laura's name is not mentioned in the original, where she appears more distant than in Smith's version. Petrarch's interest focused on line 13, 'still I shall be what I have been, shall live as I have lived', in order to stress that his love will endure but, above all, that his painful frustration will also continue (l. 14). Smith's Petrarch sounds more optimistic: she omitted the original line 13 and simply cried out his unshakable love, where it remains unclear whether it was frustrated or not.

This version was added in the fourth edition of *Elegiac Sonnets* probably to reinforce the point made in the following sonnet, 'Erano i capei d'oro a l'aura sparsi', Petrarch's most famous compliment to Laura. As in the previous version, Smith drew Petrarch and Laura closer than they were in the original:

> Loose to the wind her golden tresses stream'd,
> > Forming bright waves with amorous Zephyr's sighs;
> > And tho' averted now, her charming eyes
> Then with warm love, and melting pity beam'd.
> Was I deceiv'd?—Ah! surely, nymph divine!
> > That fine suffusion on thy cheek was love;
> > What wonder then those beauteous tints should move,
> Should fire this heart, this tender heart of mine!
> Thy soft melodious voice, thy air, thy shape,
> > Were of a goddess—not a mortal maid;
> > Yet tho' thy charms, thy heavenly charms should fade,
> My heart, my tender heart could not escape;
> > Nor cure for me in time or change be found:
> > The shaft extracted does not cure the wound!

Petrarch's original:

> *Erano i capei d'oro a l'aura sparsi*
> *che 'n mille dolci nodi gli avolgea,*
> *e 'l vago lume oltra misura ardea*
> *di quei begli occhi ch'or ne son sì scarsi;*
>
> *e 'l viso di pietosi color' farsi,*
> *non so se vero o falso, mi parea:*
> *i' che l'ésca amorosa al petto avea,*
> *qual meraviglia se di sùbito arsi?*
>
> *Non era l'andar suo cosa mortale,*
> *ma d'angelica forma, et le parole*
> *sonavan altro che pur voce humana:*
>
> *uno spirto celeste, un vivo sole*
> *fu quel ch'i' vidi; et se non fosse or tale,*
> *piagha per allentar d'arco non sana.*[23]

Daniel Robinson states that Smith's translation 'is a sharp critique of the hyperbolic Petrarchan lovers who raise women too high on an ideal pedestal, thus robbing them of their humanity'.[24] Though Robinson's observation is emphatic, it is true that Smith, like most readers of her time, must have found Petrarch's idealisation of Laura unlikely. As we have seen before, much more radical reservations about the figure of Laura and the quality of Petrarch's love were expressed by some poets and scholars in Smith's time. Whereas the original sonnet describes Laura in the third person, Smith's Petrarch addresses Laura in the second person in both translations, thereby making her less aloof. Her Laura responds to Petrarch's sentiment, as Smith made her blush 'with warm love' (l. 4) besides the original pity, a concept reiterated in Smith's line 5. She specifies that Petrarch's 'tender heart' was fired by Laura's 'beauteous tints' (ll. 6–7), that is, by the fact that Laura also seemed to feel something for him. In the original, it was Laura's physical beauty, with only a vague touch of pity, which made Petrarch fall in love. In the conclusion, Smith expanded the original last line and a half into four lines, which she evidently considered an essential point. More emphatically than the original, her Petrarch affirms that his love will never wane, even when Laura's beauty should fade.

The noteworthy point of Smith's two versions from Petrarch is not that their form is 'illegitimate' or that they question Laura's deification and aloofness, which hardly anyone could believe in Smith's time; the essential point is that they imagine Laura involved in Petrarch's passion. In the light of the biographical debate on Petrarch and Laura, Smith's versions seem to state that adulterous love, if genuine, can be admired and justified on both sides. This was their real moral novelty, notwithstanding the irony she may have cast on Petrarch's idealisation of Laura.[25] Significantly, Smith echoed the beginning of 'Erano i capei d'oro' in a late poem, 'The female exile', where Petrarch's words were used to give noble dignity to a desperate French lady on an English shore.[26]

Smith's point of view is confirmed by the next two translations from Petrarch, which return to the dominant elegiac mode of her collection, as they belong to the *in morte* section of *Canzoniere*. The first, 'Se lamentar augelli, o verdi fronde', is one of those sonnets where, as Robinson has rightly noted, the partial identification with Laura of a woman poet who is translating Petrarch renders the meaning of the final version difficult to disentangle:

> Where the green leaves exclude the summer beam,
>> And softly bend as balmy breezes blow,
> And where, with liquid lapse, the lucid stream
>> Across the fretted rock is heard to flow,
> Pensive I lay: when she whom Earth conceals,
>> As if still living to my eyes appears,

> And pitying Heaven her angel form reveals,
>   To say—"Unhappy Petrarch, dry your tears;
> Ah! why, sad lover! thus before your time,
>   In grief and sadness should your life decay.
> And like a blighted flower, your manly prime
>   In vain and hopeless sorrow fade away?
> Ah! yield not thus to culpable despair,
> But raise thine eyes to Heaven—and think I wait thee there."

> *Se lamentar augelli, o verdi fronde*
> *mover soavemente a l'aura estiva,*
> *o roco mormorar di lucide onde*
> *s'ode d'una fiorita et fresca riva,*

> *là 'v'io seggia d'amor pensoso et scriva;*
> *lei che 'l ciel ne mostrò, terra n'asconde,*
> *veggio et odo et intendo ch'ancor viva,*
> *di sì lontano a' sospir miei risponde:*

> *«Deh, perché inanzi 'l tempo ti consume?*
> *– mi dice con pietate – a che pur versi*
> *degli occhi tristi un doloroso fiume?*

> *Di me non pianger tu; ché' miei dì fersi,*
> *morendo, eterni, et ne l'interno lume,*
> *quando mostrai de chiuder, gli occhi apersi».*[27]

Robinson based his reading on the fact that Smith's Petrarch is not 'sitting in thoughts of love and writing'; he only says, 'Pensive I lay' (l. 5). According to Robinson, Smith's omission was a way of underlining the fact that Laura was not a verbal creation of Petrarch, but a real woman who 'appears out of nowhere'. In my opinion, this reading is strained. It is true that *for us* Laura exists only in Petrarch's writings; however, *for him* she did not exist only in his poetry. His sonnet states, precisely, that he could hear her voice in the sounds of nature or, rather, that the sounds of nature in the places where he used to see her evoked her presence (ll. 1–4). In Smith this link seems more threadbare and, as often in her poetry, there seems to be no empathy between nature and the melancholy poet.

If in the 'I' of the first lines we inevitably feel Petrarch's and Smith's selves overlap, the invocation of Petrarch's name in the speech of Smith's Laura (l. 8) sounds as if Smith, from this point, identified with Laura and told Petrarch what she thought of his attitude. The most visible change in these lines was her extension of Laura's reproach to Petrarch that he should stop wasting away in grief his 'manly prime', an addition of Smith's which eroticises Petrarch's self-pitying.[28] The most important change, and in my opinion the most significant point of the translation, comes in the penultimate line, which renders the original 'Do not weep for me' as 'yield not thus to culpable despair'. 'Culpable' may mean either that Smith understood Petrarch's incurable love for Laura as an effect of an unjustified sense of guilt – and she advised him to forget about it – or that she felt he was really guilty because he loved a married woman. The former interpretation is more consistent with Smith's previous translations; in any case, it is interesting that she pointed to guilt as the cause of Petrarch's haunting love. Petrarch did not refer to guilt in this sonnet, and where he mentioned it, he gave it a specific religious value, in that he loved a creature rather than her Creator. Smith's reading of Petrarch's feelings was psychological rather than metaphysical.

However, a religious perspective comes out in the last line, where Smith's Laura says that Petrarch must not yield to despair because she is waiting for him in Heaven. Smith omitted the original antithesis that Laura opened her eyes on the inner light when she seemed to close them and, more clearly than Petrarch in this sonnet, Laura told him that they would meet again. Though Smith usually curbed all ultramundane expectations, in this case she was more hopeful than Petrarch. However, such optimism was short-lived and it might have been devised only to highlight the greater pessimism of her last version from *Canzoniere*, 'Valle che de' lamenti miei se' piena':

> Ye vales and woods! fair scenes of happier hours;
>   Ye feather'd people, tenants of the grove;
> And you, bright stream! befringed with shrubs and flowers,
>   Behold my grief, ye witnesses of love!
>
> For ye beheld my infant passion rise,
>   And saw thro' years unchang'd my faithful flame;
> Now cold, in dust, the beauteous object lies,
>   And you, ye conscious scenes, are still the same!
>
> While busy Memory still delights to dwell
>   On all the charms these bitter tears deplore,
> And with a trembling hand describes too well
>   The angel form I shall behold no more!
> To heaven she's fled! and nought to me remains
> But the pale ashes which her urn contains.
>
> *Valle che de' lamenti miei se' piena,*
> *fiume che spesso del mio pianger cresci,*
> *fere selvestre, vaghi augelli et pesci,*
> *che l'una et l'altra verde riva affrena,*

> *aria de' miei sospir' calda et serena,*
> *dolce sentier che sì amaro riesci,*
> *colle che mi piacesti, or mi rincresci,*
> *ov'anchor per usanza Amor mi mena:*
>
> *ben riconosco in voi l'usate forme,*
> *non, lasso, in me, che da sì lieta vita*
> *son fatto albergo d'infinita doglia.*
>
> *Quinci vedea 'l mio bene; et per queste orme*
> *torno a vedere ond'al ciel nuda è gita,*
> *lasciando in terra la sua bella spoglia.*[29]

Smith rearranged the internal structure of the original, highlighting from the beginning the opposition between happy past and painful present, a theme that, as we have seen, was most dear to her. The following line, 'Ye feather'd people, tenants of the grove', clarifies the reason why those were 'fair scenes of happier hours': 'tenants' is a significant addition which hints at a time when Smith herself was a landowner. Petrarch does not mention private property and his 'wandering birds' (l. 3) are the exact opposite of Smith's version. Her Petrarch is also different from the original. He feels less sorry for himself and, above all, the reason for his sorrow is not only love, which is cited in the following passage. Smith condensed Petrarch's story in three lines, from the rise of his 'infant passion' (again, a *double entendre* on childhood), to his 'faithful flame', to the 'dust' where now 'the beauteous object lies'. Smith introduced Laura here rather than at the end of the sonnet, as it is in the original. The effect is the same as in line 1, that is, the immediate formulation of the conflicts embodied in the sonnet rather than the gradual development from a happier past to a sorrowful present. Moreover, 'beauteous object' is a periphrasis for Laura which contains an evident element of criticism. Smith felt that Petrarch's attitude to Laura was fetishistic and perhaps bordering on necrophilia in his sentimental evocation of her 'bella spoglia' ('beautiful vesture', l. 14, in the sense of 'beautiful corpse').

Smith's Petrarch concludes the second quatrain by mentioning the 'conscious scenes' of his favourite landscape, which 'are still the same' in opposition to his tragically changed self. In comparison to Petrarch, Smith's translation, in Daniel Robinson's words, 'is colored by her own tenacious faith in nature'.[30] Her landscape is 'conscious', a strange definition whose meaning is not completely clear to me. Did she mean that her landscape was somehow aware of what had happened to her? If so, in what sense, and how? Whatever her phrase may mean, it is clear that, in order to contradict Petrarch, Smith expressed a sort of Wordsworthian belief in the responsiveness of nature to human fate which she usually denied. In most of her poems nature does not reflect human misery. Her standard attitude is like that of

'Zephiro torna', where the joy of natural life only serves to highlight the despair of the melancholy poet more bitterly.

In fact, that consolation is only a momentary illusion, as the sestet of Sonnet 16 leads to a different conclusion. Smith added a sort of mental dissociation between 'Memory', a personified power which 'delights to dwell' on past charms, and the memory of his body, which 'deplores' them in 'bitter tears'. This prosopopoeia was probably meant as a compensation for her significant omission of 'Amor' leading Petrarch around his valley (l. 8). Moreover, Smith added in here the reference to writing she had left out in the previous sonnet. However, her Petrarch does not control his writing skills; it is his Memory which 'with a trembling hand describes' Laura, 'the angel form' he could not see any longer.[31]

In the final couplet, Smith modified Petrarch's neat antithesis between the heaven Laura's soul had fled to and the earth where she had been buried. Laura's physical dissolution in the ground was a sort of seal on all the associations between her and that landscape, where her life and death were forever mixed up. On the contrary, Smith's Laura was preserved in an urn, so that the places where Petrarch saw her were only associated with her life – hence, perhaps, his illusion of their greater sympathy with his sorrow. However, if Petrarch was left only with his recollections, Smith's Petrarch was left with Laura's urn and her 'pale ashes'. In the end, the two sonnets terminate in the opposite of what they seemed to promise. In the original, Laura's left her 'bella spoglia' ('beautiful vesture') on earth, which was the reason why Petrarch could still find his familiar landscape pleasurable, albeit tragically so. In Smith, Petrarch was left with something, but this was Laura's uninspiring 'pale ashes', whereas her 'bella spoglia' had become a colder 'beauteous object' buried in unspecified 'dust'. Smith's landscape promised more and maintained less, as in her version the only place where Petrarch could really conjure Laura up was his Memory, described, however, as an uncanny power over which he had no control.[32]

Bereavement and the threat of dissociation were the right preliminaries to the poems which in the early editions completed Smith's reflections on love. After Petrarch, she elaborated on another major love story of her time, Goethe's *Werther*. In the later editions, these two groups of sonnets were separated by three others on friendship and literary ambition, a lighter *intermezzo* between two tragic episodes. Originally, the Werther sonnets read like the fatal conclusion of the consuming passion described in the Petrarch versions. If Smith was in part sceptical about Petrarch's hyperbolic idealisation of Laura, she took its possible consequences seriously. The main theme of the Werther sonnets is the effect of the loss of reason out of despair. Smith contradicted Werther, who in the episode of the lunatic said that humans seem to be happy only before possessing their reason or after losing it.[33] In two of the Werther sonnets, as well as in many other texts, Smith warned against maddening passion, linking it to subjects like the opposition between past happiness and present despair, as in Sonnet 23.[34] This theme is not alien to Sonnet 24, 'Make there my tomb, beneath the lime-tree's shade', the last poem in the early editions of *Elegiac Sonnets*. Here Smith elaborated on Werther's desire to be buried under a lime tree, adding to the original some lines which imagine Lotte weeping on his tomb. Adela Pinch and others have noted that Smith exploited her homonymy with Lotte, so that the final lines of the poem can be referred to both women.[35] However, as Smith had no dead Werther to mourn, it is not clear what she was lamenting. Although here Smith identifies with Lotte, in the other Werther sonnets we tend to forget that the speaking 'I' is that of Werther, and we hear him and Smith at the same time. In other words, I believe that Smith identified with both Werther and Lotte, just as in the Petrarch versions she had put on the masks of both Petrarch and Laura.[36] In the last sonnet of her collection, Smith staged her personal tragedy, in which an adult, rational Charlotte wept over the tomb of a weaker, more immature self, overwhelmed by passion and misfortune.[37]

The response to Smith's tragedy of estate was sensational and, within a few years, she was even hailed as the supreme model for the English sonnet, as Shakespeare was for drama and Milton for epics.[38] Since her versions from Petrarch were the most frequently reprinted in her time, it is not surprising that they enlivened the debate which had risen from the sonnet form.[39] In particular, Anna Seward, possibly the most authoritative woman critic of the time, attacked Smith's sonnets for their excess of quotations.[40] Later, Seward focused on form, affirming that they were 'three elegiac stanzas closing with a couplet'. The legitimate sonnets were those of Milton, Petrarch, and Warton.[41] She wrote to Hayley, who was also Smith's friend and initial patron, that she disagreed with her – and Johnson, whom she detested – about the idea that the legitimate sonnet was unfit for the English language.[42] In sum, Smith's were 'everlasting lamentables, which she calls sonnets, made up of hackneyed scraps of dismality [. . .] Never were poetical whipt syllabubs, in black glasses, so eagerly swallowed by the odd taste of the public.'[43]

Seward's attitude was based on personal, moral and aesthetic grounds. She had known Petrarch for many years and she celebrated him and Vaucluse, albeit conventionally, in some texts.[44] In 'To Mr. Henry Cary, on the publication of his sonnets' she mentioned Cary, Petrarch and Milton as her models, and the sonnets she wrote from the early 1770s were mainly of the Italian type.[45] She certainly played a significant role in the sonnet revival and resented being overshadowed by Smith. However, though in form and theory Seward was more Italianate than Smith, in substance she was less Petrarchan than her rival.

As we have seen before, Seward's criticism of Smith focused on three points: her borrowings from other poets, the form of her sonnets, and the monotony of her subjects. The first remark was very strange, and it is even stranger that so many scholars have recently responded to it as though it was actually well founded. In these essays, of which McGann's *The Poetics of Sensibility* is possibly the most famous, Smith has become a precursor of post-modernity, and her use of other writers – echo, quotation, translation or imitation – has been interpreted using present-day notions like ventriloquism, parody and patchwork. This is quite licit, since anachronism can prove to be a powerful hermeneutic perspective; however, one should not put the cart before the horse. Before interpreting old authors as though they were contemporaries, we should try our best to study their works in the light of the writing practices of their time. What was, then, the common attitude to borrowing, translation and imitation in Smith's age?

Few scholars among those who have turned Smith into a kind of poetic Sterne seem to remember that in the eighteenth century, as in any period of neoclassical aesthetics, poets had to show in the first place that they knew their trade. Allusions to other poets, explicit or implicit references, echoes, quotations, translations and imitations meant first of all, 'I can write because I have read.' Quoting from and referring to other poets was a way of proving one's qualifications. This was all the more important for a woman, whose literary education could not be taken for granted. Translation and imitation, which are to a text what echoes are to a line, were not second-rate compositions, but the very condition of poetry. However, Smith lived in a time when these ideas were beginning to be questioned and slowly replaced by the Romantic concept of originality. Seward's strictures reflected the new ideas and were shared by few reviewers. Her ideas were not convincing because her poems were much more conservative and contained those writing practices for which she blamed Smith, that is, frequent echo, translation and imitation. Smith's quotations and imitations need not be minimised, as Stuart Curran does in his footnotes, using the Romantic ideas he and others have been trying to revise; nor can they be justified only as ironic ventriloquism and rhetorical masks used by Smith to avoid speaking in the first person, a major virtue for post-modern critics.[46] However post-modern Smith may be, her writings fully belong to the eighteenth-century poetic modes. What was changed from earlier in the century were the authors imitated, not the way in which they were quoted and rewritten.

If Seward's accusations of plagiarism and lack of originality were exaggerated and even self-contradictory in the light of her poems, her strictures on Smith's formal irregularity and thematic monotony deserve greater attention. Like other readers, Seward could not admit of the morbid excesses of Sensibility, and she found extreme distress and suicide distasteful subjects for verse. She disapproved of Smith's sonnets from Petrarch and Werther: 'Ah, never let thy lyre superior dwell / On themes thy better judgement must disdain! / It ill befits that verse like thine should tell / Of Petrarch's love, or Werther's frantic pain!'[47] Seward did not confine herself to criticism. In her poems she included one sonnet in the mode of Petrarch and three based on a passage of Goethe's *Werther* as alternatives to Smith's sonnets from the same sources.[48]

'Petrarch to Vaucluse', as Seward specified in a footnote, 'is not a Translation or a Paraphrase, but is written in the Character of Petrarch, and in imitation of his manner.'[49] This sonnet is a kind of fantasia on some of the sonnets Smith had translated, and it was probably meant to show how Petrarch should have been Englished:

> Fortunate Vale! exulting Hill! dear Plain!
>   Where morn, and eve, my soul's fair Idol stray'd
>   While all your winds, that murmur'd thro' the glade,
>   Stole her sweet breath; yet, yet your paths retain
> Prints of her step, by fount, whose floods remain
>   In depth unfathom'd; 'mid the rocks, that shade,
>   With cavern'd arch, their sleep.—Ye streams, that play'd
>   Around her limbs in Summer's ardent reign,
> The soft resplendence of those azure eyes
>   Ting'd ye with living light.—The envied claim
>   These blest distinctions give, my lyre, my sighs,
> My songs record; and, from their Poet's flame,
>   Bid this wild Vale, its Rocks, and Streams arise,
>   Associates still of their bright MISTRESS' fame.

Seward's gesture is clear. She rewrote Smith's translation of 'Valle che de' lamenti miei se' piena' keeping the original in mind, but leaving out half of either sonnet. In different ways, Petrarch and Smith recalled the places of their earlier happiness only to highlight the excruciating pain of its absence in their present condition of distress. On the contrary, Seward stopped at the first half of the story. She celebrated the places associated with Laura, which, as she emphasises in the last section of the sonnet, remained alive thanks to her verse. It is a conventional praise of poetic power as a form of survival; the tragedy of death, which appears only implicitly, is simply ignored. There is no past happiness opposed to present despair, no definitive absence to be mourned. Seward follows the sonnet form of the original, but her respect is merely formal. Her sonnet suggests that, in her opinion, Smith's elegiac reading of Petrarch is an exaggeration, since Petrarch was essentially a literary man, in love with the poetic laurel, whose existential tragedy should not have been taken too seriously. It is the formalist view of Petrarch which, as we have seen earlier on, has had many supporters over the centuries. Though Petrarch seems more moderate and acceptable than other love poets like Sappho, Catullus and Shakespeare, his message has proved disturbing to many readers who have considered it seriously. Romantic readings like Smith's teach us to reassess the image of Petrarch as a quintessentially conservative member of the literary canon, a harmless poet for inexperienced youths, which sounds like a sly way of neutralising him rather than a fair interpretation.

Seward's uneasy attitude can be found again in her Werther sonnets, which can be read as polemical answers to Smith's use of the same novel. As we have seen earlier on, in her sonnets Smith did not justify suicide and firmly stuck to reason in order to resist it, even though we know that she entertained the idea of suicide in the most distressing moments of her life.[50] Seward did not choose the last part of Goethe's novel, but an earlier, famous episode in which Werther was watching a flooded vale. As in the original, she compared the stormy landscape with Werther's soul (Sonnet LXXXVIII). However, he could not find the courage to commit suicide even though he would have wanted to (Sonnet LXXXIX).[51] Seward did not imagine Werther after death, as Goethe and Smith had. In the third of Seward's sonnets, Werther found in the remembrance of the happy days of his past the motive for laying aside the idea of suicide. Unlike Smith, who repeated to death that past happiness never returns, and unlike Goethe's Werther, who in that episode compared himself to an old woman prolonging 'her feeble and miserable existence', Seward argued that there can be a cheerful time in the future just as there had been one in the past.[52] Seward rejected extreme pessimism and seems to have found it ultimately incomprehensible, which may have been due, among other things, to the fact that her adult life was more pleasurable than that of Smith's.

In the end, even Seward's adherence to the regular sonnet form was not as full as it may seem.[53] Despite her admiration for Petrarch, she was opposed to subjecting the 'flowing line' of English verse to foreign 'taste or tales' like those of Petrarch and Werther: 'Let not foreign taste or tales enchain / The genuine freedom of thy flowing line.'[54] In spite of her apology of the 'legitimate' sonnet, her own sonnets contain many formal irregularities and, in fact, she came to believe that British poets should not imitate the Italians. Even Milton was dull when he imitated Petrarch.[55]

As an epitome of Seward's ideas, 'Advice to Smith' evidences what in any case may be deduced from Seward's sonnets and poems: that her interest in Petrarch and what he represented in her time was slight. Besides the reservations already discussed, she disliked other Romantic aspects of Petrarch such as the cult of solitude and the idealisation of 'Valclusa's charming fair', who was 'Bright as its laurels, as its fountain cold'.[56] Neither the themes nor the tone of Seward's sonnets are Petrarchan in any significant way – which makes her insistence on the legitimate form of the sonnet more puzzling. One is tempted to explain it away as an effect of her envy of Smith's success.

Paradoxically, it turns out that Smith was one of the most genuinely Petrarchan poets of the time, even though – or just because – she took from Petrarch what suited her interests. Smith's adversaries always complained of the monotony of theme and mood in *Elegiac Sonnets*. In effect, this variation on a fixed underground pattern is fully Petrarchan, since at first sight *Canzoniere* gives exactly the same sense of repetitiousness on few, haunting ideas. Smith's obsessions were not the same as Petrarch's, but the overall effect of her collection on the reader is undoubtedly Petrarchan. We should not only listen to Smith's enemies but also to her admirers, like William Preston who praised her for reviving the intensity of Petrarch's sentiment.[57]

Seward was a better translator and adaptor of texts from the Asiatic tongues. She versified several prose translations of Persian poems she found in the work of Sir William Jones and others. In fact, her view of Petrarch was strongly influenced by Jones, since she, like him, associated Petrarch's love poetry with the Persian tradition for their passion, their images, and the sinuousness of their syntax, as is showed by her 'Invocation to the Shade of Petrarch, and to the Spirit of the Persian Poets, on their compositions being translated into English by Sir William Jones'.[58] The surprising thing in Seward's versions from the Oriental tongues is their open sensuousness, which furnishes a deeper explanation of her uneasiness with Smith, Laura and Petrarch. Seward disliked indulging in melancholy and unrequited love, like Petrarch's and Werther's, but her fancy was triggered off by poems where sensuous desire was expressed with strength and clarity. There is nothing morbid in the Persian poems she re-worked. The women who speak in them are waiting for their distant lovers, and though they feel the pain of loneliness, it is not the sorrow of Petrarch's torments or Werther's immature idealism.[59] Though the context is still that of unfulfilled desire, in Seward's case it is an explicitly physical desire rather than the often disembodied ravings of the mainstream love poetry of her age.

An interesting contrast is provided by 'Harold's Complaint', a version of Seward's from Old Norse. While Persian women begged their men to come back from the war as soon as possible, Scandinavian women were, as a note taken from Alexander's *History of Women* goes, 'chaste, proud, and tenacious of their lover's glory, despising such as spent their life in obscurity'.[60] In the north, fighting was a way of wooing, of which Seward did not seem particularly fond. In comparison to the prose version she versified in her translation, she made the Russian maid look more disdainful but also sillier.[61] At the same time, the Norwegian hero was made to express both sentimental suffering and resentment for the girl he loved. There could not be a greater difference from the atmosphere of the Persian and Arabic poems, which Seward seems to have liked better than their Northern counterparts.

Though Seward's Petrarchism was superficial, many modern scholars have written on the form of Smith's sonnets from perspectives which, intentionally or not, strongly recall that of Seward. Many would agree with Daniel Robinson that 'Smith appears to be making perverse fun of Petrarch's forms' in her translations, which are two elegiac sonnets (Sonnets 15 and 16) and 'two wildly irregular ones' (Sonnets 13 and 14). This is not as exact as it might seem.[62] It is true that Smith did not use the strict sonnet form, but it should not be forgotten that a critical debate developed only after the publication of *Elegiac Sonnets*. Before that, as we have seen above, the discussion took place between a party of adversaries of the sonnet *in any form* and supporters of the sonnet *especially in the Italian form*.[63] The average awareness of form cannot have been great, since in 1807 Susanna Dobson called 'sonnets' the poems of Troubadours and Minnesinger.[64] Though Smith's Sonnet 13, in octosyllabics, may have been added to the fourth edition of her collection as a sort of polemical answer to the reviews which had blamed the irregularity of her sonnets, her other versions from Petrarch – and her sonnets in general – cannot be considered wildly irregular. In fact, the form of Smith's sonnets must not be compared to those published after her collection. In comparison to the British translations from Petrarch published before 1784, Smith's versions must have first struck English readers for the regularity of their form. She certainly respected the sonnet form, and adhered to it more closely than the great majority of the earlier translators who often turned Petrarch's sonnets into elegies in rhyming couplets or wildly irregular poems of approximately 14 lines.

Another historical misunderstanding is the view, embraced by several scholars, that Smith played Shakespeare against Petrarch, the English against the Italian sonnet form. This seems extremely unlikely because, as we saw in the previous chapter, the sonnet tradition of the English Renaissance remained marginal and practically unknown up to the end of the eighteenth century, and it began to circulate timidly in the early 1810s, as Lofft's *Laura* shows. There are no traces anywhere in Smith that she intended to revive one tradition *against* the other. Her models were the common ones in her time, Petrarch and Milton filtered through their earlier eighteenth-century admirers, as the echoes and quotations in her poems and footnotes show. Smith never ceased to consider Petrarch as the good genius of the sonnet if in 1791 she quoted him again in *Celestina*, and in 1797 she chose a passage from *Canzoniere* as a motto to Volume II of *Elegiac Sonnets*.[65] The interest of this motto, however, goes beyond this.

Stuart Curran argued that Smith's often imprecise quotations from Petrarch could indicate 'an Italian either insecure or so fluent as to be stored in her memory'.[66] The precise details of Smith's studies are unknown, but certainly the Italian language was a suitable subject for a young upper-class girl like her. Loraine Fletcher affirmed that Smith might have taken Italian lessons at school at Kensington, or that she began to learn Italian at Southgate round 1770, when she had already borne four children. At any rate, 'she was proficient in Italian [. . .] and read Petrarch and Metastasio with pleasure.'[67] Smith's interest in Italian was lifelong, as in 1796 she wrote to Cadell and Davies asking for Baretti's *Italian Library* and Bottarelli's dictionary.[68] Her translations, quotations and echoes in *Elegiac Sonnets* point to an anthological knowledge of Petrarch, intensive rather than extensive. The sonnets she referred to are anthology pieces, texts a teacher would typically use to introduce Petrarch to new readers and students of Italian. There is one exception to the rule, and that is the source of the motto mentioned above. 'Che debb'io far?', a *planctus* (weeping song) at the beginning of the second part of *Canzoniere*, is a rare text whose only Romantic translator was John Nott in 1777. Smith may well have used Nott's edition, which seems to be the source of a couple of points of her translations.[69] It is most unlikely that she read the poem at school; other *canzoni* are simpler, more famous and pleasant than this gloomy meditation begun by Petrarch the very day he got to know of Laura's death.

The passage Smith selected was an apt motto for her collection as well as her life: 'non t'appressare ove sia riso o canto, / canzon mia no, ma pianto / non fa per te di star fra gente allegra, / vedova sconsolata in vesta negra', that is, 'do not approach where there is laughter and singing, my song, no, but where there is weeping; it is not fitting for you to be among cheerful people, disconsolate widow in black garments.' After the death of some of her children and the separation from her husband, Smith too was a sort of 'disconsolate widow', though she enjoyed none of the legal advantages of real ones. Wherever Smith may have found this passage – be it Nott's 1777 edition or a biography of Petrarch – her use of 'Che debb'io far?' shows that in her maturity she continued reading Petrarch and thinking about him.[70] The different editions of *Elegiac Sonnets* can give us the false impression that Petrarch was to Smith a preliminary model she progressively outgrew, leaving behind herself translations and imitations on behalf of 'original' sonnets. Her later quotations and the Petrarch motto to *Elegiac Sonnets*, Volume II, inserted when her remarkable fame made a poetic patron unnecessary, prove that Petrarch was to her a point of reference and a faithful companion rather than a cumbersome precursor to be discarded as soon as possible.

Smith's was an elegiac Petrarchism, nourished by the tone of the *in morte* part of *Canzoniere*. Love, the centre of Petrarch's poetics, was not Smith's primary preoccupation, in spite of the space *Elegiac Sonnets* gave to Petrarch, Werther, and Pope's 'Eloisa to Abelard', three essential components of the love poetry of her time.[71] Smith's collection opened up new possibilities which other poets, the Della Cruscans and above all Mary Robinson, exploited thoroughly in the years which followed.

4
The Della Cruscans and Mary Robinson

Petrarch was one the numerous Italian poets who drew the attention of the Della Cruscans, both the original group, which gathered in Florence in 1785, and the second wave, which developed later round the periodical *The World*. Historically, their interest remains a significant stage in the Romantic revival of Italian literature. The enthusiasm that the most sensational school of poetry of the 1780s and early 1790s showed for Italian verse, which inspired their writings in Florence and London, played a significant role in establishing Italian as the most fashionable foreign literature of the time, following a trend which had been growing since the mid-century.

The Della Cruscan interest in Petrarch was not as specific as Charlotte Smith's. For them, Petrarch was only one – though, sometimes, a favourite one – of the Italian classics they admired and rewrote. The *Florence Miscellany* (1785), the first Della Cruscan anthology, contains imitations and translations from an impressive number of Italian poets, ranging from Dante to contemporaries like Metastasio and Parini. The Della Cruscans experimented with several stanzaic and metrical forms, including the sonnet which, however, was not their main concern. Though Petrarch appears in several points of the *Florence Miscellany*, he attracted above all the attention of Bertie Greatheed and William Parsons. Hester Thrale Piozzi's 'Song' describes a council summoned by Jove to give Florence a name where Pallas 'talk'd of Petrarca her favourite son, / Said GREATHEED should finish what *he* had begun: / Then nam'd his two Friends, but there Jove stopt her tongue, / Or the Goddess had lengthen'd till midnight her song.'[1] In other words, Piozzi saw Greatheed, though jokingly, as a disciple of Petrarch who was going to complete the work of his master, a daring enterprise which was stopped at the initial stage. In fact, the only Petrarchan texts Greatheed wrote were two sonnets in Italian, an English sonnet for an Emma he fell in love with in Florence, and an 'Ode to Apathy' where he blamed the political inertia of contemporary Italians, who did not react against the decadence in which they lived. He wished they awoke from their slumber, bringing back the glory of Latin Rome to the 'proud land of old renown'd, / Which Appennines divide, and Alps and seas surround'. The last line is borrowed from a sonnet of Petrarch which, however, has nothing to do with politics. The quotation looks more ornamental than substantial, as it does not produce a meaningful intertextual link with its source.[2] It was a nice way of bringing the ode to a close rather than a means for corroborating a message of political rebellion which, in any case, was a commonplace complaint.

Petrarch's indignation against the moral decadence of Italy was also cited by Parsons, the best Italian scholar in the group and, perhaps not coincidentally, the poet whose response was most lively to Petrarch's verse. His 'Epistle from Rome, to Robert Merry, Esq. at Florence' is a long descriptive letter on Roman history and culture where, like many British travellers before and after him, he talked of the vices of Cardinals, 'Such vices as from PETRARCH's Lyre / No longer tun'd to soft desire, / Call'd tones of harsh reproof upon, / This new and impious BABYLON'. The predictable conclusion defines Rome as a dreadful example, because the present decadence of its race is much greater than its past glory.[3] Politics, however, was not the main reason for Parsons's interest in Petrarch. *The Florence Miscellany* included other texts which were later reprinted in *A Poetical Tour* together with some additional Petrarchan poems, which, however, did not modify his attitude in the essential.

Parsons's Petrarchan contributions to *The Florence Miscellany* were an imitation of 'Levòmmi il mio penser in parte ov'era' (*PC*, 302), and 'Stanzas on Reading Petrarch's Sonnets on the Death of Laura', which was his clearest statement on Petrarch. The 'Sonnet imitated from Petrarch' is, in reality, a translation which does not stand out in the mass of eighteenth-century versions from Petrarch. Parsons's translation respects the original rhyme scheme but it does not display an original view. There are paraphrases, such as 'Fancy's wing' for 'penser' ('thought', l. 1), additions as the conventional 'Death took me from a world of pain' for 'et compie' mia giornata inanzi sera' ('and completed my day before evening', l. 8), and omissions as 'te solo aspetto' ('I only wait for you', l. 10), so that in the English text it is not clear if Laura is waiting for Petrarch in Heaven. Though the Della Cruscan style has recently been praised for its theatricality, Parsons left out Laura's rhetorical gesture in line 12, 'Deh perché tacque et allargò la mano?' ('Ah, why did she then become still and open her hand?'), replacing it with a briefer 'She ceased' (l. 13).[4] Parsons's scholastic version shows that, despite his sincere admiration, he must have found Petrarch's idealism baffling, a view confirmed by the next poem in the anthology, his 'Stanzas on Reading Petrarch's Sonnets on the Death of Laura'.

Parsons' musings on Petrarch's *in morte* poems shows that he and his friends were aware of Smith's *Elegiac Sonnets*, the most sensational novelty on the British literary scene at the time. It is no coincidence that the first stanza of Parsons's poem is paraphrased from both Petrarch's 'Vago augelletto' and 'Quel rosignuol', two favourite Romantic sonnets, and from Smith's nightingale sonnets, one of which, as we saw before, is a translation of 'Quel rosignuol'.[5] Parsons compared Petrarch to the nightingale, which, unlike other birds, sang out of woe. Petrarch's poetry for his dead beloved

> Does far, far more our thoughts engage
> While sad we turn th'infectious page,
> Than Bards in whose more labor'd lines
> The glare of wit for ever shines,
> Who only boast, great summit of their art,
> To raise the transient smile, not fire the throbbing heart.[6]

Parsons's praise of Petrarch's passionate simplicity is strange, as the last four lines, which were probably referred to Augustan poetry, are also a good definition of the Della Cruscan style, laboured and witty, aimed at light sensual pleasure rather than intense sentiment. Parsons's eulogy of Petrarch unwittingly damned himself and his friends.

In spite of this unintentional paradox, Parsons found Petrarch's lays 'congenial', as he, like Petrarch, was 'a slave to Love' and often proved 'his restless torments'.[7] He hoped, at least, that his suffering might inspire his poetry. In the last stanza Parsons, like Smith in the first of her *Elegiac Sonnets*, cited Pope's Eloisa, who argued that they paint sorrow best who feel it most. Here, however, Parsons's reading parted company with Smith. If the price to be paid for composing great poetry was so high, Parsons would be content to write worse verse and suffer less:

> May no such sad excess of woe
> E'er prompt my mournful strain to flow,
> Ne'er may I see my Stella's breath
> Like Laura's yield to ruthless Death[.][8]

As Jerome McGann, Judith Pascoe and other critics have pointed out, the Della Cruscans practised poetry as a theatrical game, a literary world of surfaces which kept at distance the painful reality in which poetry is often rooted. Poetry was not worth a tormented life like that of Petrarch: 'Ere such event my feeble song inspire, / Stop'd be my vital flood, and quench'd the Muse's fire!'[9] Parsons could hardly run such risk, as in the version of the poem he included in *A Poetical Tour* 'Stella' was replaced with 'Miranda'.[10] Consolation proved to be easy to him or, in any case, easier than to Petrarch or Charlotte Smith, who understood Petrarch's dramatic lot much more deeply than Parsons and Greatheed.

Parsons's other references to Petrarch confirm his attitude of genuine, though cautious attraction. In 'Epistle from Florence, to the Marquis Ippolito Pindemonte, at Verona' he recalled the nights they spent together in Florence reading favourite poets like Ariosto, Tasso, Dante and Petrarch, though elsewhere he specified that he liked Petrarch better than Dante.[11] In *Fidelity, or*

Love at first Sight (1798) Parsons included a section of sonnets with a preface which summarises his views, the limited ones of an amateur, as he himself was keen on acknowledging. He believed that the sonnet was like the classical epigram, and its rules had been fixed by Boileau. He disliked English Renaissance epigrams and wrote his own sonnets only for fun. Parsons echoed the contemporary debate in the conclusion, where he maintained that his were not sonnets, but three elegiac stanzas with a couplet, a definition which recalls the derogatory judgements of Smith's adversaries.[12] In Sonnet VII, 'To a friend in Love, and writing Sonnets', Parsons told his friend that if he renounced material pleasure, he might compete with Petrarch's fame, though, hopefully, he would not end up like Petrarch: 'But not like *his*, in LOVE, be thy reward, / If thou so long canst from loose joy abstain: / For of all fates, it, certes, is most hard, / To serve like him – *three 'prenticeships – in vain!*'[13] Parsons's view of Petrarch's obsessions as unreasonable reflects an opinion which, as we saw before, was common in the eighteenth century before the Petrarchan vogue.

Petrarch's life led him to a misanthropy which Parsons could not share, given the sociable character of Della Cruscan verse. This is evident in Parsons's version of Petrarch's 'Ne la stagion che 'l ciel rapido inchina', a *canzone* which met Romantic taste, as it contains many rural and natural images.[14] The theme of the poem is the opposition between the peaceful sleep enjoyed by common people like a pilgrim, a peasant, a shepherd and a sailor, and the tormented nights of the anguished lover, who is sleepless and hopeless.[15] In the last stanza Petrarch invites his song to keep away from other people, because its main preoccupation must be the poet's miserable sentimental condition. Parsons replaced this misanthropic conclusion with another one taken from 'Qual più diversa et nova' (*PC*, 135), in which Petrarch asks his song to tell its readers that he is living isolated in Vaucluse, where he can be seen only by Love and the image of Laura he carries in his heart. In other words, Parsons rejected absolute isolation and replaced it with a retreat where Petrarch, albeit at a distance, remained in contact with his readers. Parsons disagreed with a growing cult of solitude and a Romantic reading of Petrarch which, for many poets, proved to be a pose more than a necessity.[16]

Parsons's *A Poetical Tour* is a good metaphor for the Della Cruscan aesthetics. A group of polite English fellows in Florence, the Della Cruscans visited Italian places and books with the superficial enthusiasm of tourists. Parsons went round many Italian places, which he described in the first part of his collection, whereas in the second part he visited several Italian poets in imitations and translations, in most cases with no other driving interest than curiosity and a particular attention to love poetry understood as elegant society verse. From the perspective of this book, the main merits of the Della Cruscans was their attention to Italian poetry and their contribution to a renewed interest which had been growing for three decades. Since they wrote a good deal of love poetry, Petrarch naturally became one of the authors they took into account. However, as might be expected, they did not establish any special relation with him. He was only one in a series of Italian poets they used in various ways, from echo to literal translation. Their idea of love poetry as a polite conversational exchange in a masquerade of pseudonyms, both in *The Florence Miscellany* and *The World*, and the drawing-room agnosticism underlying their ornamental poetics, were too remote in any sense from the seriousness of Petrarch's idealism to have anything substantial in common with it. Petrarch's rhetorical mask was far too complex, both in form and content, for their amateur theatricality. Parsons's commonsense views barely touched the surface of Petrarch's discourse, which was ignored in the love epistles Robert Merry, Hannah Cowley and others exchanged in the pages of *The World*.[17] It is no coincidence that only Mary Robinson, the most talented poet and the only professional actress of the group, entered into a real dialogue with Petrarch, since she understood that a pleasurable game of poetic epistles may have opened up new possibilities, in particular for women poets, but it was not enough to renew love poetry radically. Tradition could not simply be eschewed; it needed to be faced and reread. This is what Robinson tried to do in *Sappho and Phaon* and a few other poems on the same subject.

4.1 Mary Robinson

Amorous discourse in later eighteenth-century poetry hinged on three main figures: Sappho, Petrarch and Werther. Sappho was the great classical example of a lover and poet whose passion was not reciprocated. Petrarch was its late-medieval version. Like Sappho, he was an unfulfilled lover and a great lyrical poet. Werther was a mask of Goethe, and his story added some important variants to the theme of melancholy, tragic love. In his novel the amorous triangle, implicit in other stories of unrequited love, is made overt. Besides, the pantheist link between love for a person and love of nature becomes a central issue. Werther is an *amateur*, both in art and life, which rendered the readers' identification with him easier. His suicide revives Sappho's legendary leap in Leucadia, but it shows its horrible side: Sappho's romantic jump from a cliff into the sea is replaced by Werther's miserable agony in his room. Goethe seized on Gothic horror before it became popular and, ironically, he deconstructed it from within.

There is another basic component to the love poetry of the period, that is, the tradition of the Ovidian epistle. Ovid's *Heroides* did not only furnish the single most influential version of Sappho's story in 'Sappho Phaoni'; they were also the model for a form which remained influential till the early nineteenth century. Pope's 'Eloisa to Abelard', possibly the most widely admired love poem of the century, was cast in this mode. Abelard and Eloisa, in fact, are the last couple that must be added to our list. They were the archetypes of the medieval lover, and they were later replaced by Dante and Beatrice. Pope's poem is the primary referent for the other eighteenth-century re-writings of Abelard and Eloisa, which seldom went back to the original sources of the story.

The work in which all these themes mingle and interact is Mary Robinson's *Sappho and Phaon*. This collection has been generally analysed as part of the Sapphic tradition, which is reasonable and justified. However, it should not be forgotten that Robinson's plan was much more ambitious, because her collection was a sort of *summa* of the main trends of the love poetry of her time. Keeping this in mind, I am going to focus on the Petrarchan element in her poetry. In fact, Robinson's involvement with Petrarch did not begin and end with *Sappho and Phaon*.

After the publication of her juvenilia in the 1770s, in 1790 Robinson made her début as a poetess in the Della Cruscan journal *The World* under the pen-name of 'Laura', as she recalled in her *Memoirs*.[18] This was not an isolated episode, as she used this name and a variant, 'Laura Maria', throughout her life – in 1800 her last published poem was signed 'Laura Maria'.[19] Robinson used other pseudonyms – at least eight – for poems of different character: for example, Oberon was used to pay homage to other women, whereas Tabitha Bramble was her mask for harsh satire. Many intriguing essays have recently commented on Robinson's multi-faceted, theatrical self and her rhetorical strategies, especially in opposition to Wordsworth's idea of the transcendental unity of the ego.[20] However, the meaning of those literary masks has received scant attention. Why was a pseudonym chosen at a certain time? What did that character represent to the British public in that period?

As we saw in the previous chapters, by the late 1780s scholars, translators and poets had made Laura's name familiar to British readers. We saw, also, that Laura's reputation was not unconditionally good. Even several enthusiasts found her aloof and unreal, whereas most sceptical readers of Petrarch lamented the immorality of her behaviour. However strange it may sound to us today, at the time of Robinson's poetic début Laura was no more recommendable a name than Sappho, though for different reasons. Robinson's choice was bolder than it may seem, if we remember that she was mainly known for her past liaison with the Prince of Wales, who, incidentally, headed the impressive list of subscribers to her first important volume of poetry, published in 1791. On top of that, her first poems came between Della Crusca (Robert Merry) and Anna Matilda (Hannah Cowley), who had been flirting in verse on the pages of *The World* for a few months. Her intervention created a triangle which disrupted their verbal idyll. Mary 'Perdita' Robinson, the most notorious mistress of the age, had the nerve to début in a literary triangle with the pseudonym Laura, the most fashionable poetic mistress of the time. This may mean two different things: on the one hand, that she did not find that role as suffocating and unpleasant as many contemporary scholars have argued; on the other, that she fully accepted her role, however unpalatable. She would neither hide nor be ashamed;

rather, she was ready to speak out from the position in which society had confined her.[21]

Though Robinson was not primarily interested in identifying with Laura, and though she did not draw on Petrarch in her poetical correspondence with Merry, during her Della Cruscan phase she composed a specific poem on Petrarch and Laura, which was published in her first significant collection in 1791. The poem, 'Petrarch to Laura', comes in the last part of the book, after several texts for which Robinson used Laura as pseudonym.[22] Though it is clear that in this poem Petrarch is talking to his Laura, inevitably it sounds as though he was also addressing Robinson, who, as the author of the poem, is in fact using Petrarch's voice. In other words, Robinson is playing a complex game, in which she is identifying with both characters, though only partially with each of them.

'Petrarch to Laura' is an epistle in heroic couplets, preceded by a motto from Pope's 'Eloisa to Abelard'.[23] The form shows that at this date Robinson was reading Petrarch through Pope's interpretation of the Ovidian tradition. She was familiar with the sonnet and, significantly, she placed 15 of them immediately before 'Petrarch to Laura', but preferred to re-write Petrarch's story as a verse epistle.[24] Most likely, the Della Cruscan correspondence in verse must also have played a decisive influence on her choice. 'Petrarch to Laura' extends the Della Cruscan game back to a remote past, creating an ancestry which, however fictitious, has a grain of imaginative truth in it.[25] It is a way of looking at Petrarch which recalls Sir William Jones rather than the more modern approaches of John Nott and Charlotte Smith. However, though Robinson's text was formally conservative, it was innovative in its perspective and content.

The subheading of 'Petrarch to Laura' specifies that the poem is 'Supposed to have been written during his retirement at Vaucluse a short time before her death'.[26] At a time when the *in morte* poems of *Canzoniere* were the centre of British attention to Petrarch, Robinson focused on the *in vita* poems. She did not concentrate on the aftermath of passion and the phenomenology of loss, like Smith and most British Petrarchans; her primary interests were the psychology and ideology of love. Her Petrarch was a lover, albeit an anguished one, rather than a mourner, as most Romantics saw him.

In her epistle, Robinson paraphrased several passages from Petrarch's sonnets, linking them together by adding some personal comments. Robinson learned Italian at school and may have met John Nott in Bristol, but her main source was Dobson's biography of Petrarch rather than the poems directly.[27] Though her source was a common one, her interpretation of Petrarch's love story was innovative. Robinson began her poem with a lonely, despairing Petrarch in a gloomy natural setting inspired by both Petrarch's poems and the opening of Pope's 'Eloisa to Abelard'.[28] Even the more pleasant, Petrarchesque nature of the second paragraph looks as despondent as the poet, and it cannot soothe his pangs of love. Solitude seems to be the only consolation: 'No more for ME your sunny banks shall pour / In purple tides Autumn's luscious store; / No more for ME your lust'rous tints shall glow, / Your forests wave, your silv'ry channels flow; / Yet 'midst your heav'n my wounded breast shall crave / One narrow cell, my SOLACE and my GRAVE.'[29] The fact that nature reflects the feelings of the protagonist but it does not console him is a variant on the unromantic view that Robinson found in Petrarch's poems such as 'Zephiro torna', where nature blatantly contradicts the mood of the poet.[30]

The following paragraph consists of a series of anguished questions, in which Petrarch wonders where and how his anxiety can be cured: 'Where, LAURA, shall I turn, what balsam find / To soothe the throbbings of my fev'rish mind?'[31] Petrarch's memory goes back to the beginning of his involvement, when he first saw Laura in a church at Avignon, an episode for which Robinson drew on Dobson's biography.[32] The emotional effect of Laura's heavenly beauty on Petrarch's mind is described in the next paragraph with an imagery typical of the Gothic novel rather than Petrarchan poetry:

> ALL, ALL WAS LOVE! while thro' my burning brain
> Rush'd a fierce torrent of convulsive pain;
> From my dim eyes celestial radiance stole,
> While howling demons grasp'd my sinking soul,
> Guilt's writhing scorpions twining round my heart,
> Enflam'd each wound, and heighten'd every smart[.]

He tried to cling to religion, but 'The priestess frowning on my impious pray'r, / Check'd the bold suit, and hurl'd me to despair.'[33]

Petrarch rebukes Love and Laura for laying him such a trap, that is, love which cannot be reciprocated: 'Why, soft enchantress, spread the fatal snare / That lures thy struggling victim to despair?' In a footnote to this section, Robinson quotes a passage from Dobson which describes Laura's behaviour with Petrarch as a mixture of attraction and coyness. Unlike Sade and Dobson, Robinson found it far from touching and justifiable: 'Why with meek smiles my wand'ring sense reclaim? / Why feed with pitying looks my hopeless flame?'[34] Her Petrarch entreats Love to cool down his passion and lead him back to God – a request Petrarch makes only in the very last texts of *Canzoniere*, as he generally described his love for Laura as a means to reach God.[35]

Laura's image haunts Petrarch, who sees her everywhere, as he himself says in his sonnets: 'Where'er I fly, where'er my frenzy roves / [...] Still on my shatter'd brain thy form appears, / Steals to my heart, and glistens thro' my tears'.[36] Though, as he had already said, he is sceptical of the healing power of solitude, he retires to Vaucluse trying to pray to God and forget Laura, but 'holy vows were lost in warm desires / LOVE drop'd a tear that quench'd religion's fires' – again, Robinson's addition, as Petrarch believed in the exact opposite.[37] Robinson did not find Petrarch's deification of Laura ridiculous or disgraceful, as many British readers did; she simply described an effect of Catholic belief on the psychology of love in order to understand its ideology.

Petrarch's passion turned Vaucluse from a peaceful retreat into an Ossianic place where he wandered tormented by hellish despair almost like an 'ancient mariner'.[38] His poetic and scholarly work gave him both rapture and peace, a combination which could not be found in his passion for Laura.[39] Since Vaucluse had become a nightmare, he decided to travel in France, Germany and Italy, but, unfortunately, Love went along with him. He ended up in Rome, where he melodramatically identified with the Christian martyrs buried there, 'For O! eternal MARTYRDOM I prove, / Heav'n's doom'd APOSTATE – my fell tyrant, LOVE!'[40]

Rome, however, was also the city of his poetic coronation, a favourite Romantic episode which could not be missing in Robinson's poem. Even during that picturesque and pleasant ceremony, Petrarch could not forget Laura,

> For who but THEE, transcendent Angel! taught
> The flame to live, which kindled every thought?
> For who, like THEE, could heavenly themes inspire,
> Or touch the sensate mind with hallow'd fire,
> Mingling with mortal dust the spark divine,
> That bade my verse with deathless glories shine.[41]

This passage is extremely significant because Robinson, who had so far concentrated on the evils of passion, seemed to acknowledge that love alone can generate that mental and emotional energy which is necessary to create great poetry. The classical idea of the inspiring Muse, as her Romantic Petrarch rephrased it, brings forward a paradox in which all poets seem to be caught: poetry is not only a technical game, but requires a genuine emotional intensity which, more often than not, brings a good deal of trouble along with its creative power. For this reason Petrarch cherished the passion which tormented him. Also, the passage seems to suggest that, in Robinson's opinion, the ultimate reason for Petrarch's passion was poetical rather than personal: Laura was a muse rather than a real woman.

Robinson, however, had reservations about Petrarch's view, though in this poem she expressed them only implicitly. The next section portrays Petrarch playing his lute at the fountain of Vaucluse, where he falls asleep and has a vision of Laura in Heaven surrounded by angelic choirs, of which Robinson caught the theatrical quality, as seen in many Baroque frescos. In Robinson's sceptical opinion, Heaven seems to be a spectacle among many others. It is here, however, that Laura speaks directly to Petrarch, as she sometimes does in *Canzoniere*. However, the tone of her speech recalls, more than Petrarch's collection, that of Ariel in Pope's *The Rape of the Lock*. Laura tells Petrarch that she is waiting for him in Heaven but, in the meantime, she is waiting upon

him like one of Pope's sylphs. The soul 'once purified, awaits on those /
who toil amidst a wilderness of woes: / It guards the partners of its mortal hours, / when anguish threatens, or despair devours, / Shields the frail
bosom with a cherub's wing, / And robs they tyrant DEATH of EV'RY STING.'[42]
This echo from Pope's mock-heroic poem obviously deflates the earnestness
of Petrarch's original vision, turning a golden altar-piece into rococo china.
Laura's language is not that of a Muse, because it echoes Pope's Ariel, the
soul of a coquette turned into a sylph after death.[43] In this passage, Robinson
sounds like a poetic version of Tytler, who in his essay on Petrarch defined
Laura as a coquette.

The conclusion of Laura's speech is not more encouraging. If Paradise is the
future she promises Petrarch, the present awaiting him is a 'wild'ring vale to
rove, / The mourning victim of disast'rous love'. Not even Laura can find
a good word for Petrarch's love; her 'last fond hope is this, / To meet her
PETRARCH in the realms of bliss'. At this point Petrarch wakes up from this
dream only to find himself in trouble as ever. The future might be heaven,
but the present is certainly hell.[44]

Seen in the clear daylight of reason, Petrarch's vision looks less promising
than in a dream. The obscurity of death threatens even the hope of immortality he expected from his verse: 'My once bright laurels doom'd, alas! to fade /
On the pale forehead of a ling'ring shade. / A living spectre drooping and
forlorn, / A star obscur'd of all its lustre shorn'.[45] This is going to make his
life even more solitary, hopeless and unbearable than before: 'Toiling thro'
tedious years unseen, unblest, / Eternal thorns corroding in my breast; / I fast,
I pray, and yet no comfort find.' The conclusion he draws is an extraordinary
line in which Robinson managed to condense the experience of Petrarch and
many other poets: 'Heaven on my lips, but hell within my mind!' A pinch of
hope, however, seems to emerge in the last lines:

> Or, if by chance one pitying ray of rest
> Warms the sad inmate of my throbbing breast;
> 'Tis but a gleam of INTELLECTUAL light
> That feebly glances o'er my MENTAL sight,
> And for a moment dissipates the gloom,
> To point my weary footsteps TO THE TOMB.[46]

The only consolation Petrarch can find is intellectual, but this does not relieve
his suffering, which is physical as much as psychological. Unlike the original Petrarch, who in the conclusion to his collection found in the Virgin
the solution for his tormented story, Robinson's Petrarch is aided solely by
reason, which, however, points to death as the only place where he can find
peace. Such death, however, is not heaven but the tomb, the place of material
disintegration rather than spiritual afterlife.

Robinson's poetic version of Petrarch's life is extremely pessimistic. The
love of her Petrarch is almost only torment rather than a bittersweet mixture

of pain and joy, as in the original. It is a gloomy Petrarch for whom unreciprocated love is true hell. Art and religion are partial and uncertain consolations,
while reason, which cannot stem the overwhelming power of his passion, can
only point to physical death as liberation. However, Robinson found some
points of this story unconvincing. As we have seen, Laura was in her opinion
a sort of coquette, a silly narcissist who tormented her lover. But the fault did
not lie only with her. In *A Letter to the Women of England*, Robinson recalled
that, according to tradition, Laura 'could neither *read* nor *write*! Petrarch was
a poet and a scholar; I will not so far stigmatize his memory, as to attribute
his excessive idolatry to the intellectual obscurity of his idol. Yet from the
conduct of some modern philosophers, (in every thing but love), the spirit
of cynical observation might trace something like jealousy and envy, or a
dread of rivalry in mental acquirements.'[47] Whatever the social conditions
may have been in Petrarch's time, celebrating a model of woman like Laura in
the eighteenth century was a way of perpetuating discrimination in learning
and work.[48]

Robinson was suspicious of Petrarch's obsessive passion. Its unusual length
was at odds with her experience, which taught her that emotional ecstasy
was given 'To prove EARTH, a transient HEAV'N', but, also, that 'like a METEOR,
glimm'ring through a shade, / TOO EXQUISITE TO LAST! the FLEETING FORM
DECAY'D.'[49] Emotional intensity did not automatically mean faithfulness and
duration. In 'Lines to Him Who Will Understand Them', Robinson described
a type of love which was both impetuous and fickle: 'Thy wild impetuous
passions trace / O'er the white wave's tempestuous space: / In every changing season prove / An emblem of thy wav'ring LOVE.'[50] In texts like this,
which elaborated her experience as a mistress of powerful aristocrats, betrayal
and unfulfilled promises loom large, and it is no coincidence that the poem
immediately preceding 'Petrarch to Laura' is 'Where, thro' the starry curtains
of the night', a nightingale sonnet in which Robinson, unlike Smith who
may have inspired it, found a precise reason for 'the luxury of tender grief':
'TRUANT LOVE'.[51]

Robinson's 1791 collection suggests that Petrarch's love for Laura was lifelong because it remained unfulfilled and, as 'Petrarch to Laura' indicates,
because it was motivated by literary ambition rather than by a genuine
attention to Laura as a real woman. Petrarch's interest in her was unlikely
because, as Robinson wrote later, Laura was too ignorant to attract as learned
a man as Petrarch, though her very ignorance allowed him to turn her into an
idol and a Muse. But, whereas Petrarch, as the epitome of the male lyric poet,
stated in 'Petrarch and Laura' that he could write only if his Muse inspired
him, Robinson demanded neither a Muse nor amorous frenzy to compose
poetry. In 'The Adieu to Love' – a significant title – she told Love that she
renounced his 'tyrant sway' and mocked his 'fascinating art' for a calm 'unruf-
fled day, / That brings no torment to the heart' and leaves the imagination
free to create poetry.[52] In 'To the Muse of Poetry' she begged the Muse to

grant her 'no fierce terrific strain, / That rends the breast with tort'ring pain, / No frantic flight, no labour'd art, / To wring the fibres of the heart!', whereas in 'Ode to Despair' she hoped that her 'calm retreat' was a place 'Where Bliss congenial to the MUSE / Shall round my Heart her sweets diffuse, / Where, from each restless Passion free, / I give my noiseless hours, BLESS'D POETRY, TO THEE.'[53]

Robinson's attitude towards Petrarch, like that of her Della Cruscan friends, is clear. It was a call for reason, self-control and technicality in poetry which stemmed from the commonsense tradition of eighteenth-century England we have already found in other critics, translators and imitators. There was one problem with this theory: however absurd Petrarch's love appeared, he remained one of the supreme lyric poets of Western literature. Robinson must have found this disturbing if, keeping Petrarch in mind, she returned to the theme through the most famous lovelorn poet of classical antiquity: Sappho.

* * *

In *Sappho and Phaon* Robinson rewrote the story of Sappho but, in lieu of an Ovidian epistle, she chose the form of a sonnet sequence, the only one to appear in the Romantic period. Precisely, Robinson's subtitle speaks of 'a Series of Legitimate Sonnets', a definition explained in detail in her Preface.[54] In the first paragraph, Robinson dismissed the 'modern sonnet, concluding with two lines, winding up the sentiment of the whole', because it limited the fancy and ended the argumentation abruptly. Conversely, she praised the ancient or legitimate sonnet, as it 'is generally denominated', which can be used to compose a long narrative text in 'a series of sketches'.[55] In other words, English sonnets, as those fashionable in her time, were formally so unbalanced that, in her opinion, they could not be organised in sequences.

Robinson affirmed that she composed Italian sonnets 'not presuming to offer them as imitations of PETRARCH, but as specimens of that species of sonnet-writing' seldom attempted in England despite the sublime example of Milton, whose sonnet to the nightingale she quoted as an example. Whereas invoking Milton was commonplace, her sentence about Petrarch was not due to modesty, real or simulated; rather, it was a way of distancing herself from the growing number of British poets who imitated Petrarch's melancholy musings in loose sonnets, as the next passage clarifies. Very few of the innumerable sonnets published in her time 'deserve notice', and when they do, the form is so discredited that it 'scarcely excites attention'. In fact, poems of any length have improperly been called sonnets.[56]

However, Robinson could not easily dismiss an authority like Johnson and a popular sonneteer like Smith, who had reservations about the Petrarchan sonnet in English. Shrewdly, Robinson cited a passage from *Elegiac Sonnets* where Smith mentioned Hayley's sonnets as evidence that legitimate sonnets could successfully be written in English, provided that their author was talented enough. In this way Robinson, who may well have chosen the Petrarchan form to escape Smith's pervasive influence, had Smith praise the achievement of *Sappho and Phaon* against Smith's own poetics.[57] Robinson emphasised the difficulty of her undertaking by reiterating that only ignorance and vanity can generate 'the non-descript ephemera from the heated brains of self-important poetasters', all published, whatever their form may be, 'under the appellation of SONNET!'[58] This barbed comment was aimed at the romantic superstition that upsetting passion is enough to write poetry. Her insistence on formal control was part of her view of rational self-control as the necessary condition to compose poetry.

At this point, it is clear that the basis of Robinson's hostility to formal looseness was not only aesthetical but also moral and social. Undervaluing form and overvaluing emotion was an obscurantist way of degrading talent and the social respectability of poetry. In fact, poetry has both 'the power to raise' and 'the magic to refine'. In the past it was admired as a prophetic art, but even in the present it 'ought to be cherished as a national ornament', because the times when poetry was generously patronised were the 'most polished and enlightened'. Poetry helps purify the language of a nation, as the case of Waller's verse shows in comparison to 'all the labours of monkish pedantry, since the days of druidical mystery and superstition'.[59] Though Robinson celebrated the prophetic character of poetry, she insisted that an element of rationality ought to be preserved. The revival of ancient poetry must not become a cult of irrationality.

Unfortunately, poetry was neglected in England in her days, and poets were surrounded only by malice and envy. This was not accidental, since 'It is the interest of the ignorant and powerful, to suppress the effusions of enlightened minds'. When only monks could read and write, the ruling class enslaved the rest of the population. The progress of learning slowly liberated humanity from that condition, and a time was coming when this process would be completed, provided that knowledge found adequate support. In the remote past, poetry was venerated as a prophetic art; later, it was admired and honoured by the powerful, as when 'Petrarch was crowned with laurels, the noblest diadem, in the Capitol of Rome: his admirers were liberal, his contemporaries were just; and his name will stand upon record, with the united and honourable testimony of his own talents, and the generosity of his country.' Robinson provokingly emphasised that Catholic Italy in the Middle Ages was more enlightened and liberal than contemporary Britain, which neglected its poets, especially women poets, to whom Robinson, as a conclusion to her Preface, paid homage for their courage and perseverance.[60]

To sum up, the Preface to *Sappho and Phaon* is dedicated to the sonnet, the meaning of form, and the social status of poetry. It is a Petrarchan entrance to the palace of Sappho, whose story fills the remaining part of the introduction to the poems. Theoretically and materially, Robinson placed Petrarch before Sappho, as a lens through which the Greek poet needed to be read in the late eighteenth century. This is confirmed by the next section, 'To the Reader', where Robinson explained that Sappho struck her fancy because it was an example 'of the human mind, enlightened by the most exquisite talent, yet yielding to the destructive control of ungovernable passions'. As in 'Petrarch to Laura', the focus of Robinson's interest was the relation between passion and creativity, love and imagination. But whereas 'The unfortunate lovers, Heloise and Abeilard; and the supposed platonic, Petrarch and Laura, have found panegyrists in many distinguished authors', Sappho's passion for Phaon has been celebrated by Ovid and Pope, whose poems, however, 'are replete with shades, tending rather to depreciate than to adorn the Grecian Poetess'. There are two noteworthy points for us in this passage. The first is the definition of Petrarch and Laura as 'supposed platonic', which places Robinson unequivocally in that minority of British readers who did not believe in the merely ideal character of Petrarch's love. On the opposite side, her remark on the 'shades' cast by Ovid and Pope probably refers to their lines on Sappho's lesbianism. In short, Robinson rejected from the start both the ideal, platonic character of Petrarch's love and the homosexual element in Sappho, turning both into physical, heterosexual passions.[61] Theirs were not unrequited loves in the strict sense; rather, they were love stories which, for different reasons, were reciprocated only for a short time, which left their narrators hopelessly anxious and unsatisfied.

There were probably other reasons behind Robinson's choice of Sappho as a subject for her sonnets. As a poetess, it was more natural for her to identify with Sappho than Petrarch, Laura or Eloisa. However, the most interesting point is not her identification, which is obvious, but the limits of her identification. I am not only referring to the homosexual element in Sappho, which was ruled out from the start, but to the stormy character of her passion, with which Robinson found it more difficult to cope than it may seem. Despite the epithet of 'British Sappho' attributed to Robinson, her strategy did not aim at immediate identification. Her attitude is the opposite of Smith's, whose sonnets invite autobiographical interpretation. The theatrical quality of Robinson's sequence creates a distance between the characters and their author but, at the same time, they do not conceal the autobiographical element completely. Like Sappho, Robinson was a celebrated poet; unlike her, she had been the most famous beauty of her age, though by the time she composed *Sappho and Phaon* she had become a crippled, elderly lady. Like Sappho, Robinson had been loved and abandoned, by the Prince of Wales in the 1780s and by Banastre Tarleton in the 1790s.[62] Like Sappho though in different ways, Robinson, the notorious mistress of many powerful men, was considered a woman of abnormal sexuality.[63] Defending Sappho was a way of defending herself.

Robinson's 'Account of Sappho' summarises the dominant eighteenth-century versions of her life. Sappho was a wealthy lady of limited beauty who was wedded early to Cercolus of Andros.[64] Her talent for describing the 'passions of the human mind' was so extraordinary that her writings have always been considered as the standard 'for the pathetic, the glowing, and the amatory'. As Addison said, if more of them had survived, they would have been dangerous reading. 'They possessed none of the artificial decorations of a feigned passion; they were the genuine effusions of a supremely enlightened soul, labouring to subdue a fatal enchantment; and vainly opposing the conscious pride of illustrious fame, against the warm susceptibility of a generous bosom.' Again, Robinson saw a radical opposition between powerful love and poetic creativity. Sappho's poems were the 'genuine effusions' of her rational mind ('enlightened soul') struggling against an overwhelming passion. Clearly, Robinson would have never believed that poetry is the lava of imagination.[65] The problem, however, was not merely aesthetic.

Though in the eighteenth century Sappho's image had been conveniently sanitised, Robinson felt the necessity to defend her in the last part of the introduction. Anything 'which might tend to tarnish her reputation', that is, the erotic and lesbian elements in her texts, were added by the malice of mediocre poets, copyists and translators.[66] She must have been a virtuous woman, otherwise she would not have blamed her brother for the passion he had for Rhodope, a notorious courtesan. If her writings were sometimes 'too glowing for the fastidious refinement of modern times', British readers would admire the liberality of the Greeks, who venerated the genius of the muse over the limits of the woman. The conclusion was left to the Abbé Barthélemy, Robinson's main source alongside Ovid and Pope.[67] Barthélemy argued that Sappho instructed and loved her female disciples 'to excess' because she was extremely passionate. This was due to the 'extreme sensibility of the Greeks', who used to apply 'the impassioned language of love' to 'the most innocent connections'. Sappho was only the epitome of this custom: 'The sensibility of SAPPHO was extreme! She loved PHAON, who forsook her; after various efforts to bring him back', she committed suicide in Leucadia.[68] 'Extreme sensibility', the eighteenth-century phrase for uncontrollable erotic desire or powerful passion, drove Petrarch almost mad for four decades and led Sappho to suicide. It is obvious that William Gifford and other conservatives found Sensibility subversive, as it was for them an individual form of Jacobinism; it is less obvious that Robinson, who is usually considered a champion of Sensibility, should also find it so disturbing. Extreme sensibility was dangerous, but Sappho and Petrarch were the greatest lyrical poets of the tradition. Robinson tried to come to terms with this conundrum in *Sappho and Phaon*.

British interest in Petrarch developed at a time when the dominant image of Sappho was that of an ugly young lady or a despairing old woman abandoned by the man she loved, whom she in vain tried to conquer.[69] When this was only a part of a complex narration of bisexual love, as in Ovid and Pope, the result was a story of abandonment and betrayal.[70] On the contrary, when the sexual element in Sappho was laid aside or drastically downplayed, as in Robinson and many of her contemporaries, what was left was a story of unfulfilled heterosexual love, whose scanty surviving fragments of text were inevitably pieced together following a Petrarchan pattern.[71] Addison referred to Sappho as an alternative to Petrarchan love poetry as was understood in the seventeenth century but, though it may sound odd, eighteenth-century Sappho was in large part a Petrarchan Sappho.[72] Robinson's *Sappho and Phaon* is perhaps the clearest example of this, also because Robinson believed, as we have seen, that Petrarch and Laura were not platonic lovers.[73] Of course, one must not expect a wealth of Petrarchan details in the events of the story, for which Robinson drew on Barthélemy, Ovid and Pope.[74] It is the form which is Petrarchan – but form itself, obviously, is meaning.

Robinson quite rightly understood that Sappho's life, as was available in the 1790s, demanded to be told as a Petrarchan story, which meant first of all in sonnets. Just as her Preface on the sonnet was a preliminary to her outline of Sappho's life, the Petrarchan sonnet were the inevitable form in which Sappho's story had to be cast. Robinson's choice of the Petrarchan sonnet form, therefore, goes beyond the local diatribe on regularity and irregularity. The autobiography of a poet in love was a 'genre' that Petrarch had fixed once and for all in modern times. Robinson's choice was a way of operating critically within a tradition and, at the same time, a way of criticising the contemporary vogue for the irregular sonnet, which, in Smith and many others, was the canonical form for the melancholy meditations of a lonely figure in a landscape. To make her viewpoint clear from the beginning, Robinson chose for *Sappho and Phaon* the following motto from Ovid and Pope: 'Love taught my tears in sadder notes to flow, / And tun'd my heart to elegies of woe.'[75] Robinson wanted her sonnets to be elegiac in a completely different way from those of Smith's, the elegiac sonnets *par excellence* in that period.[76] Robinson did not believe in depression with no specific cause: as we saw above, her nightingale sonnet 'Where, thro' the starry curtains of the night', a *topos* of that mode, pointed to a clear reason for despondency, that is, sentimental betrayal. By returning to Petrarch's most specific form and usage of the sonnet, Robinson reaffirmed the disturbing core of Petrarch's discourse, which was evident in criticism and biography, whereas in poetry it was obscured by the particular way in which the sonnet was generally used in her time, for moral meditation rather than love poetry. Robinson's use of the legitimate sonnet in *Sappho and Phaon*, however, is simultaneously traditional and innovative. In fact, her sonnets are dialogic and combine the Petrarchan with the Ovidian tradition. They are 'letters' that incorporate the Ovidian epistle into the Petrarchan sonnet. Finally, the Wertherian element of the collection is Sappho's conclusive suicide, seemingly an un-Petrarchan gesture.[77]

There are two other elements in *Sappho and Phaon* which are indebted, at least in part, to the Petrarchan tradition. The first is the general structure of the sonnet sequence, which is divided into two parts, the former *in presentia* of Phaon in Lesbos (Sonnets I–XXII), the latter almost always *in absentia*, after their departure for Sicily (XXIII–XLIV). This corresponds roughly to the division of *Canzoniere*, though Laura's death makes her distance more radical and definitive. The other significant component derived from the Petrarchan tradition is the extreme concentration on the speaking subject, which is also a characteristic feature of Sappho's poetry, as is clear from the fragments found in the last two centuries.[78] Though Jerome McGann has described Robinson's Sappho as a politically correct reformer of men's behaviour, prophesying a future of equality and mutual attention, in *Sappho and Phaon* interest in Phaon is close to nil. Much more than Laura, Phaon is a silhouette, a Hollywood beauty she describes in a Petrarchan *blason* which does not appear in her sources.[79] Phaon does not find Sappho's mental brightness erotically attractive, nor is Robinson able to explain why he ought to, since Sappho herself does not fall in love with him for his mind, about which nothing at all is said in the poems. The distinctive impression we receive is that Phaon is not worthy of Sappho's devotion, but this is the crucial point of the story, just as it was for Petrarch. Without some sort of asymmetry there is no idealisation, and without idealisation there is no powerful eros. There can be other, pleasurable forms of love, but no strong passions.[80]

Robinson's Sappho is a prey to a devastating passion, which does not help her work as a poet. In the 'Sonnet Introductory', Robinson specifies that

> Well may the mind, with tuneful numbers grac'd,
> To Fame's immortal attributes aspire,
> Above the treach'rous spells of low desire,
> That wound the sense, by vulgar joys debas'd.
> For thou, blest POESY! with godlike pow'rs
> To calm the miseries of man wert giv'n;
> When passion rends, and hopeless love devours,
> By mem'ry goaded, and by frenzy driv'n,
> 'Tis thine to guide him 'midst Elysian bow'rs,
> And shew his fainting soul,—a glimpse of Heav'n.[81]

The point made here, that there is a drastic opposition between poetic creativity and physical desire, between imagination and eros, is repeated throughout the book. I disagree with McGann, who read the last lines as though they were addressed to men only, so that the passage would be Robinson's plan for reforming men's sexual ideology. If this was the case, I cannot see why Robinson chose exactly the same pattern of behaviour for her Sappho. The significant difference, I believe, is another.

Whereas tradition said that Sappho wrote her first poem after seeing Phaon naked at an athletic game, Robinson, who did not mention that episode, believed that unfulfilled sexual desire blocked Sappho's poetic creativity: 'Mute, on the ground my Lyre neglected lies, / The Muse forgot, and lost the melting lay; / My down-cast looks, my faultering lips betray, / That stung by hopeless passion,—Sappho dies!'[82] In *Sappho and Phaon* this concept is repeated many times in different ways. The most frequent is Sappho's invocation to reason, that it may return and defeat the anguish of unrequited love. The characteristics of love (Sonnet VI) and her invocation to reason which, like art, nature and solitude, is ultimately impotent against the power of her passion (Sonnets VII and VIII), sound like a paraphrase of Petrarchan commonplaces.[83] However, the relevant difference is that Petrarch, both in *Canzoniere* and in 'Petrarch to Laura', said that his poetic power stemmed from his love for Laura, whereas Robinson's Sappho maintained that her creativity was paralysed by her passion for Phaon.[84]

This attitude of Robinson's Sappho has been interpreted in two different ways. Joan deJean has noted that Sappho's original poetry is mainly concerned with desertion but, whereas desertion by beloved girls stirred her imagination, desertion by Phaon, according to Ovid, blocked it. Unfortunately, the scanty surviving fragments of Sappho's works do not allow us to decide whether Ovid made up his statement or found it in Sappho's texts.[85] Unless more of Sappho's poems come to light, deJean's remark will remain a conjecture.[86] A different perspective was taken by McGann, who pointed out that the existence of Robinson's sonnets contradicts Sappho's supposed incapability to write. Robinson's Sappho said that her love for Phaon froze her imagination, but the very sonnets where she said so contradict her statement because they are admirable works of art. In other words, McGann presents a Petrarchan Robinson, who disguised her belief in the necessity of a Muse for poetic writing under a mask of decency and longing for self-control, as behoved a respectable woman in her time.[87] Though McGann's interpretation is suggestive, I have found Robinson's position more ambiguous, especially in the light of her attitude to Petrarch and her other love poems.

Robinson's longing for self-control can be seen as part of the rhetoric of unrequited love but, also, it acquires another meaning in the light of gender. Robinson learned from experience that women could not indulge their passions in the same way as men did. The double standard of sexual morality rendered the explicit expression of desire socially destructive for women.[88] Sappho's life – and Robinson's – was exemplary in this sense. Though the loves of Sappho and Petrarch were in many ways similar – especially in Robinson's version – it was only Sappho who, as legend had it, committed suicide. It is true, also, that interest in her leap in Leucadia grew from the 1760s, when suicide became a fashionable subject with the rise of the culture of Sensibility.[89] In comparison to Werther, the other main literary suicide of the age, Sappho's behaviour was more acceptable, since she lived in pre-Christian times.

As Joan deJean has pointed out, Sappho's interpreters can be divided into two main groups: those who see her as the 'Ur-woman at one with nature and with her feminine nature spontaneously sobbing out' her poems, and an opposite party which emphasised her 'controlled, *never* spontaneous, depiction of desire'. Without forgetting the former, Robinson clearly sympathised with the latter, who, like 'the original modern philologists', considered artistic control 'implicitly synonymous with the absence of erotic drive, Sappho's heterosexuality, and even her asexuality'.[90] Caught in the permanent conflict between head and heart, technique and inspiration, Classicism and Romanticism, Robinson tried to find her way in the Sappho history, depicting passion while envisaging self-control. In comparison to her sources, Robinson expanded the principle, because she argued that passionate love was psychologically and socially harmful to women's imagination. She invariably underlined the destructive side of powerful love, as, for instance, in her Petrarch poems and in her free version of Sappho's fragment 31, familiarly known in English as 'Peer of the Gods'.[91] Only occasionally did she celebrate the 'luxury of woe': the bittersweet taste of unrequited love, so characteristic of Petrarch, was a luxury too dear for women in her time.[92] Rather than a foretaste of heaven, amorous rapture was for women, as Anne K. Mellor has pointed out, a prelude to desertion, social disgrace, pregnancy and sometimes a career of prostitution.[93] As Robinson's Sonnet XXVIII says, 'He never lov'd, who could not muse and sigh': as the pun implies, man ('He') needed a Muse to love and think, but women poets might hopefully do without one.

* * *

Robinson returned to Petrarch in one of her last poems, the sonnet 'Laura to Petrarch', which was a long-overdue answer and a synthesis of the views analysed in this chapter:

> O SOLITARY wand'rer! whither stray
> From the smooth path the dimpled pleasures love,
> From flow'ry meadow, and embow'ring grove,
> Where Hope and Fancy smiling, lead the way!
> To thee, I ween, full tedious seems the day;
> While lorn and slow the devious path you rove,
> Sighing soft sorrows on the garland wove
> By young desire, of blossoms sweetly gay!
> Oh! blossoms! frail and fading! like the morn
> Of love's first rapture! beauteous all, and pure
> Deep hid beneath your charms lies mis'ry's thorn,
> To bid the feeling breast a pang endure!
> Then check thy wand'rings, weary and forlorn,
> And find friendship's balm sick passion's cure.[94]

Robinson's Laura addresses a Romantic Petrarch, the 'solitary wand'rer' of 'Solo et pensoso' who many of her contemporaries admired as model and precursor. Laura, however, did not join in. The most lavishly praised mistress in literary history wrote a sonnet which celebrates friendship over love, and social life over solitude. The quatrains contrast the 'smooth path' of mild, social feelings to the 'devious path' of a solitary, lovelorn Petrarch. In Burkean terms, Robinson clearly preferred the feminine, calm beauty of the first quatrain, the 'dimpled pleasures' of smiling friendship, to the masculine, tormented sublime of the second quatrain. Robinson did not believe that the sublime opened up new possibilities and unexpected views. The 'devious path' of the sublime only led to a 'full tedious' life. The 'garland' of 'blossoms sweetly gay', that is, Petrarch's expectations and recollections, were woven by 'young desire', not by sublime solitude, which was only able to sigh 'soft sorrows' on them. Those 'blossoms' were 'frail and fading' just 'like the morn / Of love's first rapture', with a pun on 'morn' which makes Robinson's point clearer. Since a garland of blossoms is a traditional image for a collection of poems, Robinson maliciously insinuated that the best part of Petrarch's poetry derived from his early hopes rather than his late despair, those *in morte* sonnets her contemporaries liked so much. Significantly, in 'Laura to Petrarch' Fancy smiles and leads the way only when it is associated with Hope in the tranquillity of affectionate friendship (l. 4), whereas there is nothing particularly imaginative in anxiety. In other words, Robinson suggested that, aesthetically, the sublime was a parasitic condition of sterility rather than the climax of creativity, as the Romantics believed.

Psychologically, those blossoms of 'love's first rapture' were not only 'frail and fading', but also treacherous. Beneath their deceiving charms lay 'misery's thorn', an unpleasant legacy of enduring pain which was a poor counterpart to an initial moment of ecstasy. It should be noted that 'beauteous all and pure' (l. 10) can be referred both to love's rapture and to misery's thorn in the heart, a clear reference to the nightingale as a symbol of the suffering poet. In other words, Laura did not dismiss the romantic cult of melancholy as nonsense; even though she argued against it, she acknowledged its moral value. In short, Robinson made readers wary of the danger of passionate love. The cure she proposed for it was not roving 'weary and forlorn', but using 'friendship's balm' – social life rather than romantic isolation, openness to other people rather than concentration on oneself. Ultimately, Laura's judgement on Petrarch's attitude to her was firmly critical: the 'disast'rous love' of 'Petrarch to Laura' became 'sick passion' in 'Laura to Petrarch'. Amorous rapture was a natural foretaste of heaven which could not last long; if it did, as in Petrarch, it must have contained an element of pathological immaturity: it was, literally, 'sick passion'.

'Laura to Petrarch' is a neat summary of the views contained in 'Petrarch to Laura', *Sappho and Phaon* and Robinson's other love poems. It is an anti-Romantic perspective based on the commonsense tradition of the eighteenth century, however laced with the ideas of the culture of Sensibility. For Robinson, it was calm, affectionate friendship rather than momentary ecstasy which made life acceptable and pleasant. She believed, also, that fancy was not stimulated by extreme sentimental conditions; rather, creativity required the presence of reason and self-control, and it fared better on the 'smooth path' of mild, social feelings than on the 'devious path' of melancholy love, a subject with which she became more and more disillusioned. Her late poems often point out the cynical side of love, and sometimes her attitudes and turns of phrase anticipate Byron.[95] The similarities between them, however, end here. For Byron, life was worth living only as an uninterrupted series of extreme experiences, as a hyperbolic, orgasmic progress of unheard-of events which should leave his bourgeois readers agape. Robinson, whose life was as eventful and unusual as that of Byron, celebrated the mild feelings of friendship and became increasingly critical of romances.[96] As her Laura wrote to Petrarch, the continuum of everyday life made more sense, even aesthetically, than rapturous moments. However, when Robinson composed 'Laura to Petrarch', Wordsworth had already written the first draft of *The Prelude*, which consists mainly of 'spots of time' episodes. Spots of time, Illuminations, Epiphanies, Moments of Being, *Occasioni* and so forth: Romanticism had begun, and with it the idea that life made sense only thanks to some special instants. For a long time, Robinson's views would be thrown aside as the outdated heritage of an irrelevant tradition.

5
Charles Lloyd and
Samuel Taylor Coleridge

5.1 The 1790s

As sonnets, together with ballads and blank-verse narratives, were fashionable forms in the 1790s, Petrarch inevitably drew the attention of Coleridge and his friends in their formative years. Their longest theoretical statement on the subject still is Coleridge's preface to *Sonnets from Various Authors* (1796), which presumably reflects shared opinions in the circle of his friends. In the preface, Coleridge took sides in the debate on the sonnet, supporting the irregular practices of Smith and Bowles against the 'Italianate party' of William Preston, Seward and Petrarch – or what Coleridge thought Petrarch represented. Boileau and Preston codified sonnet-writing in rules based on the practice of Petrarch, but Coleridge had 'never yet been able to discover either sense, nature, or poetic fancy in Petrarch's poems; they appear to me all one cold glitter of heavy conceits and metaphysical abstractions.' The models he brought forward as alternatives were Smith and Bowles, 'who first made the Sonnet popular among the present English'.[1]

Coleridge thought the sonnet a poetic form 'in which some lonely feeling is developed'; and such feelings are developed best in the context of 'the scenery of Nature.' Sonnets which develop 'no lonely feeling' should 'be entitled Odes, or Songs, or Inscriptions', like most of Warton's sonnets, which ought to be called epigrams. In fact, the number of lines in a sonnet is 14 only to distinguish it from the shorter epigram and the longer elegy. Also, a poet is free to decide about metre and rhymes – 'many or few, or no rhymes at all'. English sonnets in the Italian form are often tortuous in syntax and unnatural in vocabulary, since the rhyme scheme of the Italian sonnet is not suited to the English language. Therefore, they can hardly be the proper forms for bursts of passion, as Preston claimed.[2] Bowles's sonnets, conversely, 'domesticate with the heart, and become, as it were, a part of our identity', that is, they offer those sympathetic feelings which Coleridge expected from a sonnet.[3]

In Coleridge's opinion, therefore, the essential characteristics of a sonnet are organic unity and empathic sentiment. A sonnet is not defined by its metrical form, which is almost accidental, but by its subject, which turns out to be only one: 'some lonely feeling'. These statements show how deeply imbued Coleridge was with the aesthetics of the sonnets of Sensibility but, also, how unaware he was of the role Petrarch played in that tradition. In fact, all Coleridge's tenets can be traced back to the sources discussed in the previous chapters. The view of the Italian sonnet as unsuited to the English language goes back at least to Dr Johnson and Charlotte Smith; the naive idea that passion is incompatible with complex metrical forms is part of the rhetoric of Sensibility; and the conviction that sonnets only have to do with solitary meditation, and that they are short elegies, obviously stem from Smith and her followers. A complete discussion of Coleridge's view of Petrarch, however, must take into account other writers who influenced it, that is, Bowles, Preston and Lloyd.

Bowles was the only sonneteer of Sensibility to whom Coleridge paid homage even in his maturity, primarily in Chapter 1 of *Biographia Literaria*. Beneath the surface of the argument, critics have read that chapter both as a reflection of his enduring friendship with Bowles and as a way of down-playing Wordsworth's early influence.[4] From our perspective, it is extremely significant that even Bowles, who was considered as a quintessentially British sonneteer, included an imitation of Petrarch in his poems. The text was first published in *Sonnets, Written Chiefly on Picturesque Spots, During a Tour* (1789), the second edition of his collection.[5] Bowles took its start from Petrarch's 'Solo et pensoso', which he imitated in the first quatrain:

> LANGUID, and sad, and slow, from day to day,
>   I journey on, yet pensive turn to view
>   (Where the rich landscape gleams with softer hue)
> The streams, and vales, and hills, that steal away.

This passage echoes 'Solo et pensoso i più deserti campi / vo mesurando a passi tardi et lenti' (ll. 1–2) and 'sì ch'io mi credo omai che monti et piagge / et fiumi et selve' (ll. 9–10), whereas the rest of the sonnet is completely different.[6] The original describes Petrarch's withdrawal to solitude to hide his shameful love from other people's irony, though Love followed him everywhere. Bowles turned it into a sonnet on adult reflection on childhood, which he described as an idyllic time, like the landscape of the opening lines. However, when adults turn back, they see that those joys were only an illusion:

> So fares it with the children of the earth:
>   For when life's goody prospect opens round,
>   Their spirits beat to tread that fairy ground,
> Where every vale sounds to the pipe of mirth.
> But them, vain hope and easy youth beguiles,

> And soon a longing look, like me, they cast
> Back on the pleasing prospect of the past[.]

The conclusion, however, is reassuring, as other pleasant days may lie ahead:

> Yet Fancy points where still far onward smiles
> Some sunny spot, and her fair colouring blends,
> Till cheerless on their path the night descends![7]

In Bowles, Petrarch's desperate anxiety for his haunting love became a far more relaxed meditation on the progress of human life, which the obvious truth of the concluding line did not manage to darken. Bowles's landscape is a cosy place gleaming with life and colour rather than Petrarch's 'deserti campi' ('deserted fields'). Landscape reflects the essence of human life and gives it consolation, albeit illusory. In comparison to Petrarch's anguished flight from other humans, Bowles's solitude was a pleasant retreat into a pastoral bower. His distance from Smith, who also echoed 'Solo et pensoso', could not be greater. The opposition between happy youth and desperate maturity was a central theme of Smith's but, unlike Bowles, she found no 'sunny spot' in her adult life. I believe that Bowles's pastoral optimism is a crucial reason why several Romantics preferred to acknowledge their debt to him rather than Smith, whose extreme pessimism was felt to be like a blind alley.[8]

Another reason was certainly gender, as Coleridge praised Bowles's 'manly Pathos' and 'manliest melancholy'.[9] Smith's self-pity and obsessive insistence on unhappiness, no matter how justified by her life, were evidently embarrassing for some male poets, who needed a more detached form of melancholy. This sounds strange if we remember that later Coleridge blamed Bowles precisely for lacking the passion a genuine poet needs. In any case, as Esther Schor noted, Bowles's imitation from Petrarch was inserted at the beginning of his collection to pinpoint the allegorical value of the tour described in the other sonnets.[10] Their journey is the journey of life, and it is significant that Bowles chose Petrarch to create such an allegorical frame. Bowles did not specify the Petrarchan source of his sonnet, but many readers probably recognised it all the same, given the popularity of the original.[11] As often happens, the source discreetly reveals what the imitation conceals. Bowles's tour through Scotland and his collection of poetry originated, in truly Petrarchan fashion, in sentimental disappointment. His ailment, however, was more easily cured than Smith's melancholy, and he never returned to Petrarch and amorous depression.[12]

Unlike Bowles, William Preston had an interest in Petrarch as a love poet which he manifested openly. As early as 1781, he included in his *Poems on Several Occasions* a section of sonnets, some of which were translated from Petrarch.[13] In fact, love is the central subject of his collection, which is written in the main modes of that time, that is, elegies on the model of Ovid and Pope, and – a greater novelty – sonnets on the Petrarchan model. Preston translated mainly from *Canzoniere*, Part I, anticipating the taste of the 1790s with 'Solo et pensoso', 'La gola e 'l somno' and 'Vago augelletto'.[14] As a translator, he tried to preserve the original rhyme schemes, a choice which obliged him to alternate between literal translation and imitation, sometimes within the same sonnet.[15] Petrarch appears also in other poems of the collection, like 'Elegy 3. Petrarch, A Vision to a Friend' and 'Verses Written in the Dargle in the Country of Wicklow'.[16] These texts were reprinted, with another translation, more Petrarchan fictions and a preface, in Preston's *Poetical Works* (1793), where Coleridge read them.[17]

In the 1793 edition, some of Preston's sonnets are dedicated 'To the Untimely Death of a Young Lady', the 'Clara' of his poems.[18] In 'Elegy 11. A Fragment' Preston invokes Petrarch saying that his former lover was his only love. His present mistress, however kind, cannot replace her, because kindness cannot generate love. His ruling star is absent, and 'It rules, but chears not, my disastrous days.'[19] In the following passage, Preston asks Petrarch's heavenly protection. Like him in the Sorgue, Preston sheds tears in his Irish river. However tragically imperfect, Preston's love was beneficial, as it wakened his poetic talent and most noble thoughts. Over the years, however, his hopes and feelings faded, and his life became increasingly bad.[20] The last of his sonnets is an invitation to keep away from worldly forms and pleasures, including love, which are only transitory and mixed goods.[21] In short, Preston openly identified with Petrarch for autobiographical reasons, as is evident in these and other poems, such as 'To a Lady. With Petrarch's Sonnets'.[22]

However unoriginal, Preston's preface is more balanced than Coleridge's response to it would lead one to believe. Preston considered Petrarch 'far above all other poets, who have ever written on love'. His sonnets were the most perfect in the tradition.[23] Many of those who criticised Petrarch never read him, or, if they did, they could neither feel his 'beauties' nor understand his sentiments. Petrarch was not merely 'the feeble songster of an effeminate passion', since he 'perpetually soars the noblest flights'. He combined masculine and feminine elements, 'a daring sublimity, and a strain of moral instruction, with melting tenderness.'[24] Preston also defended Petrarch from another common stricture, that the obscurity of his Platonic conceits is essential to the composition of the sonnet. Petrarch's Platonism simply requires a congenial mind to be understood, whereas puns and conceits are occasional defects counterbalanced by 'the most pure and pathetic simplicity'.[25] In other words, Petrarch was sometimes obscure and abstruse, but also as simply tender as eighteenth-century readers desired.

Pathetic simplicity is also the keynote of Lloyd's Petrarch, which, like Coleridge's, followed Bowles and Smith in tone and themes. Like them, Lloyd wrote sonnets on melancholy and landscape but, unlike Coleridge, he included eight translations from Petrarch in the section of 15 sonnets which opens his *Poems on Various Subjects*. With the exception of 'Solo et pensoso', the texts selected by Lloyd are *in morte* sonnets. However, his attention did not focus on the core of those sonnets, which are laments for a dead lover, but on other romantic elements. He chose sonnets like 'Ite, rime dolenti', which describes Laura's tomb and can be read in the light of graveyard poetry and Gray's 'Elegy'.[26] Another sonnet which could not be missing is 'Solo et pensoso', that anticipation of the Romantic wanderer which, as we saw above, was imitated by Bowles. Like Bowles, Lloyd romanticised Petrarch, making landscape more prominent than it was in the original. Lloyd's beginning focuses on landscape rather than the wandering poet ('Where Nature frowns uncultur'd and forlorn, / I love alone to wander, sad and slow'), and his conclusion reiterates the point. He suppressed personified Love talking to Petrarch and replaced it with, 'And still so changeless is my amorous pain, / That varied Nature's wildest scenes assail / My heart (a prey to passion) all in vain.'[27]

Troubled love seems to have been beyond Lloyd's imagination at this date, as his translations sometimes make us forget that they were written to mourn Laura's absence. A good example is 'Gli occhi di ch'io parlai sì caldamente', whose version blurs the figure of Laura so much that it is not clear why and who Petrarch was mourning. Lloyd overlooked Petrarch's psychological complexity, as for instance in the line 'che m'avean sì da me stesso diviso' ('that had so estranged me from myself', l. 3), which became 'Which won this soft impassion'd heart of mine'.[28] The same attitude emerges in 'Quel rosignuol' and 'Vago augelletto'. In 'Quel rosignuol' it is not clear who the nightingale is addressing, as Lloyd mentions neither 'suoi figli' ('his children') nor his 'cara consorte' ('dear consort'), but only 'The ills that life's uncertain state must prove'.[29] In this sonnet, Lloyd is vague even in the definition of natural details like 'il cielo' ('the lingering gale' for 'the sky') and 'le campagne' ('the scene' for 'the fields'). He omitted Petrarch's belief in Laura's immortality and simplified the original sestet (ll. 8–14). Lloyd left out Petrarch's self-pity and the references to Laura, while he repeated the original conclusion throughout the sestet, that is, that 'nulla qua giù diletta et dura' ('how nothing down here both pleases and endures!')[30] In fact, at this date friendship interested Lloyd much more than love, as is showed by his version of 'Vago augelletto', which emphasises the mutual consolation of Petrarch and the bird.[31] Their sympathy is such that the bird seems to sing Petrarch's sorrows, whereas in the original it merely shares Petrarch's torment: 'If thou'rt like me with whelming woe oppress'd, / Our mutual griefs in mutual love shall join, / Thy liquid notes shall soothe my pensive breast, / And with thy sorrows thou may'st warble mine.'[32] The anguish of Lloyd's Petrarch was considerably more bearable than the original. His tragedy could find easier religious consolation probably because the translator had no idea what that tragedy meant.

'Vago augelletto' is the most literal of Lloyd's versions from Petrarch. Otherwise, he paraphrased abundantly and sometimes made Petrarch's language
more explicit and direct, as translators often do. Formally, Lloyd's sonnets
are a compromise between Smith's elegiac sonnets (in the octave) and the
Petrarchan sonnet (in the sestet), though he also used the Shakespearean
form in his first two texts. Some of his additions point to a moral attitude
which will emerge more forcefully in the translations he published in the
1810s. In 'Che fai? che pensi?' Lloyd translated 'Cerchiamo 'l ciel, se qui
nulla ne piace; / ché mal per noi quella beltà si vide' ('Let us seek Heaven, if
nothing pleases us here; for we ill saw that beauty') with 'Far loftier cares my
doating heart should fill. // Forget the fair! better she ne'er were given'.[33] The
addition of 'doating' contains an evident element of criticism. 'Sento l'aura
mia anticha', Lloyd's freest and worst version, is an epitome of his attitudes.
It is a landscape poem of melancholy reflection, in which he added some
Romantic, sublime details and condensed Petrarch's interior torments:

> With sad delight I breathe these well known gales,
> And mark those hills, whose summits pierce the skies,
> With sad delight, those solitary vales
> That witness'd love's deceitful hopes arise.

> *Sento l'aura mia anticha, e i dolci colli*
> *veggio apparire, onde 'l bel lume nacque*
> *che tenne gli occhi mei mentr'al ciel piacque*
> *bramosi et lieti, or li tèn tristi et molli.*

I feel the old breeze, and I see appearing the sweet hills where the light
was born that kept my eyes full of desire and gladness, while it pleased
Heaven, and now keeps them sad and wet.[34]

In the sestet, he did not understand that Petrarch imagined Laura visiting
his own tomb, and he turned the passage into the more conventional hope
that Laura's grave might soothe Petrarch's pain. In the conclusion, Petrarch
complained that Love was a stingy master because he rewarded him neither
when Laura was alive nor when she was dead. Lloyd moralistically observed
that he mourned 'each earthly hope, an empty show'.[35]

Despite such traces of uneasiness, it is clear that in 1796 Lloyd's admiration
for Petrarch was greater than Coleridge's, and he did not manage to get him to
change his mind. Coleridge excluded Lloyd's translations both from *Sonnets
from Various Authors* and the second edition of his *Poems*, which contains
texts by Lamb and Lloyd.[36] Considering the romanticised version of Petrarch
created by Smith, Bowles and Lloyd, one wonders how Coleridge developed
his negative view of Petrarch and the Italian sonnet.[37] Lamb may have helped,

as in 1796 he asked him not to call his sonnets 'love sonnets'. Love 'was a weakness, concerning which I may say, in the words of Petrarch (whose life is now open before me), "if it drew me out of some vices, it also prevented the growth of many virtues, filling me with the love of the creature rather than the Creator, which is the death of the soul." '[38] The passage is taken from Dobson's *Life of Petrarch*, whose story could hardly be attractive for a circle of radical utopians.[39]

In the 'Preface' to his *Poems* (1796), Coleridge responded to the accusation of 'querulous egotism' which was frequently levelled against sonnets, especially those of Smith's. Coleridge did not deny that sonnets were based on egotism; he argued that egotism was offensive only where it was out of place, as in history or epic poems. On the contrary, shorter poems are necessarily based on personal feelings: 'After the violent emotions of Sorrow, the mind [. . .] can endure no employment not connected with those sufferings.'[40] However, some forms of egotism are unacceptable. 'There is one species of egotism which is truly disgusting; not that which leads us to communicate our feelings to others, but that which would reduce the feelings of others to an identity with our own.' Examples of this centripetal egotism are an atheist who despises religious worship; an old man who 'speaks contemptuously of love-verses'; and the happy and wealthy who 'condemn all "melancholy discontented" verses.'[41] In other words, Coleridge defended the moral basis of lyric poetry, but he was fully aware of its dangers. The fact that he called his sonnets 'effusions' at the end of the 'Preface' can be read as a self-defensive strategy, considering the negative surge of contemporary criticism against the sonnet.[42]

Going back to Coleridge's *Sonnets from Various Authors*, it is evident that, though they contain four texts on lost maids, they avoid the extreme self-absorption of lovelorn Petrarch.[43] At the same time, as J. C. C. Mays puts it, they 'celebrate nature, withdrawal, pathos', turning away from Coleridge's earlier sonnets.[44] In effect, Coleridge's view of the sonnet as based on some lonely feeling is strangely self-contradictory or, at least, it implies a sort of recantation. The sonnets he had published the same year in his *Poems* are public, political and rhetorical rather than private, psychological and sentimental.[45] In the later pamphlet, Milton and Petrarch were laid aside, whereas Smith and above all Bowles were taken up as models. In Mays's words, '*Sonnets from Various Authors* arises from circumstances which the Preface characteristically obscures. The pamphlet commemorates a set of hopes entertained about a way of life more than an achieved position concerning the technicalities of a specific verse-form.'[46] Coleridge scanty interest in amorous, 'unmanly' melancholy, rather than formal preoccupations, was the reason for his attitude to Preston and Petrarch.

As everyone knows, the utopian hopes of Coleridge and his friends were short-lived. The tensions that came up within the circle and the natural development of his moral and political thought led him to a twofold reaction against his earlier attitudes. In November 1797 he parodied the 'affectation of unaffectedness, of jumping & misplaced accents in common-place epithets, flat lines forced into poetry by Italics [...] puny pathos, &c &c' in three 'Sonnets Attempted in the Manner of "Contemporary Writers"', which he signed 'Nehemiah Higginbottom'.[47] Beside irritating his friends, these sonnets laid bare the ideological basis and the moral hypocrisy of the aesthetic of simplicity, two points which were also made by political conservatives, from Dr Johnson to *The Anti-Jacobin*.

In short, between 1796 and 1797 Coleridge took an 'intensive course' in the sonnet, rapidly embracing and rejecting what at the time passed for the best sonnet-writing, political propaganda and melancholy musing in the countryside, boisterous rhetoric and sentimental simplicity. Behind both, there was an engrossing interest in political utopianism, which left no space for Petrarch's sentimental complications. Friendship rather than love was their main interest, though their idea of friendship, as scholars have showed, was wide enough to encompass experiences that today we would label as amorous and political.[48] Domestic affections were to be the bases of reformed social life. As Richard C. Allen points out, Lloyd, like Wollstonecraft, believed that marriage ought to be founded on mutual esteem rather than passionate love.[49] Besides, friendship was a protection against the 'ardent flame' of sexual desire, as Lloyd wrote in a sonnet addressed to Coleridge included in *Poems* (1797).[50] In such an ideological milieu, Petrarch's story was inevitably seen as a celebration of what the group of young friends wanted to overcome, that is, the aristocratic ethic of adultery and egotistic self-absorption.[51]

Coleridge's reaction did not stop at parody. He also rejected the opinions on Petrarch he had expressed in the introduction to *Sonnets from Various Authors*. He wrote in a copy of the 1797 edition of *Poems* that his former judgement was

> a piece of petulant presumption, of which I should be more ashamed, if I did not flatter myself that it stands alone in my writings. The best of the Joke is that at the time, I wrote it, I did not understand a word of Italian, & could therefore judge of this divine Poet only by bald Translations of some half dozen of his Sonnets.[52]

The marginal note, which according to Mays dates from between 1808 and 1810 (*PW (CC)* I:2, 1295), expresses the attitude to Petrarch and Italian lyric poetry which Coleridge developed during his sojourn in the Mediterranean. Lloyd's conventionality and Coleridge's uneasiness signal the crisis of an attitude to Petrarch which had dominated British literature for over 20 years. Petrarch remained a major source of inspiration for another 30 years, but in very different terms. The development of Lloyd's and Coleridge's views is emblematic in this respect.

5.2 Later developments

In their maturity, Lloyd's and Coleridge's attitudes to Petrarch were for the most part a recantation of their former views, both aesthetically and ethically. Lloyd's *Nugae Canorae* (1819) contains a large section of sonnets, with new translations from Petrarch dating from 1806-07 and an interesting introduction. Unlike Coleridge, Lloyd specified that, with few exceptions, he followed the Italian model, since he considered Smith's sonnets epigrams. Lloyd took from Coleridge's preface the other main feature of the sonnet, that is, its 'oneness of thought and feeling'.[53] The best subjects for a sonnet were not those mentioned by Coleridge; the sonnet was an ideal form for recording single 'impressions of life', which over the years could build up a 'sentimental biography' of their author. Clearly, Lloyd was thinking of Petrarch's *Canzoniere*, the most complex sentimental autobiography of this kind.

At this point, Lloyd unexpectedly introduced some paragraphs taken from Coleridge's old preface, which contradict some of the principles he formulated before. In particular, he cited Coleridge's opinions that sonnets have 14 lines only by accident, and that the association between lonely feelings and nature is the best pre-condition for writing a sonnet.[54] Despite these evident discordances, Lloyd disagreed explicitly only with the next section of Coleridge's preface, where Coleridge describes the rhyme schemes and the structures of the Italian sonnet as unfit for both the English language and the spontaneous expression of feeling. Lloyd replied that some of the best English poets, like Milton, Warton, Seward and Wordsworth, used the Italian sonnet form, which is not more difficult or artificial than the form used by Smith, once a poet has made himself at home with it. But Lloyd's most barbed comment came in the conclusion, where he defended Preston from Coleridge's attack. Lloyd noted that Coleridge's strictures were gratuitous because they blamed only a caricature of Preston, who always considered the sonnet 'a severe and terse composition' rather than a form fit for momentary bursts of passion.[55]

Lloyd's introduction is a polemical answer to Coleridge as much as a disinterested reflection on sonnet-writing. Like Coleridge, Lloyd had come a long way from his earlier opinions, rejecting simplicity – and the ideological radicalism linked to it – for a more mature sense of poetic craftsmanship and existential complexity. Behind his introduction is an undeniable element of personal friction with Coleridge, which was still alive 20 years after the publication of *Edmund Oliver*.[56] But Lloyd's distance from their earlier beliefs came out above all in his poems.

After the first sonnets, a reprint of those published with Lamb and Coleridge, Lloyd's new texts revisit old themes from new perspectives. His earlier attitude to solitude was changed radically, whereas his view of love was a development of that implicit in his juvenile sonnets. These themes intertwine in his version of 'O cameretta che già fosti un porto'.[57] Lloyd sensed a hovering double entendre in the text and he suppressed every trace of the possible sexual innuendoes of the original. The sonnet celebrates Petrarch's dear sleeping-room, a refuge which had become a prison, as his torments came out forcefully whenever he was there alone at night. Unlike many other sonnets, where he retired to solitary places to escape the unpleasant company of common people, in this text he dreaded to be alone. Lloyd, who in 1795 had translated 'Solo et pensoso', Petrarch's most famous eulogy of loneliness, chose this sonnet as part of his campaign against the Romantic celebration of solitude, which, he had come to believe, could not cure anything. Sonnets 37 to 39 in *Nugae Canorae*, immediately after the Petrarch translations, deal with the drawbacks of solitude, which, as in the translations, cannot be separated from the theme of love.[58]

Lloyd cleared the text of 'O cameretta' of some physical details which might hint at an embarrassing reason for Petrarch's fear of solitude. Alberto Moravia maliciously noted that this text expresses Petrarch's anxiety about masturbation. In particular, the second quatrain contains a significant hint: 'O letticciuol che requie eri et conforto / in tanti affanni, di che dogliose urne / ti bagna Amor, con quelle mani eburne, / solo ver' me crudeli a sì gran torto!' ('O little bed that used to be a rest and comfort among so many labors, with what sorrowful urns does Love bathe you, with those ivory hands cruel only toward me, and so unjustly!' Petrarca 2001, 234). However we read these lines, the image of the urns is bizarre, and hands have not only to do with tears.[59] Though this interpretation remains only a hypothesis, Lloyd seems to have been of this mind, since he meticulously omitted every dangerous detail: 'Oh couch, where common griefs are laid aside, / How oft thy shelter did my pangs allay? / Now bath'd with tears, my sighs to thee betray / A cureless passion to despair allied.' The 'little bed' became a 'couch', and he omitted 'di dogliose urne' (l. 6) and 'Amor, con quelle mani eburne' (l. 7), the most problematic phrases. He also left out that those pangs were inflicted upon Petrarch 'a sì gran torto!' ('so unjustly', l. 8). Earlier, Lloyd had changed 'fonte se' or di lagrime notturne' ('now you are a fountain of nocturnal tears') into 'Thou seest me now to pining care a prey'. Lloyd's Petrarch was more guilt-ridden than the original: he felt 'consuming woe / My tortur'd soul, my insuppressive foe!' (ll. 10–11) rather than 'mio pensero' ('my thoughts'). Line 11 insists on the same point, modifying the original idea that those sorrows sometimes made Petrarch's imagination soar high.[60] Lloyd seemed to believe that they could only drag him further and further down. In comparison to his former cult of solitude, his present desire to be with other people was a 'humbling change', Lloyd's moralistic version of 'chi 'l pensò mai?' ('whoever thought it?')

Lloyd's moralism is particularly evident in his last version, 'Amor, io fallo, et veggio il mio fallire', where his changes were all pejorative.[61] If Petrarch 'saw' his transgression, Lloyd 'consciously' transgressed (l. 1); 'man' became 'the wretch' (l. 2); his reason 'già quasi vinta dal martire' ('almost overcome by suffering', l. 4) became 'Till cureless agony complete my doom.' 'Solea frenare il mio caldo desire' ('I used to rein in my hot desire', l. 5) became 'Some little check to importunate distress / The fear inspired', which belittled Petrarch's resistance and made its cause more negative and weighty. His desire brought 'a gloom' on Laura's 'sweet hours of peace', which is stronger than 'per non turbare il bel viso sereno' ('as not to darken her clear face', l. 6). But the greatest changes came in the sestet, which Lloyd re-wrote freely:

> Of reckless ravings, petulant and wild,
>   'Tis thou, not I, oh Love, the guilt must bear,
>   Who thus dost every power of thought perplex,
> So that to airy nothings, like a child,
> And worse than airy nothings, I repair–
>   Oh, pardon thou who thus my heart dost vex.

The original runs as follows:

> *Però s'oltra suo stile ella s'aventa,*
> *tu 'l fai, che sì l'accendi, et sì la sproni,*
> *ch'ogni aspra via per sua salute tenta;*
>
> *et più 'l fanno i celesti et rari doni,*
> *ch'à in sé madonna: or fa' almen ch'ella il senta,*
> *et le mie colpe a se stessa perdoni.*

Therefore, if my soul hazards herself beyond her usual style, you are doing it – who so inflame and spur her that she attempts every difficult way toward her salvation – // and even more those heavenly, rare gifts which my lady has. Now at least make her perceive it, and make her pardon herself for my transgressions.

(Petrarca 2001, 236)

'Her reckless ravings, petulant and wild' is a negative vision of 'beyond [the soul's] usual style', and it implies, aesthetically and morally, a severe judgement on a considerable part of Petrarch's sonnets. Lloyd did not accept that such daring was a means for saving the soul; rather, he added that it perplexed 'every power of thought'. He also omitted that Laura's rare, heavenly gifts were greatly helpful to his soul's flight. For Lloyd, Petrarch repaired 'to airy nothings', but he added, 'like a child, / And worse than airy nothings' in case the Shakespearean quotation might seem too ennobling a compliment to Petrarch's poetic labour. Lloyd's last line was more like the original, even though his 'thou' referred to Love rather than Laura, who was blotted out of the poem.[62]

Lloyd's uneasiness at love poetry is evident in other texts, where he argues for a Stoic, puritanical resistance to desire which recalls the attitude of Wordsworth's maturity. In Sonnet 38, 'To Solitude', Lloyd wrote that 'we must buy / Our peace on earth with arduous victory / O'er all that Passion to her heart would bind.'[63] Sonnet 34 begs pardon to God for the 'tears of nature' that 'swell' and the 'trait'rous wishes' that sometimes unsettle his mind and heart. Lloyd is referring to sexual temptations, expressed obliquely in the first quatrain, which describes how hard it is 'To wear the look of coldness, nor embrace / The dear and proffer'd blessing of regard' when friendship 'sweetly smiles on me again'.[64] Moreover, in Sonnet 41, 'Let those to whom Love ne'er his raptures dealt', Lloyd argued that those who never felt the pangs of real love should not write about it. None the less, even those who felt them, like Petrarch, should learn to love God rather than an earthly being, who can never fulfil the human need of love completely.[65]

As often happens, however, good intentions and reality do not coincide. In Lloyd's collection there are a few sonnets (50 to 53), dating from 1807, addressed to a Miss with whom he seems to have fallen in love, since he hoped his sentiment was not unreciprocated. He did not seem to notice that these sonnets contradict the moralistic view of love of his versions from Petrarch and other texts on the same subject. Despite these exceptions, love poems, even those of Petrarch, were ultimately seen by Lloyd as a useless, childish delirium without moral justification. Though it sounds odd for a translator of Ovid's *Metamorphoses*, the only amorous feelings he admitted in his poetry were domestic, like those for his wife and children, and religious, like those described in Sonnet 41.[66] The rest were condemned squarely. Even Petrarch, the only poet he took into account in dealing with physical passion, had became unacceptable by the early 1810s, as his version of 'Amor, io fallo' shows. This is not surprising, since Petrarch's love, adulterous and unsettling, was incompatible with the Biedermeier idyll created by Lloyd. From an auto-biographical point of view, it is understandable that someone like Lloyd, who experienced insanity several times in his life, should argue against the danger of intense passion and envisage peaceful domestic sentiment as an ideal.

Though in Lloyd the radical projects of the 1790s evolved into a middle-class ideal of a quiet family life, his earlier hopes were preserved in one last sonnet influenced by Petrarch, 'Ye buds obedient to the breath of spring':

> Ye buds obedient to the breath of spring,
>> Why with no wonted smile are ye caress'd?
> Thou soul of Love that, borne on zephyr's wing,
>> Dost steal unseen within the soften'd breast,
> Who, blessing and tormenting, know'st to bring
>> Soft sighs, inquietudes, and many a guest
> That hint of dangerous joy, why dost thou *wring*,
>> Not *sooth* my spirit to delicious rest?

> 'Tis that I seek what human heart ne'er found,
>   A world where Love, Truth, Peace, their laws maintain;
> 'Tis that I ask on this polluted ground,
>   For wells of living water! Spring-tide train,
> Urging a hopeless wish, 'tis thus ye wound,
>   To seek the more for what I seek in vain.

The poem was inspired by Petrarch's 'Zephiro torna' and Gray's sonnet to West, whose kinship was felt by Lloyd. The first part describes the return of spring's breath and the reawakening of the soul of Love borne on Zephyr's wings (ll. 1–4). More neatly than Petrarch, however, Lloyd emphasises the 'dangerous joy' of desire, which brings about 'inquietudes' rather than peace (ll. 5–8). Above all, his despondency, unlike Petrarch's, did not have an individual but a social cause. Lloyd was waiting for 'A world where Love, Truth, Peace, their laws maintain' (l. 10). However, his wish was 'hopeless'. Unlike Shelley's West Wind, which announced that social change was ahead, Lloyd's zephyr only kept old suffering alive, since, in Gray's words, it urged him 'To seek the more for what I seek in vain'.[67] This was a remarkable re-writing of Petrarch's and Gray's sonnets, the only one I know that adapted their amorous and existential troubles to society at large. Evidently, in 1803 Lloyd was still haunted by the millenarian ideas of the circle of his friends, though their expectations had waned and he, like many of them, had turned a conservative Christian. The early hopes continued to exist only as a painful memory of something impossible.

* * *

In comparison to Lloyd and, indeed, any other British writer of the age, Coleridge's mature approach to Petrarch was as free and original as could be conceived by a genius. Like his contemporaries, Lloyd always talked of Petrarch with reference to the sonnet; Coleridge was the only British poet who realised that Petrarch was an infinitely more complex writer. I have described the complete story in detail in another book; here I shall recall its essentials in a different context.

Coleridge returned to Petrarch when he began learning Italian with a view to his journey to Malta in 1804. Though his sojourn in the Mediterranean has often been considered as escapist, he had several good reasons to leave: his bad health, the presence of Napoleon elsewhere on the Continent, a moment of emotional bewilderment (his relationship with Sara Hutchinson), an interest in Italian poetry and philosophy, a fresh enthusiasm for the fine arts, and two literary plans (an essay on prosody and *The Soother of Absence*) for which new knowledge was required. Poetry, philosophy and art, to which the tradition of the Grand Tour and fashion can be added, since Italian culture attained the height of its popularity in the first two decades of the nineteenth century.[68]

In Malta and Italy, Coleridge's exploration of Italian literature focused on two subjects: love poetry, with an eye to his *Soother of Absence*, and metrics, for the planned essay on prosody. Renaissance lyric poetry was the natural ground for his research, though it was not his sole reading.[69] *The Soother of Absence* was conceived in 1802 as a long topographical poem, and it soon evolved into a collection of short love poems.[70] The project was linked to Coleridge's passion for Sara Hutchinson, and although it was never completed, it underlies much of his reading and writing between 1804 and 1808. The Malta notebooks show that his frustrated passion preoccupied him, and his peculiar psychological condition must be kept in mind as we approach the topic. His attitude is perceivable in a note he made on his journey to Malta:

> In my Soother of Absence to note my utter want of Sympathy with all the ordinary Love-poems, complaining of the Cruelty of the Mistress, of her attachment to another &c – in short, all that supposes that I could love with no knowledge of being loved in return – or even with the knowledge of the contrary. – In short, I shall have abundant matter for contemplation on the Subject in my Perusal of the Italian Love-poems.[71]

Ironically, the bold tone of the note is at odds with his sentimental condition, since his intense feelings for Sara were not reciprocated. His dissatisfaction with the love poetry he was familiar with and his desire to read Italian lyric poetry are relevant to the present argument. He fulfilled his desire in Malta, where he began to read Italian poetry as soon as he could; that is, after improving his knowledge of the language. Given his project, Petrarch was one of the first poets on his reading list.

After the critical attitude of *Sonnets from Various Authors*, Coleridge turned to Petrarch in 1803, when he borrowed William Sotheby's complete edition of Petrarch.[72] Though it is not clear what he read before leaving for the Mediterranean, the discovery of Petrarch's Latin writings was a turning-point. He must have found Petrarch's introspection congenial, and it is noteworthy that he returned to the Latin works after his sojourn in Italy, where he experienced Petrarch's poetry and the Petrarchan tradition more deeply. It must not be forgotten that Coleridge's knowledge of Italian in 1803 was not sufficient for him to read Petrarch's Italian poetry in the original, whereas Latin was not a problem. Nothing demonstrates that he read or scanned Petrarch's poems in the fourth volume of the Basle edition at the time.[73]

Coleridge probably bought and read his edition of Petrarch's poems in Malta or in Italy.[74] I say probably because there is no chronological certainty: only internal evidence and contemporary reading suggest such a date.[75] The marginal notes in the volume are short, like most of his early marginalia, but they reveal a new attitude to Petrarch. He divided the poems which struck him as 'good', 'pleasing' and 'dignified', and commented briefly on some.

The group classified as 'good' includes sonnets and one *canzone*. Some of Petrarch's masterpieces are part of the list, as Sonnet I of *Canzoniere* and 'La gola e 'l somno'. Most of his preferences, however, are love poems in the strict sense. Coleridge was struck by 'Quando fra l'altre donne' (*PC*, 13), which expresses a view of the poet's woman as a mediator between man and God – a concept repeated by the *canzone* 'Gentil mia donna' (*PC*, 72), which treats the theme of the mistress's eyes. 'Vergognando talor' (*PC*, 20) is a rhetorical statement on Petrarch's poetic skill: his mistress is so beautiful that he is not able to write about her as he wished, a problem Coleridge was facing in his *Soother of Absence*.

Coleridge did not neglect Petrarch's moral meditations. 'La gola e 'l somno', which was popular in the 1790s, is included in the list. 'S'io credesse' (*PC*, 36) anticipates Hamlet's proverbial monologue and argues that the poet would commit suicide to stop his torments, if death meant peace; since he does not know, he lives on. The theme is repeated in a passage of *canzone* 'Perché la vita è breve' (*PC*, 71, ll. 37–45), which Coleridge admired for its 'vigour & chastity' – it is, actually, unusually vigorous for Petrarch.[76] Other poems he marked, the sonnet 'Quanto più m'avicino' (*PC*, 32), which echoes 'Voi ch'ascoltate', and the *canzone* 'Si è debile il filo' (*PC*, 37), deal with the vanity of human hopes and the transitoriness of things. The only political poem he noted was 'O aspectata in ciel' (*PC*, 28), a *canzone* to Giacomo Colonna for the Crusade. Coleridge seems to have ignored Petrarch's 'patriotic' poems like 'Italia mia', which were popular with other readers, from Jones to Shelley.

Unlike his contemporaries, Coleridge seems to have preferred the first part of *Canzoniere*; the only poems of the *in morte* section he commented upon are three sonnets and two *canzoni* (*PC*, 268 and 270) which deal with writing as consolation.[77] He regarded the former as superior to the latter, even though he did not like some of its images. The poem is a plea to Love, that he may bring Laura back to life, since Petrarch feels free but melancholic, and it anticipates sixteenth-century taste in the paradoxical nature of its argument and imagery, which Coleridge disliked. He would have deleted 'half a dozen Conceits & Petrarchisms of *Hooks*, *Baits*, *Flames*, and *Torches*'.[78] Such disparaging observations on Petrarchism lead to the conclusion that the note was written before summer 1805, when his judgement changed.[79] Finally, the three *in morte* sonnets he marked are 'La vita fugge' (*PC*, 272), which touches once again upon the theme of suicide in dealing with the brevity of human life and the change of the poet's character over the years; 'Datemi pace' (*PC*, 274), where Petrarch begs his heart to stop tormenting him; and probably 'Dolci durezze' (*PC*, 351), which thanks Laura for saving his soul by rejecting his love.

Coleridge's notes focus on poems of love and moral reflection – subjects prominent both in *Canzoniere* and Coleridge. The marginalia relate to the first 100 pages of *Canzoniere*, Part I, and the beginning of Part II. *Canzoni* attracted his attention more than sonnets; he found the ballad 'Lassare il velo' (*PC*, 11) pleasing, but was not struck by any *sestina*. Coleridge's disregard for pre-Dantesque poetry has perhaps something to do with his indifference toward highly complex poetic structures, although the *stilnovo* poets were not popular in his time.

Though Coleridge's notes might look sketchy and unimportant, they are the signal of a significant change in his attitude to Petrarch and love poetry. In the 1817 edition of *Sibylline Leaves*, the love poems were arranged in a section to which the following motto was prefixed:

> *Quas humilis tenero stylus olim effudit in ævo,*
> *Perlegis his lacrymas, et quod pharetratus acuta*
> *Ille puer puero fecit mihi cuspide vulnus.*
> *Omnia paulatim consumit longior ætas,*
> *Vivendoque simul morimur, rapimurque manendo.*
> *Ipse mihi collatus enim non ille videbor:*
> *Frons alia est, moresque alii, nova mentis imago,*
> *Voxque aliud sonat –*
> *Pectore nunc gelido calidos miseremur amantes,*
> *Jamque arsisse pudet. Veteres tranquilla tumultus*
> *Mens horret, relegensque alium putat ista locutum.*

You peruse the causeless cares that once in my tender youth my humble pen poured forth. You read here of tears and how the quivered boy wounded me, a boy, with piercing barb. Advancing time devours all things by degrees, and as we live we die, and as we rest we are hurled onward. For if I am compared with myself I shall not seem the same. My face is changed, my ways are changed, I have a new kind of understanding, my voice sounds otherwise – With cold heart now I pity hot Lovers, and am ashamed that I myself burned. The peaceful mind shudders at past tumults, and reading again thinks that some other wrote those words.[80]

The motto is an excerpt from Petrarch's metric epistle to Barbato da Sulmona, which Coleridge read and transcribed in 1813.[81] Since a motto is a way of establishing a link with an author and a tradition, a way of pointing to a cultural horizon within which a text ought to be read, there must be a good reason why Coleridge chose Petrarch after the disparaging views he had expressed in the 1790s. The new attitude depended in part on his reading in Petrarch's Latin writings and in part on Petrarch's philosophy of love, which he found congenial in his maturity.

Though by the early 1800s Coleridge had written a good deal of love poetry, he was not well-read in the Petrarchan and Renaissance tradition. Between 1803 and 1810 he discovered not only poetic modes he had so far underrated; he also realised that there was a close kinship between his ideas and

Petrarch's philosophy of love, a Christianised Platonism mixed with courtly elements. To be more precise, I believe that Coleridge found in Petrarch not only congenial ideas on love, but above all a congenial blend of them, both in the poems and the Latin writings. In short, the ratio between the body and the spirit, between Christianity and Platonism, in Petrarch's vision of love was the closest to Coleridge's ideal. This is confirmed by his reaction to other poets, like Dante and Shakespeare, who might have been his models in this field.

The philosophy of love has a crucial place in Coleridge's ethics. In his numerous annotations on the subject, Coleridge reacted against two seemingly opposite views of love. On the one hand, writers like Pope, Sterne, Ariosto and Boccaccio acknowledged the importance of love for human behaviour, but regarded it as a mere corporeal phenomenon. Petrarch, 'the final blossom & perfection of the Troubadours', inherited a chivalrous view of love which distinguished him from the materialist sensuousness of the Italian narrative poets.[82] Love was for them an embellished form of feeling and sensation – what Coleridge called lust.[83] On the other hand, Spinoza, Kant, Godwin and Wordsworth – that is, Stoic ethics – also regarded love as an offspring of feeling, but found it undesirable or morally meaningless. In a marginal note to Kant's *Metaphysik der Sitten* Coleridge wrote:

> If, I say, I doubt this independence of Love on the Will, and doubt even Love's being in its essence merely eine Sache der Empfindung, a mere matter of *feeling*, i.e. a somewhat *found* in us which is not of and from us/Emp. – (= in sich) – Findung, I mean only that my Thoughts are not distinct much less adequate on the subject – and I am not able to convey any grounds of my Belief of the contrary. But the contrary I do believe. What Kant affirms of Man in the state of Adam, an ineffable act of the will choosing evil & which is underneath or within *consciousness* tho' incarnate in the *conscience*, inasmuch as it must be conceived as taking place in the Homo *Noumenon*, not the Homo *phainomenon* – something like this I conceive of *Love* – in that highest sense of the Word, which Petrarch understood.[84]

Coleridge adjudged those ideas immoral and illusory. Feeling was everything to the former group of writers and nothing to the latter: both refused to see any sacred or transcendental value in love. If his reaction against the former view was predictable, his ethical disappointment with German philosophy and Wordsworth was not the least reason why he turned to Italian culture around 1802. The paradoxical aspect of his admiration for Petrarch's philosophy of love was that he overlooked that the Petrarchan tradition is an uninterrupted hymn to adultery. Despite the failure of his own conjugal life, Coleridge continued to believe in the religious and institutional value of marriage.[85]

Coleridge's attempt at reviving a metaphysics of love may seem anachronistic or a consequence of his prudery. It was certainly an isolated episode in his time, but it must not be forgotten that Shelley tried to do something similar, even though his approach to the same tradition was different. Both were intrigued by the philosophical implications of love; but whereas the tone of Shelley's best love poetry is high and lofty, Coleridge's is intense and intimate.[86] Another important difference between them is frustration. Sara Hutchinson, Coleridge's only true passion, did not return his love, though their friendship compromised his marriage. Coleridge had mocked love poetry 'complaining of the Cruelty of the Mistress', yet he painfully discovered that there could be a grain of truth even in trite conventions.

Coleridge was affected both by Petrarch's vision of love and his poetic technique. His responses may seem independent of one another, since they concern different areas of knowledge, but they stem from the same experience. His interest in Petrarch's Latin works and his formal interest in the Petrarchan tradition show the importance the experience had to him. Coleridge planned what became *The Soother of Absence* as

> a *series* of Love Poems – truly Sapphic, save that they shall have a large Interfusion of moral Sentiment & calm Imagery on Love in all moods of mind – Philosophic, fantastic, in moods of high enthusiasm, of simple Feeling, of mysticism, of Religion – /comprize in it all the practice, & all the philosophy of Love.[87]

In 1801 he did not realise that a 'truly Sapphic' love poetry, which combined Classical polish, powerful passion and detailed psychological analysis, had been introduced into modern Europe by Petrarch and adapted by his numerous followers. As Coleridge found out in the following years, *Canzoniere* was the most complete and influential 'Soother of Absence' in the Western tradition. In any case, the note shows that Coleridge was looking for a new style in love poetry beyond the ballad form, which he had used so successfully in the 1790s. Such a style characterises the later phase of his love poetry, and is easily distinguished from the ballad: it is analytic and descriptive rather than narrative, and it borders on abstract thought rather than story-telling. As such, it fitted Coleridge's taste after 1800, which had become more philosophic. Some of his best poems were written in forms which derived from a reinterpretation of medieval tradition; Renaissance poetry was not equally fruitful for his poetic writing, though it underlies much of the love poetry he composed in his maturity.

Coleridge's serious love poems may seem to have little in common with Petrarch, since they rarely imitate his imagery and structures. However, Petrarch's influence on Coleridge must not be read only in these terms. In fact, his approach has two sides which can be analysed separately, though their coexistence should always be kept in mind. Coleridge had a specific interest in

Petrarch's view of love, education and other moral themes, whereas Petrarch's Italian poetry interested him as part of the Renaissance tradition. However strange, Coleridge considered Petrarch the thinker individually, whereas he read his poetry only in the context of his followers. In other words, the impact of Petrarch as an Italian poet on Coleridge is inseparable from the impact of the Petrarchan lyric tradition up to the Renaissance. Coleridge's *formal* interest in Petrarchism is testified by some of his poems and Chapter 15 of *Biographia*; his *philosophical* interest in Petrarch emerged in *The Friend* and the lectures on literature and philosophy.[88] His two interests, however, are ultimately inseparable and fostered each other at least up to 1810. It was his admiration for Petrarch as a thinker which made him understand that the Petrarchan tradition was not only an empty formal game of puns and antitheses, as might appear in several epigones.

Starting from poetry, the new, intimate and meditative mood first appears in the Asra poems that Coleridge composed between 1801 and 1810, when *The Soother of Absence* was abandoned. As the project never went beyond its preliminary stage, the poems are extremely fragmentary, both individually and collectively. They show how hard Coleridge struggled to appropriate a different tradition of love poetry, with which he could never make himself at home entirely. The character of his interest in the Petrarchan tradition became clearer in the following years, when he talked of frustrated love and hope, and mentioned flushing cheeks, smooth necks, shining eyes, in sum, the stock-in-trade of Petrarchism.[89] These images and concepts were used not only seriously, but also ironically in texts like 'An Anagram on Mary Morgan's Face'.[90] I am not suggesting that Coleridge became a sort of Petrarchist, which would be absurd. From his journey to Malta onwards, his approach alternates irony and serious interest, parody and direct use of a tradition which he could no longer ignore or dismiss, as he had in the 1790s.

Though the relation between Coleridge's poems and Petrarch might appear superficial, an accurate reading shows the profound affinity of their vision, due to their common Christian and Platonic background. For example, Coleridge's idea that the lover regained himself through the other underlies the poems dealing with spiritual exchange, of which the exchange of hearts is a favourite image, as in 'The Exchange of Hearts' or in the fragment 'Lines Inscribed in Benedetto Menzini'.[91] Many poems are concerned with the symbolic value of the body, which reveals its soul in love; but the idea did not lead him to extensive descriptions of the body, as in the Renaissance. He focused on a few general images, repeating time and again that love spiritualises the body and makes the spirit shine through and around it.[92] Beauty is such revelation of the essence of things:

> O Beauty, in a beauteous Body dight!
> Body! that veiling Brightness becom'st bright/

> Fair Cloud which less we see, than by thee see the Light!
>   in avvenenti spoglie
> Bellissim' Alma![93]

A short poem written in the 1820s summarises his attitude:

> 'Tis not the lily brow I prize,
> Nor roseate cheeks, nor sunny eyes,
> Enough of lilies and of roses!
> A thousand-fold more dear to me
> The gentle look that love discloses,
> The look that love alone can see![94]

It is obvious, however, that gentle looks, exchanged hearts and shining souls belong to the Provençal and Petrarchan tradition as much as roseate cheeks and lily-brows. Coleridge seems to have dismissed the descriptions of the Petrarchan tradition and to have focused on few concepts. His approach accounts for the limitations of his love poetry after 1800, which, far from including 'a large Interfusion of moral Sentiment & calm Imagery on Love in all moods of mind' and comprising 'all the practice, & all the philosophy of Love' as he had planned in 1801, does not manage to turn love into the catalyst of a complete view of the world. Despite Coleridge's opinions in philosophy and despite his celebration of speculative constancy, he was incapable of Petrarch's idealisation of his mistress. His original contribution to the genre, as Mays points out in his editorial Introduction, has to do with affection-love and mutual, delicate sympathy rather than overwhelming passion or Platonic idealism.[95] This is evident even in his late poems, which became more epigrammatic and often consist of one or two rhymed quatrains, even though in the late 1820s he successfully returned to longer poetic forms in 'Alice du Clós' and 'The Garden of Boccaccio'.

In comparison to these narrative modes, Coleridge's relationship with the sonnet remained problematic. As Daniel Robinson has argued, the sonnets are the most personal and intimate part of Coleridge's poems, which, I believe, explains why he was always uneasy about the form.[96] As he soon realised, *The Soother of Absence* would have required a detailed and ruthless analysis of his sentimental situation, as Petrarch did in *Canzoniere*. Though no one can question Coleridge's depth as a thinker, he was loath to expose his most intimate feelings and preoccupations in this field. The section of 'Love Poems' in *Sibylline Leaves* (1817) is a self-defensive manoeuvre much more than a representative display of his output at that date. Most of the poems are narrative or impersonal, and those which do not conceal their autobiographical origin are light pieces or relatively harmless and generic poems.[97] Only the Latin motto from Petrarch pointed unambiguously to a painful, personal involvement of the author; but Coleridge had a moral reputation to defend, and his most intimate fragments were either published very late in life or they remained in his notebooks. In fact, most of his late sonnets, just as many unpublished epigrams on love, deal with the most painful aspect of his life, that is, his sentimental failures, at whose core, explicitly or implicitly, was always Sara Hutchinson. Most of his later poems on love, including a couple of serious sonnets, refer to one theme: hope and love. All of them repeat that 'WORK without Hope draws nectar in a sieve; / And HOPE without an Object cannot live.'[98]

It is interesting to see how far Coleridge's idea of the serious sonnet was still influenced by Smith and Bowles even in his later years. As Robinson notes, 'Work without Hope' draws on themes and images characteristic of both Coleridge's early sonnets and Smith and Bowles.[99] All of them mention capitalised Hope, symbolic rivers and garlands of flowers. Moreover, the dramatic opposition between joyful nature in spring and the poet's melancholy sounds like yet another variation on 'Zephiro torna', that sort of archetype of the English Romantic sonnet. The form of Coleridge's poem is irregular, as octet and sestet are inverted, as though premise and conclusion were turned upside-down. Besides, 'Work without Hope' was taken from a longer poem, whose remaining part is another sonnet which refers explicitly to the occasion of their composition. The suppressed lines specify that, growing old, Coleridge felt as though 'The World her spidery thread on all sides spun', isolating him more and more from the world without. His Faith, which hung like a mirror together with 'One Sister Mirror' on the opposite wall, enlarged the suffocating space woven by the world round him. However, the Sister Mirror 'is broke! And with that bright Compeer / I lost my Object and my inmost All— / Faith *in* the Faith of THE ALONE MOST DEAR!'[100] This refers specifically to his relation with Anne Gillman, which he felt was growing strained after nine years at Highgate. It is significant that he used a 'double sonnet' to speculate on his sentimental situation in the 1820s, even though the text he published – 'Work without Hope' – became a general reflection, secretly encompassing his experience with Sara Hutchinson.

Coleridge found two consolations for his torments, duty and faith. Duty is the subject of a text which, as Mays puts it, 'might qualify as a sonnet in Coleridge's loose categorisation'. Given the subject, I believe that the form is not accidental:

> Unchanged within to see all changed without,
> Is a blank Lot and hard to bear, no doubt:
> Yet why at others' Wanings should'st thou fret?
> Then only might'st thou feel a just regret,
> Hadst thou withheld thy love or hid thy light
> In selfish fore-thought of Neglect and Slight.
> O wiselier then from feeble Yearnings free'd,
> *While*, and *on whom*, thou may'st—shine on! nor heed,

> Whether the Object by reflected light
> Return thy radiance, or absorb it quite:
> And tho' thou notest from thy safe recess
> Old Friends burn dim, like Lamps in noisome Air,
> Love them for what they *are:* nor love them less,
> Because to *thee* they are not what they *were.*[101]

The sonnet is Coleridge's most general reflection on sentimental relationships, either with friends or lovers. Whereas in other late poems he repeated that love survives only when reciprocated, here he argued that one should not regret the fact of loving someone, even though that love remains unrequited: 'shine on! Nor heed / Whether the Object by reflected light / Return thy radiance, or absorb it quite.' The last lines apply the concept only to friends, but one cannot help referring them also to Sara Hutchinson, especially in the light of a notebook entry he made in the same period. Though he had repeatedly praised the constancy to an ideal object, he came to suspect that there was a basis of narcissism in any fixed idea, for 'this is always a *Self*-love – tho' the Conscience may be duped by the alterity & consequent distinct figurableness of the *form* – As sure as it is cyclical, and forms the ruling *Eddy* in our mind, so surely does it become the representative of our Self, and = Self.'[102]

If Coleridge became wary of haunting passions for worldly objects, he found his ultimate consolation in faith, which is the subject of two sonnets, 'My Baptismal Birth-Day' and 'Dewdrops are the Gems of Morning'. The story of this sonnet is complicated and will be analysed later on. 'My Baptismal Birth-Day' is his last sonnet, in which he took up Donne as a model, discarding Bowles and Smith. The idea expressed in the poem is not original, as it argues that physical death is not a definitive end, but only a liberation from the woe of material life: 'Is that a Death-bed, where the CHRISTIAN lies? / Yes!—But not *his*: 'tis DEATH itself, *there* dies.'[103] From our perspective, it is worth pointing out that, again, Coleridge used the sonnet to deal with an intimate theme of extreme importance.

Given the association in Coleridge's mind between the sonnet and the most painful and momentous aspects of his life, it is not surprising that he tried to exorcise the form through parody and satire.[104] A case in point is 'The Irish Orator's Booze: A Sonnet', a parody of 'The Old Man's Sigh: A Sonnet', which he sent to two rival magazines in 1832.[105] The texts are preceded by introductory notes, respectively 'What is an Irish Orator?' and 'What is an English Sonnet?', which are Coleridge's last critical statements on the subject. The splenetic note on the sonnet reflects his earlier uneasiness at the 14 lines structure but, also, at the view of the sonnet that the press had popularised in his time. For bourgeois readers, Milton was a 'bigoted Aristocrat' who 'contra-distinguished the Populace, the Political Unions, from the PEOPLE', whereas Petrarch, 'otherwise called Plutarch', presumably by the pseudo-cultured public which mixed them up, was treated with equal severity: 'the TIMES will soon dish up his business with Laura, and finish him in the Duke of Cumberland style.'[106] The note could not be clearer. The new middle-class public deemed Milton a classist intellectual for his hierarchic view of society, and it reduced Petrarch's *Canzoniere* to a poetic soap opera, whose only interest was its plot. Coleridge was irritated by the contemporary approach to Petrarch, which, both in poetry and criticism, focused only on his sentimental life to judge his morals. Petrarch was made into a second Duke of Cumberland, a hideous figure whom the reading public and the contemporary press, that new court of modern customs, were ready to indict.[107] Of course, we have seen that behind such morbid interest in the sensational aspects of Petrarch's story and the presumed scandal it represented, there was a serious debate on the relationships between men and women, their social roles and their sexual liberty. But Coleridge, probably, did not approve of this either, and he reacted both against the literal meaning of the sensational interest in Petrarch and its ideological implications.

The next part of Coleridge's critical note is a conclusion which only ironically follows from his sarcastic premise on Milton and Petrarch. The sonnet he is introducing is the

> Out-slough, or hypertrophic Stanza, of a certain poem, called 'Youth and Age,' having, by a judicial Ligature of the Verse-maker's own tying, detached itself, and dropt off from the poem aforesaid, assumes the name and rank of an integral Animal, and standing the test of counting the lines, twice seven exactly, is a legitimate English Sonnet, – according to the critical Code established since the happy and glorious separation of the *British* Press (four-fifths Scotch and Irish) from the Literature of break *England* – and the virtual extinction of the latter in the noonday blaze of the former.[108]

The formalism of the critical debate on the sonnet was evidently unconvincing to an organicist like Coleridge, who polemically underlined that sonnets were 'found' rather than written. He frequently pointed out the occasional character of his sonnets, which in some cases were composed 'on the spur of the moment', as he wrote in a letter.[109] This view stems from the tradition of Sensibility, whose poets and fictional characters often 'break into' a sonnet when their emotions run high. The formal irregularity of the sonnet which follows Coleridge's introduction was both a way of supporting his organicist view and, given its parodistic extremism, of blaming the poetic practices of his contemporaries, which were partly a consequence of organicism.[110]

In fact, the debate on the sonnet was the formal counterpart of the superficial approach to the content of Petrarch's *Canzoniere* that Coleridge had denounced in the first part of his critical note. The source of both was the press, who did not understand poetry and, none the less, created new rules and a specific taste for poetry. Coleridge was defending the space of literary criticism from the invasion of the rising mass-media, which were usurping a role that, he felt, should have been played by poets rather than journalists. The note of xenophobia against Ireland and Scotland must not conceal the dramatic truth underlying Coleridge's preoccupation about the marginal status of poets in our society.

Though the introductory note is sarcastic, the sonnet is serious and, significantly, it deals again with the meaninglessness of life 'where no Hope is', a condition which 'only serves to make us grieve, / In our Old Age!' For those who lead such life, death is not a frightening end, but a way of liberating 'selfless *Mind*' from a burden.[111] This is the message of 'Work without Hope' taken a pessimistic step further – or optimistic, for those who agree with the final lines. Though a true Christian, Coleridge felt the need to exorcise the anxieties voiced in the sonnet with a parody.

'The Irish Orator's Booze: A Sonnet' is the satiric, playful twin of 'The Old Man's Sigh: A Sonnet'. As Mays explains, the background of the text is the 1830 Beer Act, which repealed the tax on beer in England and Wales while leaving in place the tax on spirits, thus favouring the national drink against Ireland and Scotland. The dispute touched on the moral meaning of drinking and drunkenness, for which the Scots and the Irish still have a solid reputation. Moreover, the immediate background was the heated discussion on the Reform Bill. In his introductory note, Coleridge wondered what an Irish orator was, just as he had speculated about the English sonnet in the other introduction. Milton and Petrarch were replaced by O'Doherty and Hogg. The former, who had written parodies of Coleridge's poems in *Blackwood's Magazine*, was a pseudonym used by D. M. Moir, J. G. Lockhart and others, even though William Maginn was long thought to be the culprit; Hogg had collaborated with these writers for the same magazine in a series where Coleridge was often mentioned and lampooned. Whereas in the note on the sonnet Coleridge had defended Milton and Petrarch, describing them in the silly terms of the press, in the note on the Irish orator he attacked O'Doherty and Hogg, two champions of the detested Irish and Scottish press, as two drunkards. Anyone who is born in Hibernia and talks, preferably nonsense, 'with a touch of the brogue' is an Irish Orator. In the passage parallel to the conclusion of the note on the sonnet, Coleridge wrote

> that the following onslaught, or hyperbolical Stanza, of a certain poem, called 'Farce and Flummery,' having by a suicidal Ligature of the Verse-maker's own tying, detached itself, and bolted away from the rhymes aforesaid, assumes the name and rank of an intolerable Hanimal, and standing the test of reading the rhymes twice seven times exactly, is a descriptive Irish oratorical Sonnet, – according to the convivial Rules established since the happy and glorious reduction of the *Beer*-tax

> (four-fifths English) from the favourite beverage of England – and the
> virtual extinction of sobriety in the noon-day blaze of drunkenness.[112]

In this case, the irregular, organic sonnet is not a provocation against the
formalism of the Petrarchan sonnet, but a symbol of Irish politics and Scottish
criticism. Both of them are so gross that they seem to be inspired by alcohol.
The noon-day blaze of drunkenness is parallel to the noon-day blaze of the
Irish and Scottish press, and the decay of sobriety to the decay of English
literature. The two critical notes reinforce each other, even though it sounds
odd that a drug addict and a drinker like Coleridge should have penned them.
   After the introduction, the Irish orator's sonnet is a parody of 'The Old
Man's Sigh'. Instead of a depressing lack of hope, there is now 'good Drink',
which 'only serves to make us brave / In our old age'. Read against the despair
of the other sonnet, and against Coleridge's habits, this sounds like a confes-
sion, however disguised in the comically bold tone of the Irish orator. In the
conclusion the Irish orator, like the old man, invokes death, though for different reasons: 'O! might Life cease! and folk be blind, / Whose total *Tipple* is
Tea, their thirsty souls to bind!'[113] If in the other sonnet death was a liberation
of the selfless Mind, here forced teetotalism is represented as a sort of spiritual
enslavement, a blind rejection of the pleasures that make life endurable.
   In sum, Coleridge's sonnets show that he refused to identify Petrarch with
the sonnet, as his contemporaries were wont to do. Probably, there was an
element of self-defence in his attitude towards the sonnet, a form which was
normally used for introspective themes of embarrassing intimacy. Coleridge's
admiration for Petrarch's formal perfection was great, but it never led him to
imitation. However, Coleridge's response to *Canzoniere* represents only a part
of his interest. The meaning of the Latin motto in *Sibylline Leaves* can be fully
understood only in the light of his reading in Petrarch's Latin works, which
is linked on the one hand to Petrarch's Italian poetry, and on the other to his
interest in neo-Latin poetry and prose.
   Coleridge's reading of Renaissance Latin, though in itself not very extensive, was considerable, and it made him acquainted with essential features
of Renaissance poetry and poetics. The debate on rhetoric, the imitation of
the classics and other themes characteristic of Renaissance poetics helped
him develop his sense of Renaissance culture and, by extension, his view of
poetry in general. The problem of imitation, in particular, is inevitable in
neo-Latin writing.
   Among Italian poets in Latin, Coleridge most admired Petrarch, whom he
read during and after the period in the Mediterranean. In Lecture III of the
1818 course he discussed *Africa*, which he held in low regard. Its Latin was
rude and its versification harsh and feeble, despite the 'endless centos and
ends of lines from Virgil, Ovid, and Statius'. But such flaws were tolerable in
comparison to the poverty of its imagery and the absence of any beautiful
passage, which were all the more surprising in a poet whose Italian works,

even 'the most indifferent of them', always possess 'a fascinating delicacy in the choice and position of the words and the flow of metre'. Coleridge considered it an example of the interference of scholarly prejudices on poetic genius.[114]

His response to Petrarch's metric epistles was different. Classical learning is not so prominent in them as in *Africa*; the rhetorical element is still evident, but is not an end in itself as in the epic poem, since it is counterbalanced by the subjects, which are characteristic Petrarchan musings on life and experience. Coleridge was enthusiastic about the first letter, to Barbato da Sulmona, which he transcribed and quoted.[115] The epistle would have been a classical gem, 'had Petrarch lived a century later, and retaining all his substantiality of Head, & Heart, [had] added to it the elegances & manly Politure of Fracastorius, Flaminius, Vida, & their Corrivals'.[116] Renaissance Latin poetry was impeccable in terms of style, but was inferior to Petrarch's in intellectual intensity; none the less it deserved to be better known.[117]

Leo Spitzer argues that whereas Petrarch 'shows himself to us as a spirit torn between two civilizations which he felt his duty to harmonize', Renaissance poets like Poliziano 'embody the independent existence [...] of two distinct poetic climates, ancient and modern'. The problem was to 'give the flavor of new personal emotion to the traditional Latin vocabulary'.[118] Coleridge was struck by Petrarch's metric epistles and in general by the letters, whereas he disliked the excesses of rhetoric, whether they led to *Africa* or that letter of Petrarch containing '177 phrases of human life, chiefly of 2 words each'.[119] Living in a time when neo-Latin writing has become exotic for everybody except scholars, we might be tempted to dismiss Coleridge's interest as a waste of time on a subject from which he seems to have learned hardly anything. This would be a mistake for various reasons. Coleridge himself practiced poetic imitation – an eminently neoclassical form of writing – throughout his life. He was perhaps referring to himself when he noted that

> To a Translator of Genius, & who possessed the English Language, as an unembarrassed Property, the defects of Style in the original (i.e., Petrarch's epistle to Barbato da Sulmona) would present no obstacles: nay, rather an honorable motive in the well-grounded Hope of rendering the Version a finer Poem than the original.[120]

Coleridge always regarded Latin, including metrical composition in Latin, as a necessary part of education. Since he was aware that Latin was no longer so common as in the fifteenth century, he recommended students first to learn to develop their thoughts, then to embody them in a mosaic of passages borrowed from the classics. The style of poetry which consisted of translating 'prose thoughts into poetic language' – the style of Pope and his followers – 'had been kept up by, if it did not wholly arise from, the custom of writing Latin verses', which was regarded as basic in the school.[121] The negative tone of the remark does not conceal his admiration for some Latin poems, even though the point should not be overstated.[122] Coleridge observed that the 'prejudice in favor of classical learning' was so strong in Italy that Dante and Ariosto intended to write their poems in Latin, while Petrarch 'expected fame from his Latin works rather than his Italian poems'.[123]

Coleridge admired Petrarch as a moral philosopher as much as a poet, and he gave him a significant place in his *Philosophical Lectures*. Petrarch's Latin works were part of Humanistic prose, which, together with Dante's *Convivio* and *De vulgari eloquentia*, made Coleridge acquainted with the theoretical component of the Italian Renaissance. This tradition did not exist for many of his contemporaries, whereas it stimulated his thinking on the problem of imitation and it widened his historical horizon. Coleridge called Petrarch 'great in every respect because he was likewise eminently good and desirable', although he was aware that Petrarch was not a philosopher: 'He had, in truth, too much of inward reality, too much of tenderness, too much of interest for his human brethren, to find any gratification in forms of any sort, in mere forms.'[124] However, Coleridge was right in including Petrarch in his course of lectures. Dante, who had a philosophic mind, is paradoxically less important than Petrarch in the history of philosophy. Dante's philosophic writings are digests of medieval knowledge and only have a bearing on his own intellectual life; Petrarch's Latin works, though not philosophic in the technical sense, embody a new, epoch-making perspective on culture and therefore on philosophy, as his followers made evident.

Coleridge's opinions were based on a first-hand knowledge of Petrarch's Latin writings, which changed his attitude to Petrarch in 1803. They induced him to read Petrarch's Italian poetry, which in turn stimulated him to take up again the Latin works after his sojourn in Italy. Between 1808 and 1813 he transcribed and marked long passages from *De vita solitaria*, *De origine et vita sua*, *De remediis utriusque fortunae* and the letters.[125]

Though Coleridge never discussed Petrarch's Latin works in detail, it is worth observing what aspects struck him most, since he quoted them in support of his own opinions in *The Friend*, *Biographia Literaria* and *Sibylline Leaves*. His excerpts, most of which were taken from *De vita solitaria* and the letters, mainly deal with the social role of intellectuals. *De vita solitaria* describes a way of life for the poet and the scholar which became a model in the following centuries. Petrarch opposed his life of knowledge both to monastic isolation and the emptiness of commercial life in town. His idea of solitude was closer to the classic *otium literarium* than medieval asceticism,[126] but he believed he had achieved a kind of balance between them, as the numerous references to Christian authors and figures in *De vita solitaria* show.[127] His ideal was aristocratic and elitist: he was aware that his model did not suit everybody, but only the chosen few.[128] Petrarch proudly emphasised that he was self-taught, and the universities play a secondary role in his view of education and scholarship, whereas they were the centres of knowledge in the late Middle Ages.[129]

Coleridge's interest in the story of Giovanni da Ravenna shows that he was struck by Petrarch's idea of education. Petrarch's letters on his disciple were Coleridge's favourite and led him to overvalue Giovanni's role as a mediator between Petrarch and the later humanists.[130] Coleridge considered these epistles as the most interesting documents of the relation between a teacher and a pupil: he admired, evidently, the model of education, a form of transmission of knowledge which became common in the Renaissance, and which suited his own view of intellectuals in society.[131] Although Petrarch did not influence any aspect of Coleridge's thought in particular, the fact that his reflections on the life of the intellectual struck Coleridge has significant implications: it suggests that the affinities between them were profound and involved poetry and the philosophy of love as well as education, ethics and politics. It should not be forgotten that Coleridge's political interests, as he expressed them in *Lay Sermons* and *Church and State*, focused on the relation between intellectuals – the 'clerisy' – and society. The answer he gave to the problem has significant analogies with Petrarch's, though his reading of the Humanist tradition was influenced by the political theories of seventeenth-century England.

Coleridge's response to Petrarch has a bearing on the question of his acquaintance with literary criticism and scholarship in the Renaissance. The Renaissance reputation of Petrarch's Latin works, which preceded in this respect his Italian poetry,[132] rested on the fact that he propounded again the figure of the literary scholar by profession for the first time since the end of the Classical world.[133]

Coleridge did not pay much attention to the passages in Petrarch's Latin works which concern poetics. Giorgio Barberi Squarotti argues that Petrarch never wrote a treatise of poetry because 'moral problems prevailed and absorbed into their context any occasion of meditation on poetry'.[134] However, Petrarch may have influenced one aspect of Coleridge's thinking on poetry: the distinction between copy and imitation. Kathleen Coburn points out that Petrarch developed his ideas on imitation, a central theme for any classicist, in a letter to Boccaccio concerning Giovanni da Ravenna.[135] The imitator must produce something similar, not identical, to the original ('simile non idem'); the resemblance must be like that between father and son, something indefinite which painters call 'aerem' ('air, look').[136] Seneca and Horace argued that one should write as bees produce honey: not by picking up flowers, but by turning them into honey, so that various elements are melted into one, different and better.[137] If we remember that Petrarch's letters on Giovanni da Ravenna were Coleridge's favourite among the Latin writings; that he was reading them before leaving for Malta and Italy; and that his first distinction between copy and imitation was made in Malta in

1804 (*CN* II, 2211), we can infer that Petrarch may well be one of his sources, even though Metastasio was the actual catalyst.[138]

Coleridge expressed his general view of neo-Latin writing in a note he made on Petrarch:

> The Latin of Petrarch is the Language of modernized Europe in Latin words – doubtless, the great Purifiers of Latin Eloquence, Laurentius Valla, & his learned tho' inveterate opponents, contributed greatly to prevent the Latin from becoming the Lingua Communis – by confining it to classical Purity they both impoverished it, & made the writing in it a sort of Pedantry – for in order to write Ciceronianly we must *think* in the age of Cicero. Erasmus fought nobly against this; but the fine gentlemen of Classical literature, in Italy, were too hard for him. Perhaps, if some great Philosopher had arisen, laid down the foundations of philosophical Language, cleansed from Idioms; & made it the sole Law of Latin Style, that it should be equally intelligible to a Swede as to a Sicilian, &c., something might have been done – we might have escaped the French.[139]

The view of language expressed in the passage recalls, in its essentials, the historic ideas of the German Romantics. Language and thought are inseparable: 'in order to write Ciceronianly we must think in the age of Cicero.' Besides, language is historical, and the exact reproduction of past styles is impossible: 'The Latin of Petrarch is the Language of modernized Europe in Latin words.' The later Humanists, however, thought otherwise, and their Latin was more distant than Petrarch's from everyday reality. The failure of Erasmus's attempt deprived Europe of the learning of a common tongue – a problem which the English language has partially resolved today.

Coleridge's observations are correct, but give too much emphasis to the opposition between the various phases of Humanism. His knowledge of Valla and the later Humanists was not comparable to his knowledge of Petrarch, so that he overlooked important facts – in particular Erasmus's debt to Valla. The true object of Erasmus's polemic was not early Humanism, but sixteenth-century Ciceronianism.[140] However debatable Coleridge's opinion is, the note makes clear that he regarded Latin writing not merely as an erudite exercise, but as a vital philosophical issue.

At this point, Coleridge's poetic, moral and philosophic interest in Petrarch can be re-examined in the wider context of Petrarch's Platonism. Since Coleridge considered the Renaissance a Platonic age, Petrarch gave an essential contribution to forming his view of an epoch which influenced both his idea of poetry and the fine arts.[141] Although Petrarch's direct knowledge of Plato was confined to the few dialogues available in Latin in the Middle Ages – that is, *Timaeus*, *Phaedo* and *Meno* – he changed decisively the prevailing view of Plato. The reason for his anti-Aristotelianism was moral: he reacted both against the scientific interests of natural philosophy and 'the tendencies to reduce any problem to a matter of terms, all fields of knowledge to a refined logic', as in Ockhamism.[142] True philosophy had to show 'the way in salvation; ethical, not logical, perfection is its object', for to will the good is wiser than to know the truth.[143]

Aristotle erred in the most important points, those which concern our salvation; he did not have any idea of true happiness.[144] Plato was the Classical philosopher who came nearest to the Truth, as many Stoic, Neoplatonic and Christian philosophers acknowledged.[145] Charles Trinkaus points out that 'Petrarch's more pressing concern is in showing Plato's compatibility with Christianity.'[146] There is no doubt, as Augustine believed, that Plato would have been a Christian had he lived in Christian times; the conversion of several Platonists contemporary with Augustine demonstrated it – a point Coleridge also made in the *Philosophical Lectures*.[147] Raymond Klibansky argues that

> the Augustinian origin of these ideas is obvious, and similar conceptions may be found in earlier mediaeval authors. But the significance they acquire for Petrarch is a different one. [...] the notion of Plato as the guide in Christianity which had been, for earlier thinkers, a bold construction of history, was for Petrarch an unquestionable truth confirmed by Augustine's life and dominating his own.[148]

Aristotle and Plato, therefore, were in Petrarch's mind the watchwords for two different attitudes in philosophy and knowledge; but though Petrarch's philosophical expertise was limited, the change he brought about was decisive.[149] His programme, as summarised in *De sui ipsius et multorum ignorantia*, consisted of Platonic wisdom, Christian dogma and Ciceronian eloquence, and became a powerful model for Italian and European Humanism. As Paul Oskar Kristeller argues, he showed that it was possible to reject Scholasticism

> while remaining convinced Christians, and to reconcile [...] classical learning with religious faith. He is thus an early, Italian forerunner of that 'Christian Humanism' which recent historians have emphasized in the works of Colet, Erasmus, More, and other Northern scholars.[150]

Petrarch anticipated the Reformation in other aspects of his thought, mainly because of Augustine's influence. He developed the idea of salvation by grace alone; he endorsed the primacy of will over intellect; and his introspection precedes the Protestant solitary struggle with the conscience.[151] However, Petrarch's affinity with the Reformation must not be exaggerated; he always remained a convinced Roman Catholic – he took minor orders around 1330 – in spite of occasional invectives against the Church.

Coleridge's definition of Petrarch as a Platonist and a father of the Platonic revival of the Renaissance was historically grounded.[152] His admiration did not prevent him from pointing out that Petrarch's hostility to Scholastic philosophy was excessive, even though it was more comprehensible than the neglect in which Scholasticism was held in nineteenth-century England.[153] If Scholastic philosophy was ignored, Petrarch's prose works were also not read, as we saw in the previous chapters. Coleridge was certain of their value and tried to attract public attention by quoting them. The mottos for *The Friend* were selected with great care, because mottos 'are known to add considerably to the value of the Spectator'; and 'of two mottos equally appropriate', he always preferred 'that from the book which is least likely to have come into my Readers' hands'.[154] He specified that he quoted

> Petrarch often in the hope of drawing the attention of Scholars to his inestimable Latin Writings. Let me add, in the wish likewise of recommending a Translation of select passages from his Treatises and Letters to the London Publishers. If I except the German writings and original Letters of the heroic Luther, I do not remember a work from which so delightful and instructive a volume might be compiled.[155]

The meaning of Petrarch's Latin lines prefixed to the love poems in *Sibylline Leaves* should be clearer now. From *The Soother of Absence* onwards, Coleridge's love poems expressed increasing disillusion with frustrated love. Absence and separation characterise them from the beginning, and in the long run took over his hopes, as an impressive number of poems shows.[156] The motto from Petrarch expresses in a more prosaic form concepts often repeated in *Canzoniere*, as for example in the opening sonnet: the force of love and its vanity, its irresistible fascination and its cruelty. Unlike many sonneteers before him, Coleridge did not use a passage of Petrarch's Italian poems for his motto. In fact, he was interested in the content of the excerpt, that is, in Petrarch's philosophy of love, but he wanted to stay clear of the sonnet. This was due in part to the disturbing meaning the sonnet as a form had to him, and in part to the way in which the sonnet was seen in his time – a view of which he could never get rid entirely.

But the excerpt from Petrarch's Latin poems means more than this. In fact, Coleridge cited it also in *Biographia Literaria*, which was composed in the same period as *Sibylline Leaves*. Petrarch's lines, with some variants, appear at the end of Chapter 10, where Coleridge describes the development of his political and religious opinions together with some anecdotes, whose aim is to ease the tension of an argument of extreme seriousness. Coleridge tries to show that his principles remained unchanged over the years, concealing his involvement with radical thought in the 1790s. Despite his insistence on the consistency of his opinions, he ends the chapter with a quotation from Petrarch, whose point is that everyone changes incessantly as time goes by.

When we look back, we hardly recognise ourselves, and we feel the urge to apologise for what we wrote in our youth. As happens with other quotations, Petrarch's lines reveal that Coleridge was not as proud of all his past as he claimed throughout the chapter.[157]

Coleridge has taken us a long way from the image of Petrarch we have found in Jones, Dobson, Tytler, Smith, Seward, Robinson and Lloyd. Coleridge's late view of the sonnet and his interest in Petrarch's scholarly works were two sides of the same coin. As his late sonnets show, he was always uneasy about the form, which in his mind bore the mark of the poets of Sensibility, remaining embarrassingly intimate, and even feminine and sentimental, despite Wordsworth's revision of the form.[158] His insistence on Petrarch's Latin writings was genuine, but it was also a way of displacing a sensational view of Petrarch as a lovelorn sonneteer which he found unacceptable for poetic and moral reasons.

6
Epilogue: From Romantic to Victorian Petrarch

6.1 Displacing Petrarch

Petrarch continued to be an important figure well into the 1830s, even though the Petrarchan fashion had begun more than 60 years earlier. Poets and critics still felt the need to express a personal opinion of Petrarch and Laura, critically or sympathetically. Their comments were not only a direct response to Petrarch, but also to the Petrarchan fashion of their time. As in the Renaissance, the Petrarchan vogue generated a wave of anti-Petrarchism, a counter-discourse which opposed and distorted the dominant fashion. Coleridge's rereading of Petrarch was unique, but its pattern was a common one in the early nineteenth century, especially with male writers. The simplest form of counter-discourse is direct reaction, whose champion in Romantic times was Lord Byron.

Byron's attitude to Petrarch was unusual, as he embraced the views of both the supporters and the adversaries of Petrarch to demolish them mutually. This complex strategy was not a novelty, since it was first employed by Beckford in *Modern Novel Writing* (1796) and *Azemia* (1797), which make fun of both Gifford and sentimental literature.[1] But whereas Beckford admired Petrarch, Byron disliked him from the start. When Byron first read Petrarch's sonnets, he emulated them, but he soon found out that the form was not his cup of tea.[2] He wrote in his journal that he would compose no more sonnets, 'the most puling, petrifying, stupidly platonic compositions. I detest the Petrarch so much that I would not be the man even to have obtained his Laura, which the metaphysical, whining dotard never could.'[3] This aggressive attitude was expressed fully only in *Don Juan*. Before then, Byron referred to Petrarch in a different tone. This was in part due to Teresa Guiccioli, who was an ardent admirer of Petrarch.[4] Her temporary absence prompted Byron, who was passing the River Po, to compose his 'To the Po. June 2nd 1819', a poem which echoes Petrarch's 'Rapido fiume che d'alpestra vena'.[5]

Even before meeting Teresa, Byron celebrated Petrarch, like Dante and Tasso, as one of the poet-heroes of oppressed Italy in Canto IV of

Childe Harold's Pilgrimage (1818). Harold does not visit Vaucluse, like other eighteenth-century Petrarchists, but Petrarch's tomb at Arquà in the Euganean Hills.[6] Petrarch is conventionally described as a melancholy lover and a scholar who founded Italian lyric poetry dispelling barbarism. The tomb is a sort of sanctuary to his admirers ('The pilgrims of his genius', l. 266), who are familiar with his 'well-sung woes' (l. 265). Byron's lines are as bombastic and sentimental as those of many eighteenth-century Petrarchists (ll. 269–70): 'Watering the tree which bears his lady's name / With melodious tears, he gave himself to fame.' Stanza 31 praises the affectionate attention with which local people look after Petrarch's tomb and house, whose simplicity suits Petrarch better than the grandeur of a pompous monument. His 'soft quiet hamlet' is ideal for 'those who their mortality have felt' (l. 282). It is the conventional celebration of the simple delights of the country, which can be felt only by those who are aware of the transitory nature of material goods (ll. 285–93). Of course, this eulogy is captious, as Petrarch was a well-to-do man and Byron a British aristocrat, however impoverished. In any case, solitude has its morality, as it teaches us to die (l. 295): 'alone – man with his God must strive' (l. 297). However, man must also strive with demons. They 'seek their prey / In melancholy bosoms' (ll. 299–300), who feel doomed to suffering and frustration.[7] Byron's rehearsal of Romantic commonplaces on Petrarch continues in stanzas 56–57, where he blames the Florentines for their ingratitude towards Dante, Petrarch and Boccaccio.[8] But a reference to Petrarch's coronation could not be missing, and Byron talked of 'the crown / Which Petrarch's laureate brow supremely wore', though he had to wear it abroad (ll. 510–11).[9] The autobiographic implication of the passage is evident: Petrarch is a metaphor for Byron, another genius ill-treated by his countrymen.

Byron was aware of the ongoing critical debate on Petrarch, as Hobhouse's note to these stanzas of *Childe Harold* shows.[10] Significantly, the note focuses on one theme: Laura's identity and the nature of Petrarch's passion. Hobhouse summarised Tytler's argument and ironically pretended he agreed with it. 'Thanks to the critical acumen of a Scotchman', who attacked 'the discoveries of the Abbé de Sade', 'we know as little of Laura as ever.' In other words, Byron and Hobhouse found Tytler's arguments unconvincing and pointed out several comic contradictions. For example, they noted that Petrarch wrote in a letter that he repented of his earlier life when he was 40; however, in that period his illegitimate daughter was born. Even weaker was Tytler's argument on the purity of Petrarch's love – that only this kind of love lasts beyond the death of its object. Hobhouse thought that only bigoted or inexperienced people could find the idea convincing.[11] 'What is called vindicating the honour of an individual or a nation, is the most futile, tedious and uninstructive of all writing', though it always receives public approval. There is always a malicious desire to reduce great men 'to the common standard of humanity', which is what happened to Petrarch and, of course, Byron. Tytler's vindication of the morality of Petrarch was unconvincing. Tytler may have been right 'in retaining his favourite hypothetic salvo, which secures the author, although it scarcely saves the honour of the still unknown mistress of Petrarch'.[12] In sum, Hobhouse and Byron turned Tytler's argument inside out. They showed how irrelevant and contradictory it was while, at the same time, they used it to back up the idea that uncommon men cannot be criticised on the basis of common morality. Petrarch's morals were aristocratic rather than bourgeois, unlike those of his sentimental admirers.[13]

In the following years, Byron's attitude to Petrarch grew more hostile, as part of his campaign 'to tell the truth' by stripping human behaviour of moral illusions. His satirical strategy became more sophisticated than in *Childe Harold*. On the one hand, he endorsed the discourse of the admirers of Petrarch, when he wrote that Petrarch would not have written his poems, had Laura been his wife. Byron extolled Petrarch's illicit passion as a virtue rather than defending it timidly, as many eighteenth-century Petrarchans had done.

> There's doubtless something in domestic doings,
> Which forms, in fact, true love's antithesis;
> Romances paint at full length people's wooings,
> But only give a bust of marriages;
> For no one cares for matrimonial cooings,
> There's nothing wrong in a connubial kiss:
> Think you, if Laura had been Petrarch's wife,
> He would have written sonnets all his life?[14]

Marriage is the tomb of love; love poetry can only come from adultery and illicit passion. One should note that Byron never questioned the genuine quality of Petrarch's love, though he disliked it. He did not believe that a merely literary love for the muse could lead to great poetry. As he stated in 1822, 'For a man to become a poet (witness Petrarch and Dante) he must be in love, or miserable.'[15] Petrarch's lifelong love for his mistress confirmed Byron's paradoxical statement that Italians took adultery more seriously than marriage. Italians were more faithful to their lovers than their wives and husbands.[16]

At the same time, Byron took up the anti-Jacobin view on the eighteenth-century Petrarchans. Of course, the reason for Byron's attack was the opposite of Gifford's. Whereas Gifford and his friends considered the poets of Sensibility as socially subversive, Byron attacked their sentimentalism as a hypocritical, petty-bourgeois view of love.[17] Though sometimes the anti-Jacobins expressed positive judgements on poets like Smith and Robinson, they usually complained about sonnet-writing. First of all, Gifford was irritated by the popularity of the sonnet. In *The Mæviad* Phoebus asks Gifford to sweep away the heap of 'soft sonnets' which fill every corner of his room;

but when Gifford is getting down to work, 'Reams of outrageous sonnets, thick as snow, / Flew round my head; yet, in my cause secure / "Pour on," I cried, "pour on, I will endure."—'[18] This blizzard of sonnets was all the more intolerable because women were fond of them. This is evident in the motto of Gifford's *Baviad*: '*Impune ergo mihi recitaverit ille* SONETTAS, *Hic* ELEGOS'. The remarkable point is the word 'sonettas', used by Renaissance critics to indicate 'bad sonnets'.[19] Though *sonetto*, the Italian word for sonnet, is masculine, 'sonettas' is feminine. This must have pleased Gifford, because the sonnet was strongly associated with women writers and readers and, as criticism has showed, the feminisation of poetry was perceived not only as an aesthetic, but also a political danger. The *Anti-Jacobin* satirised the 'Wearisome Sonnet-teer, feeble and querulous, / Painfully dragging out thy demo-cratic lays'.[20] Sensibility and its morbid attention to feeling was for individuals what the French revolution was for society, that is, a subversion of traditional rules in the name of Rousseau and revolutionary progressivism.[21]

Byron radicalised the anti-Jacobin views, though the moral aim of his battle was different. Byron, who admired Gifford as satire's 'regular physician', repeated his strictures against the Della Cruscans, sonnet-writing, women poets and their patrons.[22] Class and gender played a central role in Byron's aggressive response to these writers. Scholars have showed that Byron's relation to the Della Cruscans, Staël and Hemans was more nuanced than he would have us believe. However, what is relevant here is that Byron's attack was addressed not only to eighteenth-century sonneteers, male and female, but also to their sources.[23] That is why his scourge fell on Plato and Petrarch, who had escaped the anti-Jacobins.[24]

> When amatory poets sing their loves
> In liquid lines mellifluously bland,
> And pair their rhymes as Venus yokes her doves,
> They little think what mischief is in hand;
> The greater their success the worse it proves,
> As Ovid's verse may give to understand;
> Even Petrarch's self, if judged with due severity,
> Is the Platonic pimp of all posterity.[25]

Even Petrarch, the chastest of poets, is not harmless, given that his *Canzoniere* often played the role of a *galeotto* book, to use the words of Francesca in Dante's Hell.

> I therefore do denounce all amorous writing,
> Except in such a way as not to attract;
> Plain–simple–short, and by no means inviting,
> But with a moral to each error tack'd,
> Form'd rather for instructing than delighting,

> And with all passions in their turn attack'd;
> Now, if my Pegasus should not be shod ill,
> This poem will become a moral model.[26]

Byron was creating a new type of lover, the Byronic hero, and a new way of seeing sentimental relationships. Clearing the way from previous models was indispensable to the success of his project.[27] His 'moral model' did not repress or titillate amorous feelings; rather, it told what they were like, that is, a dangerous game of power, sex and feelings. 'Plain–simple–short' means that his poetry would talk about that core of human relationships rather than something else, as love poetry often did. However, Byron was aware that comic didacticism and love poetry were incompatible. Anacreon, Sappho and Pope in 'Eloisa to Abelard' were blamed as immoral, but they were much better than the modern sentimental writers.[28] German drama, Rousseau, Staël and the poets of Sensibility reasoned on passion and killed it, whereas poetry itself is passion.[29] It was the dilemma of the modern mind, which, in Schiller's terms, was sentimental though it strived to be naïve. *Don Juan* is the splendid result of Byron's naivety in masquerade – the only naivety granted to a sentimental mind.

However strange it may sound, the closest ally of Byron was William Wordsworth. Wordsworth's attitude to Petrarch was seemingly very different from Byron's. Wordsworth expressed admiration for Petrarch, translated one of his sonnets, used mainly a variation of the Petrarchan form for his own sonnets, and quoted Petrarch's Latin works.[30] However, Wordsworth's displacement of Petrarch was more radical and lasting than Byron's. While Byron's attack on the Petrarchist view of love was a preliminary part of his campaign to impose a new way of seeing sexual relations, Wordsworth skipped the first stage and started directly from 'part two' of the process, substituting Milton for Petrarch as a model for the sonnet.

Wordsworth's apprenticeship, like that of many poets of his time, includes some Petrarchan experiments. His first published poem is a sonnet to H. M. Williams (1787) which, together with a few other texts he wrote in the late 1780s, is based on the conventions of sentimental poetry. In the same period or perhaps a little later he composed 'If grief dismiss me not to them that rest', a free and unremarkable translation of Petrarch's 'Se la mia vita da l'aspro tormento'.[31] Wordsworth must have discussed his version with Coleridge, who sent it to the *Morning Post* in 1798, and with his friend Francis Wrangham, who in the 1790s was translating Petrarch.[32] In the following years, however, Wordsworth's and Coleridge's attitudes to Petrarch evolved in opposite ways.

Wordsworth rediscovered the sonnet thanks to Milton in the early 1800s, when Coleridge began to reconsider Petrarch both as love poet and scholar. Wordsworth's epiphany is so famous that it does not need repeating here. Milton's sonnets struck him because they were 'in character so totally different from the Italian, and still more so from Shakespeare's fine Sonnets'.[33] Wordsworth's argument is worth following despite its inaccuracy. In fact, when he told this story, he must have been aware that Milton's tone and subjects can be found in Italian Renaissance poets like Della Casa, and ultimately in Petrarch's political sonnets, which Wordsworth knew and admired. However, historical accuracy was the least of Wordsworth's concerns in that moment. His mythical account of that afternoon was part of his campaign to present himself as the fountainhead of the new English sonnet, a role which demanded an unambiguous ancestry.

Some of Wordsworth's later statements on the sonnet must be seen in the same light. A good example is a letter he wrote to Landor in 1822, where he affirmed that he used to think the sonnet 'egregiously absurd' before reconsidering those of Milton in 1802.[34] Even the form of Milton's sonnets was the most satisfactory he knew. In a later letter again, he wrote that he never reflected much on the form of the sonnet. He believed, however, that the sonnet should have a threefold structure (beginning, middle and end), but the Italian form was divided into two parts (octave and sestet). He liked best an orbicular, organic form resembling a dew-drop, which he found in Milton, rather than the traditional Italian form.[35] Again, Wordsworth was defending his organicist aesthetics and reiterating his connection with Milton rather than providing a genuine history of the form, given that the sonnet was used as a unified stanza by several early Italian poets and in the Renaissance. Wordsworth's formal view of the sonnet is a practical application of the principles put forward by theorists like Coleridge, who argued that the main feature of the sonnet was unity of subject and feeling. Wordsworth's ideas naturally led him to sonnet sequences like *The River Duddon*, in which the sonnet is used as the stanza of a narrative poem.[36]

However, form is not the main issue. Criticism, especially in the past, has often reduced the story of the sonnet in the Romantic age to a formal battle between 'regular' and 'irregular' sonneteers. Wordsworth did more than anybody else to change the main modes of sonnet-writing in his time; however, he continued to use the Petrarchan sonnet, though in an adapted, Miltonic form. The formal problems are only a part of the matter, and they can be understood fully in the wider context of style and meaning. The crucial change brought about by Wordsworth does not concern the form, but the content of the sonnet. Wordsworth turned away drastically from the main theme of the sonnet tradition, that is, love. In Wordsworth's opinion, it was obvious that many of Petrarch's love poems had flowed 'I do not say from a wish to display his own talent, but from a habit of exercising his intellect in that way rather than from an impulse of the heart.' It was otherwise 'with his Lyrical Poems, and particularly the one upon the degradation of his country: there he pours out his reproaches, lamentations, and aspirations like and ardent and sincere Patriot'.[37] One could hardly find a more typical expression of Wordsworth's personality. Petrarch's love poems are only a display of rhetoric; they come from the intellect rather than the heart. On the contrary, his political poems are ardent and, therefore, sincere – the highest virtue Wordsworth could find in poetry. Wordsworth repeated the opinion of several eighteenth-century readers and expressed it in its most radical form. The opposition with the writers of Sensibility could not be neater. Petrarch the love poet was for him a rhetorician and a liar, whereas Petrarch the conservative opportunist became a sincere patriot.

Wordsworth's dismissal of Petrarch's love poetry includes the rejection of the achievement of the sonneteers of Sensibility. Wordsworth believed that the sonnet should not be used for melancholy musing on personal subjects, but for manly reflection on themes of public interest. The tone had to be oratorical rather than intimate and plaintive. It is surprising that in the 'Preface of 1815' Wordsworth included the sonnet in the 'Idyllium' section, which comprised poems descriptive 'of the processes and appearances of external nature', 'or of characters, manners, and sentiments', 'or of these in conjunction with the appearances to Nature'. It is a miscellaneous group which does not seem to be particularly coherent.[38] In any case, the paradoxical thing is that the objective and 'heroic' style Wordsworth recommended for the sonnet, which would normally be described as rhetorical, was put forward as the chief vehicle of individual sincerity, whereas the intimate tone of the Petrarchan tradition was described as the result of a rhetorical exercise. That is why it was crucial to avoid referring to Petrarch, though the sonnets Wordsworth wrote are variations of the Petrarchan form.[39] The association between Petrarch and the sonneteers of Sensibility was so strong and automatic that even Milton's obvious debt to Petrarch had to be ignored. Coleridge's interpretation must have convinced Wordsworth that it was high time to find a new place for Petrarch and his Romantic followers, though the place Wordsworth had in mind for them was marginal. A good example of this is provided by Wordsworth's judgements on Charlotte Smith.

Wordsworth met Smith on his way to France in 1791, when he received from her a letter of recommendation to H. M. Williams in Paris. He bought a copy of Smith's *Elegiac Sonnets* in 1789 and was reading them in 1802, when he took up the sonnet again, but he was reticent about them for many years.[40] Later in life, however, he praised Charlotte Smith for reintroducing the sonnet to English literature. In a note to his 'Stanzas Suggested in a Steamboat off St. Bees' Head, on the Coast of Cumberland' (1833), whose stanza is taken from Smith's 'St. Monica', she is defined as

> a lady to whom English verse is under greater obligations than are likely to be either acknowledged or remembered. She wrote little, and that little unambitiously, but with true feeling for rural nature, at a time when nature was not much regarded by English poets; for in point of time her earlier writings preceded, I think, those of Cowper and Burns.[41]

This would seem to be a just though late atonement for his earlier forget-fulness. In fact, there is more than a pinch of malice in his words, not only because he was aware that Smith wrote neither little nor unambitiously, but also because the hundreds of sonnets he had been writing in the meantime made her poems look like a false start in comparison to the true origin of the new English sonnet, which Wordsworth was attributing to himself.[42] A poetic version of his claims can be found in one of his best-known sonnets:

> Scorn not the Sonnet; Critic, you have frowned,
> Mindless of his honours; with this key
> Shakespeare unlocked his heart; the melody
> Of this small lute gave ease to Petrarch's wound;
> A thousand times this pipe did Tasso sound;
> With it Camoëns soothed an exile's grief;
> The Sonnet glittered a gay myrtle leaf
> Amid the cypress with which Dante crowned
> His visionary brow; a glow-worm lamp,
> It cheered mild Spenser, called from Faery-land
> To struggle through dark ways; and, when a damp
> Fell round the path of Milton, in his hand
> The Thing became a trumpet; whence he blew
> Soul-animating strains – alas, too few![43]

There are some strange points in this poem, which is one of the masterpieces of the Romantic meta-sonnet. One is struck by its untimely date of composition, as in 1827 the sonnet did not need defending. The form had won its battle for respectability, and complaints concerned its overabundance rather than the form itself, as happened in the eighteenth century.[44] The aim of the poem must have been different, and a good way of finding it out is to look at the poets mentioned by Wordsworth. Despite Wordsworth's scanty interest, Petrarch could not be omitted from a sonnet story, however brief. It is clear, though, that Wordsworth preferred Milton's trumpet over the lute he conventionally attributes to Petrarch. Above all, Wordsworth's list of poets gives the impression that they form a sort of self-evident ancestry of the English sonneteer, as though they had always been available to English readers and writers. In fact, most of them had disappeared from English literature a long time ago, and it had taken writers and critics a great deal of work to call them back. Wordsworth could read those poets and mention them in his sonnet thanks to the eighteenth-century sonneteers, whom he ignored in his text. It can be argued that in such a miniature history of the sonnet there is space only for the main figures. However, Wordsworth had written several multiple sonnets on one subject, whenever he wanted to express his thought fully. The point is that in this case the brevity of the sonnet was a good excuse for writing a history of literary giants, the latest of whom was Wordsworth himself.

'Scorn not the Sonnet', in fact, was only a poetic moment in Wordsworth's lifelong campaign of erasure, which had begun much earlier. His famous attack on Gray's sonnet in the 1802 'Preface' to *Lyrical Ballads* can be seen in a new light. Wordsworth's dismissal of Gray may well have been due not only to the style (the notorious 'poetic diction'), but also to the content of the sonnet to West. As Roger Meyenberg notes, Wordsworth identified Gray as an early example of the revival which had led to Smith, Robinson and their colleagues.[45] Criticising Gray's sonnet was a subtle way of dismissing the sonneteers of Sensibility without mentioning them.

The effects of Wordsworth's strategy can be seen in an anthology, *Specimens of English Sonnets*, edited by Alexander Dyce in 1833. Dedicated to Wordsworth, the volume includes a generous selection of Renaissance English sonnets, followed by some 50 pages of eighteenth-century texts, and another 30 by Romantic poets. Wordsworth is the contemporary author who is given most space. His sonnets are described as the only ones as powerful as those of Shakespeare and Milton. This familiar judgement, however, is uttered in a note, almost sotto voce, and the eighteenth-century sonneteers, from Smith to Russell, Seward and Bowles, are still there.[46] Wordsworth's battle was not won easily, even in an anthology edited by an admirer, and only in the Victorian age did his primacy as a sonneteer become undisputable.[47]

As far as Petrarch is concerned, the effects of Byron's and Wordsworth's displacing readings are evident in Thomas Campbell's biography of Petrarch, which appeared in 1841. Campbell's main source was Sade, but even a short comparison with Dobson's abridgement shows how greatly the cultural climate had changed in 70 years. Whereas Dobson's Petrarch was a melancholy lover, and his life a sort of novel of Sensibility, Campbell's Petrarch was a scholar, a traveller, a politician, a patriot, and accidentally an Italian poet.[48] Campbell minimised Petrarch's work as a poet because he took for granted that anyone knew about that. However, he discussed the character of Petrarch's love and, surprisingly, he took sides with Laura rather than Petrarch.[49] As a politician, Petrarch was not a sycophant to kings and emperors. He was fascinated by Giovanni Visconti because the Duke of Milan 'was the Bonaparte of the fourteenth century'.[50] Campbell's image of Petrarch is Coleridgean, though he added some elements which turn Petrarch into a sort of Victorian intellectual.[51] But Campbell's biography is noteworthy for other reasons. It shows that public interest in Petrarch in the 1840s was still great enough for a new biography, which ran through two reprints. It also shows that Petrarch had not become a subject for scholars only, if a poet like Campbell could invest a considerable amount of time in the compilation of a critical biography. Finally, even an enthusiast like Campbell remained sceptical about the quality of the Petrarchan sonnet in English.[52] The Victorian poets who revived the love sonnet sequence a few years later, drawing on Petrarch and other sources, undertook daring experiments even from a formal point of view, despite the long-standing popularity of the sonnet. But

the Victorians were influenced not only by Wordsworth's and Byron's views
of the sonnet. Other Romantic readings of Petrarch were more important
for them.

6.2   Re-placing Petrarch

If we drew a literary map of Romantic England on the basis of the responses to
Petrarch, our traditional geography would be greatly modified. Responding to
Petrarch proved to be problematic and it often forced writers to part company
from their friends. In fact, though Wordsworth and Byron played a major role
in overshadowing the Petrarchan sonnet and its themes, they did not win
everyone over to their cause. The Wordsworthian sonnet and the Byronic
lover were not the only influential models in their fields, as literary histories
have taught us. Though influenced by Byron and Wordsworth, several poets
continued to see in Petrarch a stimulating source of inspiration. They found
a new place for him rather than blotting him out, as Wordsworth and Byron
tried to do. The group which took up the baton of the sonneteers of Sensibility
was, as William Maginn called them, the second Della Cruscan School, that
is, Shelley, Hunt and Keats.[53] Considerable critical attention has been paid
to their responses to Petrarch, which, however, still need to be placed in the
context of the other Romantic reactions to Petrarch to be understood fully.

   Shelley's reading of Petrarch is much closer to Coleridge's than Byron's.
Shelley was one of the few poets of his time to develop a serious interest
in Petrarch's philosophy of love, which most of his contemporaries found
either baffling or ridiculous. Like other Romantics, the young Shelley began
to read Petrarch with two women, who considered him as the greatest love
poet.[54] Even in the lyric poets of ancient Greece 'nothing has been discovered
[...] equivalent to the sublime and chivalric sensibility of Petrarch', which
is a great compliment on the part of a Philhellene like Shelley.[55] Only with
Christianity 'Love became a religion [...] and a paradise was created of the
wrecks of Eden.' Provençal poetry led to Petrarch, 'whose verses are as spells,
which unseal the inmost enchanted fountains of the delight which is in
the grief of love'.[56] Petrarch's love was neither immoral nor preposterous, as
many readers in Shelley's time believed. Shelley was aware of the debate on
the morality of Petrarch's relationship with Laura, but he never referred to
it, probably because he found it beside the point. Adultery was a concept
which did not apply to Petrarch's idealistic love, just as it was unacceptable
for the idealised relationship described in 'Epipsychidion'.[57] Besides, it is
noteworthy that Shelley found some aspects of Dante objectionable, whereas
he could see no defects in Petrarch. Shelley did not even mention conceits
and puns, which were defended by few Romantic readers. On the contrary,
he highlighted the incantatory quality of Petrarch's music, which he could
relish better than most English readers thanks to his familiarity with the
Italian language.[58]

For Shelley aesthetic pleasure is never separated from morality and politics; thus, he argued that it is impossible to feel Petrarch's poems 'without becoming a portion of that beauty which we contemplate'. Shelley repeated the humanist belief in the civilising power of poetry, which many of us today would find dubious: 'it were superfluous to explain how the gentleness and the elevation of mind connected with these sacred emotions can render men more amiable, and generous and wise, and lift them out of the dull vapours of the little world of self.'[59] Love is the central moral agent together with the imagination, because it opens up the self. Love is the *trait d'union* between the individual and the world, and between individual happiness and political justice. An ideal of perfection is necessary to both poets and politicians, as Shelley argues in 'Lines Written among the Euganean Hills', a poem composed after visiting Venice and Petrarch's house at Arquà in 1818. The poem is based on Petrarch's and Dante's favourite image of life as a perilous sea-journey.[60] The Po plain is described in the poem as a green sea whose islands are cities and hills. In the central part of the text, Shelley compares Byron to Homer, Shakespeare and Petrarch, whose love from his 'urn / Yet amid yon hills doth burn, / A quenchless lamp by which the heart / Sees things unearthly'. The quenchless lamps of love embodied in the greatest human creations are fragments of the eternal light symbolised by the sun, which fills the world and 'floats up the sky / Like thought-wingèd Liberty', whose hovering presence frightens Tyranny.[61]

Shelley's later works are the climax of this combination of individual love and political expectations, for which he found the form he needed in Petrarch's *Trionfi*.[62] Here we are not concerned with the details of Shelley's borrowings, which have been studied by several scholars.[63] For our purposes, it is noteworthy that Shelley did not draw on *Canzoniere*, like all the Romantic admirers of Petrarch. Though it lacks Byron's polemical tone, Shelley's interest in allegory is a radical revision of the common Romantic readings of Petrarch. Shelley showed that most Petrarchans had concentrated on one side of Petrarch, and even so their readings could have been subtler. Despite the widespread popularity of Petrarch's sonnets, his philosophy of love was seldom paid serious attention. Shelley showed that learning from Petrarch as a love poet meant more than imitating his sonnets. One could be a Petrarchan poet without using the sonnet. In fact, there was another Petrarch ignored by most Romantics, with the exception of Coleridge and few other readers. This was Petrarch the Latin rhetorician and the politician, whose poetic voice could be found in the *Triumphs*.

Shelley's perspective on Petrarch is original for another reason. His use of allegory in 'The Mask of Anarchy' and 'The Triumph of Life' is a combination of Dante and Petrarch. This achievement must be highlighted, since scholars have often emphasised the importance of one source against the other. Dante's influence has usually been considered more relevant, perhaps as a result of T. S. Eliot's influential view of 'The Triumph of Life' as the greatest Romantic homage to Dante.[64] This judgement is misleading, because 'The Triumph of Life' can be understood only as a combination of Dantean and Petrarchan modes. I am referring not only to some images, which are evidently borrowed from Petrarch's *Triumphs*, but to the form of allegory and the structure of the Triumph used by Shelley. In fact, Shelley was interested in the elements Dante and Petrarch had in common rather than those which separated them. For this reason, he read and translated Dante's sonnets, which were unknown in his time, besides Petrarch's sonnets; and he was attracted by Petrarch's allegories besides *The Divine Comedy*. This is not as obvious as might seem, because critics normally contrast Dante's use of allegory with Petrarch's.

The results of Shelley's intuition are his most characteristic poems, from 'The Mask of Anarchy' to 'The Triumph of Life', which Peter Vassallo has defined as 'a *rifacimento* of Petrarch's Trionfi in terms of Dante's *Inferno*.'[65] Rather than a conclusion to the *Triumphs*, as Charles Robinson argued, or a response to a single *Triumph*, as other scholars believed, Shelley's poem reads like an attempt to answer the progress of Petrarch's work, from the triumph of Love (*Cupidinis*) to the triumph of Eternity through Chastity, Death, Fame and Time.[66] Shelley picked out elements from Dante's *Purgatory* and Petrarch's *Triumphs*, especially the 'Triumph of Death' and the 'Triumph of Time', the two main challenges to the humanist belief in the value and permanence of poetry.[67] Though, as Charles Robinson points out, in this phase of his life Shelley believed that 'Life would triumph even over Eternity', he failed to find an alternative solution to Dante's and Petrarch's eternity, since 'The Triumph of Life' reverses the materialistic optimism of former works like *Hellas* and *Prometheus Unbound*. Unlike Dante and Petrarch, there is no final illumination. As Vassallo notes, Light (enlightenment) guides Rousseau to disenchantment. His progress is from Terrestrial Paradise to an infernal vision. However, as Ralph Pite argues, Shelley's uncertainty is logical, because the poem 'refuses to assert the victory of either oppression or liberty.'[68]

Shelley's response to Petrarch can be placed halfway between the discourse of the eighteenth-century Petrarchans and the anti-Petrarchism of Byron and Wordsworth. Shelley was sensitive to some points made by the anti-Petrarchists but, at the same time, he responded enthusiastically to Petrarch's poetry and philosophy of love. The compromise he worked out was unique. He did not imitate Petrarch in his sonnets, which are modelled on Dante, Shakespeare, Milton and Wordsworth, but he turned to Petrarch's *Trionfi*. This Dantean Petrarch, a synthesis of his two favourite Italian poets, allowed Shelley to find an accomplished form for his late concerns in politics and metaphysics, and to create an image of Petrarch as a visionary idealist which, at last, gives poetic justice to Petrarch's multi-faceted personality.

Hunt's and Keats's approach to Petrarch, even more than Shelley's, is rooted in the sentimental tradition of the eighteenth-century sonnet. This does not mean that their readings were banal. Their longer involvement in

Della Cruscanism did not prevent Keats from achieving results as original as Shelley's. In fact, it is fair to say that Keats's achievement evolved from the sonnet of Sensibility combined with other sources. Though the relation of Keats's sonnets with the Petrarchan tradition is the only part of the Romantic reception of Petrarch which has been studied adequately, its character and contours will be clearer if re-examined in the context of the other Romantic responses to Petrarch.

In comparison to Dante, Boccaccio, and Tasso – not to mention the poets of classical antiquity – Petrarch would seem to be a marginal presence in Keats, who mentioned him rarely. However, this first impression is wrong. Scholars have shown that Keats had a permanent interest in the sonnet form, which led him to experiment with different types of quatorzains. The Petrarchan sonnet was his starting point and the type he used most frequently. However, since Keats's Petrarchan sonnets were composed before he began the study of Italian in 1819, it is necessary to find out the sources on which he drew. What ideas of Petrarch and the Petrarchan sonnet did he come across? Since there were more than one in his time, it is not enough to say that he used, criticised and modified the Petrarchan sonnet.

Though Keats had already written several Petrarchan sonnets, he first mentioned Petrarch in 'Keen, fitful gusts are whispering here and there', a sonnet he composed to celebrate one of his early visits to Hunt's cottage in Hampstead. The last lines describe 'lovely Laura in her light green dress, / And faithful Petrarch gloriously crowned', that is, a portrait of the two lovers Hunt had in his house.[69] The picture is described in greater detail in 'Sleep and Poetry':

> Petrarch, outstepping from the shady green,
> Starts at the sight of Laura; nor can wean
> His eyes from her sweet face. Most happy they!
> For over them was seen a free display
> Of out-spread wings, and from between them shone
> The face of Poesy: from off her throne
> She overlooked things that I scarce could tell.

Keats did not linger on Petrarch's melancholy. The couple is described as 'most happy' because love conjures up the invisible wings of Poesy, as Keats will call them in his 'Ode to a Nightingale'. At this date Keats did not pay much attention to the price to be paid to compose love poetry. But in Hunt's room there were other literary portraits. 'Sleep and Poetry' mentions Alfred the Great, Tadeusz Kosciusko and, significantly, a bust of Sappho.[70]

These early references show that Keats got acquainted with Petrarch through Hunt, who associated Petrarch with Sappho. This combination was common with the poets of Sensibility, as we have seen, and it proved to be very important to the women poets of Hunt's time, as we shall see below.

Since Keats received his idea of Petrarch from Hunt, a few words on Hunt's view of Petrarch will be helpful.

Hunt had a lifelong interest in the sonnet, but he expressed his critical views in a systematic way only in 1867, when he wrote a long introduction to *The Book of the Sonnet*, a two volume anthology he edited together with S. Adams Lee. Despite the late date of publication, the ideas expressed in Hunt's essay reflect the cultural climate of the early decades of the century rather than the 1860s. Since his late views agree with those he put forward occasionally early in life, we can assume that they were the ideas Keats learned from him.

The starting point of 'An Essay on Cultivation, History, and Varieties of the Species of Poem called the Sonnet' is that the sonnet is a specifically Italian form.[71] Hunt was a staunch supporter of the Petrarchan rather than the Shakespearean sonnet. While his position was common early in the century, in the 1860s it was often disputed as a result of cultural nationalism and the growing popularity of Shakespeare's sonnets. In any case, Hunt points out that he wants to further the knowledge of both English and Italian poetry.[72] Hunt notes that Italian sonneteers are innumerable, and many of them are women. As a way of countering the idea that the sonnet is effeminate, he pinpoints that most sonneteers have been politically active.[73]

Section II, 'On the nature and properties of the sonnet, particularly the sonnet called legitimate', discusses the origins of the sonnet and its association with music.[74] Hunt's preface becomes prescriptive when it affirms that only legitimate sonnets can be perfect works of art. The sonnet must be based on one idea, and the conclusion must not be epigrammatic, unless it is really necessary.[75] Section III presents the fathers of the legitimate sonnet, Guittone d'Arezzo, Dante and Petrarch. Petrarch is more moderate than Dante, whose sonnets are sometimes even better than Petrarch's. However, Petrarch's poetry was more popular up to the late eighteenth century, a time of new revolutions which rendered Dante's extremism attractive. Petrarch looks monotonous, but he has always been a great favourite with ladies, though not only with them.[76] He freed the sonnet from metaphysics (i.e., the philosophical framework of the *stilnovo* poets), he gave it a finer music, refined the language of the tribe, and made the form popular with women. He furnished a moderate model to Italians, who are prone to war, lust and superstition. Petrarch's conceits are a defect, but they are occasionally employed by all lovers.[77] In short, Hunt's view of Petrarch's aesthetics is part of the mainstream Romantic Petrarchism, though the observation on Petrarch's suppression of metaphysics is due to Hunt's empiricist frame of mind. His opinion of Petrarch's character and politics is that of the Romantic liberals from Foscolo to Byron. Unlike them, however, he does not blame Petrarch for his political moderation.

Petrarch's moderation does not apply to his morals. In Section VI, 'Of English Sonnets, and of the Sonnet illegitimate or Quatorzen', Hunt notes that the sonnet tradition revolves round 'illegal attachments'.[78] Dante, who deified both Beatrice and himself, never mentions her husband. The same happens with Petrarch. 'Nobody would dream, from his three hundred sonnets, that there was a gentleman of the name De Sade, who had a right to ask him "what he meant."' Petrarch and Laura ignored her husband, both on earth and in heaven. Della Casa was an ecclesiastic who addressed his poems to a married lady, and Alfieri's sonnets are addressed to the wife of the second English Pretender.[79] Hunt hastens to argue that the sonnets in his anthology – even Shakespeare's – contain nothing objectionable, though he does not explain why.

Hunt does not spend much time on Shakespeare's sonnets, even though he commends them.[80] After a brief discussion of Donne, Daniel, Drayton, Drummond and Milton, he moves on to Gray, the British restorer of the sonnet. Between Gray and Wordsworth the sonnets are of poorer quality. However, some of them influenced important poets like Coleridge, whose sonnets, though, are worse than those of Bowles. Hunt praises Seward, H. M. Williams, and C. Smith. Many eighteenth-century sonnets were of illegitimate type, but Wordsworth put an end to this fashion.[81] Hunt's praise is double-edged, because Wordsworth is presented only as the restorer of the Petrarchan sonnet form, whereas nothing is said about the style and content of his 'heroic' sonnets. Wordsworth is described as a part of the Petrarchan tradition rather than a radical alternative to it, as Wordsworth himself went out of his way to state. After Wordsworth, Hunt praises Coleridge, and above all Keats, Shelley and C. Lamb. The only living poet he mentions is Barrett Browning, whom he considers the greatest poetess who ever lived.[82]

Though Hunt's views are not particularly original, they provided Keats with a critical and ideological framework for writing sonnets and understanding Petrarch.[83] In fact, we do not know whether Keats read Petrarch's poems and, if so, what translations he used. The only poem he must have read is Hunt's version of 'Chiare, fresche et dolci acque', which appeared in *The Examiner* in 1816 under the Romantic title, 'Laura's Bower'.[84] Above all, Keats's background must be completed considering the way in which sonnet-writing was practised in Hunt's coterie.

Though Hunt wrote that the Della Cruscans were mere idlers, and was not keen on being associated with them, Lockhart, Crocker, Maginn and the other reviewers who called Hunt and his friends a second Della Cruscan school were not completely wrong. The link with Della Cruscanism is particularly evident in the way the sonnet was used in the Hunt circle, as several scholars have noted.[85] Even more than Hunt's, Keats's early sonnets are based on modes employed by their late-eighteenth-century precursors. Most of Keats's sonnets were conceived during poetic contests, or as compliments addressed to his friends and brothers. They are short epistles in verse which celebrate the value of friendship, conversation and social life. Unlike Smith and Bowles, Keats rarely writes about solitude and melancholy, and when he does, he argues that they can be enjoyed only by 'two kindred spirits'.[86]

Besides sociability, another central theme of Keats's sonnets is poetic fame, which looms large in both Petrarch and the Della Cruscans. A couple of sonnets record a mock coronation with laurel which took place at Hunt's.[87] Later, Keats was ashamed of the pleasure he took in it, and he even specified that he 'would reject a petrarchal coronation – on accou[n]t of my dying day, and because Women have Cancers', which probably means that Petrarch's poetic idealisation of Laura and the prize he won for it are unworthy of the human condition, which is characterised by suffering and mortality.[88] Keats's judgement was part of his more mature view of life in 1818, but his critical tone may have been influenced by the fact that Petrarch's coronation on the Capitol was becoming more and more important to women writers, as we shall see below. Moreover, we hardly need recall how haunted Keats was by poetic fame, notwithstanding coronations on the Capitol. Besides these similarities, there are significant differences between Keats's early sonnets and the Della Cruscans. Keats addressed some complimentary sonnets to young women, but seduction is not for him the central theme it was for the Della Cruscans, at least before meeting Fanny Browne. Unlike the Della Cruscans, Keats's greatest achievements can be found in literary meditations like the Chapman's Homer sonnet.[89]

Keats's Petrarchism was a matter of form rather than content. If the themes of his early sonnets and their modes of circulation recall the Della Cruscans, his formal interests are in part independent of them.[90] The most interesting of Keats's early celebrations of female beauty is 'Woman! When I behold thee flippant, vain', a mini-cycle of three sonnets in which the use of the eighteenth-century version of Petrarchan conventions is serious and ironic at the same time. In Keats's 1817 *Poems*, the three sonnets are printed as one text, which anticipates his invention of the 'sonnet stanza' in his later odes. These stanzas evolved as a *crescendo* from his interest in the sonnet form, as Bate and other scholars have shown, following Garrod's intuition.[91] The story is well known and need not be repeated in detail. When Keats outgrew Hunt's poetics, he abandoned the Petrarchan for the Shakespearean sonnet form, which, in Bate's words, was 'temptingly unpopular'.[92] Keats wrote that Hunt 'has damned Hampstead [and] Masks and Sonnets and italian tales', which is an interesting remark because it shows that Wordsworth had not changed the reputation of the sonnet, since it had been impaired again by a new wave of sentimentalism sponsored by Hunt.[93] But it is noteworthy that Keats, like Hunt, considered Milton and Wordsworth as part of the Petrarchan sonnet tradition rather than as an alternative to it.[94]

However, Keats soon grew dissatisfied with the Shakespearean sonnet. In a famous letter dating from May 1819, he said he was trying to discover a 'better sonnet stanza' for his poems. 'The legitimate does not suit the language over-well from the pouncing rhymes – the other kind appears too

elegi[a]c – and the couplet at the end of it has seldom a pleasing effect.'
In other words, Keats found the Petrarchan or 'legitimate' sonnet unsuited to
the English language, because the language contained few rhyming words.
The hammering repetition of few sounds was unpleasant to him.[95] On the
other hand, the 'illegitimate' sonnet was metrically loose and sounded like
an elegy more than a rigorous stanza form. Of course, the 'illegitimate' sonnet was not intrinsically elegiac. Keats's view was influenced by the fact that
it had been associated with elegiac themes from Smith onwards. But Keats
was dissatisfied with the structure of the Shakespearean sonnet, whose final
couplet was too separate from the preceding quatrains.[96] As an alternative,
he included in his letter a specimen of his new sonnet, 'If by dull rhymes our
English must be chained':[97]

> If by dull rhymes our English must be chained,
> And, like Andromeda, the Sonnet sweet
> Fettered, in spite of painèd loveliness,
> Let us find out, if we must be constrained,
> Sandals more interwoven and complete
> To fit the naked foot of Poesy:
> Let us inspect the lyre, and weigh the stress
> Of every chord, and see what may be gained
> By ear industrious, and attention meet;
> Misers of sound and syllable, no less
> Than Midas of his coinage, let us be
> Jealous of dead leaves in the bay wreath crown;
> So, if we may not let the Muse be free,
> She will be bound with garlands of her own.

It was but a short step from this irregular sonnet to the ode stanzas, which,
as Garrod and Bate have shown, are an outgrowth of the Petrarchan and
Shakespearean sonnets.[98] Keats's stanzas are variations on the sonnet form,
with a different ratio of Petrarchan and Shakespearean components in each
ode.[99] Keats desired something slower, wider and more intense than the epigrammatic speed created by the 'pouncing rhymes' of the traditional sonnet,
whose influence, none the less, has been detected even in the major odes.[100]

There is, however, an intriguing *coda* to Keats's involvement in the sonnet.
He returned to it in the last months of his life, when his tormenting love
for Fanny Browne reached its climax. In fact, there was a reason for Keats's
lack of interest in the content of Petrarch's poems which has not yet been
mentioned. Keats was loath to talk of his sentimental life. He was annoyed
when his friends gossiped about his relationship with Fanny.[101] In a sonnet
inspired by the Paolo and Francesca episode in Dante, he dreamed that his
spirit was ravished in that circle of hell where 'lovers need not tell / Their sorrows' (ll. 11–12). Like Coleridge, Keats was tormented by a passion which did

not satisfy him fully, since Fanny's feelings were not as strong as Keats's. Like Coleridge, Keats was embarrassed with the outspoken expression of intimacy which found in the sonnet its most popular vehicle. Scholars have long shared his attitude, since many of them have found Keats's poems to Fanny embarrassing, with the exception of 'Bright Star!'. These critical judgements derive from the idea that a great poet is never supposed to lose self-control. Keats's attitude, too, was in part the result of social pressure, since most critics, including those who attacked the Cockney school, thought that indulging one's sentiments was an effeminate attitude.

Though Keats tried to keep this use of the sonnet at distance, he could not help taking up his 'old sins' again.[102] He had already conceived of fame as a coy lover, for example in the first of his sonnets 'On Fame', where he argues that Fame is unpredictable as a disdainful lover (ll. 11–14): 'Ye love-sick bards! repay her scorn for scorn; / Ye artists lovelorn! madmen that ye are, / Make your best bow to her and bid adieu – / Then, if she likes it, she will follow you.' Now his passion for Fanny forced him to see the problem literally instead of metaphorically. Keats, who 'never was in love', called Love 'my Religion' and used sacred terms to describe his sentiment and Fanny, as Petrarchan poets typically do.[103] 'The day is gone, and all its sweets are gone!' and 'I cry your mercy, pity, love – ay, love!', two sonnets written in late 1819, belong to the Petrarchan tradition of the plea to the beloved.[104] As Susan Wolfson argues, these sonnets to Fanny, like Coleridge's sonnets to Asra, contain 'the language of loss and frustration [...], a Petrarchan fate that Keats's writing in Shakespeare's form does not succeed in avoiding.'[105] However unreal, it is fascinating to imagine what might have happened to Keats's attitude to Petrarch had Keats lived longer.

Keats's interest in Petrarch is singular. It was a formal interest, in which the content of *Canzoniere* and the love story of Petrarch and Laura, which his contemporaries found so exciting, played a marginal role. The reason for his interest was partly psychological, and also due to his embarrassment towards sentimental intimacy. The result was that Keats, like Shelley, found the sonnet form constraining and unbalanced, and eventually broke it up.[106] Like Shelley, he developed an ode stanza from the sonnet. We might say that their reading of the sonnet was etymological. Keats's ode stanzas, which developed out of his experiments in the sonnet form, brought the sonnet back to its origins, since the Sicilian poets created the sonnet from a stanza of a *canzone*. Oddly, Keats was not inspired by *canzoni*, whose intricate metrical patterns could have met his desire for forms 'more interwoven and complete'. It cannot be excluded that they were in his mind when he worked out his odes, since he was familiar at least with 'Chiare, fresche et dolci acque' in Hunt's translation. In any event, the natural outcome of a formal interest carried to extremes is meta-poetry. For this is the direction to which Keats's sonnet-writing points. The self-enclosed pattern of the sonnet was ideal for musing on the nature of rhyme, poetic form, and language. When the speculation on the self-reflecting structure of the sonnet took the opposite direction, extolling self-enclosure rather than breaking it up, the result was Mallarmé's Petrarchism.

6.3 Replacing Petrarch

Recent criticism has argued that the typical Romantic poetess adopted the mask of the *improvvisatrice*, insisted on the primacy of love and domestic affections, rejected fame and embraced the Burkean aesthetics of the beautiful. At the same time, the Romantic poetess subverted these ideals and resisted the dominant representations of feminine subjectivity by identifying with 'such female personae as Philomela's nightingale, the Greek Pythia, or the inspired Sappho'.[107] This is only a partial truth, since her identification with Petrarch was equally important. In fact, though the Sapphic tradition is usually presented as a radical alternative to Petrarchism, they continued to foster each other in the Romantic age. Mary Robinson's combination in *Sappho and Phaon* was not an isolated episode. Those traditions were mixed up by many early nineteenth-century women writers, and none of them was more successful than Madame de Staël with *Corinne*.

The epigraph of *Corinne ou l'Italie* is taken from *Canzoniere*. On the novel's title-page, Corinne, Italy, and Petrarch look like synonyms. After an introductory chapter on Oswald, the male protagonist, the novel describes the coronation of Corinne on the Capitol in Rome. This long chapter – for Ellen Moers 'the most important' in the book – re-elaborates many of the *topoi* we have met in our story.[108] Corinne was the most famous woman poet of ancient Greece after Sappho. I believe that Staël used Corinne for three reasons. Firstly, Sappho was too predictable a protagonist for a novel written by a woman in the 1800s, as fictions of Sappho had become commonplace; secondly, Corinne allowed Staël to bypass the dangerous problem of lesbianism; thirdly, Sappho was not used as a name, not even as a pseudonym, in eighteenth-century Italy, where the story takes place.[109] It is extremely significant that the most influential image of the woman writer of the Romantic age consists of a mixture of Corinne and Petrarch. Or, to put it in another way, that Corinne – a variant of Sappho – was reread through Petrarch a decade after Robinson's *Sappho and Phaon*.

Nobody could miss the subtext of Corinne's coronation, since Petrarch on the Capitol in Rome was one of the favourite episodes of his life with the Romantics. In any case, Staël specified that the ceremony had been 'consecrated by the names of Petrarch and Tasso'.[110] Staël rewrote the episode to lay claims which repeat and expand Robinson's reading of the same event in the preface to *Sappho and Phaon*. But the meaning of Staël's claim can be fully understood only if we go back briefly to the social implications of Petrarch's achievement. Petrarch struggled hard to reaffirm in Christian times the social status poetry and poets had enjoyed in classical antiquity. For him, poetry possessed a sacred value, and it was not a dangerous waste of time in comparison to theology. Poets were no mere entertainers; governors should have listened to their advice. In a passage of Corinne's improvised ode to Italy, Petrarch is praised not only for his merits as a scholar, but also as a patriot: 'his native land inspired him better than Laura herself.'[111] Like some eighteenth-century readers and Wordsworth, Staël found Petrarch more involving as a political than a love poet.[112] In short, Petrarch's coronation was the symbol of a renewed social role for poetry and poets.

When Staël made her Corinne repeat Petrarch's gesture, she was claiming for women what Petrarch had claimed for poets in general, though in his time 'poets' automatically meant 'men'. Male writers from Gibbon to Landor could afford to blame the gaudy display of vanity in Petrarch's coronation in Rome because Petrarch's hard-won battle for the social respectability of men of letters had made their snobby attitude possible. On the contrary, the social respectability of women writers was far from secure. For this reason, they found the coronation of Petrarch so attractive that most of them felt the need to re-write and comment on it from a female viewpoint. As Staël specified, 'There was certainly nothing more contrary to the customs and opinions of the English than this publicity given to the fortunes of a woman.'[113] In fact, this public celebration of a woman was unusual not only to the English. The real Italian *improvvisatrici* normally performed for select, private audiences and avoided public spaces and the common folk, which were potentially harmful to the reputation of a lady.[114] The coronation of the Italian *improvvisatrice* Corilla Olimpica in 1776, the unacknowledged model for Staël's episode, raised so much popular protest that her procession to the Capitol had to be cancelled to avoid riots.[115] In any case, the political meaning of the ceremony went beyond this. Staël pointed out that Oswald, the Scottish protagonist, had seen some pageants for military victories, but he had never seen the public celebration of the peaceful value of genius – female genius, at that.[116] Corinne's coronation was a Triumph which celebrated that kind of genius rather than an abstract, allegorical Virtue, as in Petrarch's *Trionfi*, or an army for a military victory.[117]

Whenever Romantic women poets rewrote Petrarch's coronation in Rome, they were laying claims to social status, despite the fact that they often affected to despise fame. In most cases, their modesty was lip service paid to the idea that women should not aspire to public fame and a literary career. Their stubborn interest in Corinne's and Petrarch's coronations, and in Petrarch's poetic exchange with Giustina Levi-Perotti, shows that their ambition was far from modest. Petrarch was a poets' poet, a writer who spent his entire life rediscovering forgotten texts and winning back social prestige for poetry. The Romantic women poets who followed his example were demanding the same thing. More often than Sappho, Petrarch was invoked by women poets whenever the meaning of poetry and the value of fame were at stake. It is no coincidence that Petrarch appears in the other key episode of *Corinne* on the social status of poets, that is, the visit to the countryside around Naples. Here Oswald and Corinne visit Virgil's tomb, where Petrarch planted a laurel tree, as he alone 'was worthy of leaving a permanent mark of his visit'.[118] The passage is followed by Corinne's improvisation at Cape Miseno, where she reiterates and expands the argument of her performance at the coronation on the Capitol.

Given the enormous success of *Corinne*, it is hardly surprising that Byron and other writers attacked Madame de Staël together with Petrarch and sonnet-writing in the years that followed. The success of *Corinne* may well have been one more reason why Tytler decided to publish a longer version of his essay on Petrarch in 1810, whereas in the same period Wordsworth began his campaign of erasure of Petrarch from the sonnet tradition.

As well, Anne Mellor has argued that the tradition of the poetess based on the model of *Corinne* does not account for all the women poets of Romantic Britain. Hannah More put forward a different and equally influential model which embodied the virtues of protestant domesticity, warning British women against mixing with Mediterranean culture.[119] Though Mellor's observations are fully justified, it should not be forgotten that More's argument was hardly a novelty. More's points about the degeneracy and effeminacy of the South had been made many times before her. As we saw above, all the critics who disliked Petrarch voiced similar ideas. But, though the Petrarchan tradition and Staël had many adversaries, they could not be neutralised easily. Few writers, however, were ready to embrace those models as fully as Letitia Elizabeth Landon.[120]

When at 22 Landon published her second book, *The Improvisatrice, and Other Poems* (1824), her starting-point was, once again, Petrarch associated with Sappho. Landon's choice was not only the immature repetition of a cliché; rather, it was a deliberate way of continuing a tradition. Wordsworth's indifference to Petrarch and Byron's hostility to Staël, Petrarch and the sonneteers of Sensibility cannot have escaped Landon, who was heavily influenced by Byron, especially at her début. Her book was a Byronic building, but its entrance was emphatically different, since it drew on a tradition Byron had fiercely opposed. Landon's polemical gesture was a claim to autonomy from her main male model.

The title of Landon's collection would lead one to expect Romantic spontaneity, which contemporary criticism considered the hallmark of women's poetry. However, her poems are the spontaneous overflow of literary reminiscences, as they are full of echoes of the main poetic modes of the age.[121] Landon's *improvvisatrice* is a young, pretty, passionate Italian poet, painter and musician. In the first pages of the poem she describes the first two canvasses she has exhibited. Their subjects are noteworthy. The first painting represents a 'festival' in a 'gorgeous hall', where Petrarch, lonely and despondent, admires Laura from afar – an imaginary episode which had never been used previously.[122] The second canvass is a portrait of another 'minstrel', that is, Sappho wasting away because of her unrequited love for Phaon.[123] Landon's models can be easily traced.

Whereas Robinson and Staël had depicted themselves as Sappho and Corinne, Landon represented herself as a poet-artist-musician who painted Petrarch, Laura and Sappho. Their portraits are the patterns of the other tragic stories told in Landon's long poem. Petrarch's presence is all the more significant considering that he is the only man whose unrequited love is included in *The Improvisatrice*; all the other victims of love and abandonment are women. Landon's self-portrait looks like Mary Robinson and Madame de Staël to the power of two.[124] Like them, Landon mixed up Petrarch and Sappho, placing Petrarch before Sappho, that is, seeing Sappho through a Petrarchan lens.[125] As late as 1825, Petrarch was still an inevitable starting-point for a woman poet – in this case, the most talented figure of her generation.

In fact, Petrarch was not only a starting-point for Landon. Her interest was lifelong, since she wrote poems on him before and after *The Improvisatrice*. For example, 'The Vow of the Peacock', the long title poem of a collection published in 1835, is a fiction of Petrarch set in medieval Venice.[126] However, when Landon mentioned Petrarch, Sappho was often nearby. That is why 'The Vow of the Peacock' is followed by a section of 'Classical Sketches', the first of which is 'Sappho'.[127] But Landon's most original poems on Petrarch are the first and the last, 'Vaucluse' and 'Petrarch's Dream'. 'Vaucluse' (1820) describes the River Sorgue and the local valley drawing on the River Alph and the landscape of Coleridge's 'Kubla Khan'. 'Tall rocks begirt the lovely valley', making it a gloomy place where:

> An angry river came; at first it traced
> Its course in wrath, and the dark cavern rang
> With echoes to its hoarse and sullen roar;
> But when it reach'd the peaceful valley, then,
> Like woman's smile soothing wild rage away,
> The sunlight fell upon its troubled waves –
> It made the waters, like a curbed steed,
> Chafed and foamed angrily but softly flowed,
> A bright unbroken mirror, for the kiss
> Of the fair children of its fragrant banks,
> And close beside uprose the tree whose form
> Had once been beauty's refuge – sacred shade!
> Which even the lightning dares not violate,
> The hero's trophy and the bard's reward –
> The faded laurel –
> Vaucluse! Thou hast a melancholy charm,
> A sweet remembrance of departed time,
> When love awoke the lyre from its long sleep,

> Unbound the golden wings of poetry,
> And in thy groves the graceful Petrarch sought
> A shelter where his soul might wander free,
> Dwelling on tender thoughts and minstrel dreams,
> All that the bard can feel in solitude.
> Thy name is in his song, and it will be
> Remembered, when thy woods shall wave no more.[128]

Landon's reading is extraordinary because it links two places and traditions which seem to have nothing in common. Her allusion to a demonic element in Petrarch's story makes 'Vaucluse' the most Romantic re-writing of Petrarch. The poem suggests that a disturbing, uncontrolled element exists both in the relationship between Laura and Petrarch and in poetry-writing, though sunlight, 'like woman's smile', eventually calmed it down.

The landscape of Vaucluse must have had a special meaning to Landon, since she returned to it in 1836 with 'Petrarch's Dream', the opening text of the uncollected *Subjects for Paintings*. The poem is the first illustration of a principle introduced by the motto, which argues that the imagination makes ancient names and stories more real than the present time. 'Petrarch's Dream', in fact, is a reflection on the power and meaning of poetry. As in 'Vaucluse', the starting point is the Sorgue, a real and symbolic river which flows from a laurel grove where Petrarch creates all that can escape the grave: 'Fame, song, and love' (Stanza I). Petrarch leaves his 'feverish bed' and falls asleep where the laurels shed dew 'O'er his charmed sleep' (St. II). His passion has left its mark on him, who is pale and has lines on his forehead, because 'We must feel to think' (St. III). He is haunted by the vanity of his enterprise, as poets struggle to win learning and love, which are ultimately void, and song, whose core is the poet's 'innermost despair' (St. IV). This darkness is effaced by an image drawn by the heart in a morning dream (St. V). It is a group of young people who warm up the air and make flowers spring up when they tread on them (St. VI). These youths are 'starry Spirits', who 'attend the radiant day' when the soul breaks away from 'the clay / Of its prison wall' (St. VII). One of them has got in her eyes a heavenly love which 'is too true to die' (St. VIII). It is an angel look that 'purified the earthly leaven / Of a beating heart. / She has breathed of hope and love, / As they warm the world above; – / She must now depart' (St. IX). Love has power even 'at the spirit's dying hour', sharing its immortal dower and 'Mastering its doom: / For that fair and mystic dream / By the Sorgia's [sic] hallowed stream, / Kindled from the tomb' (St. X).[129]

Landon's use of Petrarch confirms some of the main trends that have emerged in this research. Like many of her contemporaries, Landon found Petrarch an ideal character for speculating on the philosophy of writing. After 'Vaucluse', 'Petrarch's Dream' is another text where Landon, like Coleridge in 'Kubla Khan', traced the sources of poetry to love, death and dreaming. And to poetry itself, of course, since the text describes a poet dreaming of poetry as

it gathers literary echoes ranging from Petrarch to Coleridge. Equally importantly, Landon's frequent association between Petrarch and Sappho shows
that women poets did not consider women as their only precursors. Divid-
ing 'grandmothers' from 'grandfathers', focusing only on women writers as
models for women, writing on Sappho as the only relevant myth for women
poets is an ideological simplification which leads to a partial – if not a fictional – history of literature. The range of interests and the variety of reading
of the Romantic women poets were richer and more nuanced than those of
their present-day exegetes.

One might think that Petrarch and Sappho were obvious names for a love
poet such as Landon, who must have been an isolated case in her time. However, sceptics can turn to Landon's female contemporaries, and they will find
out that all of them had a specific interest in Petrarch. This is not surprising
in a time of raging 'sonnettomania', as an 1821 article in *The New Monthly
Magazine* called the enduring popularity of the form.[130] Even Felicia Hemans,
the singer of domestic love and politico-historical romances, translated two
of Petrarch's sonnets and cited him several times in her poems.[131] However,
the most intriguing example is Elizabeth Cobbold's 'Sonnets of Laura', which
appeared in her *Poems* (1825).

Cobbold drew on a popular point of Petrarch's biography, the debated question of Laura's tomb and the sonnet found in it. Rather than a sonnet of
Petrarch, Cobbold found three sonnets of Laura, who at last was given right
of word.[132] The first sonnet, 'Reproach', was probably inspired by a passage of
Petrarch's *Triumphs*, and it shows us Laura in love with Petrarch rather than
the usual beauty devoid of feelings.[133] In the sonnet she argues that Petrarch
has 'little cause' to complain (l. 1), as he 'boasts his wound' and 'vaunts the
smart', whereas she is struggling to conceal her pain 'Derived from silence
and a bursting heart' (l. 4). She does cherish Petrarch and his poems to her,
but 'this avowal meets no human ear' (l. 6), nor does anyone see her in pain
(ll. 7–8). In other words, Petrarch's wooing cannot be answered because she is
a married woman, who is compelled to suffer in silence and to wear a mask of
indifference (l. 11). As the final couplet argues, 'The world shall sympathize
with Petrarch's woe, / While night and silence only Laura know.' Petrarch,
who as a male was allowed to speak, could at least take advantage of a tragic
amorous situation; her grief was more terrible because it could not be told
to anyone. Laura was denied both the consolation of literary fame, however
vane, and the therapeutic power of speech.

Sonnet II, 'The Veil', is a direct answer to Petrarch's madrigal 'Lassare il
velo o per sole o per ombra' (*PC*, 11), where he complains that Laura never
shows him her face, which he is yearning to contemplate. Cobbold's Laura
praises her veil, which allows her to conceal her true feelings for Petrarch and
preserve her honour. However, her praise is ironic. 'The Veil that shades the
face obscures the mind, / And love is ever fearful to believe' (ll. 3–4), which
means that the respect of oppressive conventions is harmful both to her and

her beloved. Her 'unguarded smile', the pleasure she feels 'when you were nigh', and 'The tear of rapture' would otherwise tell 'a fond tale that you should never learn' (l. 9), that is, her fears, hopes and joys as a lover. Though oppressive, the veil is a protection against the uncertainty of passion, but also, given the existing social status of women, a 'Guard of my pride, my honour, and my fame'.

Sonnet III, 'Absence', touches on a central theme of the Petrarchan tradition, of which Cobbold's Laura, again, has an original opinion. She argues that her love is alive even when Petrarch is absent because it does not derive from the presence of his body, but from the quality of the sentiment he felt for her. It was 'that rich and ever varying mind, / With ev'ry just and gen'rous feeling fraught, / That ardent love, by sentiment refin'd, / That spoke in ev'ry look, and ev'ry thought' (ll. 9–12). A result of it was his poetry, which speaks for him even though he is looking for peace elsewhere (ll. 13–14).

Cobbold's sonnets are remarkable because they re-elaborate some crucial points of Petrarch's biography. Cobbold concentrated on Laura at a time when most poets neglected her and focused on Petrarch, a character who served their interests better. Thirty years after Robinson, Laura could speak again. While Robinson's Laura advised Petrarch to cultivate friendship rather than melancholy passion, Cobbold's Laura blamed him overtly. She told him that complaining about unrequited love was a luxury that she, as a woman, could not afford. She was forced to conceal both her body and her mind, but he should not have blamed her for that. He should have known better, if his love was as high as he claimed. True love, she argued in her last sonnet, can endure even without physical presence and need not turn into melancholy.

* * *

Though a discussion of Victorian Petrarch is beyond the scope of this book, it is worth remembering that English interest in *Canzoniere* and its author did not die out in the Romantic period. Despite the fact that other foreign poets, from Dante to Goethe, became more popular than Petrarch, the views analysed in this chapter continued to circulate almost unchanged throughout the Victorian age. This is evident in two influential anthologies of the 1870s, Charles Tomlinson's *The Sonnet* and David Main's *A Treasury of English Sonnets*. Tomlinson's anthology is an updated version of Lofft's. The preface contains a history of Italian sonnets, and it argues how and why they are better than English sonnets. Petrarch is described as the supreme master of the Italian sonnet. Milton's sonnets exerted scanty influence, and the true reviver of the form was Bowles. Tomlinson even argues that many of Wordsworth's sonnets are not sonnets. After this historical excursus, Tomlinson discusses the character of Petrarch's love and Laura's identity, taking Tytler's sides against Sade. The essay ends with a section of translations, which are meant as examples, since Tomlinson believed that Petrarch had made little impression on English readers because he had never been trans-lated properly.[134] In opposition to Tomlinson, David Main's anthology is a proud expression of the self-sufficiency of the English sonnet tradition. In his long annotations, Main ignores the question of foreign influence and con-structs a history which climaxes in Wordsworth, whose sonnets are given more space than Shakespeare's.[135] In short, Tomlinson and Main are the Vic-torian metamorphoses of one of the central themes of our story, the diatribe between the supporters of regularity and irregularity in the sonnet form.

The Victorian period was a golden age of the love sonnet, and Petrarch played a relevant part in it. Too much credit has been given to the opinions of critics like Macaulay, who in 1830 argued that the loves of Petrarch and Rousseau had become outdated, uninteresting and even ridiculous.[136] This kind of view, based on Byron's and Wordsworth's interpretations of Petrarch, was by no means dominant. Writers such as Staël, Landon and Cobbold handed over to their Victorian successors an interest in Petrarch, Laura and the sonnet which bore extraordinary fruit. Elizabeth Barrett Browning's and Christina Rossetti's revisions of the love sonnet tradition was anticipated, both in form and content, by the women poets discussed in the previous chapters.[137] The differences are due to Barrett's and Christina's greater talent and deeper knowledge of the Italian and English sonnet traditions, which had become available thanks to all the critics, translators and imitators discussed in this book.

The novelty of Barrett's *Sonnets from the Portuguese* and their importance in the history of women's poetry have been assessed firmly. Coming to her son-nets at the end of this book, one is struck by their boldness. However, recent criticism has often blamed them for not breaking radically with the Petrar-chan and courtly tradition.[138] Unfortunately, the myth of the 'radical break' – an academic application of avant-garde principles – has obscured the import of Barrett's gesture. Reviving the love sonnet as she did was, among other things, a challenge to Wordsworth and Byron who, with the help of critics like Macaulay, were becoming the arbiters of contemporary taste. Barrett's early view of Petrarch was identical to Macaulay's,[139] but eventually, even before meeting Robert, she retraced her footsteps and began to reread and translate Petrarch.[140]

In reviving the Petrarchan conventions, Barrett made several important points.[141] First of all, she argued that women must have a say in traditional love poetry. It was suspicious that the two most influential male poets of her time were in such a hurry to lay that tradition aside, when women poets were just beginning to reread it.[142] Barrett was strong enough to profit from Wordsworth and Byron without accepting their views uncritically. Like Mary Robinson, she understood that the love sonnet tradition could neither be ignored (Wordsworth) nor ridiculed (Byron). Women poets had to go across it, if they wanted to reshape the image of the ideal woman and the rela-tion between the sexes. Her reinterpretation of the love sonnet sequence was an epoch-making innovation. She did not simply swap the characters' roles, turning the woman into the lyric 'I' and the man into the object of her passion, which would have been predictable. She redoubled those roles, blurring the distance between subject and object, and making each actor play both Petrarch's and Laura's parts.

However, even such complicated masks were not enough. The sentimental autobiography of a woman poet remained a problem, and not only for the conservatives outside the literary milieu. For example, Barrett's sonnets made her husband so uneasy that he advised her to pretend that they were translated from the Portuguese. Translation and rewriting became one and the same thing in the sonnet cycles of the two best women poets of the Victorian age, who carried to extremes poetic modes of great importance for their eighteenth-century precursors. As Marjorie Stone has argued, 'the translation trope is a revisionary strategy serving similar ends' in both *Sonnets from the Portuguese* and *Monna Innominata*. It allowed them to express their inmost feelings 'without sacrificing the appearance of modesty'. It reflected the difficulty of communication between lovers, which is showed by the fact that the Brownings used Greek and Christina Italian as private, intimate languages.[143] Finally, they were two women translating the tradition of love poetry, which had been dominated by men, into a feminine language.[144]

Sonnets from the Portuguese answered another question raised by the eighteenth-century revival of the sonnet, that is, metrics. Barrett's sequence is innovative also in this field, which may sound strange considering that the rhyme scheme of its sonnets is simple and regular: *abba abba cdcdcd*. Besides Barrett, only Meredith used a constant, regular form for a long sonnet sequence. Barrett's gesture must have been intentional after a century of discussion on the sonnet form. She wanted to show that the renewal of the tradition was not a formal issue, but it depended on the poet's perspective. It was a question of vision rather than mere form. One could use a single, Petrarchan rhyme scheme and renew the love sonnet tradition. Also, she demonstrated once and for all that the regular Italian sonnet was suited to the English language.

A household where no one ever doubted that Italian forms could be used in English was that of the Rossettis. Though it may sound odd, Dante Gabriel continued the work begun by Byron and Wordsworth, in part as an answer to Barrett's sonnets. Dante Gabriel replaced Petrarch with Dante and the early Italian poets as models for love poetry, but his *House of Life* shows that they were not viable models in the nineteenth century.[145] Though his work has always been described as a monument of Victorian Dantism, its spirit is strikingly un-Dantesque. Rossetti took from Dante many stylistic and rhetorical devices, from allegory to imagery; however, Dante's metaphysics of love proved to be untranslatable. Like other Victorians, Rossetti was looking for an antidote to the fragmentation of the self brought about by the decline of religion. Rossetti turned to Dante not only for aesthetic reasons. He knew that Petrarch was the first poet whose central theme was the fragmentation of the self. Time, change, anxiety and uncertainty abound in *Canzoniere* despite its unified, religious structure. The certainties of Dante's metaphysics of love seemed to Rossetti to be a good solution but, eventually, he found out that it was an illusion. Dante's philosophy of love could not exist outside its theological framework, which remained beyond the reach of the Victorians, with the exception of Rossetti's sister and Hopkins. Petrarch was perhaps an unlikely model for love poetry; Dante was an impossible one. *The House of Life*, a poem of mutability and ghastly fragmentation, shows that it was infinitely more difficult to re-write *Vita nova* than *Canzoniere*. Rossetti's use of allegory often feels like a method for covering up his private life, which was morally dubious by Victorian standards, rather than the technical imagery of a philosophy of love, as was with the early Italian poets. Allegory makes sense as an objective code if it refers to a system of values and beliefs shared by a group of poets. If it is the private vocabulary of a single writer, object-iveness leaves room to subjectiveness, metaphysics to psychology, Dante to Petrarch.[146]

Christina Rossetti's personality was far more Dantean than that of his brother. However, if Dante Gabriel contrasted Dante and the early Ital-ian poets with Petrarch and Petrarchism, Christina understood that, for a woman, they were two sides of the same tradition, which had created the images of the ideal woman and the conventions of ideal love. Christina's reinterpretation of them in *Monna Innominata* was the climax of a lifelong involvement in the sonnet, both Italian and English, which began in 1857 with a surprising entry on Petrarch she wrote for John Francis Waller's *Imperial Dictionary of Universal Biography*. The entry contains a biographic outline of Petrarch and, as a conclusion, a discussion of Laura's identity – the only point developed after the chronological sequence of events of Petrarch's life. Christina endorses Sade's thesis, and adds that Laura 'was, in fact, my own ancestress, as family documents prove'. She recalls that there are other hypotheses, and mentions Tytler's essay.[147] She records that some scholars noted the inaccuracies of Petrarch's chronology of his encounter with Laura on 6 April 1321, which was a Monday rather than Good Friday. Christina, however, was one of those who preferred 'a flesh and blood Laura to a mysterious impersonation'.[148]

Though Christina rejected her father's reading of Beatrice and Laura as political allegories, she inherited a pinch of his talent for forgery. Even Jan Marsh, Christina's biographer, wondered why she chose to make public the odd claim that she was Laura's descendant.[149] After following the long debate on Petrarch which originated in Sade and Tytler, we are now in a better pos-ition to understand the meaning of Christina's gesture. Like Mary Robinson, Christina decided to wear the mask of the descendant of a character who caused much gossip over the centuries. Whereas Robinson used Laura to ennoble her own role as a mistress of the Prince of Wales, Christina was interested in other aspects of Laura's image. Her strategy was perfected in *Monna Innominata*, after further reading and writing in the sonnet tradition.

In the late 1870s, Christina helped Charles Cayley complete his edition of *Canzoniere*.[150] As Jan Marsh points out, she corrected his translations, which were later echoed in some lines of *Monna Innominata*. As Cayley was more than a friend to Christina, Petrarch found himself, yet once more, in the position of Byron's 'Platonic pimp', even though he was unsuccessful in their case. In the same period, Christina attended Tomlinson's lectures on Dante at UCL. She also read Tomlinson's sonnets, original and translated, and his essay on the sonnet.[151] Finally, she and Dante Gabriel gave Main's *Treasury of English Sonnets* as a present to their mother on her eightieth birthday.[152] She wrote a dedicatory sonnet to her, in which she argued that 'sonnets are full of love'. It is clear that Christina was not interested in the displacement of the sonnet tradition enacted by Wordsworth, Byron and the other male Romantics mentioned above. This does not mean, however, that she turned to the love sonnet uncritically. Her dedicatory sonnet contains the core of her view.[153] It is addressed to her Mother, 'on whose knee / I learnt love-lore that is not troublesome' (ll. 5–6). This could be either domestic or religious love; in any case, it was the opposite of the problematic love she eschewed, that is, love for a man. This attitude was illustrated in detail in *Monna Innominata*.

This sonnet sequence is preceded by an introductory note which Christina clarified in a letter to his brother. She wrote that her observations on Barrett's *Sonnets from the Portuguese* in her preface to *Monna Innominata* had been misunderstood. Christina meant that, had Barrett worn the mask of a 'donna innominata', her sonnet sequence would have been unsurpassable. 'The Lady in question, as she actually stands, I was not regarding as an "innominata" at all, – because the latter type, according to the traditional figures I had in view, is surrounded by unlike circumstances.'[154] Barrett's sonnets cycle would have been more powerful had its story been 'surrounded by unlike circumstances', that is, the miraculous coincidences and impossible situations of many sonnet cycles. Most of them were stories of frustrated or impossible love. They had no happy end, which, as Isobel Armstrong argued, for a Victorian woman meant marriage.[155] With the exception of Spenser, the sonnet cycles of 'traditional figures' never ended up in marriage. Rather, they developed outside and against marriage, from Dante and Petrarch to Shakespeare. The 'traditional figures' Christina had in mind were 'a bevy of unnamed ladies, "donne innominate"', sung by the Troubadours, who could not answer the poems which celebrated them.[156] Christina's observation is intriguing despite its partial inaccuracy, because some poems of female Troubadours have come down to us, as she knew.[157] In the previous paragraph she argued that famous ladies, such as Beatrice and Laura, are unattractive because Dante and Petrarch, 'a great though an inferior bard', have made them too perfect and aloof.

It is noteworthy that Christina chose to identify with a mistress of medieval Provence or Italy rather than Renaissance Italy.[158] She was probably thinking of a *trobairitz* or a *stilnovo* poetess, just as her precursors were intrigued by Giustina Levi-Perotti. I believe that Christina's ambiguity was intentional. Although the Troubadours idealised their lovers, they did not exclude sexuality from their relationships, unlike many of their Italian followers. Though Provençal relationships did not end up necessarily in physical intercourse, they are never read as merely allegoric or literary experiences, as has happened with Dante's and Petrarch's loves. For this reason Christina wrote that, had one of those Provençal ladies spoken for herself, 'the portrait left us might have appeared more tender, if less dignified, than any drawn even by a devoted friend.'[159] Christina did not want to exclude idealisation completely from love poetry, but, at the same time, she rejected the excessive idealisation characteristic of the love sonnet tradition, which turned lovers into lifeless statues or allegories, as did her father. In this sense, there was no difference between Dante and Petrarch. But, despite her mask as a *trobairitz*, the poetic form she employed was the sonnet, which did not exist in medieval Provence. It was the main form of the love poetry that developed out of Provençal poetry. Therefore, *Monna Innominata* appears as an ambitious rereading of the mainstream love poetry from the Middle Ages to the nineteenth century. After all, the subtitle of *Monna Innominata* was *A Sonnet of Sonnets*, that is, the essence of love-sonnet writing.

Christina described a relationship in verse where 'the barrier between' the lovers 'might be one held sacred by both, yet not such as to render mutual love incompatible with mutual honour'.[160] Though Christina assumed a specifically female perspective on her theme, the basic problem she was facing was the same one discussed in all the essays on Petrarch and Laura analysed so far: how could passion and honourable behaviour coexist? We have seen that most critics writing on Petrarch answered that they could not. Christina subscribed to the same opinion, though from a new point of view.

Christina's insistence that the greatest love poetry can be written only out of unhappiness makes the perspective of *Monna Innominata* different, and probably more conservative, than that of *Sonnets from the Portuguese*.[161] The programmatic distortion of Dante and Petrarch, whose sonnets have furnished the mottos for Christina's texts, only serves to reconfirm their views, that sentimental fulfilment on earth is impossible. It can only be sublimated into an allegory, or deferred to the otherworld after death. Its trajectory from earthly to heavenly love repeats, in a more rapid and radical form, that of Petrarch's *Canzoniere* and Dante's *Comedy*, which had been reversed in Dante Gabriel's and Barrett's sonnet sequences. I agree with Marjorie Stone that Christina's poem partly takes up and partly opposes both her ancient and immediate precursors.[162] *Monna Innominata* turns upside-down some central *topoi* of the traditional sonnet cycles, but it suggests that the only way of getting rid of them is refusal. Christina's disillusioned parody stems from the nihilistic suppression of her feelings, and it preaches self-denial. The revision of the tradition offered by *Sonnets from the Portuguese* is formally less aggressive, but ideologically more radical than that of *Monna Innominata*.

However, there is another poem where Christina disfigured the tradition even more: *Goblin Market*. D. M. R. Bentley has noted that the protagonists' names, Laura and Lizzie, gesture 'in directions that are both similar and different – Laura towards Petrarchan love (the love of a sanctified woman) and Lizzie's – that is, Elizabeth's (meaning the oath of God) – towards Saint Elizabeth of Hungary', who was the subject of other poems of Christina's.[163] Though I have not noticed specific references, it can hardly be a coincidence that the name of a protagonist is Laura. Christina was too aware of the Italian tradition to use it at random, especially in a period when she had just written her entry on Petrarch for the *Imperial Dictionary of Universal Biography*.[164] Since we are now aware of the way Laura was seen in Romantic and Victorian times, Bentley's insight can be taken a step further. Laura was not only 'a sanctified woman', but also a mistress with a debatable position in a notorious love affair. That is why Christina chose her name for the character who in her poem represents the fallen woman. The Laura of *Goblin Market* is the opposite extreme of an innocent interpretation of Petrarch's mistress. Petrarch's Laura is ethereal and has no body; Christina's Laura is disturbingly material – she is all body. In *Goblin Market*, Laura is the girl who probes the limits of conventions, whereas Lizzie embodies order. The literary echoes contained in Laura's name are continuously subverted by the orgiastic, uncontrolled behaviour of the protagonist of *Goblin Market*. At last, Laura is given back a physical life, but it is immature and almost disgusting.

Christina Rossetti furnishes a convenient conclusion to our story, because she is a sort of interface between the Romantic and the contemporary receptions of Petrarch. Though she was partly anticipated by poets such as Robinson, Cobbold and Barrett Browning, her response to Petrarch and Laura was dramatically different from theirs. The critical identification of the Romantics was replaced by her disfiguring refusal of the mainstream love-sonnet tradition. This attitude was taken up and radicalised even further by many poets – especially women – in the twentieth century. However, the anti-patriarchal readings of Anne Sexton, Sylvia Plath, Amelia Rosselli and many others is not the only recent approach to the Petrarchan legacy. Another influential trend, running from Mallarmé to Ungaretti, Celan and beyond, is there to remind us that Petrarch's presence in contemporary poetry is more relevant than most readers would allow. Petrarca is indeed in sight, though it would be naïve to believe that our sight is more impartial and unprejudiced than the Romantic-era fascination with the romance of Petrarch and Laura.

Notes

Introduction

1. The examples are numerous; see, e.g., Anna Seward, who found *Inferno* tedious, horrifying and morally useless (Seward 1936, 31 and 289–90).
2. Gardini 2001, 23.
3. Stanton 1987, 393 and 396.
4. Figures remained between 40 and 70 up to 1834. Before 1808 the number was always below 40. See the interesting graph of books published by women per year in Jackson 1993, 394.
5. Curran 1988, 188; see also Mellor 1993, 7.
6. The same can be said of Milton's role in the revival of the sonnet. Even R. D. Havens, who minimised the Italian and Petrarchan element in the revival, acknowledged that 'the main influence was certainly Italian.' In spite of this, Havens believed that the sonnets of Hayley, C. Smith, Mary Robinson and others who used the form freely gave no evidence of Italian influence. Havens's view of these authors and the Della Cruscans belongs to the disparaging trend initiated by Gifford (Havens 1922, 491 and 503–5).
7. Foscolo 1953a, 153.
8. Fontenelle 1773a and 1773b; Fontenelle n.d., 45–50 ('Dialogue II. Sapho, Laure'). Part I of the work appeared in 1683, Part II in 1684; 'Sapho, Laure' comes from part I. The Macaroni Club in London was an association of well-travelled young men who shared an interest in foreign food and fashions. A Macaroni could be an ironic epithet for anyone with dandyish and eccentric tastes.
9. Fontenelle 1773a, 31.
10. Fontenelle 1773a, 32.
11. Fontenelle 1773b, 54. This part of the dialogue contains many Petrarchan ideas.
12. From this point to the conclusion, the translator broke down Laura's last intervention into small parts, adding in comments to each of them.
13. Fontenelle 1773b, 54.
14. This was entirely added by the translator.
15. Fontenelle 1773b, 55.

1 Writing the Biography of Petrarch: From Susanna Dobson (1775) to the Romantics

1. Foscolo 1953a, 153 (the concept is reiterated on p. 155). He also criticised the absurdity of some translations which strayed from the original (Foscolo 1953b, 119).
2. Sade was aware that his work was sensational, as he published it without his name and with a false place of publication (the real one was apparently Avignon). The Abbé was the affectionate uncle of the Marquis de Sade, who knew the *Mémoires* and in jail had a dream of Laura, based on a passage of Petrarch's *Triumph of Death*, which remains a famous episode in his life (see Hayes 2000, 119, 128, 134). Together with Voltaire and Rousseau, Sade was the only French scholar who wrote on Petrarch to find an audience in England. His work was received better

in England and Italy than in France. However, though some magazines reviewed and recommended each volume of his essay, it was known only to a handful of erudite readers before 1775, when Dobson's translation was published. Her translation was hailed as a major event in all magazines, which commended it without exception. Some of them reprinted long excerpts, while others extracted a series of articles from it (Mouret 1976, 22, 26–9, 151–3, 301).

3. Evidence and documents, reproduced mainly in the Appendix to vol. I of Sade's *Mémoires*, were destroyed during the French Revolution. Laura's identity remains an open question, though her identification with Laura de Sade is considered plausible today. See the two major biographies of Petrarch (Wilkins 1985; Dotti 1987), Jones 1984 and, above all, Jones 1992.

4. *Mémoires* I, 127–8.

5. 'Aux François amateurs de la poésie e des belles-lettres', *Mémoires* I, xcvii–xcviii.

6. *Mémoires* I, 81, 86.

7. According to Dobson, it was 'clearly proved' (a phrase not in Sade) that Laura was married. Sade was right; it was the other scholars who fictionalised Petrarch's life (*Life* I, 39–40). Dobson also mentioned Laura's will and contract of marriage, which were kept in Sade's house (*Life* I, xxvi–xxvii).

8. *Mémoires* I, cxii–cxiii.

9. *Mémoires* III, 609–12.

10. *Life* I, xxii–xxiii, which are a sort of paraphrase of *Mémoires* I, xcvii–xcviii. Besides inspiring many British poets, the view of Petrarch as a man of feeling found an interesting echo in the *Encyclopædia Britannica*. The entry 'Petrarch' in the third edition summarises the main events of his life drawing on Gibbon and Dobson with extensive quotations. In the last paragraph Petrarch is compared with Sterne's Yorick. Both 'had great wit and genius, and no less imprudence and eccentricity; both were canons, or prebendaries'; both lived in France; both were familiar with bishops. 'In their attachments to Laura and Eliza, both married women, these two prebendaries were equally warm, and equally innocent.' After death, the bones of both Petrarch and Yorick – it was rumoured – were stolen, Petrarch's to be sold, whereas Yorick's skull was exhibited at Oxford (*EB* vol. 14).

11. *Life* II, 559.

12. *Life* II, 560.

13. *Life* I, xix. Three articles, made mostly of translated passages from Petrarch's poems, anticipated the core of the English interest, which concentrated on his love story and marginalised the rest. They were taken from Sade, as is showed by the French spelling of Petrarch and the repetition of some of his theses. The author of the articles, who signed the first as 'Lucia', only added some details, such as an excursion round Vaucluse when Laura met Petrarch and asked him, ' "have you ceased to love me?" ' (Lucia 1774b, 417). The articles end with Laura's death. See Lucia 1774a, 1774b, 1774c.

14. *Life* I, xx–xxi.

15. Sade pointed out that, in comparison to the classical love poets, Petrarch has been admired mainly for the delicacy and honesty of his passion, which was of a Platonic purity. 'Sa manière de traiter l'amour, lui donne encore un grand avantage sur les Anciens, c'est que *la Vierge la plus scrupuleuse peut le lire d'un bout à l'autre sans rougir.*' (The italicised phrase is by Francesco Panigarola, Bishop of Asti in the sixteenth century. *Mémoires* I, c–ci.) Analogously, Sade defended the *Decameron*, which was written in a very particular period, after the Black Death, and did not need to be censored later (*Mémoires* III, 609–12). He argued that it was

composed to entertain the fair sex, whereas Dobson more cautiously said that it was written as a *divertissement* (*Life* II, 421).

16. *Life* I, 33–4. When Dobson talked about Petrarch's son, she did not mention the fact that he was illegitimate (*Life* I, 386–7). This was part of her campaign to render the story morally suitable for her contemporaries.

17. *Life* I, 36–7: 'Her person was delicate, her eyes tender and sparkling, and her eyebrows black as ebony. Golden locks waved over her shoulders whiter than snow; and the ringlets were interwoven by the fingers of Love. Her neck was well formed, and her complexion animated by the tints of nature, which art vainly attempts to stimulate. [...] Nothing was so soft as her looks, so modest as her carriage, so touching the sound of her voice. An air of gaiety and tenderness breathed around her, but so and happily tempered, as to inspire every beholder with the sentiments of virtue: for she was chaste as the spangled dew-drop of the morn.' Dobson's description, supposedly the first impression Laura made on Petrarch, is a patchwork of lines from his poems. Dobson only added the last sentence (from 'for she was chaste'; see *Mémoires* I, 122–3).

18. *Life* I, 118.

19. *Life* II, 421.

20. *Life* II, 419–20. This was Dobson's version. In fact, Sade only stated that eventually she went back to him, as he convinced her of his innocence (*Mémoires* I, 294–5).

21. Dobson 1807, 335–6. For Sade, see *Mémoires* I, 117–18, a passage omitted by Dobson.

22. Dobson 1807, 373–4.

23. *Life* I, 538.

24. *Life* I, 117.

25. *Life* II, 553–6. This section was entirely added by Dobson.

26. *Mémoires* I, 44 (Appendix); *Life* I, 289.

27. *Life* I, 421, which corresponds, with that characteristic interpolation, to *Mémoires* I, Appendix, Note VI. On his part, Sade argued that, out of sympathy with Laura, Petrarch too aged quickly (*Mémoires* II, 62–3).

28. *Mémoires* II, 68, which refers to Giovannini's *Li due petrarchisti* (Venice, 1623).

29. *Mémoires* III, 80 (Appendix, Note XXI, 'Sur la nature de l'amour de Pétrarque').

30. *Mémoires* I, 11. This part was omitted by Dobson.

31. *Life* I, xxix.

32. *Mémoires* I, cvii–cviii.

33. See, e.g., *Mémoires* I, 178 ff., on Petrarch's puns and sonnets on Laura/lauro; and *Mémoires* I, 182 for an extremely condensed version of *PC*, 148.

34. See Watson 1967, 41.

35. The complete text runs as follows (*Life* II, 159): 'Zephyr returns; he brings with him the mild season, the flowers, herbs, and grass, his dear children. Progne warbles, Philomela sighs, the heavens become serene, and the valleys smile. Love re-animates the air, the earth, and the sea: all creatures feel his sovereign power. But alas! this charming season can only renew my sighs! The melody of the birds, the splendour of the flowers, the charms of beauty, are in my eyes like the most gloomy deserts; for Laura is no more!' For Sade's version, *Mémoires* III, 209. See Chapter 2 in this volume for the Italian text and its English translation.

36. *Mémoirs* I, 189–90; *Life* I, 69–70. The passage is italicised in Sade; Dobson translated it closely.

37. Sade relied on Giacomo Filippo Tomasini's authority about the authenticity of the sonnet and its author (*Mémoires* I, 190). The story of Giustina Levi-Perotti is

symbolic for many women writers of the remote past. She was first published as a poet in the seventeenth century by Tomasini, whose authority was not questioned till the late nineteenth century, when several scholars – above all Medardo Morici – tried to demonstrate that she was a fictional figure. Recently, however, Giuseppe Perotti showed that Morici's archival research was incomplete, as there are many more written references to Giustina than Morici affirmed (Perotti 1999, 221–30). Giustina wrote other sonnets, one of which, on the decadence of the Avignon court, was sent to Pope Innocence VI while Cola di Rienzo was heading his *coup* in Rome.

38. *Life* I, 70.
39. She omitted 'de bonne heure' after 'Parnassus', turned 'l'immortalité' into 'the life' she desired, 'de m'y livrer' into 'to devote myself to them', and above all, left out 'qui ne veut pas que les femmes fassent des vers' after 'vulgar minds'.
40. *Life* I, 71. See Chapter 2 in this volume for the Italian text and its English translation.
41. *Mémoires* I, 191: 'La gourmandise & la paresse ont chassé du monde toutes les vertus. Tout est changé. Nous n'avons plus de lumiere qui nous guide. On montre au doigt un homme qui fait de vers. La vile populace qui ne songe qu'à gagner de l'argent, dit: a quoi bon couronner sa tête de myrte ou de laurier? La Philosophie est abandonnée, & va tout nue. O vous que le ciel a doué d'un esprit aimable! que ces propos ne vous rebutent pas! suivez la route que vous avez prise, quoiqu'elle soit peu fréquentée.' Sade and Dobson made the conclusion more emphatic and placed l. 11 (from 'the vile populace' to 'interest') near the middle of their versions.
42. *Mémoires* I, 191: 'Mais dans le fond le Sonnet de Justine ne vaut pas mieux que celui de Petrarque; & combien de fois a-t'on vu les femmes l'emporter sur les hommes, dans toutes les opérations de l'esprit, qui ne demandent que de la finesse & de l'agrément!' Sade argued that Petrarch wrote the sonnet using her rhymes rather than the opposite.
43. Sade noted that Petrarch never mentioned Laura's poems; in fact, he said that Laura 'non curò giammai rime né versi' ('never cared for rhyme or verse'). Besides, there is no Laura among the troubadours. *Mémoires* II, 471–2; *Life* I, 540. Sade, however, pointed out that Laura played an actively intellectual role towards Petrarch when she spurred him to cultivate his poetic talent instead of living for superficial pleasure, as he did as a young man (*Mémoires* I, 116).
44. In 1780 Dobson told Fanny Burney that she earned the remarkable sum of £400 with her *Life* (Burney 1904–05, I, 369).
45. Volume 3 (1781) of Warton's *History* contains a long section on the *Divine Comedy*, whereas his comments on *Canzoniere* were brief. He emphasised the debt of Petrarch's love poetry to the troubadours, even though he believed that Petrarch, 'inspired with the most elegant of passions, and cloathing his exalted feelings on that delicate subject in the most melodious and brilliant versification, had totally eclipsed the barbarous beauties of the Provencial [*sic*] troubadours' (Warton 1998, I, 463; II, 409–10). However, Warton disliked the Metaphysical element in Petrarch, who 'would have been a better poet had he been a worse scholar' (Warton 1998, III, 12). Sade was Warton's main source on Petrarch.
46. Gibbon drew on Sade extensively in the section on Petrarch, though he noted that in *Mémoires* Petrarch's life was often lost in a sea of historical details (Gibbon 1996, II, 784 n. 1).
47. *The Decline and Fall* was published between 1776 and 1788. The last three volumes, where he discussed Petrarch, appeared in 1788.

48. Gibbon 1996, II, 479, 523–5, 582. Gibbon remarked that Petrarch's celebrated attack on the viciousness of Avignon was beside the mark, since the problem was not due the place but to the Papal court (Gibbon 1996, 582). Petrarch was cited again in the conclusion of the book, when Gibbon pointed out that the Romans themselves, rather than foreigners, were the main cause of the decline of Rome (Gibbon 1996, II, 595).

49. Gibbon 1996, II, 573 and notes. In particular, Gibbon warned the reader against the Romantic idealisation of Vaucluse, which was a retreat for hermits rather than a picturesque grotto for two lovers (Gibbon 1996, 784 n. 5).

50. Gibbon 1996, II, 573 and 785 n. 12.

51. Gibbon 1996, II, 573–5.

52. Another, minor figure who drew on Sade and Dobson was Thomas Penrose, who also used Baretti, the two Wartons, and some French and Italian scholars as sources for Penrose 1790. This hackneyed essay, which appeared without its author's name, testifies to an ever-increasing public interest in the life of Petrarch in the late eighteenth century.

53. Tytler 1810, dedicated to T. J. Mathias, was reprinted in 1812. Tytler stated that some Italian friends spurred him to publish it to correct some common errors in Petrarch biographies (Tytler 1810, vi–vii). An intermediate version of the essay, based on a lecture he gave in 1797, appeared in 1805 (see Mouret 1976, 331).

54. Tytler 1810, 4–5.

55. Tytler 1810, 47–8.

56. Tytler 1810, 54 note. To refute Sade, Tytler drew especially on an influential reprint of Castelvetro's edition of Petrarch's poems (Venice, 1756).

57. In Tytler 1784 his confutation of Sade's evidence for Laura's marriage was contained in a long note on pp. 24–39. In Tytler 1810 (pp. 59, 84–5, 89–94) he also talked of the conjectural discovery of Laura's tomb in Avignon in the sixteenth century, which he believed was not hers. Two other famous documents were for him forgeries: a sonnet found in Laura's tomb, and a marginal note on Laura's death in Petrarch's Virgil, which contradicted many passages in Petrarch's letters and poems. He also questioned Sade's reading of an abbreviation in a letter where Petrarch talked of Laura's 'crebris partubus' or, since the last word was abbreviated, 'perturbationibus' (i.e., that she was tormented by her passions, which Sade thought impossible as she was a virtuous woman; see *Mémoires* I, Appendix, Note II). Tytler preferred the latter to the former interpretation (Tytler 1810, 135–77), even though the news that Laura was worn out by her several deliveries came directly from Petrarch, who talked about it in his *Secretum* (see Dotti 1987, 57).

58. Tytler 1810, 119 ff.

59. Tytler 1810, 128–9.

60. Tytler 1810, 130–3.

61. Tytler 1810, 134–5.

62. Tytler 1810, 161–3.

63. Tytler 1810, 206–10. One such poem is *PC*, 237.

64. The idea that Petrarch's passion was mere fiction goes back to his friend Giacomo Colonna, who asked him whether Laura really existed. Petrarch answered in a letter that Laura and his passion were all too real (Wilkins 1985, 23). Some major scholars, probably influenced by the formalism of the mid-twentieth century, still believe that Laura is a fictional figure invented by Petrarch, among other things, to cover up his illicit affairs with the women who bore him two children (see, e.g., Billanovich 2001, 82). I agree with Petrarch's major biographers, such as

Wilkins and Dotti, who never questioned the real existence of Laura. As F. J. Jones put it, Petrarch 'was fundamentally a realist, transfiguring and intensifying but not inventing his love-situations as he filtered them through memory' (Jones 1984, 45).

65.   Tytler 1784, 43–4. In Tytler 1810, this section was expanded and replaced by another one on the non-Platonic character of Petrarch's love.

66.   Tytler 1810, 16.

67.   Tytler 1810, 14. Tytler cited *PC*, 174, which he translated in the Appendix.

68.   Tytler 1810, 28.

69.   Tytler 1810, 194 ff., which includes passages from *PC*, 334, 347, 348, a part of 366, and a sonnet of Boccaccio for Petrarch, 'Or se' salito, caro Signor mio'.

70.   Tytler 1810, 34 and 36.

71.   Tytler 1810, 35. He referred in particular to *PC*, 292 and 300, which he translated in the Appendix as 'Those eyes' and 'O earth'.

72.   The form is mainly Shakespearean and sometimes Petrarchan or irregular. Occasionally he translated more literally, as in his version of *PC*, 162, 'O happy flowers' (Tytler 1810, 107–8). He did not draw on Sade for his versions.

73.   A good example is quatrain 2 (ll. 5–8) of 'Zephiro torna', 'Ridono i prati e 'l ciel si rasserena; / Giove s'allegra di mirar sua figlia; / l'aria et l'acqua et la terra è d'amor piena; / ogni animale d'amar si riconsiglia' ('the meadows laugh and the sky becomes clear again, Jupiter is gladdened looking at his daughter, the air and the waters and the earth are full of love, every animal takes counsel again to love', Petrarca 2001, 310): 'And thou, sweet Philomel, renew'st thy strain, / Breathing thy wild notes to the midnight grove: / All nature feels the kindling fire of love, / The vital force of spring's returning reign' (Tytler 1810, 265). L. 5 has been moved and paraphrased in l. 4 ('And tender green light-shadows o'er the plain'); 'Philomel' appears in l. 3 of the original together with 'Progne', whom Tytler omitted; 'sweet', 'Breathing', 'wild' and 'midnight groves' are not mentioned in the original; l. 6 was omitted, probably on account of its mythological and erotic content (Jove's daughter is Venus); l. 8 is a paraphrase of the original, which is sanitised by the scientific language employed by Tytler.

74.   Tytler 1810, 268–9.

75.   'You who hear in scattered rhymes the sound of those sighs with which I nourished my heart during my first youthful error, when I was in part another man from what I am now: // for the varied style in which I weep and speak between vain hopes and vain sorrow, where there is anyone who understands love through experience, I hope to find pity, not only pardon. // But now I see well how for a long time I was the talk of the crowd, for which often I am ashamed of myself within; // and of my raving, shame is the fruit, and repentance, and the clear knowledge that whatever pleases in the world is a brief dream.' (Petrarca 2001, 1) Unless otherwise indicated, all modern English translations of Petrarch's poems are taken from Petrarca 2001 (refs given by poem number).

76.   The irregular metrical scheme, the different position of some phrases, like those in l. 1 that correspond to the original l. 7, and other changes are not germane to our discussion.

77.   Eighteenth-century English translators found the stammering pun on 'me' in l. 11 particularly distasteful, since most of them paraphrased or omitted it.

78.   Tytler 1810, 269.

79.   See Tissoni 1993, 102–5. Zotti's translation of Tytler's essay is contained in vol. 3 of his edition.

80. *Histoire* II, ch. 12 deals with Petrarch.
81. *Histoire* II, 334–5 note.
82. *Histoire* II, 505.
83. *Histoire* II, 382.
84. Wilkins (1985, 35) points out that none of Petrarch's friends seems to have found the fact scandalous. In fact, at that time it was not unusual to have illegitimate children; rather, it was uncommon that they were raised and educated by their father, as Petrarch later did with his son (born 1337) and daughter (born 1343).
85. *Histoire* II, 303–4.
86. *Histoire* II, 500.
87. *Histoire* II, 489–90.
88. *Histoire* II, 502–3.
89. *Histoire* II, 566–7 note.
90. 'Solo et pensoso', which he quoted with a verse translation, was the most moving of his sonnets. Another excellent text was 'Di pensier in pensier', which he partially translated (*Histoire* II, 508–9, 523). Other prose and verse translations were included in his essay. Also, he paraphrased sonnets to describe some episodes of Petrarch and Laura's love, though he was concise on some popular points such as their first encounter, which most scholars described profusely.
91. *Histoire* II, 519. Following the classicist tradition, he mentioned the so-called 'three sisters' (*PC*, 71, 72, 73) as poems in the purest Italian (*Histoire* II 525).
92. *Histoire* II, 534, 540. 'Levòmmi il mio pensiero' was even better than 'Solo et pensoso'.
93. *Histoire* II, 553 ff.
94. Sismondi 1819, I, 430, and Sismondi 1818, V, 292.
95. Sismondi 1818, V, 292.
96. Sismondi 1819, I, 409–10. Sismondi cited *PC*, 1 to show that Petrarch himself was not so keen on his Italian poems. None the less, Sismondi believed that Petrarch turned Italian into a language as polished as Greek and Latin (Sismondi 1819, I, 431).
97. Sismondi 1819, I, 427.
98. Sismondi 1819, I, 408; Sismondi 1818, V, 296.
99. Sismondi 1818, V, 298. *Canzoni* were longer than their original models, the Provençal *chansons*, and what they gained in speculative complexity they lost in liveliness. Sismondi translated 'O aspectata in ciel', the best of Petrarch's poems and the closest to the strength of classical poetry (Sismondi 1819, I, 422–3).
100. Sismondi 1819, I, 413, 431. Besides Sade, Sismondi referred to Ginguené.
101. Sismondi 1819, I, 414–15. Sismondi included the translations of some poems (pp. 416 ff.): *PC*, 16, 19, 90 (in verse), 292, 320.
102. Sismondi 1819, I, 428–9.
103. Hallam 1818, II, 509. Hallam drew on Sade, as his notes show.
104. Hallam 1818, II, 600–1. On Cola di Rienzo see also Hallam 1818, I, 297 note.
105. Hallam 1818, II, 601, where he also recalled the *vexata quaestio* of Laura's 'partubus' or 'perturbationibus'. Hallam did not go into it, but he found Sade's solution the most convincing.
106. Hallam 1818, II, 602.
107. Hallam 1818, II, 601–2.
108. Hallam 1818, II, 603.

109. Hallam 1818, II, 603.
110. In 1825 he wrote to Landor (Rome, 9 April): 'I bought a little Florentine edition of Petrarch and Dante the other day, and have made out one page' (cited in Howe 1947, 344). His critical remarks on Petrarch were published long before this late attempt at the Italian language. Interestingly, Howe believed that the translations included in Hazlitt's review of Sismondi may have been done by Leigh Hunt (Howe 1947, 167; and 'Sismondi's Literature of the South', in Hazlitt 1931–34, XVI, 421–2 notes).
111. 'Sismondi's Literature of the South' (Hazlitt 1931–34, XVI, 24, 31).
112. Hazlitt 1931–34, XVI, 32, 35.
113. Sismondi believed that Dante was neither pure nor correct, but he was a creator (Hazlitt 1931–34, XVI, 41–2). Hazlitt read Dante, 'the father of modern poetry' (Hazlitt 1931–34, V, 17), in Boyd's version (Hazlitt 1931–34, XVI, 422). He also discussed Dante in his *Lectures on the English Poets*.
114. 'Sismondi's Literature of the South' (Hazlitt 1931–34, XVI, 43).
115. Hazlitt 1931–34, XVI, 43.
116. Hazlitt 1931–34, XVI, 44.
117. Hazlitt 1931–34, VI, 186, 299.
118. Hazlitt 1931–34, VI, 298–9.
119. The poems he cited were 'I know that all beneath the moon' and 'Fair moon, who thy cold' (Lecture VI of *Lectures on the Dramatic Literature of the Age of Elizabeth* (1820), Hazlitt 1931–34, VI, 299).
120. Hazlitt 1931–34, VI, 300–1.
121. 'On Milton's Sonnets', Essay 28 of *Table Talk* (1821) (Hazlitt 1931–34, VIII, 174).
122. Hazlitt 1931–34, VIII, 175.
123. Hazlitt 1931–34, VIII, 176. There was at least one exception to Hazlitt's dislike of contemporary sonnets, as he wrote that W. L. Bowles was an excellent sonneteer. Incidentally, in the same essay he said that his favourite passage in Byron's *Childe Harold's Pilgrimage* was the description of Petrarch's tomb. See 'Pope, Lord Byron, and Mr. Bowles' (1821) (Hazlitt 1931–34, XIX, 69); and 'Childe Harold's Pilgrimage' (1818) (Hazlitt 1931–34, XIX, 38–9).
124. Hazlitt 1931–34, XVII, 204.
125. Hazlitt 1979, 233–4 (Feb. or early March 1822).
126. 'On the Disadvantages of Intellectual Superiority', in *Table Talk* (1821) (Hazlitt 1931–34, VIII, 280); the correct phrase is 'singular da l'altra gente' (*PC*, 292). The general principle he wanted to affirm in his essay was that it is better to be neither above nor beneath average intelligence. In his review of Sismondi, Hazlitt mentioned Petrarch's Latin poetry and scholarly works in a long quotation, probably because he knew little about them ('Sismondi's Literature of the South', Hazlitt 1931–34, XVI, 44).
127. Hazlitt 1931–34, VIII, 45.
128. 'On Manner', in *The Round Table* (1817) (Hazlitt 1931–34, V, 45–6). The essay was originally published in *The Examiner* (3 Sept. 1815) without the paragraph 'Grace has been defined [...] Arabian Nights' and without the polemical note on Wordsworth. The 1815 version contained another long, more generic note omitted in 1817.
129. See Butler 1984; Fulford 1999, especially pp. 233–41.
130. See, e.g., Hazlitt 1931–34, IX, 162 (*Liber Amoris: Or, The New Pygmalion*).
131. Foligno, Introduction to Foscolo 1953b, xxi.
132. Foligno, Introduction to Foscolo 1953b, xxv.

133. Foligno, Introduction to Foscolo 1953b, xxix. Gifford suppressed the initial passages on love in ancient Greece, which were too lascivious, a lyrical description of Vaucluse, and a section on the prevalence of political feelings over personal gratitude in Petrarch.
134. Foligno, Introduction to Foscolo 1953b, xxxi. Sade and Dobson seem to have been the most important sources.
135. Foscolo 1953a, 153, 156–7. Foscolo pointed out that Sade made many discoveries about Petrarch and his time, but he was not a professional scholar and naively presented several well-known facts as novelties. He ignored some of Petrarch's crucial essays while he spent too much time on the sonnets, which he wisely did not analyse, since his translations show that he did not understand their style.
136. Foscolo 1953a, 158–9. Foscolo pointed out that, however reluctantly, Italian scholars agreed with the core of Sade's argument.
137. Foscolo 1953a, 159–62. These strictures were omitted in the version of the essay published in the *Quarterly Review* and in volume.
138. However mediocre, Mme de Genlis sometimes succeeded in creating lively fictions out of some episodes in Petrarch's life, such as his famous first meeting with Laura. In general, Mme de Genlis attributed to Petrarch 'those qualities chiefly which she fancies she herself has in common with him'. Foscolo 1953a, 163–5.
139. Foscolo 1953a, 160–2.
140. Foscolo 1953a, 166.
141. Foscolo 1953b, 5–6.
142. 'Dalle Appendici' (Foscolo 1953b, 141).
143. Foscolo 1953b, 12.
144. The letter is dated 3 Feb. 1821 (Foligno, Introduction to Foscolo 1953b, xxxiv).
145. Foscolo 1953b, 30–1, 33.
146. Foscolo 1953b, 39–43.
147. Foscolo 1953b, 41.
148. Foscolo 1953b, 45–7.
149. Foscolo 1953b, 48–9. See Chapter 2 in this volume.
150. Foscolo 1953b, 53.
151. Foscolo 1953b, 58–9.
152. Foscolo 1953b, 64–5.
153. Foscolo 1953b, 86–9.
154. Foscolo 1953b, 109–22.
155. Foscolo 1953b, 125.
156. Foscolo 1953b, 131, 136.
157. Foligno, Introduction to Foscolo 1953b, xxxv.

2 'Englishing' Petrarch: The Translators' Role

1. Mouret 1976, 53.
2. On the effeminacy of Italian, see Zuccato 1996, Appendix, especially 230–1.
3. Baretti 1757, xxi. He added that this was only his own opinion. For his defence of the manliness of Italian poetry, see Baretti 1753a, 49 ff., where he cites the Ugolino episode from Dante.
4. Baretti 1753b, 14; and Baretti 1776, 150. Baretti argued that if more of Sappho's works had survived, scholars would have compared them to Petrarch endlessly.
5. Baretti 1753b, 14.

6. Baretti 1753a, 53. Petrarch's most 'most pathetic Descriptions of his Passion for the beautiful *Laura*, does not equal the Sweetness' of Dante's hymns in *Paradiso*.

7. Baretti 1936, I, 98 (London, 15 April 1754). Petrarch and Berni, a sixteenth-century burlesque poet, no longer seemed to him the climax of human understanding. Baretti added, however, that the average Englishman was already serious as a young man; just imagine, then, 'che implatonito animale debb'essere' ('what a Platonified animal he must be') later in life. For Petrarch's style, see Baretti 1776, 150.

8. Baretti 1776, 89. He believed that the same problems existed for Metastasio, La Fontaine and Shakespeare, who had been assassinated by Voltaire's translation.

9. Warton 1782, I, 66. Warton, who referred to Petrarch in the context of his discussion of the ode, believed that Metastasio was a much better lyric poet. Later, however, Warton changed his mind at least in part, thanks to Sade or Dobson. In the chapter that opened vol. II of the third edition of his *Essay* (1782), he mentioned the 'very entertaining Memoirs of the Life of Petrarch' (Warton 1782, I, 350).

10. Hume 1875, I, 283–4. Hume continued with a reference to Boccaccio, whose thanksgiving to his ladies and God at the end of his tales was equally ridiculous. Hume was thinking of Petrarch's 'Movesi il vecchierel canuto et bianco' rather than the *canzone* 'Vergine bella', as Watson believed (Watson 1967, 40).

11. *Essai sur les mœurs* (Voltaire 1877–85, XI–XIII; for his version, XII, 59). The book appeared in 1756, the English translation in 1761. See also his letter to Le Comte d'Argental, 30 June [1764] (*Correspondance*, vol. XI, Voltaire 1877–85, XLVIII, 259): 'je n'aime point Pétrarque, mais j'aime l'abbé de Sade.'

12. 'Lettre aux auteurs de la *Gazette littéraire*', 6 June 1764, in *Mélanges*, IV, Voltaire 1877–85, XXV, 486, 489. Ariosto was a much better poet, and Sappho's ode was more powerful than any of Petrarch's poems.

13. Letter to Le Comte d'Argental, 22 June [1764] (Voltaire 1877–85, XLVIII 249, *Correspondance*, vol. XI).

14. *Essai sur les mœurs* (Voltaire 1877–85, XII, 59).

15. See Hayes 2000, 133. In any event, Voltaire argued that it did not matter whether Laura had existed or was a fictional character, as he believed ('Lettre aux auteurs de la *Gazette littéraire*', Voltaire 1877–85, XXV, 489).

16. The novel contains the partial translation of nine poems by Petrarch. The first translation into English appeared in Dublin in 1761 without the translator's name; the French original was published in the same year. According to the *DNB*, William Kenrick (1725?–1779) was a weird character: a notorious libellist, a violent man and a drinker, a quick writer and a prolific translator. He received the degree of LL.D. from Marischal College and the University of Aberdeen for his *Eloisa*.

17. Rousseau 1989, I, 90 (Letter XII, to Eloisa). Eloisa was also advised to abandon French and take up Italian music. A quotation from Petrarch illustrated his suggestion that she learn to sing in the Italian style (Rousseau 1989, I, 223, Letter XLVIII, to Eloisa).

18. Rousseau 1989, I, 92 (Letter XII, to Eloisa).

19. Quotations are especially frequent in vol. I of the book. Several of them appear within eulogies of mountain landscape or in celebrations of the simplicity of rural life. Rousseau never specified who their authors were; they are from Petrarch, Tasso, Metastasio and other poets. They are given in the Italian original with an English translation.

20. Mouret 1976, 21.

21. See Morton 1905; and Havens 1922, ch. XIX and pp. 685–6.

22. Mary Monk taught herself Latin, Spanish and Italian and translated, besides Petrarch, Filicaia, Della Casa, Guarini, Marino and Tasso. After her death, her father published her poems under the name of Marinda (Marinda 1716). Some of her translations were reprinted in *PEL* II, 185–96 and later in *Laura* II (CCXXXII Petrarch; CCXVI Della Casa).

23. Though not a masterpiece, Monk's version is reasonably good. She used rhyming couplets and triplets, with which she formed two quatrains and a sestet; she condensed ll. 13–14 and omitted the fact that the protagonist of the sonnet talked with Love. Monk's additions, like those of many translators, sometimes explain the original (*Laura* II, CCXXXII). Interestingly, another early translation of the same sonnet made by an anonymous 'Lady' appeared in *The Poetical Calendar* in 1763 (Anonymous 1763). It is a pleasant, literal version accompanied by *PC*, 132 and imitations from other Italian poets.

24. Recently, for example, in Feldman and Robinson 1999, 26. The popularity of Gray's sonnet is curiously at odds with his critical judgement on the poem, which he thought 'bad' (Mack 2000, 317).

25. See Gray 1969, 65–8; and Gleckner 1997, 120–6. As Lonsdale indicates, Sir Egerton Brydges noted in 1821 that Gray had 'deeply studied the images, the sentiments, the language, and the tone' of 'Zephiro torna' (Gray 1969, 66).

26. 'Zephyrus returns and leads back the fine weather and the flowers and the grass, his sweet family, and chattering Procne and weeping Philomena, and Spring, all white and vermilion; // the meadows laugh and the sky becomes clear again, Jupiter is gladdened looking at his daughter, the air and the waters and the earth are full of love, every animal takes counsel again to love. // But to me, alas, come back heavier sighs, which she draws from my deepest heart, she who carried off to Heaven the keys to it; // and the singing of little birds, and the flowering of meadows, and virtuous gentle gestures in beautiful ladies are a wilderness and cruel, savage beasts' (Petrarca 2001, 310).

27. As Lonsdale pointed out, the conclusion to West's 'Ad Amicos' is especially relevant to Gray's sonnet, as West imagined that on his death only his dearest friend would remember him, whereas nature would remain indifferent (Gray 1969, 65, 328).

28. Gray 1971, I, 202 (to West, 8 May 1742). The force of Gray's interest is confirmed by Nicholls, who recorded that Gray was 'a decided, and zealous admirer' of Petrarch (Mack 2000, 201). In 1766 he read Sade's biography of Petrarch, which he found 'not well written, but very curious' and interesting as a cultural history of the fourteenth century (Gray 1971, II, 922). Gray planned a history of poetry which included in Part I a section on Provençal poetry later brought to perfection by 'Dante, Petrarch, Boccace, & others'. He passed his notes over to Warton, who found them very useful for his *History of English Poetry* (Mack 2000, 660–2). A phrase of Petrarch's *canzone* for the crusade (*PC*, 28, l. 48) was mentioned together with Virgil as a source of a line of Gray's 'The Progress of Poesy' (II, 2, l. 54). Gray reversed the meaning of the original phrase: whereas Petrarch described the north-eastern peoples of Scythia as absolute barbarians whom his friend Giacomo Colonna would meet on his way to Jerusalem, Gray pointed out that the spirit of poesy visited even the parts of humankind which lived 'In climes beyond the solar road'. Gray's footnote to the next stanza points out that Chaucer, Wyatt, Spenser and Milton were disciples of Dante, Petrarch and other Italian poets.

29. Notes on the metre of Petrarch and other Italian poets were made around 1755 (Gray 1969, 66). See his essay 'Metrum', section 'The Measures of Verse' (Gray

1884, I, 349, 'Sonnets of Fourteen, on Five Rhymes'). Gray lists other types of sonnets, used by Milton, Spenser, Wyatt and Surrey. A note taken from Crescimbeni on 'Sonnets of Fourteen, on Five Rhymes' specifies: 'This, and the fourth kind [i.e., sonnets of four rhymes], are the true Sonnet of the Italians. Petrarch uses only these two measures.' The note also argues that the invention of the sonnet was probably due to Guittone d'Arezzo about 1250, whereas the Provençal *sonet* was only a short *canzone*. In the text Gray mentions some of Milton's sonnets as English examples of 'true sonnets' in this sense. Petrarch is also mentioned under the heading 'Stanza of Fourteen, on Seven Rhymes. Spenser's Visions of Petrarch, Bellay, &c.', a stanza which is like 'the last kind of Sonnet', that is, a sonnet of seven rhymes (Gray 1884, I, 350).

30. It is useful to remember that vanity, which is so prominent in Gray's sonnet, is a crucial concept in Petrarch, as is clear from *PC*, 1.

31. On the imitations from Tibullus and Propertius, Gleckner 1997, 59–65, 107–10. On Gray's homoeroticism, besides Gleckner's and McCarthy's excellent studies, see Hagstrum 1974; Haggerty 1992; Jung 2000.

32. Schor 1994, 59. The title of the poem in Lonsdale's edition is a compromise between the two options: 'Sonnet [on the Death of Mr Richard West]' (Gray 1969, 64).

33. The translation was first published by T. J. Mathias in 1814.

34. See, e.g., Mack 2000, 200–3. Gray began the study of Italian in 1736–37. In that period he translated Tasso and Dante into English, and Petrarch into Latin.

35. 'Alas, I burn and I am not believed; rather all believe me except for her, who is above all others and whom alone I wish to believe me; she does not seem to believe it, but still she sees it. // Infinite beauty and little faith, do you not see my heart in my eyes? If it were not for my star, I should surely find mercy at the very fountain of pity. // This ardor of mine, which matters so little to you, and your praises in my well-known rhymes, could perhaps yet inflame thousands; // for in my thought I see, O my sweet fire, a tongue cold in death and two lovely eyes closed, which after us will remain full of embers' (Petrarca 2001, 203).

36. Gray 1969, 308–9.

37. Ong 1962, 211.

38. See Hutchings 1995. He points out that only 'With the death of West, Latin [became] a dead language' for Gray, who did not compose other Latin poems of equal emotional intensity after 1742 (Hutchings 1995, 139).

39. It is worth recalling that in Florence Gray translated into Latin a disturbing epigram by Giuseppe Maria Buondelmonte ('Spesso Amor sotto la forma', 'Lusit amicitiae interdum velatus amictu'), who argued that love appears in many forms, such as pleasant sexual attraction, rage, despondency and friendship, but in fact it is always the same god in different disguises (Gray 1969, 316). Significantly, he called the epigram 'a pretty little Sonnet', probably owing to its subject (Gray 1971, I, 183, 21 Apr. 1741).

40. Gray 1969, 133–4. In his Latin version, Gray followed Petrarch line by line as far as l. 11; then he expanded the last tercet into his ll. 12–16. Gray's l. 12 ('when we two will each be no more than a handful of ashes') is a paraphrase of 'dopo morte' ('after death') in graveyard style, whereas his l. 15 ('the ill-starred Muse will breathe out eternal love') made explicit the theme of the posthumous survival of passion thanks to poetry which was only implicit in Petrarch's conclusion. In the 'Elegy', however, Gray returned to his source and left the rationale for his statement unexpressed.

41. In the first version of the 'Elegy', 'thee' clearly referred to Gray; in the last version, which is cited here, the referent is more ambiguous. Also, the first version of l. 92 was 'And buried Ashes glow with social Fires' (Gray 1969, 134 n.). The correction rendered the antithesis Ashes/Fires neater, whereas 'wonted' for 'social' gave 'Fires' a wider meaning, encompassing public as well as private love.

42. *PC*, pp. 711–12. The lines cited are 12–14.

43. Gray 1985, 106.

44. J. Hagstrum noted that later Gray used the phrase 'trembling anxiety' in a letter to Bonstetten, in which the context is undeniably one of homoerotic jealousy (Hagstrum 1974, 10–11).

45. Gray 1969, 113–14. See also White 1998, 61.

46. Langhorne 1770a, I 45.

47. Langhorne 1770a, I, 50–1. Langhorne, who was a curate, specified that, though he would be pleased to live like a philosopher, he 'should choose to love like a man'.

48. The novel contains a translation of Petrarch's sonnet 'Aventuroso più d'altro terreno' (Langhorne 1770a, I, 139–40). In the novel Eleonora is especially fond of quoting Petrarch to illustrate her feelings (see, e.g., Langhorne 1770a, I, 118, 121).

49. Langhorne's second wife also died in childbearing in 1772.

50. Langhorne 1770b. The first, shorter edition appeared in 1763; vol. II contains the letters supposedly found in her convent after her death. The references to Petrarch were added in 1770.

51. He translated four sonnets, which were printed together with the original texts. Unfortunately, 'Se lamentar augelli', probably his worst translation, full of awkward inversions and clumsy lines, was reprinted in several anthologies (Langhorne 1804, II, 175–81). He found Petrarch's sufferings mannered ('I hate the languor of your lenient strain, / Your flow'ry grief, your impotence of pain') and he affirmed that those men whose passion remain only ideal do not know what the agonies of real love feel like. They are as violent as sublime nature rather than, as in Petrarch, delicate as pastoral landscape ('Verses in Memory of a Lady', Langhorne 1804, II, 100).

52. Langhorne 1770a, I, 121. Langhorne's translations were among the first not to be made as part of someone else's work.

53. Jones 1970, II, 759 (28 Aug. 1787), and 784 (10 Oct. 1787). Anna Maria Jones (1748–1829), Sir William's wife, began her literary career in India, where she published *The Poems of Anna Maria* (1793), which includes sonnets, before going back to England after her husband's death. She mentioned 'PETRARCH's shade', which 'still loiter nigh, / To lisp his cruel LAURA's Sigh' in her 'Ode. Inscribed to Della Crusca', i.e., Robert Merry, whom she erroneously thought dead. She asked him to guide her 'through the hallow'd Glade / Where Learning's sons', like Virgil, Sappho and Petrarch, are laid (Jones 2002, 46).

54. Jones 1970, II, 761–2 (16 Aug. 1787). Jones thanked John Shore for sending them 'the tender strains of the unfortunate Charlotte, which have given us pleasure and pain; the sonnets which relate to herself are incomparably the best'.

55. Jones 1970, II, 582 (23 Oct. 1782). The lines he cited are the conclusion to 'Italia mia': 'among the magnanimous few who love the good; say to them: "Who will protect me? I go crying: Peace, peace, peace!"' (Petrarca 2001, 128).

56. Jones 1970, II, 816–17 (24 Sept. 1788) and Cannon's note.

57. Jones 1970, II, 583–4 (24 Oct. 1782); and II, 703 (7 Sept. 1786), where he cited a passage of the first poem of *Canzoniere*, Part II.

58. Jones 1970, I, 27 ([April] 1769); and Jones 1772, I, v. The poem on the fountain of Vaucluse is probably Jones's version of Petrarch's 'Chiare, fresche et dolci acque',

though his 'Elegy' also contains a passage, in part imitated from a poem of Mme Deshoulieres, which describes the fountain (Jones 1772, I, 90–1).

59. Jones 1772, I, iv–v.

60. Voltaire, who did not compare Sa'di and Petrarch, argued that Oriental people never had good taste. They had a strong spirit of servitude and their works were like the titles of their monarchs, full of suns and moons. They had no delicacy because women were excluded from social life. There was neither order nor method in them, as each poet followed his imagination in solitude. They had never known the real eloquence of Cicero and Demosthenes. As an example of Oriental poetry, he translated in blank verse a passage of Sa'di which resembled the prophets of the Bible (*Essai sur les mœurs*, Voltaire 1877–85, XI, 62–3). Jones later mentioned the passage in a letter (Jones 1970, I, 447, ?1780).

61. Jones 1772, I, vii–viii.

62. The contents of Jones 1772 are: 'Solima, an Arabian Eclogue'; 'The Palace of Fortune, an Indian Tale'; 'The Seven Fountains, an Eastern allegory'; 'A Persian Song of Hafez'; 'An Ode of Petrarch'; 'Laura, an Elegy'; 'A Turkish ode on the spring'; 'Arcadia, a pastoral poem'; 'Caissa, or, The Game of Chess' (the last two are Jones's juvenile poems). The texts are followed by the two essays.

63. Jones 1772, 77–8.

64. Jones used a regular six-line stanza rhyming aabccb for Petrarch's more elaborate stanza. He expanded, moved and paraphrased the original lines in many places. Jones 1772, 77–83.

65. Jones changed Petrarch's landscape by drawing on neoclassical pastoral poetry. The voice of his Petrarch is less intimately lyrical and more melodramatically public than the original.

66. Mme D'Arblay's paraphrase of Burney's diary says that he studied Italian on horseback while riding his mare in the Norfolk countryside in the early 1750s. He made himself at home with Italian thanks to Dante, Petrarch, Ariosto, Tasso and Metastasio and a dictionary his Italian teacher had compiled for him. Immediately after the death of his wife, he annotated in despair (London, Autumn 1762): 'for a fortnight did nothing but meditate on my misery. I wrote elegyac [*sic*] Verses on her Virtues & Perfection. Tried to translate 2 or 3 of Petrarca's most touching Sonnets on the death of Laura—but was at length obliged to plunge into business' (Burney 1988, 113, 145). His daughter specified that the only thing Burney could do in that period was writing verse in memoriam or 'imitations, adapted to his loss, and to her excellences, from some selected sonnets of Petrarch, whom he considered to have loved, entombed, and bewailed another Esther in his Laura'. Also, he took to the study of Dante and translated in prose a part of *Inferno*, which remains among his unpublished papers (Burney 1832, I, 150–1).

67. See Burney 1904–05, II, 210 (Dr Burney to Mr Crisp, 12 Apr. 1783).

68. Burney 1958, II, 633 (vol. II was first published in 1782).

69. Burney concluded this section with a quotation from 'the elegant and captivating' Sade, who called Petrarch the greatest genius of Italy and the most important reformer of its tongue (Burney 1958, II, 634).

70. These sonnets, which never became popular, were printed with the parallel original text. Burney mentioned Laura explicity though her name does not appear in the Italian version. He simplified l. 3 and used l. 12 of the original as l. 14 of his version. In his discussion, he also quoted some lines from other poems (Burney 1958, II, 634–6).

71. *Laura* V, DCCCLXXXI, 'To Charles Burney, M. D. On the Sonnets in His History of Music'. Lofft specified in ll. 5–6: 'To thee [Burney] congenial the PETRARCHAN

Lays / The undulating SONNET's graceful round.' This sonnet and Burney's version are placed near the end of *Laura*.

72. France 2000, 62.
73. See, e.g., Venuti 1995, 81–95. Nott's was the first complete and uncensored translation of Catullus into English. As Venuti argued, Nott's open-mindedness towards sex was in part influenced by the aristocrats he regularly served as a physician (Venuti 1995, 95).
74. Nott 1777, v–vi. The editor's name does not appear in the book, but the attribution to Nott is certain on the basis of the evidence brought forward by Mouret (Mouret 1976, 230). Nott also commended Jones's version in the 1808 edition (Nott 1808, 239-40).
75. Nott 1787, ix–x ('Preface'). This was the only work published with his name as editor.
76. Nott 1787, x ('Some Account of the Persian Poet Hafez'). Nott referred to Virgil in Rome and later to a particular manuscript of Petrarch, 'preserved in one of the public libraries in Italy'. This should be Petrarch's Virgil in the Biblioteca Ambrosiana in Milan.
77. Nott 1777, 46–7. Another link between Hafiz and the sonnet tradition appears in a note to Nott's version of Hafiz's 'Ode XI', which recalls that Jones compared this poem to a sonnet of Shakespeare (Nott 1787, 76). Nott repeated Jones's view of translation as a way to stimulate the study of foreign languages. In addition, translation had a very important practical value. Nott believed that it was impossible to rule a foreign country merely by force. It was necessary to learn its culture if one wanted to reconcile and subdue the people's minds (Nott 1787, ii).
78. See Mouret 1976, 230–1. The manuscript was donated to Harvard Library in 1907 (Houghton MS Eng 1288).
79. Nott 1777, vi–vii.
80. In the introduction to his Catullus edition, Nott defended literal translation on the basis of historical truth. Translators must respect the manners described in the original, however strange and repugnant to their sensibility. See Venuti 1995, 85.
81. Nott sometimes modified the original order of the lines, as for example in *PC*, 1, ll. 9–11 (Nott 1777, 3).
82. A characteristic example is his version of 'Valle che de' lamenti miei se' piena' (Nott 1777, 55; for Petrarch's text, see Chapter 3 in this volume): 'Ye vales, made vocal by my plaintive lay! / Ye streams, embitter'd with the tears of love! / Ye tenants of the sweet, melodious grove! / Ye tribes, that in the grass-fring'd streamlet play! / Ye tepid gales, to which my sighs convey / A softer warmth!—Ye flow'ry plains, that move / Reflection sad!—Ye hills, where yet I rove! / Since Laura there first taught my steps to stray. / Yet all your native bloom, and mirth retain! / While I, a prey to slow-consuming pain, / No wonted youth, no former pleasures share. / Oft from yon elm-clad height these eyes survey / The spot where, seeking the bright realm of day, / Laura's fair spirit left a frame so fair!' Paraphrases are: 'made vocal', 'plaintive lay', 'tenants of the sweet, melodious grove', 'tribes', 'Reflection sad', ll. 10–11 and 13–14. He suppressed the antithesis in l. 7, omitted the original reference to 'Amor' in l. 8, and added 'embitter'd' and 'yon elm-clad height'.
83. This applies to all his translations (two *canzoni* and a *sestina*), for which he used an eight-line stanza with different types of line. In the 1808 edition he used the same method in the longer texts.
84. Nott gave no space to the political side of Petrarch. The social criticism of his version of 'La gola e 'l somno' is moderate and vague in comparison to the

translations made a few years later by Hayley, Lofft and Rickman (see below). Still, drawing on Dobson, Nott introduced the sonnet as Petrarch's answer to Giustina Levi-Perotti in both the 1777 and 1808 editions (Nott 1777, 6–7; and Nott 1808, 230).

85. Precisely, he included 23 sonnets and two *canzoni* from the *in vita* part, seven sonnets and one *canzone* form the *in morte* part.

86. In 1808 Nott referred to Italian scholars like Tassoni, Crescimbeni, Vellutello and Castelvetro, though always through other sources. He also mentioned Wyatt and Surrey as significant English Petrarchans.

87. See 'Some Account of Petrarch's Life' (Nott 1777, xi and xiii). Nott included it in his edition for those who did not want to read all of Dobson's *Life of Petrarch*. He related the story of the sonnet found in Laura's tomb, which he translated even though he found it poor in quality (Nott 1777, 104–5).

88. In a note to 'Kiss V', he indicated Secundus's line 'O! JUCUNDA MEI CALORIS AURA' as a wonderfully delicate definition of his mistress, which he compared to Petrarch's puns on *l'aura*, though Secundus's line was better and not merely written for the sake of the conceit, as in *PC*, 365 and 196. In a note to 'Kiss VII', Nott noted that, like Secundus, Petrarch attributed to Laura's smile the same power of quenching his ardent desires, citing four lines of *PC*, 17 (Nott 1778, 80 and 94). Both these notes and the references to Petrarch were added in the second edition of Secundus, after Nott translated Petrarch.

89. Nott 1777, 53: 'But she, who bears far hence my soul away; / Leaving me nought but unsubdued desires; / Ne'er cheers my night, nor glads my gloomy day.' Nott was translating l. 14 of *PC*, 291, which literally means, 'and left me nothing of herself but her name' (Petrarca 2001, 291).

90. Nott 1777, 33 and 47. Nott rendered the direct 'Tu sola mi piaci' ('You alone please me', Petrarca 2001, 205) of *PC*, 205, l. 8, as 'thou art my only care', which is less physical (Nott 1777, 39).

91. Nott 1777, 23 (ll. 10–11, *PC*, 153).

92. Nott 1777, 13. The original phrase (l. 13) runs, 'qui cangiò 'l viso', which means that the colour of her face changed. Like Nott, Durling erroneously understood it as 'here she frowned' (Petrarca 2001, 112).

93. Nott 1808 contains 51 *in vita* and 29 *in morte* sonnets.

94. Twenty-two sonnets of the 1777 edition appear also in the 1808 edition, but in a new translation. Nott's abiding interest in the Petrarchan tradition is also showed by his edition of Wyatt's and Surrey's poems (1812), which unfortunately was almost entirely destroyed by fire.

95. E.g., l. 8 of *PC*, 205 became ' "Thou only pleasest me." ' (Nott 1808, 125)

96. See Chapter 3 in this volume for the Italian text.

97. Formerly, there was only one anthology of Italian poetry (Isola 1784), a collection of students' exercises edited by Agostino Isola, an Italian expatriate who taught Italian and Spanish to several Romantic men of letters, such as Hayley and Wordsworth. Besides three anonymous versions from Petrarch, the volume included poems by Ariosto, Guarini, Tasso, Tassoni and, above all, Metastasio. In the Introductory Note, Isola pointed out that he excluded some morally unsuitable material which, however, would have enlarged and adorned the collection. Though the versions from Petrarch are not of particular interest, they show that by that date his sonnets had become part of the ordinary teaching material for students of Italian.

98. *Fiori*, vi.

99. Allen 2002, 384.

100. *Fiori*, 13. The translations are accompanied by the original text on the facing page. For Levi-Perotti's original, see Chapter 1 in this volume. Hayley added 'inglorious ease', which echoes Petrarch's answer, 'future fame' and 'Poet'.
101. The rest of Hayley's version reads as follows: 'And still to live, in spite of death, aspire / By virtue's light, that darkness cannot seize: / But, stupified by custom's blank decrees, / The idle vulgar, void of liberal fire, / Bid me with scorn, from Helicon retire, / And rudely blame my generous hope to please. / "Distaffs, not laurels, to your sex belong," / They cry—as honors were beyond our view: / To such low cares they with my spirit bent. / Say thou! who marchest 'mid the favor'd few, / To high Parnassus, with triumphant song, / Should I abandon such a fair intent?' The lowliness of women's practical work is significantly emphasised in Hayley's l. 11.
102. *Fiori*, 15. For Petrarch's original text, see Chapter 1 in this volume. Lines 1–12 of Hayley's version read as follows: 'Luxurious pleasure, and lethargic ease, / Have deaden'd in the world each bright desire: / Our thoughts no more with nature's force aspire; / Custom's cold powers the drooping fancy seize: / So lost each light that taught the soul to please, / Each heavenly spark of life-directing fire, / That all who join the Heliconian choir, / Are frantic deem'd, by Folly's dull decrees. / "What charms, what worth to laurel-wreaths belong? / "Naked and poor Philosophy we view," / Exclaims the croud, on sordid gain intent. / Associates in thy path thou'lt find but few'.
103. He quoted some beautiful passages, especially those praised by Tasso (Hayley 1782, 146, 'Notes to the Third Epistle').
104. Hayley 1782, 261–3, 'Notes to the Fourth Epistle'. A note on p. 264 mentions Petrarch in a discussion of poetic crownings.
105. Hayley 1782, 64–5.
106. *Laura* III, CCCXCV. For the original lines, see Chapter 1 in this volume.
107. *Laura* III, CCCXCVIII, ll. 4, 8, 11, where he rendered 'dice la turba al vil guadagno intesa' ('says the mob, bent on low gain', Petrarca 2001, 7) as 'How lost, how abject, in these iron days!'
108. Lofft substituted ' "Chill naked Poverty is all thy store! / March thy lone way", the sordid Rabble cry. / Thou not the less pursue thy generous Essays' for Preston's 'Yet dauntless *Clara* may thy spirit soar; / Spurn the vile croud, disdain senseless cry; / And seek, within thyself, the worthiest praise', which, also, sounds like a much vaguer support of women's right to poetry. *Laura* III, CCCXCVIII, ll. 12–14; Preston 1781, 142, ll. 12–14.
109. *Laura* III, CCCXCIX. The original reads: 'che per cosa mirabile s'addita / chi vòl far d'Elicona nascer fiume' ('that whoever wishes to make a river flow from Helicon is pointed at as a strange thing', Petrarca 2001, 7).
110. Hayley studied with Isola at Cambridge. In Hayley 1782, ll. 79–122 of 'Epistle III' deal with Dante, whose poem was praised for its bold visions but, also, blamed for its quaintness and harshness (Hayley 1782, 146). The interminable Note IV contains a biography of Dante, translations from his sonnets ('Guido, i' vorrei') and Cantos 1–3 of *Inferno* with the original text. In 1836 Wordsworth could recite from memory Hayley's version of that sonnet of Dante (Graver 1996).
111. Byron's indictment must not conceal the fact that Hayley was a respected poet in his time, as he was offered and declined the laureateship on the death of Warton. Hayley's poems were popularly successful and ran through a dozen editions. Three of his sonnets were included in Henderson 1803, section 'Sonnets Descriptive'.
112. Hayley 1789. The novel carries a motto from Petrarch.

113.   Giuliana read Petrarch's poems to her Peverell and later those poems became 'a sort of soothing magic' on her afflictions (Hayley 1789, I, 151). She quoted and translated from four sonnets (Hayley 1789, I 149–51). Peverell always carried on him a *Petrarchino*, a Renaissance miniature edition of Petrarch's poems. When he died his servant gave it to Giuliana (Hayley 1789, I, 158). She cited some passages that illustrated her condition in that moment, which impressed Seymour. The quotation is from a Letter of Seymour from Calais (Hayley 1789, I, 157). They had become 'idolaters' of Petrarch and were going to visit Vaucluse (Hayley 1789, I, 163).

114.   *DNB*, entry 'William Hayley'. On Hayley, Smith and the complex economy of poetic exchange, see Allen 2002.

115.   Collier's versions were published in vol. II of his *Poems*, which contains many translations from Latin, French, Greek, Spanish and Italian poets. Only his versions from Petrarch were printed without parallel original texts. He also imitated Petrarch in some poems of vol. I (Collier 1800, 141–2 and 181). In *Laura* Lofft included the sonnet on p. 141 and one version (*PC*, 224). Le Mesurier's translations were reprinted in some journals. They appeared as the work of 'Anonymous' in Henderson 1803, *Laura*, and Petrarca 1859.

116.   Collier's selection from Petrarch (*PC*, 338, 311, 163, 263, 224, 292) is a collection of anthology pieces rather than a personal route through *Canzoniere*. The sonnets anthologised in *Fiori* were *PC*, 224 and 338.

117.   Collier supported literal translation whenever possible in his section 'On the Sonnet' in 'Notes and Observations on Some of the Original Poems in the First Vol.' (Collier 1800, II, xii–xxii). He affirmed that the main difficulty in translating Italian verse was due to elision, in which Ariosto and Petrarch excelled (Collier 1800, II, xlvii–xlviii, note in 'On the Limits of Translation').

118.   See, e.g., his version of *PC*, 163 (Collier 1800, II, 282), which contains several emphatic additions such as exclamation marks (ll. 1, 4), 'inmost thought' for 'pensero' ('thought', l. 1), 'panting breast' for 'core' ('heart', l. 3) and others. As far as respectability is concerned, see l. 13, 'pur che ben desïando i' mi consume' ('as long as I am consumed with a high love', Petrarca 2001, 163) rendered as 'In distant homage let my life be spent'.

119.   Collier 1800, II, xviii, xxi–xxii. Collier found that Petrarch was more limited than Milton in his numbers, but he was able to vary his subject all the time. Collier wrote that the structure of the sonnet, which was a sort of serious epigram, had been explained by Tasso. A sonnet should expose an argument in the first quatrain, develop it in the second and finish it in the sestet. There must be a gradation towards a climax and unity among the parts. The sonnets of Petrarch were often deficient in gradation, as the quatrains were often better than the conclusion (Collier 1800, II, xiv, xviii).

120.   Le Mesurier 1795, iii. The volume includes two dedicatory sonnets, the second 'To Mary ******* With Petrarch' (Le Mesurier 1795, 3).

121.   Henderson 1803, xxxiv. Le Mesurier chose 13 *in vita* sonnets and 11 *in morte*, including popular texts like *PC*, 162, 311, 208, 279, 35, 353, 1, 310, which were printed with the parallel original texts. He chose none of the political poems. *Fiori* selected two of his bird sonnets, *PC*, 279 and 311.

122.   Le Mesurier 1795, iv.

123.   Le Mesurier 1795, 51. The original reads (*PC*, 353, ll. 4–8): 'se, come i tuoi gravosi affanni sai, / così sapessi il mio simile stato, / verresti in grembo a questo sconsolato / a patir seco i dolorosi guai' ('if as you know your own grievous troubles

you also knew my similar state, you would come to my unconsoled bosom to share its sorrowing groans') (Petrarca 2001, 353).

124. Le Mesurier 1795, 5 and 11. The originals read: 'Solo et pensoso i più deserti campi / vo mesurando a passi tardi e lenti' (*PC*, 35, ll. 1–2; for the English version, see Chapter 3 in this volume); 'Ma ben veggio or sì come al popol tutto / favola fui gran tempo, onde sovente / di me medesmo meco mi vergogno' (*PC*, 1, ll. 9–12; for the English version, see Chapter 1 in this volume). In this case he changed 'popol tutto' ('the crowd') into 'country'; he added 'I bow my head'; and he did not preserve the alliteration at l. 12.

125. See, e.g., ll. 1–4 of *PC*, 90: 'Loose to the breeze her golden tresses flow'd / Wildly in thousand mazy ringlets blown, / And from her eyes unconquer'd glances shone, / Those glances now so sparingly bestow'd', where 'unconquer'd glances' is a free rendering of 'il vago lume oltre misura ardea' ('the lovely light burned without measure'), and 'so sparingly bestow'd' a paraphrase of 'ch'or ne son sì scarsi' ('which are now so stingy of it', Petrarca 2001, 90). Le Mesurier 1795, 17.

126. Le Mesurier 1795, 7. Though he translated political poems of Filicaia and Rota, his reading of 'La gola e 'l somno' was moral. He mentioned neither tyranny, nor liberalism, nor social privilege.

127. Petrarch's poems, like that of the other authors, are not collected together in a section, but are scattered here and there in the anthology. The presence of Dobson's versions means that the editor wanted to include those poems for their subjects, and that she was admired as a translator despite the fact that her translations were in prose.

128. His name does not appear in the title page, but only at the end of the Dedication.

129. Henderson 1803, viii–ix. The volume frontispiece is a plate in which Laura appears to Petrarch from a cloud. Lines 12–14 from Langhorne's translation of 'Wail'd the sweet warbler' are appended below the illustration.

130. Henderson 1803, xxii–xxiii.

131. Henderson 1803, xxvii.

132. Henderson 1803, xxix–xxx.

133. Henderson 1803, xxv.

134. Henderson 1803, xxxiii–xxxv.

135. Henderson 1803, vii–viii ('Preface'). He added that he wanted to include Southey and his friends but could not for editorial reasons (Henderson 1803, ix–x).

136. Petrarch appears also in Langhorne's sonnet 'In the Manner of Petrarch' and Dimond's 'To a Myrtle. From a Volume of Petrarchal Sonnets. 1800'.

137. Russell's 'To Valclusa' is another text of Petrarchan interest.

138. Lorenzo il Magnifico, Tasso, Zappi, Filicaia, Metastasio. The translators were Mickle (Tasso), Roscoe (Lorenzo), and Le Mesurier for the others. Besides the Italians, Camoens was the only ancient poet included.

139. This drew on him violent attacks. For example, Meyenberg records that 'Charles Lamb ridiculed Lofft as a "Genius of Absurdity" and a madman who "is his own Moon" without "need of ascending into that gentle planet for mild influences"' (Meyenberg 2005, 26–9).

140. Lofft settled in Turin, an unusual location for British exiles in Italy, and died in nearby Moncalieri (he was born in 1751). He was buried at San Germano, a Waldensian village in Val Chisone. He had no contacts with other English exiles in Switzerland nor in Italy.

141. Meyenberg 2005, 33. See Lofft's 'To Mr. G. Henderson. On His Anthology; or "Selection of Sonnets"' (*Laura* II, CCXXXVII). He celebrated Henderson's

anthology, which inspired him to edit his own as a collection of flowers dear to the Muses, according to classical ideals.

142. Meyenberg 2005, 35 ff. Vols. III and IV are dated 1813. The 'Preface' specifies that it was begun in 1802 (*Laura* I, i).

143. *Laura* I, iii, v. As theorists, he mentioned Menzini, Boileau and Crescimbeni (*Laura* I, xxxvii).

144. *Laura* I, v–vi. Lofft noted that two Guidos from Arezzo were the fathers of the modern system of musical notation and the sonnet (*Laura* I, vii). Initially, Lofft had mixed up Guido of Arezzo and Guittone d'Arezzo.

145. *Laura* I, vii–viii. He noted that exact forms could be felt as chains; so they were, like all verse, but 'they are Chains which like those of LOVE a POET will not be easily persuaded to throw aside.' He then described the most common rhyme schemes (*Laura* I, ix–xi). Lofft included in the anthology Seward's version of Boileau's 'On the Structure of the Sonnet' (*Laura* III, CCCXXVIII). Here Apollo, sick of poetasters, creates new forms, first of all the sonnet. However, he affirms in the sestet that he will not give the poetic crown to the poets who write irregular sonnets.

146. *Laura* I, xxviii, xxx. Lofft mentioned Collier, who argued, on the model of Hebrew poetry, that the first tercet should answer the subject of the first quatrain, the second tercet the subject of the second quatrain. Lofft believed that the parallelism of Biblical poetry influenced the structure of the sonnet (*Laura* I, xxxii–xxxiii).

147. *Laura* I, xxxiv. At the end of the 'Preface', Lofft placed some remarks on the formal patterns of the sonnet (*Laura* I, ccli). He even included some 'tavole del sonetto' ('sonnet tables'), with mathematical combinations of the rhymes (*Laura* I, cclvi–cclvii), taken from Francesco Saverio Quadrio via an Italian grammar written by Carl Ludwig Fernow. Then he analysed irregular sonnets, most of which he considered as variants of the Spenserian sonnet (*Laura* I, cclviii). There were three main types of sonnet, 'two *proper* and one *improper*. The *Guidonian, Petrarchan,* or *musico-systematic*; the *Spenserian,* or *Disasynartete* (connected by *like* rhyme running through it) and the *Asynartete,* or disconnected throughout' (*Laura* I, cclxi).

148. *Laura* I, xliv. He also anticipated the criticism of the severe reviewers 'on the northern side of the *Tweed*', that he may believe he managed to produce perfect sonnets. Lofft did not want to boast his poems; he only wanted to emphasise that the difficulties of the sonnet were not arbitrary (*Laura* I, xli–xlii).

149. *Laura* I, xlv. Lofft was probably unaware that Greek was not known in Italy in Guittone's and Petrarch's times. Besides Crescimbeni, whom he quoted via Mathias, Lofft's other main sources for his collection were Fernow and Henry Crabb Robinson's researches in German literature (*Laura* I, xii).

150. *Laura* I, xlvii, lii.

151. On this point, see also Meyenberg 2005, 52–3, 71 ff.

152. *Laura* I, lvi.

153. *Laura* I, lvii. He added that sometimes even patriotism, philanthropy, ideal beauty and religion have proved to be excellent subjects for the sonnet (*Laura* I, lviii). In a sonnet of reply to Henry Kirk White not included in *Laura*, Lofft argued that he was not worried about the fact that 'the sublimer Muse' disdained 'the plaintive SONNET little form'; he was the 'lowliest of the sylvan train', part of a pastoral tradition of soft melody which 'soft it flows / Through the smooth murmurs of thy frequent close'. Text quoted from *CLP*, 30 August 2002.

154. *Laura* I, lix.
155. *Laura* I, lxiii–lxix.
156. *Laura* I, lxv.
157. *Laura* I, lxvi–lxviii. Though in a footnote he mentioned Tiraboschi's assent to Sade, in a note to Sonnet XI in vol. II Lofft quoted an Italian source which affirmed that everyone agreed that Laura had no husband.
158. *Laura* I, lxii–lxxiii. Lofft believed that Tiraboschi's evidence was weak.
159. *Laura* I, lxxiv. Lofft celebrated Lorenzo's as a golden age of art and poetry. He noted that his name contained the word 'laurel', which had been wonderfully influential in Italian poetry.
160. *Laura* I, cxli–clv. The English sonnet was only given a couple of paragraphs on the Renaissance at the end of the Preface (*Laura* I, cxcvi).
161. *Laura* I, ii.
162. *Laura* I, cxcii–cxciii. He hoped that the works of Roscoe, Mathias and several sonneteers of his time had already modified that derogatory view.
163. It contains mostly Italian texts, from Pier delle Vigne to Alfieri, without translations. One exception is Alfieri's sonnet on Petrarch's house in Vaucluse (*Laura* I, ccxlix). Then there are Spanish, French and English sonnets. None of Shakespeare's is included.
164. *Laura* I, cxciv–cxcv.
165. His desire to reproduce the original form and rhyme schemes sometimes led him to use an awkward syntax which does not appear in the Italian. Two examples are *Laura* IX (the translation of *PC*, 312), ll. 13–14 ('my Mind / Longs her again to see whom erst beheld I rue.') and *Laura* XI (*PC*, 187), ll. 9–13 ('Her of the Homeric, the Orfèan Lyre, / Most worthy, or that Shepherd, Mantua's Pride, / To be the Theme of their immortal Lays, / Her Stars and unpropitious Fate denied / This Palm'). Despite his admiration for the regular sonnet, in his compositions he rarely stopped at the end of l. 8, as Petrarch usually did.
166. A good example is *Laura* CCCXLIII, Smith's translation of *PC*, 301, followed by Lofft's version (CCCXLIV) of the same sonnet. Though Smith's version was freer, Lofft made several changes. He condensed in l. 3 the original ll. 3–4, and expanded to ll. 8 and 9 the original l. 9; he modified the antithesis at l. 5; he added the phrase 'Hath sunk into the Night' at l. 11; and paraphrased 'al ciel nuda è gita' ('she went naked to Heaven', l. 13; Petrarca 2001, 301) with 'dead she lay'.
167. *Laura* CCCXLVI; *PC*, 220. Lofft's facing translation (*Laura* III, CCCXLVII) includes several additions ('So radiant', l. 2; 'To tint those Cheeks', l. 3; the passage from '*He* only knows', l. 5, to the end of l. 8), expansions and paraphrases of the original (as at ll. 9 and 12–13), and omissions (e.g., of l. 11, and all the question marks after l. 4).
168. Petrarca 1996, 739 ff.
169. Petrarch composed the poem on his way back to Avignon immediately after his coronation in Rome. Lofft expanded on Petrarch's eulogy, adding that liberty was a 'Gift of Heaven' (l. 1), a 'sacred Grant' (l. 3) which, 'How high soe'er tyrannic Pomp aspire', even 'in a Cot' can 'raise the Spirit higher' (ll. 13–14).
170. These texts are included in the first part of *Laura* II. *Laura* XXVIII bears the title 'To Mrs. Lofft. A Sonnet Compos'd by Her on the Day of Petrarch's Birth XXIV July'; XLIX is a sonnet of Lofft's to compliment his wife on her sonnets; LXIV is another compliment sent to his wife with 'Petrarch's Selected Verse' on her

birthday. Her translations are XXXVII, XXXIX (a very free translation of 'Ite, rime dolenti'), and XL.

171.   *Laura* I, LXXXII, 'To Mrs. Robinson; By the Rev. Paul Colombine' mentioned the '*Lesbian* Lute' (l. 1) of the '*British* SAPPHO' (l. 3) who could move both young and old people (ll. 11–14). In a note to sonnet CVI, 'On Reading Mrs. Robinson's Poetical Works', Lofft praised her for her intelligence, her charm, her talent and her goodness of heart. In the poem, he noted: 'All these transcendant Charms avail'd thee not; / They fill'd with Misery thine envied Lot . . .' (ll. 12–13). The first sonnet in vol. III is 'To Miss Seward, on Transferring her Sonnets into this Collection'; CCLII is another sonnet on the same subject, in which Lofft affirmed: '*And softly warbling thy pathetic Lay / Canst make thy Cares, thy Anguish, all our own*' (ll. 5–6). There are several sonnets dedicated to C. Smith, such as DCLXXXIII (*Laura* IV), 'Gent. On the Death of Mrs. Charlotte Smith', an anonymous sonnet taken from *The Monthly Mirror*, 1807. On the legal difficulties Lofft met in including Smith's poems in his anthology, see Smith 2003, 718–19.

172.   Sonnet VII of 'La corona', 15 sonnets plus a conclusion placed at the end of *Laura* V, enumerates the best British sonneteers. Lines 9–14 celebrate eighteenth-century women sonneteers such as M. Robinson ('British Sappho', l. 9), Seward and Smith. Obviously, *Laura* includes also the translations of several male sonneteers, such as Boothby, Langhorne, Crowe, Russell, Burney, Preston, Nott (indicated as 'The translator of Catullus'), Le Mesurier (indicated as 'Anonymous'), Rickman and Collier.

173.   For Wyatt's version, see *Laura* III, CCCLXXXIII. Shakespeare's 'sonnets', taken from plays strongly influenced by Petrarchism, are *Laura* II, CLXXVIII, 'Sonnet from Shakespeare. Romeo. Elegiac', a story of love and death; 'From Shakespeare. Viola. Elegiac', the story of a girl whose love remained unfulfilled (the author of both is an 'Albert'; *Laura* II, CLXXX); 'Sonnet from Shakespeare. Juliet. Elegiac', on parting at dawn, based on the famous *aubade* in the play (*Laura* II, CLXXXI). Shakespeare's sonnets, albeit 'lighter QUATORZAIN[S]', were mentioned in sonnet X of 'La corona' (end of *Laura* V) as evidence against those who despise the sonnet. 'Elegiac' seems to have meant to Lofft something that had to do with tragic, unfulfilled love. Shakespeare's 'sonnets' were immediately preceded by Smith's version of 'Erano i capei d'oro' (*Laura* II, CLXXVII), and followed by 'Di Petrarca. Sonetto elegiaco', that is, Le Mesurier's version of 'Zephiro torna' (*Laura* II, CLXXXIII), almost to show what genuine 'elegiac sonnets' were. Besides these texts, the anthology includes a handful of Shakespeare's sonnets proper.

174.   The French texts were 'Se lamentar augelli', translated by La Fontaine (*Laura* III, CCLXVI) and 'Marot. Traduction. "*Lasciato ha la Morte*"' (*Laura* III, CCCLXIV). The other texts: Pindar, *Laura* III, CCXCVIII and CCC; La Fontaine, *Laura* III, CCCCXLVIII; the psalms (with transliteration and original text), *Laura* V, DCCLXI and DCCLXII; Racine, *Laura* V, DCCC; Petrarch's madrigal (in fact, a ballad), *Laura* III, CCCCLXXXVIII, which, as a footnote points out, is a sonnet 'in triplet or *terzetto* only.'

3   Charlotte Smith and Anna Seward

1.   Robinson 2003, n. 14 (cited from the database 'Academic Search Elite', with no page numbers).

2. Another early example can be found in 'To the Memory of the Same Lady. A Monody, A.D. 1747', probably by Lord Lansdown (Dodsley 1766, II, 67–78). Stanza XIV invokes Petrarch's help: 'teach my sorrows to relate / Their melancholy tale so well', so that they can move even inanimate things, like Orpheus. Stanza XV affirms that Petrarch's woes were nothing in comparison to Lansdown's. Laura was never Petrarch's wife and she could never quell his passion, nor did she wait on him in bed when he was sick, nor did she bear him children. On the contrary (st. XVI) Lansdown was now alone, as his wife died. The former stanzas of the poem mentioned several Latin poets; Petrarch was the only modern poet he invoked – and he invoked him as a poet of melancholy.

3. The first edition (1784) contained only 19 poems; nine of them were translations and imitations. The early editions contained only three versions from Petrarch; a fourth was added in the third edition (1786), which remained a little volume.

4. 'That nightingale that so sweetly weeps, perhaps for his children or for his dear consort, fills the sky and the fields with sweetness in so many grieving, skilful notes, // and all night he seems to accompany me and remind me of my harsh fate; for I have no one to complain of save myself, who did not believe that Death reigns over goddesses. // Oh how easy it is to deceive one who is confident! Those two lights much brighter than the sun, who ever thought to see them become dark clay? // Now I know that my fierce destiny wishes me to learn, living and weeping, how nothing down here both pleases and endures!' (Petrarca 2001, 311)

5. In l. 12 she spoke of 'mourning Friendship, or unhappy Love'. In the prefaces of *Elegiac Sonnets*, especially to vol. II, she referred the theme of betrayed friendship to specific events of her life (see, e.g., Smith 1993, 11). Some critics, like Anna Seward, blamed Smith for her use of unpleasant autobiographic material (see Fletcher 1998, 100).

6. Robinson 2003. I disagree with him, however, that Smith's reading was a way of questioning 'the validity of Petrarch's interpretation' of the bird's song.

7. Brooks 1992, 17. The sonnet of Petrarch that Smith imitated does not fit into Brook's typology. Though Petrarch evokes the nightingale only in the quatrains, his description implies substantial identification with the bird.

8. 'Alone and filled with care, I go measuring the most deserted fields with steps delaying and slow, and I keep my eyes alert so as to flee from where any human footprint marks the sand. // No other shield do I find to protect me from people's open knowing, for in my bearing, in which all happiness is extinguished, anyone can read from without how I am aflame within. // So that I believe by now that mountains and shores and rivers and woods know the temper of my life, which is hidden from other persons; // but still I cannot seek paths so harsh or so savage that Love does not always come along discoursing with me and I with him.' (Petrarca 2001, 35)

9. Smith expressed a concept like that of 'Solo et pensoso' in her Sonnet 62: 'While thus I wander, cheerless and unblest, / And find in change of place but change of pain' (ll. 1–2). Smith might have echoed another sonnet of Petrarch's on a wandering character (*PC*, 16) in her poems on the pilgrim like Sonnets 52 (especially ll. 1 and 3) and 75.

10. Smith admired Gray's sonnet, which she quoted in her 'Elegy', regretting that he wrote only one (Smith 1993, 81).

11. E.g., in Nott 1777 (see Chapter 2 in this volume).

12. For the text of 'Zephiro torna', see Chapter 2 in this volume. L. 3 of the sonnet mentions the nightingale ('chattering Procne and weeping Philomena').

13. The sonnets which repeat, literally or metaphorically, that spring is no cure for her despair and that, in any case, there is no second spring for her are at least Nos 2, 6, 8, 10, 27, 41, 42, 45, 53, 54, 58, 63, 64, 68, 78, 87, 89, 92.
14. Robinson 2003.
15. See Kennedy 1995; Hawley 1999. I disagree with Hawley's view that Smith's elegies 'resolutely refuse consolation' (Hawley 1999, 187). In that period, a woman of Smith's age, in her economic situation, with a number of children, had no chance of redeeming herself, either economically or sentimentally, as she sadly wrote in Sonnet 72, 'To the morning star. Written near the sea'. Venus would never announce anything joyful to her (ll. 9–14), as she does to the lover (a man, not coincidentally) mentioned in ll. 5–8.
16. Smith 1993, 119.
17. *Beachy Head*, l. 314 (Smith 1993, 230). The line did not require this footnote to be understood. None the less, Smith was keen on establishing a link with Petrarch.
18. 'April' forms a sort of diptych with the following poem, 'Ode to death', the last one in the first edition of *Elegiac Sonnets*, vol. II. The structural symmetry of the former poem with Sonnet 2 is confirmed by 'Ode to death', which recalls some specific points of Sonnet 1, in particular the central themes of betrayed friendship ('Or shun the *once* fond friend's *averted* eyes?', 'Ode to Death', l. 122) and 'unrequited love' (l. 15). A few other poems, extracted from her novels, were added after 'Ode to death' in the second edition of vol. II.
19. They are 'Imitation' of a French poem, 'Chanson. Par le Cardinal Bernis', and 'The origin of flattery'. From the third edition, they were placed after the sonnets.
20. The most relevant passage is at ll. 77 ff., where Flattery was ironically defined as 'a subtle spirit' of a power 'to cure the woes of womankind' (Smith 1993, 88).
21. 'Place me where the sun kills the flowers and the grass, or where the ice and the snow overcome him; place me where his chariot is temperate and light, or where dwell those who yield him to us or those who take him away; // place me in lowly or proud fortune, in sweet clear air or dark and heavy; place me in the night, in day long or short, in ripe maturity or early youth; // place me in Heaven or on earth or in the abyss, on a high mountain, in a deep and swampy valley; make me a free spirit or one fixed in his members; // place me in obscurity or in illustrious fame: still I shall be what I have been, shall live as I have lived, continuing my trilustral sighing.' (Petrarca 2001, 145)
22. Petrarch's 'libero spirto, od a' suoi membri affiso' means dead or alive, not 'Prisoner or free'. Smith adapted the phrase to her experience.
23. 'Her golden hair was loosed to the breeze, which turned it in a thousand sweet knots, and the lovely light burned without measure in her eyes, which are now so stingy of it; // and it seemed to me (I know not whether truly or falsely) her face took on the color of pity: I, who had the tinder of love in my breast, what wonder is it if I suddenly caught fire? // Her walk was not that of a mortal thing but of some angelic form, and her words sounded different from a merely human voice: // a celestial spirit, a living sun was what I saw, and if she were not such now, a wound is not healed by the loosening of the bow.' (Petrarca 2001, 90)
24. Robinson 2003.
25. One such point is the innuendo in 'frigid' at l. 3 of Sonnet 13. Smith's tolerant attitude to extra-marital sex for women can also be found in some of her novels, especially the first three.
26. 'Loose stream to wild winds those fair flowing tresses, / Once woven with garlands of gay Summer flowers', ll. 13–14 of 'The female exile. Written at Brighthelmstone

in November 1792', which reworks a passage of 'The Emigrants'. Smith changed the original atmosphere of delicate beauty into one of violent sublimity, which corresponded to the condition of the French woman (Smith 1993, 98).

27. 'If I hear birds lamenting, or green leaves moving softly in the summer breeze, or the faint murmuring of shining waves from a flowering and fresh bank // where I am sitting in thoughts of love and writing, I see her whom Heaven showed us and the earth hides from us, I see and hear and understand her, for, still alive, from far away she replies to my sighs. // "Ah, why do you consume yourself so before the time?" she says, pityingly. "Why do you still pour forth a sorrowful river from your sad eyes?" // "Do not weep for me, for my days became eternal by dying, and, when I seemed to close my eyes, I opened them on the internal light."' (Petrarca 2001, 279). Smith may have been attracted by the rhyme scheme of the quatrains (ABAB BABA), which show that Petrarch's sonnets were not all as regular as some English critics believed.

28. Smith's ll. 10–12, corresponding to the original l. 9.

29. 'O valley full of my laments, river often rising by my weeping, beasts of the forest, wandering birds, and fishes that these two banks rein in, // air warmed and cleared by my sighs, sweet path become so bitter, hill that pleased and now displeases me, where still Love leads me as he is wont: // I recognize in you your accustomed forms, not, alas, mine in myself, for I have become after such gladness the dwelling of infinite grief. // From here I used to see my love, and with these steps I come back to see the place whence she went naked to Heaven, leaving on earth her beautiful vesture.' (Petrarca 2001, 301)

30. Robinson 2003.

31. 'Angel form' is a periphrasis Smith took from l. 10 of 'Erano i capei d'oro', which she replaced with the more secular 'goddess' in her Sonnet 14. She also used it at l. 7 of Sonnet 15.

32. From the fourth edition of *Elegiac Sonnets*, Smith added a kind of *coda* to her translations from Petrarch, i.e., Sonnet 17 'From the thirteenth cantata of Metastasio'. 'Il nome', Metastasio's *cantata* XIII, celebrates love and poetry using Petrarch's central pun, the laurel. In Smith's imitation the pun remained concealed, as she did not specify the 'Beauteous tree' on which she carved 'Miranda's cipher' (l. 2). Smith does not express her poetic ambitions openly, though she hints at them in the conclusion which, as in the original, says that 'the nightingale shall build her nest' in the tree (l. 14). See Metastasio 1947, 720–1. The last part of the poem was set by Beethoven.

33. Goethe 1991, 169. This episode was versified in Sonnet 21. However, in Sonnet 70, 'On being cautioned against walking on an headland overlooking the sea, because it was frequented by a lunatic', Smith subscribed to Werther's view. She envied the lunatic because he, 'uncursed with reason', was unaware of 'The depth or the duration of his woe.' (ll. 13–14) Smith was no extreme rationalist and believed that reason was a limited power, which could cast only a 'dubious ray' on 'life's long darkling way' (Sonnet 86, 'Written near a port on a dark evening', ll. 13–14). However unsettling, sentiment was a necessary counterpart to the aridity that reason brought along (Sonnet 75, ll. 10–14).

34. Smith 'bid the traitor Love adieu' in her 'Ode to despair', adding that 'The wounds *he* gave, nor Time shall cure, / Nor Reason teach me to endure' (ll. 17, 21–2, Smith 1993, 79). The italicised 'he' is ambiguous: it can mean both Love and Smith's husband. She repeated in other poems that reason was no sufficient cure for a wounded heart, as in 'Hope. A rondeau. A parody on Lord Strangford's "Just like

love is yonder rose"' (Smith 1993, 306, ll. 10–14) and 'Love and Folly. From the Fables of La Fontaine' (Smith 1993, 309, ll. 31–6).

35. Pinch 1996, 61–2. The passage runs (Sonnet 24, ll. 9–14): 'And sometimes, when the sun with parting rays / Gilds the long grass that hides my silent bed, / The tear shall tremble in my Charlotte's eyes; / Dear, precious drops!—they shall embalm the dead! / Yes!—Charlotte o'er the mournful spot shall weep, / Where her poor Werter—and his sorrows sleep!'

36. In the Werther sonnets Smith probably retrieved a couple of specific references she had omitted in her Petrarch translations. In Sonnet 22, l. 12, she has the nightingale weep her fate, as Smith, unlike Petrarch, had failed to do in Sonnet 3. In Sonnet 25, ll. 5–6, her Werther expected forgiveness from those 'who know the force of hopeless care / On the worn heart', which sounds like a paraphrase of Petrarch's famous sonnet 1, 'Voi ch'ascoltate', ll. 7–8. The idea does not appear in Goethe.

37. It is not a coincidence that the texts Smith added later, immediately after the Werther sonnets, dealt with youth and the places where she grew up. In particular, there is a series on the River Arun and the South Downs. I disagree with Myers 2002, who argues that Smith subverted the traditional view of men as rational and women as sentimental beings, since her male speakers are mentally feeble, whereas her female speakers are rational, especially in the Werther sonnets. This does not apply to all the male voices of *Elegiac Sonnets*, and even in Werther's case it is true on the condition that Werther is a figure for herself.

38. Thelwall 1792 (signed J.T., probably John Thelwall). He was responding to the Reverend Henry White, a cousin of Seward's, who considered Smith's sonnets illegitimate and the English sonnet not a sonnet. Significantly, in the discussion they never mentioned the Elizabethans, but only Milton. Thelwall believed that Smith could equal Milton's sonnets, and she even surpassed them in 'To the moon' and 'Should the lone wanderer'. British poets were not to be chained by the fetters of Italian patterns.

39. They went through 35 reprints between 1784 and 1798 (Mouret 1976, 41).

40. They were 'pretty tuneful centos from our various poets, without any thing original' (Seward 1811, I, 163, To Miss Weston, 20 July 1786). Besides Smith, Seward criticised severely or had arguments with several other writers of the time, especially women, such as Clara Reeve, Helen Maria Williams, Mrs Piozzi and Hannah More.

41. Seward 1811, II ,162, To Rev. — Berwick, 6 Oct. 1788. The idea that Smith's sonnets were inspired by the stanza form of the eighteenth-century elegy was taken up again in Robinson 2003, which argues that 'elegiac' must be referred to the form rather than the content and the tone of Smith's sonnets, as scholars usually do.

42. Seward 1811, II, 233–4, To William Hayley, 29 Jan. 1789. She repeated that Smith's sonnets were unoriginal and full of borrowings. The diatribe on Johnson between Seward and Boswell was a sensational episode in the British literary life of the 1780s and 1790s.

43. Seward 1811, II, 287, To Theophilus Swift, 9 July 1789.

44. Seward first heard of Petrarch's sonnets in November 1762 from a gentleman who danced with her. She wrote that she longed 'to see a fine translation of them into our own language'. Petrarch's frustrations were better than the cynicism of many coxcombs of her time (Seward 1810, I, liv, lvi). Later, Seward read Dobson and perhaps Sade with enthusiasm (Seward 1811, I, 369, To George Hardinge, 21 Nov. 1787; Seward 1811, I, 389–90, To T. S. Whalley, 20 Dec. 1787).

45. Seward 1799, 66, Sonnet LXIV. Petrarch is mentioned in Sonnets XXV and LXXXVI.
46. On Curran's footnotes, see Smith 1993, 14, 21, and xxvi on the theatricality of some of her sonnets; on post-modern readings of Smith, see, e.g., Pinch 1996, 63–4, 69–71; Mergenthal 1997, 72; Hawley 1999, 191; Dolan 2003, 248. Pinch argues (Pinch 1996, 71) that the use of quotation to express one's feelings challenges 'our sense of what the authenticity of a feeling would consist of'. This carries the anti-Romantic stance to an absurd extreme, as though sympathy did not exist and it were impossible to find some coincidence with other people's experience, and as though authenticity and originality could only be the fruit of some Martian mind, totally different from any other.
47. 'Advice to Mrs Smith. A Sonnet', ll. 5–8, cited from Wu 1997, 4. The sonnet was originally published in *The Gentleman's Magazine* (1786) in response to the third edition of *Elegiac Sonnets*.
48. They are Sonnets LXXXVIII–XC.
49. Seward 1799, 27 (Sonnet XXV).
50. See Fletcher 1998, 46.
51. Seward 1799, 90–1. Sonnet LXXXIX is probably a critique of another fashionable literary suicide, Sappho's leap in Leucadia.
52. Seward 1799, 92 (Sonnet XC, ll. 10–14): 'lest my remorseless Fate decree / That all I love, with life's extinguish'd rays / Sink from my soul, to soothe this agony, / To balm that life, whose loss may forfeit thee, / COME DEAR REMEMBRANCE OF DEPARTED DAYS!' For the Werther quote, see Goethe 1991, 177.
53. For another view of the Smith-Seward controversy, Meyenberg 2005, 76–88.
54. Seward, 'Advice to Mrs. Smith. A Sonnet', ll. 9–10. Petrarch and Werther were mentioned in the previous line.
55. Seward 1811, II, 304, To Rev. T. S. Whalley, 7 Apr. 1789.
56. 'Alpine Scenery. A Poem, Addressed to the Rev. Thomas Sedgwick Whalley, during his residence on the continent in 1785', Seward 1810, II, 366. Seward argued against women's coyness in poems like 'Sonnet LVI. To a Timid Lady, Distressed by the Attention of an Amiable, and *Accepted* Lover' (Seward 1799, 58), and she used Laura as an emblem of coy women in 'Song' (Seward 1810, I, 141). The cult of solitude, a narcissistic remedy which could not cure the evils of social life, was blamed in Sonnet IX (Seward 1799, 11). In fact, Seward believed that Petrarch moved to Vaucluse to be closer to Laura, who used to spend her summers there, rather than to run away from her (Seward 1811, I, 389, To T. S. Whalley, 20 Dec. 1787). She also disliked conceits, which were the main cause of the decay of Italian poetry (Seward 1811, II, 333, To Mr. Cary, 19 Dec. 1789; II, 354, 21 Jan. 1790; II, 393, 16 Mar. 1790).
57. See 'Elegy 3. Petrarch, A Vision to a Friend' (Preston 1793, I). The friend he addressed was Smith.
58. Seward 1810, I, 113–14.
59. A good example is the beginning of 'Song of Roxana' (Seward 1810, II, 295–6): 'When, to thy own Roxana's arms, / Wilt thou, my lovely lord, return? / When on thy blaze of youthful charms / Shall these desiring glances turn? / Anxious I wait thee in the spicy grove; — / My eye-balls ache with watching for my love.' In comparison to the prose source, Seward made the text more sensual by adding in the 'desiring glances' and the 'spicy grove', which can be an exotic place as much as an erotic metaphor. Other such examples appear in the following stanzas and in translations like 'The Song of Zillia' (Seward 1810, II, 297–9).

60. Seward 1810, III, 29. The complete title runs, 'Harold's Complaint. A Scandinavian Ode. From Dr Alexander's History of Women'.
61. See, e.g., stanza II (Seward 1810, III, 30–1), and the burden to each stanza.
62. Robinson 2003.
63. Havens defines five typical reactions to the sonnet in the eighteenth century. Those who disliked all types of sonnets (e.g. Dr Johnson); those who liked all sonnets (Hayley); those who preferred irregular forms (C. Smith); admirers of Milton, Petrarch and the regular sonnet (Seward); those who held no opinion at all, who probably were the majority.
64. The term is used throughout Dobson 1807, which Dobson translated from the French of Sainte-Palaye.
65. They are the last four lines of *Canzone* 268 (not 'sonnet', as Curran wrote, Smith 1993, 1). The sonnet cited in *Celestina* is *PC*, 292, l. 6 (Smith 2004, 141).
66. Smith 1993, 1.
67. Fletcher 1998, 14, 36–7.
68. Smith 2003, 218. As Baretti's *Italian Library* is in one volume and she applied for a work in five volumes, she probably meant also other works of Baretti's.
69. Smith's version of *PC*, 301, 'Ye vales and woods!', is probably indebted to Nott's translation at two points: 'tenants of the grove' (l. 2), which corresponds to Nott's 'Ye tenants of the sweet, melodious grove!' (Nott 1777, 55, l. 3), and 'bright stream! befringed with shrubs and flowers' (l. 3), which corresponds to Nott's 'in the grass-fring'd streamlet' (l. 4).
70. This is shown also by her novels, especially *The Young Philosopher* (1798). As Fletcher points out, Smith depicts one of the protagonists, the despairing Laura, in the same poses of the 'I' of *Elegiac Sonnets* (Fletcher 1998, 281–2). The choice of Laura as a name for such a character is not a coincidence.
71. Smith quoted Pope's poem in her Sonnets 1, 21 (one of the Werther sonnets) and 54.

4   The Della Cruscans and Mary Robinson

1. *Florence*, 93.
2. 'Sonnet' and 'Ode on Apathy', *Florence*, 80, 129–31. One of Greatheed's Italian sonnets was translated by Parsons. The source of Greatheed's borrowing is *PC*, 146, where Petrarch wishes he were able to sing Laura's beauty to all the world, but since he cannot, his song will be heard in the 'bel paese, / ch'Appennin parte, e 'l mar circonda et l'Alpe'. It seems that Greatheed often read his translations, which remained unpublished, to his friends (Hargreaves-Mawdsley 1967, 41).
3. Parsons's note cites *PC*, 114, where Petrarch called the Avignon court a Babylon. Parsons 1787, 137–8.
4. Also, 'al suon de' detti sì pietosi et casti' ('at the sound of words so kind and chaste') became 'so rapt'rous were the strains' (*Florence*, 74; all modern trans of this sonnet from Petrarca 2001, 302). On the Della Cruscans, see the chapters on them in Pascoe 1997, McGann 1998, Labbe 2000, and also Bostetter 1956, Gamer 2003.
5. 'Stanzas on Reading Petrarch's Sonnets on the Death of Laura' (*Florence*, 75). In *A Poetical Tour* Parsons added a misleading note to the passage, arguing that the source of the stanza was a passage on Philomela in Virgil's *Georgics* (Parsons 1787, 65). Another literary echo he took up from Smith is 'the dull ear of night' (l. 2), a

phrase of Shakespeare's used in Smith's Sonnet 7, 'On the departure of the nightingale', l. 4. In *A Poetical Tour*, after his imitation of *PC*, 302, Parsons included an imitation of Metastasio's 'Scrivo in te l'amato nome', which Smith had translated freely in *Elegiac Sonnets* (Parsons 1787, 196 ff.). Like her, Parsons referred to a 'Miranda' who does not appear in the Italian text. Smith's imitation was first published in the forth edition of *Elegiac Sonnets* in 1786; *A Poetical Tour* came out in 1787.

6. *Florence*, 75.
7. *Florence*, 76.
8. *Florence*, 76.
9. *Florence*, 76.
10. Parsons 1787, 67. In *Fidelity*, he paraphrased *PC*, 183 on the variability of women's love (Parsons 1798, 32).
11. Parsons 1787, 54: 'Or lost in softer grief o'er LAURA's bier, / With PETRARCH drop the sadly-pleasing tear'. His preference for Petrarch was expressed in a footnote to Sonnet I, 'To a Lady, on her beginning to study Italian', where he pointed out that studying Italian was difficult but eventually, from the top of the volcano, she would enjoy a wonderful view of Ariosto, Tasso and Petrarch (Parsons 1798, 80).
12. Parsons 1798, 77–9, 'Preface to the Sonnets'. He pointed out the Italian origin of the term. As a dilettante, he emphasised that his job was not to write sonnets constantly, since he had got other things to do in life. *Fidelity* is an Arthurian tale in rhyming couplets whose opening contrasts the degeneracy of the present to the sanity of the past. Parsons often quotes Greek, Latin, and Italian authors (Petrarch, Ariosto, Tasso) in his footnotes and he imitates some of their lines. The tenor of the story is not Petrarchan, because it is rather explicitly erotic – for example, there is a bed scene with the illustration of the beauties of the female protagonist, for whose description he invoked the help of Solomon and Aretino (Parsons 1798, 25).
13. Parsons, 'To a friend in Love, and writing Sonnets', ll. 11–14; *'three 'prenticeships'* means 21 years; 'he', obviously, is Petrarch.
14. In a note to his *Travelling Recreations* (Parsons 1807, I, 170) Parsons wrote that he had made many more translations from Petrarch, but he preserved only this one for the sake of its beautiful descriptions of evening.
15. Like other translators, Parsons treated the *canzone* more freely than the sonnets. He used a different stanza, he omitted some lines or parts of lines, and he condensed some points and expanded others. As in his sonnet version, he added a few adjectives and changed others. For example, 'il cielo rapido' ('swift heaven') became 'the landscape', 'dì nostro' ('our day') 'light's pure beam', 'sgombra' ('lightens') 'charms'. He rendered 'eterna luce' ('eternal light') with 'ray' (Parsons 1787, 192), expanded 'Et perché un poco nel parlar mi sfogo' (l. 57, 'And – let me vent myself somewhat in speaking') into 'Since some small solace thence I find, / Still let me pour the mournful strain' (Parsons 1787, 195), and omitted 'volli' in 'Misero me, che volli / quando primier sì fiso / gli tenni nel bel viso' (ll. 63–5, 'Miserable me! What was I doing when for the first time I kept them so fixed on her lovely face', Petrarca 2001, 50), which he translated as 'ill fated was the hour / When first I saw her matchless grace' (Parsons 1787, 195).
16. Petrarch's original conclusion runs as follows (Petrarca 2001, 50): 'Song, if being with me from morning to night has made you of my party, you will not show yourself everywhere; and you will be so careless of praise that it will be enough for you to think from hill to hill how I am reduced by the fire from this living

stone on which I lean.' The conclusion of 'Qual più diversa et nova' is (Petrarca 2001, 135), 'If anyone should wish to know, Song, what I am doing, you can say: "Beside a great stone in a closed valley, whence Sorgue comes forth, he is; nor is there anyone to see him save Love, who never leaves him even for a step, and the image of one who destroys him: for his part, flees all other persons."' Parsons rendered it as, 'My song! – if any ask thee, tell / Where now retired I chuse to dwell; / In the closed vale where SORGA springs, / While Love alone approaches nigh, / Who to my thought her image brings / For whom all human steps I fly!' For Parsons, also, changing the conclusion was a way of mentioning the fountain of Vaucluse, of which, as he said in a footnote, Sir William Jones gave an elegant description in 'Laura' (Parsons 1787, 195).

17. Merry cited Petrarch only marginally in 'Il viaggio', a poetical tour through France and Italy (*Florence*, 199).

18. Robinson 1994b, 136–7.

19. In the tributary poems included in Robinson's collected poems, she is addressed as Laura nine times, and as Sappho five times (see Robinson 1996).

20. See at least Pascoe 1995; Pascoe 1997, 25, 68–70, 123–4, 173–8; Mellor 2000a. Though Pascoe defines the personalities of Laura and Laura Maria as mellifluous, she points out in a footnote that the outspokenly Jacobin poem 'Ainsi Va le Monde' appeared with the signature 'Laura Maria' in a journal in 1790 (Robinson 2000a, 103).

21. Robinson's début is recalled with pride and a touch of criticism towards the Della Cruscans in her *Memoirs*, even though this section was written by her daughter or the book's publisher (Robinson 1994b, 136-8). Though Robinson outgrew her Della Cruscan friends, she returned to the mode of epistolary exchange in her late poetic correspondence with Coleridge, who addressed her as 'Laura' and 'Sappho'.

22. See, e.g., the motto to 'Echo to Him Who Complains', 'Rinaldo to Laura Maria' and its answer, 'To Rinaldo', and 'To Leonardo' with a motto from 'Leonardo to Laura' (Robinson 1994a, 100–7, 123, 153). Rinaldo and Leonardo were two of Merry's pseudonyms.

23. Pope 1953–69, vol. II (ed. G. Tillotson, London: Methuen, 1940, rptd London: Routledge, 1993), p. 336, ll. 197–200: 'Ere such a soul regains its peaceful state, / How often must it love, how often hate! / How often, hope, despair, resent, regret, / Conceal, disdain—do all things but forget.'

24. Tillotson points out the dramatic quality of Pope's 'Eloisa to Abelard', which Robinson must have found congenial ('Eloisa to Abelard', Pope 1953–69, II, 299). In the early eighteenth century, Ovid's epistolary style was considered more natural than that of Petrarch and Donne (Pope 1953–69, II, 300).

25. McGann affirms that the Della Cruscan poetical correspondence intentionally revived the Provençal *tenso* or the *stilnovo tenzone*, but he does not provide historical evidence for his hypothesis (McGann 1998, 80–1). I have not come across any kind of evidence, and since Provençal and *stilnovo* poetry was extremely rare reading at the time, it is much more likely that the Della Cruscan correspondence evolved from Pope's verse letters and the Ovidian tradition. The last section of Ovid's *Heroides* consists of three couples of epistles with a reply on the part of each addressee. Robinson mentioned the 'DELLA CRUSCAN lyre' immediately before 'OVID's tender pain' in her 'Ode to the Muse' (Robinson 1994a, 5).

26. Robinson 1994a, 187.

27. See Robinson 1994b, 29. She also learned Latin and French. Besides Petrarch, in her poems Robinson evoked Italy as a paradise of the senses and a 'Land

of MELODY' ('Ode to Health' and 'Lines to Him Who Will Understand Them', Robinson 1994a, 13–14, 63).

28. For instance, like Pope, Robinson mentioned silence, melancholy, deepest caverns (see Pope's 'deep solitudes'), fatal fires (see Pope's 'long-forgotten heat'), and so forth. Several images also appear in Petrarch; in particular, 'Where frantic, lost, forlorn, and sad I go' is a free version of the beginning of 'Solo et pensoso'.

29. Robinson 1994a, 188. The 'narrow cell' sounds, again, like an echo of Pope's 'Eloisa to Abelard' (l. 1, 'awful cells').

30. The idea that nature can offer no real consolation to a suffering mind is repeated in other texts of the collection, like 'To Rinaldo' and 'To Leonardo' (Robinson 1994a, 104 and 153).

31. Robinson 1994a, 188.

32. The source is specified in a footnote (Robinson 1994a, 189). Dobson's angelic description of Laura is a paraphrase of some passages of Petrarch's poems. Robinson included Dobson's translation in the remarkable works by contemporary British women writers she mentioned at the end (Robinson 2005, 95–6). She erroneously indicated that Dobson's *Life of Petrarch* was translated 'from the Italian' (Robinson 2005, 100).

33. Robinson 1994a, 190.

34. Robinson 1994a, 190.

35. Robinson 1994a, 191. Petrarch's frenzy is described in physical, sensuous terms as a demonic power ('Calm my touch'd sense, and lull the fiends to rest; / Teach me each rebel passion to disown'). Robinson's emphasis on the opposition between human love and religion was probably influenced by Pope's 'Eloisa to Abelard', where the concept is a structural part of the story.

36. Robinson 1994a, 191.

37. Robinson 1994a, 192. Dotti recalls that Petrarch himself wrote in *Familiares* (VIII, 3, 13) that solitude increased his passion (Dotti 1987, 49). On her part, in 'The Adieu to Love' Robinson wrote a eulogy of solitude, where the muse and Philomela can console and inspire the despondent lover (Robinson 1994a, 115–16).

38. 'Madd'ning I see thy glitt'ring phantom rise, / Spring from the steep, and hover 'midst the skies. / I rave, I howl, from point to point I start, / While hell's worst torments riot in my heart; / I court the fiends my rending pangs to share, / And prove the PROUDEST TRANSPORTS OF DESPAIR' (Robinson 1994a, 193).

39. 'When all was rapture, all was peace, my breast / No pang endur'd, no wayward thought confess'd!' (Robinson 1994a, 193).

40. Robinson 1994a, 194. Robinson does not mention the fact that many of Petrarch's travels were undertaken for his scholarly researches.

41. Robinson 1994a, 195.

42. Robinson 1994a, 196. See Pope, *The Rape of the Lock*, especially canto I, ll. 47–114.

43. Robinson again used this image in the last sonnet of *Sappho and Phaon*, where 'capricious Fancy' was defined as a 'light sylph' (Sonnet XLIV, l. 3). Like Fancy, Laura was implicitly associated with capriciousness and volubility.

44. Robinson 1994a, 196.

45. Robinson 1994a, 197.

46. Robinson 1994a, 197.

47. Robinson 2005, 67–8.

48. Robinson noted that a learned woman was usually considered a masculine woman, as though knowledge were a territory for men only (Robinson 2005, 72).

49. Robinson 2000a, 139.
50. Robinson 1994a, 62–3. Some critics believe that the poem, which was also included in Robinson's *Memoirs*, is addressed to the Prince of Wales, others to Colonel Tarleton, Robinson's lover at the time of its composition. My impression is that the poem is intentionally vague enough to be referring to both figures. The preceding text, 'Ode to Valour', is dedicated to Tarleton. Robinson 1994a, 60; Robinson 2000a, 87.
51. Robinson 1994a, 186.
52. Robinson 1994a, 113.
53. Robinson 1994a, 109 and 28.
54. Formally, an intermediate step between 'Petrarch to Laura' and *Sappho and Phaon* was her 'Sonnet to Lesbia', signed 'Sappho' and published in *The Oracle* (5 Oct. 1793). A gossip column immediately below the sonnet mentions Colonel Tarleton and Mary Robinson. As S. Curran points out, Lesbia, like Sappho, was a pseudonym Robinson used for love poetry, 'Sappho generally the victim of her experiences with men, Lesbia with her illusions still intact' (Curran 1994, 27). The earliest reference to Robinson as a British Sappho dates from 1791 (Pascoe 1997, 25).
55. *Sappho*, 144.
56. *Sappho*, 144–5.
57. *Sappho*, 145–6. Robinson and Smith might have met at William Godwin's, who was a friend of both (Robinson 2000a, 45). However, though Robinson even wrote a 'Sonnet to Mrs. Charlotte Smith', Smith was not keen at all on meeting Robinson '& other Mistresses whom I have no passion for being confounded with' (Smith 2003, 269, 25 Apr. 1795). Robinson also mentioned William Kendall's opinion in support of her view of the sonnet (*Sappho*, 145–6).
58. *Sappho*, 146.
59. *Sappho*, 146–7.
60. *Sappho*, 148–9. Robinson argued that in the Middle Ages women's ignorance was the chief cause of 'bigotry and religious imposition' (Robinson 2005, 56–7).
61. *Sappho*, 149–50.
62. L. H. Peterson rightly noted that, though the date of publication of *Sappho and Phaon* is closer to the end of her affair with Tarleton, the physical traits and the age of the characters recalls her story with the Prince of Wales (Peterson 1994, 49).
63. In her *Memoirs*, Robinson wrote that love was the theme of her earliest 'poetical phantasies', as if, like Sappho, she was doomed to be a love poet (Robinson 1994b, 30).
64. This was Robinson's spelling for Kerkulas ('tail') from the island of Andros ('man'). The episode originated in classical Athenian comedy, in which Sappho became a character with an insatiable heterosexual appetite.
65. *Sappho*, 151–2.
66. This was a widespread critical tenet in the eighteenth century (Most 1996, 12–13). Robinson found it at least in Barthélemy 1880, 103.
67. Ovid's 'Sappho Phaoni' was usually printed along with Pope's version from the 1736 edition of Pope's works onward. Pope 1953–69, I (ed. E. Audra and A. Williams, London: Methuen, 1961, rptd London and New York: Routledge, 1994) p. 392. Significantly, Robinson ignored Barthélemy's most characteristic contribution, that is, his view of Sappho as a politically committed fighter against tyranny and an exile in Sicily (Barthélemy 1880, 646 n.). On this theme, see also deJean 1989, 157–60.

68. *Sappho*, 153–4. Barthélemy argued that Sappho's loves were as pure as those of Socrates and Plato (Barthélemy 1880, 103).
69. See Most 1996, 18–19.
70. deJean points out that 'From 1710 to 1816, Sappho's heterosexuality is uncontested', which in general is correct, even though it must not be forgotten that in the same period texts like Ovid's 'Sappho Phaoni' and Pope's translation, where Sappho's homosexuality is evident, continued to enjoy great popularity. Though *Heroides* were not as fashionable as in the seventeenth century, they were not eliminated, as deJean affirms (deJean 1989, 12–13, 129).
71. In Ovid and Pope it is clear that Sappho and Phaon were lovers for a while, before he ran away with another woman. Robinson disclosed the latter part of the story, whereas she only hinted at the affair between Sappho and Phaon. Ovid's passages of explicit eroticism (e.g. ll. 39–52, 129–30), which appear in Pope in a more moderate form, are drastically downplayed in Robinson, who omitted them completely or hinted at them with the greatest caution. The only passages of clear sensuality are Sonnet XXV, ll. 3–4, and Sonnet XV, ll. 3–4. The moral standard of her age obliged her to behave like that so as to defend her shaky reputation. Her strategy worked well, since conservative critics like Polwhele liked her poems, whereas they attacked her novels (Polwhele 1974, 17).
72. Addison was quite frank about Sappho's lesbianism, which is also clear in Ambrose Philips's translations appended to his essays. Of course, we shall never know what Robinson really thought about this. Women writers could not 'admit Sappho's bisexuality without harming their reputation'; they could not 'defend something that could damage' their status (Donoghue 1993, 245–7, 250).
73. The link between Sappho and Petrarch is motivated not only by historical circumstances. As G. Greer recalls, despite the great difference between the two poets, 'Eternal non-reciprocity, which DeJean sees as Sappho's insight into the nature of love, is a fundamental tenet of the Petrarchist philosophy of love' (Greer 1995, 132). Interestingly, in her *Memoirs* Robinson wrote that she never met 'with an associating mind, a congenial spirit, who could (as it were abstracted from the world) find an universe in the sacred intercourse of soul, the sublime union of sensibility' (Robinson 1994b, 69).
74. Some points of Robinson's text were drawn from or at least influenced by the Petrarchan tradition. For example, Sonnet XXIV includes a passage (ll. 9–14), not found in Ovid, Pope and Barthélemy, where all nature but Sappho is sleeping at night, which recalls Parsons' translation of *PC*, 50 (see above). In Sonnet XVIII, the close alliance of rapture and pain in the last lines, not present in Ovid's poem and Pope's version, is a typically Petrarchan antithesis. Two passages where Sappho expects to be understood and pitied by those who have experienced love like her sound like a Petrarchan reading of some Ovidian lines, and a Petrarchan addition: see Sonnet XVII, ll. 13–14 ('Then nymphs beware how ye profane my name, / Nor blame my weakness, till like me ye love!'), corresponding to 'Sappho Phaoni', ll. 199–204, and Sonnet XXVIII, l. 9 ('He never lov'd, who could not muse and sigh'). The relevant passage is *PC*, 1, ll. 7–8 (Petrarca 2001, 1), 'where there is anyone who understands love through experience, I hope to find pity, not only pardon.'
75. The original distich from Ovid's 'Sappho Phaoni', ll. 7–8, runs as follows: 'Flendus amor meus est; elegeïa flebile carmen; / Non facit ad lacrymas barbitos ulla meas.'
76. Smith influenced some parts of *Sappho and Phaon*, in particular Sonnet XXIV, an address to the moon which imitates 'To the moon' (*Elegiac Sonnets*, 4). Robinson adopted Smith's imagery and vocabulary ('orb', 'beams', 'silv'ry light', 'pale,

placid', 'pensive beam'), but she contradicted her in ll. 5–6 and, above all, in the conclusion. Unlike Smith, Robinson emphasised that the calm beauty of moonshine cannot soothe Sappho's tormented mind, which finds the idea of suicide (Sonnet XXIV, ll. 7–8) far less attractive and beautiful than Smith's 'weary pilgrim' (Sonnet 4, ll. 13–14). In Sonnet XXV, Sappho's 'solitary urn' may be indebted to Smith's version of *PC*, 301 (*Elegiac Sonnets*, 16, l. 14). Also, Robinson probably learned from Smith the technique of closing a sonnet with a quoted line, as in Sonnet XLII.

77. I said seemingly because Petrarch considered suicide as a way of getting rid of his torments, but commonsense and his Christian faith compelled him to reject this solution (see *PC*, 63). Robinson wrote an 'Elegy to the Memory of Werter', in which his suicide, a sin for the 'churlish priest', is forgiven by Charlotte's Sympathy and Sensibility, and his tomb is consecrated by sympathetic Nature (Robinson 1994a, 80–1).

78. Though recent feminist readings have argued for a specifically feminine value of Sappho's experience, I agree with G. Greer and G. Most, who point out how the ambiguity of gender in poems like fragment 31 and the exclusive attention on the poet's subjective feelings have made and will make Sappho's poems interesting for everyone, regardless of sexual orientation (Greer 1995, 113, 116, 132; Most 1996, 28–35).

79. *Sappho*, 162 (Sonnet X). Like the mistresses of many Renaissance sonnets, Phaon's body is depicted as a sum of precious parts, like 'melodious tongue', the 'sapphire sheath' of 'murd'rous eyes', 'smooth cheek', 'fragrant breath', 'ruby lips', 'polish'd brow', 'golden hair'.

80. On this point, I quite disagree with McGann, who wrote that, 'Following Rousseau and Goethe, Robinson turns Sappho's apparent madness to a psychological sign of a general disfunction, of which Phaon is the emblem. Her love for him therefore functions as prophecy, the forecast of a time when a Phaon might come who would be worthy of such love. In the meantime Sappho exhibits a soul tormented by the failures of time and circumstance' (McGann 1998, 101). I believe that Robinson's view of the nature of love was much closer to Sappho's and Petrarch's sense of eternal non-reciprocity than to McGann's post-modern, illusory optimism.

81. *Sappho*, 157.

82. *Sappho*, 159 (Sonnet IV, ll. 5–8).

83. Other sonnets which emphasise the impotence of the mind are XVII, XXVI (on philosophy), XXVIII. The uselessness of nature and solitude as a cure for love appears in Sonnets XXVIII, XXIX, and XXXVI, which corresponds to Ovid's 'Sappho Phaoni', ll. 135–56, and Pope's 'Sapho to Phaon', ll. 160–78. Barthélemy does not mention these themes.

84. See, e.g., Sonnets XIX and XLIII. In any event, poetry benefits readers rather than its author (Sonnets XXXIII, ll. 11–14; XXXVI, ll. 12–14).

85. See Pope, 'Sapho to Phaon', ll. 13–14 ('No more my Soul a Charm in Musick finds, / Musick has Charms alone for peaceful Minds') and 228–31 ('Alas! the *Muses* now no more inspire, / Untun'd my Lute, and silent is my Lyre, / My languid Numbers have forgot to flow, / And Fancy sinks beneath a Weight of Woe.'), which correspond to Ovid's 'Sappho Phaoni', ll. 13–14 and 195–8. Barthélemy, who does not mention this theme, writes that Sappho, like the Pythia, was possessed and agitated when she composed her poems (Barthélemy 1880, 104).

86. deJean 1989, 327–8 n. 4.

87. McGann 1998, 103.
88. Robinson pointed out the paradoxical character of libertinism. Men's laws decreed that women's chastity was of paramount importance, yet men were 'indefatigable in promoting their violation' (Robinson 2005, 74–5, 80). In her *Memoirs*, she complained about the behaviour of her husband, who at least should have observed 'some decency in his infidelities' to protect her from 'the most degrading mortifications' (Robinson 1994b, 91).
89. See deJean 1989, 175. She points out that the episode became particularly popular with painters and illustrators of Sappho's poems.
90. deJean concludes: 'For centuries, Sappho commentary has been torn between two radically opposed visions: on the one hand, Sappho the abandoned woman, the essence of unmediated female suffering and pain; and, on the other, Sappho as detached and wry commentator on the "vanity and impermanence" of *human – not* essentially female – passion.' (deJean 1989, 26–8)
91. *Sappho* 173–4 (Sonnet XXXII). Whatever Robinson's source may have been, her Sappho envies a Sicilian maid who conquered Phaon, 'The youth whose soul thy yielding graces charm; / [...] While round thy fragrant lips light zephyrs swarm, / As op'ning buds attract the wand'ring Bee!' The conclusion is especially characteristic of Robinson: 'Yet, short is youthful passion's fervid hour; / Soon, shall another clasp the beauteous boy; / Soon shall a rival prove, in that gay bow'r, / The pleasing torture of excessive joy! / The Bee flies sicken'd from the sweetest flow'r; / The lightning's shaft but dazzles to destroy!' Here and elsewhere, the sensuousness of the original was transferred from human to floral images.
92. *Sappho*, 165 (Sonnet XVI, l. 14). Here Robinson recycled the phrase 'luxury of tender grief', which she had used in 'Where, thro' the starry curtain of the night' (l. 12), the sonnet placed immediately before 'Petrarch to Laura' in Robinson 1994a.
93. This was the reason why, in comparison to the Romantic male poets, women writers were much more cautious in celebrating the romance of sexual, passionate love (Mellor 1993, 59–60).
94. Robinson 1996, III, 119.
95. See, e.g., 'For when the FANCY is on wing, / VARIETY is a dangerous thing: / And PASSIONS, when they learn to stray / Will seldom keep the beaten way' ('The Fortune-Teller', Robinson 2000a, 248). See also 'The Mistletoe', 'Deborah's Parrot' and 'Poor Marguerite'.
96. As J. Labbe argues, 'Robinson and Hemans write romances in which romance itself – as an ideology and as a lifestyle – is shown to be corrupt, where reliance on romantic love leads only to catastrophe, and where the violence suffered, by women and men, reveals the emptiness of behavioural stereotypes' (Labbe 2000, 104). Though Labbe is referring to the Gothic romance, the fictions of Petrarch and Sappho can be considered as romances.

5 Charles Lloyd and Samuel Taylor Coleridge

1. *PW (CC)* I:2, 1205.
2. As an example, Coleridge quoted Seward's sonnet on the sonnet, whose style resembled 'racked and tortured Prose' more than poetry. *PW (CC)* I:2, 1206–7.
3. *PW (CC)* I:2, 1206.
4. In Wiltshire Coleridge visited Bowles regularly while he began composing *Biographia* in spring 1815. The eulogy in *Biographia* is especially suspect

considering the substantial reservations about Bowles expressed by Coleridge in 1802, when he blamed the weakness of Bowles's passion, which led him to moralise everything (*CL* II, 864–5).

5. The title of the first edition, which was also published in 1789, was *Fourteen Sonnets. Elegiac and Descriptive*, in which his debt to Smith's elegiac view of the sonnet is evident.

6. 'Alone and filled with care, I go measuring the most deserted fields with steps delaying and slow', and 'So that I believe by now that mountains and shores and rivers and woods' (Petrarca 2001, 35).

7. Bowles 1978, 11.

8. Bowles praised the soothing beauty of landscape and the joyous thoughtlessness of youth in other sonnets, such as 'To the River Tweed', 'To the River Itchin, near Winton', 'On a Distant View of England', and the well-known 'Written at Ostend. July 22, 1787'. See also Coleridge's 'Sonnet: To Bowles', whose lines 'Their mild and manliest melancholy lent / A mingled charm, such as the pang consign'd / To slumber, tho' the big tear it renew'd' (*PW (CC)* I:1, 163, 1796, ll. 8–10). Coleridge's admiration was also due to the Christian and philanthropic ideals embodied in Bowles's verse. See Robinson 2000b, 86–7.

9. *PW (CC)* I:1, 162–3. The second phrase is taken from 'Sonnet: to Bowles', l. 8, which in 1794 ran as 'Thy kindred Lays an healing solace lent'.

10. Schor 1994, 66–8. Schor, who is unaware of the source, defines the allegory as 'Bunyanesque'.

11. Coleridge certainly knew the sonnet, as Lloyd also translated it in his *Poems on Various Subjects* (1795).

12. Bowles revealed, however generically, the autobiographical background to his collection only later, in the prefaces to *Sonnets* (1805) and *Scenes and Shadows of Days Departed* (1837), where he specified that there were two unfortunate love affairs behind the composition of his sonnets.

13. As in *Canzoniere*, Preston's are partly *in vita* and partly *in morte* sonnets for his Clara.

14. Preston 1781, 139, 142, 144, 157. 'Lonely and pensive' is 'Sonnet the First' of the series; besides these three, he translated *PC*, 12. His version of 'La gola e 'l somno', which, as we saw above, was prominent in Sade and Dobson and became a favourite text in radical circles, is more crudely critical of the 'vile croud' (l. 13) than the original, but it does not include the reference to money of 'dice la turba al vil guadagno intesa' (l. 11, 'says the mob, bent on low gain'), which became 'How lost—how abject in these iron days!' (Preston 1781, 142). 'Lonely and pensive' and 'The glutton banquet' were reprinted in *Laura*.

15. The subtitle of the two freer versions is: 'imitated from Petrarch' (Preston 1781, 142, 157).

16. In the first poem, Petrarch appears to the sleeping poet and tells him that he must love for 40 years, as he did, and then abandon everything and retire in solitude if he wants to earn fame (Preston 1781, 118–20). He tells the poet he must not despair as long as his beloved does not marry another man (Preston 1781, 121–2). In 'Verses Written in the Dargle in the Country of Wicklow' Preston compares the place to Vaucluse, whose solitude is ideal for a poet (Preston 1781, 184). *PC*, 1 was used as a motto for Preston's section of 'Love Elegies'.

17. The new translation was 'Sonnet the Twenty-Fifth' (*PC*, 19).

18. Sonnets 14–19 (Preston 1793, I, n.p.).

19. 'Elegy 11. A Fragment' (Preston 1793, I, 345).

20. Preston 1793, I, 346–7.
21. Sonnet 26, ll. 12–14 (Preston 1793, I, n.p.).
22. In Sonnet 24, l. 1, he compares himself to Petrarch as a desperate lover who 'mourns th' eternal wound' (Preston 1793, I, n.p.). He loves his lady more than Petrarch loved Laura, but she never responded. However, he hopes that Clara, like Werther's Lotte, will survive him and will shed tears on his grave.
23. Preston wrote, against Sir William Jones, that love poetry does not belong to the early stages of society. Preston did not want to use the name of love poets for those who celebrate only sensual pleasure, and especially vice, obscenity and licentiousness. Love poets have more sentiment and less sensuality, and they alone deserve the name of erotic poets (Preston 1805?, 8, 10). Of the classical poets, Propertius was the closest to Petrarch, 'in violence of passion, and energy of expression.' He was the only classical writer to have a sense of the dignity and value of women, and of 'the intercourse of mind' besides the body (Preston 1805?, 18, 22). Sonnets like 'La gola e 'l somno', 'Zephiro torna' and 'Rotta è l'alta colonna' strongly recall some passages by Propertius (Preston 1805?, 28, 30). Ovid, Tibullus and Propertius invented a new kind of poetry, which in modern times has been equalled only by Petrarch, 'whose romantic destiny, however, has contributed not a little to heighten the lustre and renown of his poetical beauties' (Preston 1805?, 34).
24. Preston 1793, I, 261–2 ('To the Reader').
25. Preston 1793, I, 262–3 ('To the Reader'). Preston also pointed out that Petrarch was a man of 'various abilities', a great scholar and a consummate negotiator.
26. Line 7 of his version of *PC*, 269 contains a quotation from Gray's 'Elegy' ('And every lingering, longing wish is vain'). Lloyd did not understand that Petrarch was mourning two separate persons, his lover and his best friend, both of whom had died of Black Death. He left out, also, Petrarch's remark about how quickly we can lose what we love. Lloyd only emphasised that death destroys the illusions of youth (ll. 13–14; Lloyd 1978, 17). Lloyd's Sonnet V is entitled 'To the Grave' (Lloyd 1978, 11).
27. Lloyd 1978, 16. The last tercet of 'Solo et pensoso' runs as follows: 'but still I cannot seek paths so harsh or so savage that Love does not always come along discoursing with me and I with him'. (Petrarca 2001, 35)
28. Lloyd 1978, 18. Also, Lloyd made Petrarch more passive, since in the conclusion he seems to stop writing because 'With hope the muses soothing dreams are flown'. In the original l. 12, it is Petrarch who decides to put an end to his singing: 'Now here let there be an end to my song of love'. All modern trans of this sonnet are from Petrarca 2001, 292.
29. Lloyd 1978, 21, l. 2.
30. Lloyd 1978, 21: 'For my "frail thoughts dallying with false surmise" / Built all their hopes of happiness below, / And still forgot how soon earth's pleasure flies! / But now alas! 'tis mine with tears to know / That every thought to purer scenes should rise, / Nor linger here with vanity and woe.' The quotation at l. 9 seems inspired by Smith.
31. The title of the 'Dedicatory Sonnet' of the collection is '*Ad Amicos*' (Lloyd 1978, 3).
32. Lloyd 1978, 20, ll. 4–8. The original: 'se, come i tuoi gravosi affanni sai, / così sapessi il mio simile stato, / verresti in grembo a questo sconsolato / a partir seco i dolorosi guai.' ('if as you know your own grievous troubles you also knew my similar state, you would come to my unconsoled bosom to share its sorrowing groans' Petrarca 2001, 353).

33. Lloyd 1978, 15. Lines 12–13 of *PC*, 273; trans, Petrarca 2001, 273.
34. Lloyd 1978, 19, ll. 1–4; *PC*, 320; Petrarca 2001, 320. The additions are at ll. 1–3 ('With sad delight', 'whose summits pierce the skies', 'those solitary vales'); the original ll. 3–4 are condensed and paraphrased in Lloyd's l. 4.
35. Lloyd 1978, 19, l. 14. The original conclusion is, 'I have served a cruel and niggardly lord: I burned as long as my fire was before me, now I go bewailing the scattering of its ashes' (Petrarca 2001, 320).
36. The complete title is, S. T. Coleridge, *Poems*, 2nd edn, *To which are now added Poems by Charles Lamb and Charles Lloyd*, Bristol: Cottle; London: Robinsons, 1797 (*PW (CC)* I:2, 1227). The book contains an 'Introduction to the Sonnets' reprinted with some variants from *Sonnets from Various Authors*.
37. At this date, Coleridge's references to Petrarch betray a generic knowledge. Laura's name appears in 'On a Lady Weeping', an imitation of Nicolaus Archius's 'De lacrimis puellae', which is in its turn an imitation of Ariosto ('Lovely gems of radiance meek / Trembling down my Laura's cheek', *PW (CC)* I:1, 71, Feb.–June 1792?); in the first-known manuscript of 'Sonnet: To an Old Man in the Snow (with Samuel Favell)', l. 9 (later replaced by 'Sara', *PW (CC)* I:1, 154, probably Nov.–Dec. 1794); in Sonnet XI 'on Eminent Characters', 'To Richard Brinsley Sheridan, Esq' ('And sweet thy voice, as when o'er Laura's bier / Sad music trembled thro' Vauclusa's glade', *PW (CC)* I:1, 168–9); in 'Lines on the Portrait of a Lady', l. 15 (*PW (CC)* I:1, 258, before 17 Mar. 1796). In 1796 Coleridge substituted Petrarch and Vaucluse for Rousseau and Ermenonville in a sonnet which was intended to be Southey's inscription for Rousseau's cenotaph at Ermenonville (*CL* I, 244–5).
38. Lamb concluded: 'Thank God, the folly has left me for ever' (Lamb 1975–78, I, 60). Lamb also held in low regard melancholy sonnets like those of Bowles and Smith, 'who can see no joys but what are past, and fill peoples' heads with notions of the Unsatisfying nature of Earthly comforts' (Lamb 1975–78, I, 144, 13 Nov. 1798).
39. George Whalley points out that Tytler's essay on Petrarch was part of Coleridge's library (Whalley 1950, II, 422). The book, however, is not mentioned in Coffman 1987, 161–2.
40. *PW (CC)* I:2, 1194.
41. *PW (CC)* I:2, 1195.
42. *PW (CC)* I:2, 1196. He specified that he avoided the term 'sonnet' because his did 'not possess that *oneness* of thought' he deemed 'indispensible [*sic*] in a sonnet' and, also, because he did not want to be compared with Bowles.
43. These are Sonnets 10–14, by Lamb, Sotheby and Coleridge (*PW (CC)* I:2, 1214–16). The feminine figures of these sonnets are allegorical more than real. In particular, Coleridge's final sonnet, which insists on the necessity of feeding Hope rather than feeding on Hope, gives them social rather than personal value. See Fairer 2002, 595–7.
44. Mays, *PW (CC)* I:2, 1201. See also Sheats 2002.
45. Daniel Robinson points out that the 'Sonnets on Eminent Characters' were the first sonnets of the Romantic revival to develop political themes at length. They were also 'Coleridge's first foray into politics' (Robinson 2000b, 95–6).
46. Mays, *PW (CC)* I:2, 1202.
47. *CL* I, 357 (*c.* 20 Nov. 1797). On these sonnets, published in *The Monthly Magazine* in November 1797, see Erdman 1958; Raycroft 1998; Taussig 2000.
48. On the ambiguities of their 'disinterested' friendship, see Fairer 1991; Allen 1996; Taussig 2000; Fairer 2002.
49. Allen 1996, 262, 274, 280–1.

50. The sonnet is 'My Coleridge! take the wanderer to thy breast'.
51. One case in point is the scandal created by Prince George, who left his wife for his mistress in 1796. Such behaviour was seen as harmful to the Constitution.
52. *PW (CC)* I:2, 1205 note. Mays points out that the reprinting of the preface as an appendix to the 1803 edition of Coleridge's *Poems* was entirely due to Charles Lamb (*PW (CC)* I:2, 1202).
53. Lloyd 1977, 168.
54. Lloyd 1977, 169–70.
55. Lloyd 1977, 172–4.
56. On this theme, see Taussig 2000; and Allen 1996, which shows that the novel was not only a satire of the Coleridge circle. Rather, it is a sort of *Bildungsroman* based on principles Lloyd learned from Coleridge.
57. Lloyd 1977, 210, 'Sonnet XXXV' (*PC*, 234).
58. Lloyd 1977, 212–14. In Sonnet 39, Lloyd affirms that it is wiser 'To chase of busy life the vanities / [...] than court [Solitude's] reign / Of deep, profoundest gloom.' Solitude is discussed also in other texts, like Sonnet 18, which emphasises that joy and love require to be shared with other humans (Lloyd 1977, 192): 'Yes, when I see that pomp of Nature, wrought / To such excess of loveliness, I seek, / Though sought in vain, a soul, whose mutual thought / May catch the gush of love which cannot speak; / Rescuing the sigh that may not be subdued / From agonies that dwell with Solitude.'
59. M. Santagata mentions two possible readings of the image of the urns: either, that Love wets the poets with many tears, shed from his eyes as though they were two urns, by means of Laura's hands; or, urns full of tears, which Love (through Laura) sheds from her hands (*PC*, p. 970).
60. Ll. 9–11: 'Né pur il mio secreto e 'l mio riposo, / fuggo, ma più me stesso e 'l mio pensero, / che, seguendol, talor levòmmi a volo'; ('Nor do I flee only my hiding place and my rest, but even more myself and my thoughts that used to raise me in flight as I followed them'. Prose trans from Petrarca 2001, 234).
61. Lloyd 1977, 211, Sonnet XXXVI (*PC*, 236; Petrarca 2001, 236).
62. Lloyd's attitude also appears in his third version (Lloyd 1977, 208, 'Sonnet XXXIII'; *PC*, 341). It is a relatively literal translation, in which he expanded the original l. 11 into his ll. 11–12 and omitted a hyperbolic description of Laura's words at l. 14. He turned Laura's direct speech of the original ll. 12–13 ('– Fedel mio caro, assai di te mi dole, / ma pur per nostro ben dura ti fui, –' ' "My dear faithful one, I am much grieved for you, but still for our good I was cruel to you" ', Petrarca 2001, 208) into indirect speech, making it sound more like a sermon: 'For, pitying, thou dost condescend to teach / That thou refusedst, but the more to bless.'
63. Lloyd 1977, 213.
64. Lloyd 1977, 209. The sonnet is placed among the translations from Petrarch.
65. Lloyd 1977, 216.
66. Lloyd translated Ovid's poem between 1805 and 1811; in 1815 he published a translation of Alfieri's tragedies.
67. Lloyd 1977, 195. This sonnet, No 21 of the series, was composed in 1803.
68. For more information, Zuccato 1996, 19–21.
69. On Coleridge and Italian metrics, Zuccato 1996, 34–7.
70. *CN* I, 1225. This section draws on Zuccato 1996, 21–31.
71. *CN* II, 2062, May 1804.
72. *Opera quae extant omnia*, 4 vols (Basle, 1554). The volumes remained at Keswick when he left for Malta, even though he intended to return them (*CL* IV, 655, 16

July 1816). In 1812 he reassured Mrs Sotheby he would return them soon (*CL* III, 364), but the following year he was still asking his wife for them (*CL* III, 431). Sotheby received his volumes back in 1816.

73. An edition full of blunders and printed in a small type (*CN* III, 3360, 1808).
74. *Le Rime di Francesco Petrarca*, 2 vols (London, 1778).
75. *CM (CC)* IV, 102. Coleridge purchased a copy of Petrarch's Latin writings, that is vols I–III (in one) of the folio edition he had borrowed from Sotheby (Whalley 1950, II, 424). In 1819 Henry Francis Cary presented Coleridge with another edition, *Il Petrarca di nuovo ristampato* (Venice, 1651) (*CM (CC)* IV, 101). On Coleridge's editions of Petrarch, see Coffman 1987, 161–2.
76. *CM (CC)* IV, 103.
77. Petrarch argues in the first poem that he would follow Laura, who is dead, but Love advises him to renounce his intention and to write on her instead. Writing as a late consolation is also the subject of *PC*, 12, which Coleridge admired.
78. He marked lines 17–19, 54–6, 76–7. He found lines 87–8 'rather flatly worded' (*CM (CC)* IV, 104).
79. According to G. Whalley and H. J. Jackson, the marginalia date perhaps from 1810–12. I believe that, at least in part, they were made before, during his sojourn in Malta and Italy. Another proto-Baroque *canzone* Coleridge found pleasing in sound is *PC*, 23, in which Petrarch sees himself turned into a laurel, a swan, a stone, a fountain and a deer. He found these thoughts ridiculous. I think it was such metamorphic imagery that reminded him of George Herbert, even though no exact imitation in Herbert has been found (*CM (CC)* IV, 102).
80. Coleridge 1990, 118 (the original passage is printed in capitals). I have reproduced with small graphic variants the translation given by *CN* III, 4178 n. The passages on death in life (ll. 44–5) and past passion (ll. 64–5) were transcribed in capitals by Coleridge. I think the motto is more than an apology to the Wordsworths, who disapproved of his passion for Sara Hutchinson, as E. H. Coleridge maintained (Raysor 1929, 308–9).
81. Lines 42–9 and 63–5 of the epistle.
82. See *Lects 1808–1819 (CC)* II, 95 (*1818 Lectures on European Literature*, Lecture 3). Following Friedrich Schlegel, Coleridge argued that the spirit of chivalry was less felt in Italy than in Northern Europe. The Prospectus announced a lecture on 'Chaucer and Spenser; of Petrarch; of Ariosto, Pulci, and Boiardo', but Coleridge dealt only with the Italian romances. See also *CN* III, 4388.
83. 'Either therefore we must brutalize our notions with Pope 'Loveust thro' some gentle Strainers well refin'd Is gentle Love & charms all womankind' – or dissolve & thaw away all bonds of morality by the inevitable Shocks of an irresistible Sensibility with Sterne' (*CN* III, 3562, July–Sept. 1809).
84. *CN* III, 3562 n. What Coleridge says about Kant on duty is equally valid for Wordsworth: 'Wordsworth is by nature incapable of being in Love, tho' no man more tenderly attached – hence he ridicules the existence of any other passion, than a compound of Lust with Esteem & Friendship, confined to one Object, first by accidents of Association, and permanently, by the force of Habit & a sense of Duty. Now this will do very well – it will suffice to make a good Husband – it may even be desirable (if the largest sum of easy & pleasurable sensations in this Life be the right aim & end of human Wisdom) [...] but still is not *Love*' (*CL* II, 305, 12 Mar. 1811).
85. On Coleridge's philosophy of love, Lockridge 1977; Barth 1985, esp. 129–32; Zuccato 1996, 24–9.
86. See Mays 1993.

87. *CN* I, 1064, Dec. 1801.
88. It was only after reading Petrarch and the Italian Petrarchists that Coleridge began to appreciate the lyric poetry of the English Renaissance, including Shakespeare's sonnets and poems, which he had ignored before. On *Biographia* ch. 15 and the role of Petrarchism in Coleridge's aesthetics, see Zuccato 1996, 41–56, 58–62, 81–4.
89. The list of Asra poems written by 1810 which contain elements of the Petrarchan tradition is long: 'The Day Dream', 'Sonnet to Asra', 'The Keepsake', 'The Picture', 'The Kiss and the Blush', 'Phantom', 'Recollections of Love', 'Constancy to an Ideal Object', 'Apostrophe to Beauty in Malta', 'Farewell to Love', 'The Blossoming of the Solitary Date-tree', 'Those eyes of deep & most expressive blue', 'Fragments Written in February 1807', 'The Pang More Sharp than All', 'The Two Sisters', 'A Motto to Accompany a Third Emblem', 'Sonnet Translated from Marino', 'Alternative Stanzas in the Manner of Marino', 'The Happy Husband', 'Lines on the Body and the Soul', 'The Visionary Hope', 'Fragment in Blank Verse'. After 1810 the dialogue with the Petrarchan tradition continued in several other poems.
90. *PW (CC)* I:2, 844 (late 1807–early 1808): 'The Blue, the rosy Red, the Black, the White' which 'charm our sight / in Woman's Face' do not respectively refer to her eyes, her lips, her hair and her teeth, as one might expect, but are mixed up, so that the lips are white, the nose blue, and hair red. The rhyme scheme is also burlesque (aabb ccdd eeffff). Mock-Petrarchism was not new in his poetry, as the 'Epigram on My Godmother's Beard' (Aug.–Sept. 1791? summer 1792?), and the 'Sonnet to a Lady' (Nov. 1797?) show (*PW (CC)* I:2, 59, 357).
91. *PW (CC)* I:2, 596 (May–Sept. 1799?); I:2, 886 (1804–12). Although the exchange of hearts is corporeally impossible, Coleridge seems to imply the contrary in 'Alternative Stanzas in the Manner of Marino', *PW (CC)* I:2, 852 (Sept. 1808).
92. The idea is expressed in 'To a Lady' (Nov. 1797?), 'Phantom' (before Apr. 1805), '"Ερως ἀει λάληθρος ἑταιρος' (before May 1827), and perhaps most clearly in the fragment 'Lines on the Body and the Soul': 'The body— / Eternal Shadow of the finite Soul/ / The Soul's self-symbol/ it's image of itself, / It's own yet not itself—', *PW (CC)* I:2, 872 (Apr.–June 1810).
93. 'Apostrophe to Beauty in Malta', *PW (CC)* I:2, 783 (May–June 1805). The *CC* editor translates the Italian as follows: 'in charming mortal spoils / A most beautiful soul'.
94. *PW (CC)* I:2, 1075.
95. *PW (CC)* I:1, xc.
96. Robinson 2000b, 82, 91–2. In particular, the sonnet form 'is the place where Coleridge expresses his mournful sensibility like nowhere else in his poetry – except for, perhaps, "Dejection: An Ode" ' (Robinson 2000b, 102).
97. The section includes: 'Love', 'Lewti', 'The Picture', 'The Night-Scene', 'To an Unfortunate Woman, Whom the author had known in the days of her innocence', 'To an Unfortunate Woman. At the Theatre', 'Lines Composed in a Concert-Room', 'The Keepsake', 'To a Lady', 'To a Young Lady', 'Something Childish, but Very Natural', 'Home-sick', Answer to a Child's Question', 'The Visionary Hope', 'The Happy Husband', 'Recollections of Love', 'On Revisiting the Sea-shore'. As Mays points out, it is difficult to see why some poems were placed in this section and others, which can also be considered love poems, were placed in the section of blank-verse poems. Besides, Coleridge told Gutch that he approved of only two of the ten poems between 'The Keepsake' and 'On Revisiting the Sea-shore', 'the others being either sickly or silly or both' (*CL* IV, 619, *c.* Jan. 1816; *PW (CC)* I:2, 1245).

98. 'Work without Hope' (Feb. 1825), *PW (CC)* I:2, 1033, ll. 13–14. The concept, with some variants, appears in other poems written from 1807 to 1833, like 'The Pang More Sharp than All: An Allegory', 'Written in Dejection, May 1810', 'The Visionary Hope', 'Fragment in Blank Verse', 'Lines on the Usury of Pain', 'Extempore Lines in Notebook 28', 'The Improvisatore' (ll. 31–4), 'The Alienated Mistress', 'Reply to a Lady's Question Respecting the Accomplishments Most Desirable in an Instructress', 'Love's Apparition and Evanishment: An Allegoric Romance'.

99. Robinson 2000b, 107–8.

100. *PW (CC)* I:2, 1031–2, ll. 13–14.

101. *PW (CC)* I:2, 1068 (Sept. 1826).

102. *CN* V, 6487 (19 Oct. 1830). The note concludes that love for one object is always excessive. Only the love of God 'is inclusive of all good & lovely' and excludes nothing but the lust of evil.

103. *PW (CC)* I:2, 1136, ll. 13–14. The sonnet was perhaps composed in October 1832.

104. The only two late texts which develop the sonnet tradition in a different direction are 'Fancy in Nubibus' (Oct. 1817), which seems to anticipate Keats, and 'Sonnet: To Nature', a Wordsworthian meditation which might date from the late 1790s (*PW (CC)* I:2, 942–3, 992–3).

105. Besides the earlier examples, another parodistic sonnet composed in the same period is 'An Elegiac Plusquam-Sesqui-Sonnet to My Tin Shaving Pot' (Jan. 1832). As Mays points out, a ' "sesqui-sonnet" would be $1\frac{1}{2}$ times a sonnet, i.e. 21 lines, and this "more than" ("plusquam") sesqui-sonnet comes to 22 lines' (*PW (CC)* I:2, 1124–5). The attribution of 'The Irish Orator's Booze' to Coleridge is uncertain.

106. *PW (CC)* II:2, 1199.

107. Coleridge was probably referring to Prince Ernest Augustus, Duke of Cumberland and later, from 1837 to 1851, King of Hanover, a fierce enemy of the Reform Bill and modern constitutions. The association with Petrarch implies that Coleridge considered both of them admirable figures.

108. *PW (CC)* II:2, 1199.

109. *CL* VI, 880 (12 Jan. 1832), commenting on the composition of 'An Elegiac Plusquam-Sesqui-Sonnet to My Tin Shaving Pot' (Jan. 1832), *PW (CC)* I:2, 1124–5. Another example is 'Fancy in Nubibus' (Oct. 1817), composed on seeing a 'glorious Sunset'. The poem 'has the character of a Sonnet – that is like a something that we let escape from us – a Sigh, for instance' (*CL* IV, 780).

110. 'The Old Man's Sigh' is mostly in tetrameters, except for l. 5 (a dimeter), l. 6 (an alexandrine) and l. 14 (a pentameter). The insistence on oneness as a central feature is clear also in a note 'On the Sonnet' presumably made round 1811–12. Coleridge was probably reading an English translation of an Italian sonnet and remarked that it was extremely difficult to preserve the original rhyme scheme, since rhymes are easier and less obtrusive in Italian. He wondered whether the result was worth the great formal effort of a 'literal' translation (*SW&F (CC)*, 283).

111. 'Album Verses: "Dewdrops are the Gems of Morning"' (1832–3), *PW (CC)* I:2, 1014–15. The poem, with an additional line, appeared in a magazine under the title of 'The Old Man's Sigh: A Sonnet'.

112. *PW (CC)* I:2, 1126–8.

113. *PW (CC)* I:2, 1128–9, ll. 3–5, 13–14.

114. *Lects 1808–1819 (CC)* II, 92. This section draws on Zuccato 1996, 114–22.

115. *CN* III, 4178; *BL (CC)* I, 14 and 222; combined with some lines from Milton's *Epitaphium Damonis* in *Friend (CC)* I, 144.
116. *CN* III, 4178 (1813).
117. In late 1809 Coleridge was still planning to 'make a Catalogue of the Greek and Latin Classics, and of those who like the author of the Argenis & Euphormio, Fracastorius, Flaminius, etc. deserve that name, tho' moderns' (*CN* III, 3656).
118. Spitzer 1955, 125, 137. Most neo-Latin poets evoked 'sentiments already exploited by the ancient poets'; only the best authors, like Pontano or Giovanni Cotta, were able to give new life to traditional conventions (Spitzer 1955, 138). For another view, see Arnaldi 1964, Introduction.
119. *CN* III, 3634.
120. *CN* III, 4178, Feb.–June 1813.
121. *BL (CC)* I, 21.
122. John Barclay's *Argenis* was a masterpiece in terms of poetry and style, of which 'it is awful to say, that it would have been well if it had been written in English or Italian verse', even if 'the Event seems to justify the Notion' (*CM (CC)* I, 221).
123. *Lects 1808–1819 (CC)* II, 91. The opinion was widespread in his time. Wordsworth, for instance, said that 'Miserable would have been the lot of Dante, Ariosto, and Petrarch if they had preferred the Latin to their mother tongue' (Toynbee 1909, II, 2). In consequence of the Romantic vogue for the Middle Ages, the revival and imitation of the Classics were frequently considered as having had a noxious effect on Italian literature.
124. *P Lects (CC)*, 425.
125. 1808–09: *CN* III, 3360, 3364, 3366 (quoted *EOT (CC)* II, 400 (1814); *Friend (CC)* I, 77 (1818 only); and *Friend (CC)* I, 7 and 9), 3467, 3633 (also *Friend (CC)* I, 75–6), 3727; see also *Friend (CC)* I, 51, *EOT (CC)* II, 270 (1811): *CN* III, 4178 (quoted *BL (CC)* I, 14; and, combined with some lines of Milton, *Friend (CC)* I, 144); *BL (CC)* I, 222 and II, 16. Coleridge was familiar with all the epistles (*Familiares*, *Seniles*, *Metricae*, and *Variae*).
126. *De otio religioso* contains the same principles as *De vita solitaria*, of which it is a kind of continuation. *De vita solitaria* is constructed on the contrast between commercial life and the life of knowledge. Some passages transcribed by Coleridge concern this point: they are ironical descriptions of people's inconstancy, greed, superficiality, and above all their unawareness of them (*CN* III, 3364, 3467, 3727). A consequence was the contrast between the city and the country – an attractive theme for Romantic sensibility. In a passage transcribed by Coleridge, Petrarch argues that nature inspires poets and philosophers. If they want to speak a superhuman language, they must be carried beyond the limits of the human mind, which happens more easily 'locis apertissimis'. In such places Cicero wrote his *De legibus*, Plato his *Republic* and Virgil his eclogues (*Prose* 366–8; *CN* III, 3467).
127. G. Martellotti, Introduction to *Prose*, p. XV. Interestingly, Coleridge ignored Book II of *De vita solitaria*, in which Petrarch related examples of saints and classical figures who lived in solitude.
128. *Prose*, 580–2.
129. *Prose*, 334.
130. See *P Lects (CC)*, 426–8. Giovanni da Ravenna lived with Petrarch between 1364 and 1368 (*Prose*, 1014–15 n.). Coleridge's information on Giovanni Malpaghini derived from Meiners and probably Tennemann. In the lecture on Dante, Giovanni was said to have read the *Comedy* as a philosophical work (see Zuccato 1996, ch. III).

131. It was for this reason that Coleridge cited some lines of Petrarch's letter to Barbato in Chapter I of *Biographia*, where he describes his own poetic apprenticeship. The lines are referred to Dr Middleton, a senior schoolfellow Coleridge admired, who first made him acquainted with Bowles's poems (*BL (CC)* I, 14).
132. Wilkins 1955, 280–1. In Italy, the wave from the Latin works 'reached its peak in the late fourteenth and early fifteenth century, diminished thereafter, and virtually disappeared in the sixteenth century'. In the Northern European countries the chronology is similar though belated. Coleridge noted that Petrarch spent most of his time on the works neglected by his posterity (*Lects 1808–1819 (CC)* II, 91, 1818; *SW&F (CC)*, 969, 1822).
133. However, Petrarch's antiquarian interests did not grow out of nothing, as he induced posterity to believe; they developed what other grammarians and scholars had begun (Billanovich 1947, 405–6). As an instance of the Humanistic image of Petrarch, Eugenio Garin mentions Johannes Herold's presentation of the 1554 Basle edition of Petrarch's works, which Coleridge used. Herold portrays Petrarch as the father of the revival of Classical learning outside the schools. Petrarch's works are an encyclopaedia of the liberal arts. Those who possess this kind of culture are philosophers, and as such they are regarded as guides and models for well-ruled cities (Garin 1988, 174–5).
134. Barberi 1968, I, 293. Petrarch's defence of poetry in the *Invective contra medicum quemdam* is unorganised and based on medieval concepts. Boccaccio developed them in his *De genealogia deorum*.
135. Coleridge 1949, 442 n. 7.
136. *Prose*, 1018 (*Familiares*, XXIII, 19).
137. *Prose*, 1018–20.
138. See Zuccato 1996, 37–41.
139. *CN* III, 3365, Sept. 1808.
140. Sixteenth-century strict Ciceronianism triumphed, in Luigi Baldacci's words, 'over the eclectic stance [...] which in the history of Humanism was linked to Poliziano's dispute with Cortese, and to the rich and conflicting ideas of Petrarch in his *Familiares*' (Introduction to Baldacci 1984, xxii). See also Zuccato 1996, 208.
141. See Zuccato 1996, chs I and II.
142. Vasoli 1968, 14. Although 'the experienced eye of the historian can discover certain subtle analogies between the extremes of Nominalism and the new philological and rhetorical interests' (Garin 1965, 24), basic differences remain (see Auerbach 1965, 273–5).
143. Klibansky 1981, 68. As Petrarch wrote in *De sui ipsius et multorum ignorantia*, humans cannot know God fully, but they can love him. The love of God is always happy, whereas knowledge is sometimes painful (*Prose*, 748).
144. *Prose*, 720.
145. *Prose*, 742, 750.
146. Trinkaus 1979, 14.
147. *Prose*, 760; *P Lects (CC)*, 429–30.
148. Klibansky 1981, 69. In a letter, Petrarch pointed out that Augustine found 'in libris Platonicorum magnam fidei nostre partem' (*Familiares* II, 9, in *Prose*, 820).
149. Klibansky argues that 'If the origin of the impulse which produced the humanist translations be sought, it appears that this is to be found, not in a foreign Greek influence, but in Petrarch's veneration of Plato, which inspired Boccaccio, and afterwards Coluccio Salutati [...] who was the first to order, from a Florentine

in Byzantium, a complete text of Plato. The admiration for Plato, which was handed down by Coluccio to the next generation of noble Florentines, accounts for Cosimo de' Medici's reception of Pletho in 1439. The fresh inspiration given by the Byzantine Platonist would hardly have borne fruit had it not fallen on ground already well prepared by a century old enthusiasm' (Klibansky 1981, 32).

150. Kristeller 1965, 12.

151. Trinkaus 1979, 24, 111, 84. The doctrine of the primacy of the will was developed by the Franciscan School, with which Petrarch was in touch. It eventually led to Ockhamism (Trinkaus 1979, 111). Some of Petrarch's works were put on the *Index* (Gerosa 1966, 360 n. 1).

152. *LS (CC)*, 173; *CL* IV, 759 (25 July 1817). He quoted from the *Trionfi*, which was not his favourite work, the lines on Plato, who 'came closest to the goal / Where to by Heaven's grace men may attain' (*CM (CC)* II, 868; *AR (CC)*, 42 n.).

153. *P Lects (CC)*, 425–6.

154. *Friend (CC)* I, 53.

155. *Friend (CC)*, I 75 n. The discussion of Petrarch in Lecture 3 of the 1818 course was brief, but a lecture on Dante and Petrarch was announced for the 1819 course on Shakespeare &c (*Lects 1808–1819 (CC)* II, 343–4). On 27 February he asked J. H. Bohte for Meiners's *Lebensbeschreibungen berühmter Männer aus der Zeiten der Wiederherstellung der Wissenschaft* (3 vols, 1795–97), probably with an eye to the lecture on Petrarch. He in fact described the book 'by saying that it contains the Life of [. . .] Johannes Somewhat, the Eleve and Scholar of Petrarch', that is, Giovanni Malpaghini da Ravenna (*CL* IV, 922). He did not receive the volumes, and only lectured on Dante, since he had never revised his notes on Petrarch and the time available was little. In 1816 he had included Petrarch in his planned reviews of old books that had caused important changes in taste or ideas (*CL* IV, 648). In the last year of his life, Coleridge still advised the new series of the *Gentlemen's Magazine* to include the learned criticism and 'the Biography of the middle age & the Restoration of Literature – Hugo de St Victore, Ambrosius, Petrarch &c &c &c' (*CL* VI, 976, 4 Jan. 1834). Coleridge did not know that Susanna Dobson had edited a selection of Petrarch's epistles, which even went through one reprint (Dobson 1797).

156. 'Recollections of Love' (Oct. 1804? 1806–07?), the sonnet 'Farewell to Love' (Aug.–Sept. 1806), 'Written in Dejection, May 1810', 'Separation. After Charles Cotton' (early 1810), 'Extempore Lines in Notebook 28' (Apr. 1824), 'The Alienated Mistress (Love's Burial Place)' (1826?), 'Love and Friendship Opposite' (1830?). Max E. Schulz describes 'Recollections of Love' as Coleridge's 'last unqualified expression of faith in the permanence of the love-sentiment' (Schulz 1964, 223).

157. *BL (CC)* I, 222. See also *Friend* I, 75–6, where he used Petrarch again in a political context. Coleridge quoted a Latin passage of Petrarch on liberty to attack the Jacobin notion of the concept.

158. In 'On the Curious Circumstance, that in the German Language the Sun Is Feminine, and the Moon Masculine, after Vernicke', a free version from the German, Coleridge wrote, probably remembering Smith, that 'cheap as blackberries our Sonnets show / The Moon Heaven's Huntress with *her* silver Bow' (*PW (CC)* I:2, 732, ll. 5–6, 1799–1802). In the 1810s he used Petrarch for his Italian lessons to his wife and Sara, who in 1819 translated *PC*, 209 and another sonnet. See the text in *PW (CC)* I:2, 706–7 and Mays's note of attribution to Sara in the site of *The Friends of Coleridge* (www.friendsofcoleridge.com/CPW). On Sara's lessons

of Italian, Potter 1934, 12; Jones 2000, 157, 172, 211; Reesman 2002. Hartley Coleridge translated two of Petrarch's sonnets (*PC*, 35 and 279), which were included in his published sonnets. In his notes to the texts, he affirms that he could not reproduce the simplicity of the Greeks and the Italians. The English can be stern, but not simple (*PW BLC*, 270, 274).

6   Epilogue: From Romantic to Victorian Petrarch

1. These novels contain sentimental sonnets written by distressed characters – especially women. They are a parody of the styles of C. Smith and the Della Cruscans, based in part on anti-Jacobin views. However, Gifford appears as a character – a moralist bore – in *Modern Novel Writing*. Beckford ridiculed love at first sight, the spontaneous outbursts of poetry, the promises of eternal love, women's ignorance of classical culture, the breakdown of class barriers brought about by Sensibility, the democratic muse which celebrates little things, etc. Ch. IX of *Azemia* deals with the literary debate on the sonnet, which is seen as an irrelevant issue. Beckford visited Petrarch's house at Arquà in the Euganean Hills, which inspired his travel mate John Robert Cozens to paint several watercolours (see Sloan 1986, 142–6). Beckford's admiration for Petrarch is not surprising in the light of his peculiar sexual taste, which made him a specialist in frustration (see Oliver 1932, 22; Mowl 1998, 90–102).
2. On what is probably the best of his sonnets, the Petrarchan 'To Genevra' (1813), see MacCarthy 2002, 206–12.
3. *BLJ* III, 240, 17–18 Dec. 1813. The form of his sonnets, with one exception, is Petrarchan.
4. His edition of Petrarch's poems (Venice, 1581) was 'Purloined from my lady's bower', Ravenna, 9 April 1820, 'but received as a gift the next day' (Byron 1980–93, VII, 117).
5. For a comparison between the two poems, see Vassallo 1984, 40–2. Byron did not parody Petrarch's sonnet, but he used it to express a different message. Byron was delighted to hear Teresa recite Petrarch's poems.
6. Byron revisited the village together with Teresa on their way to Venice in 1819.
7. On Petrarch's and Rousseau's influence on Byron's use of nature in *Childe Harold*, see Martin 1982, 74–9.
8. In stanza 114 Byron talked of Rienzi, 'The friend of Petrarch', as an Italian champion of liberty. They were the greatest idealists of their time and were haunted by their ideals of perfection.
9. The point is reinforced by two notes to the passage, which emphasise that the Florentines did not take the opportunity of Petrarch's short visit to the city to revoke the decree issued against his father. The following year they tried to call him back from Padua, but he returned to Vaucluse. The other note argues that Petrarch's fame is due to his sonnets rather than *Africa*. This depended in part on the historical situation, as the establishment of a new tongue confers 'an immortality on the works in which it was first written' (Byron 1980–93, II, 241, 243). Byron translated some lines of *Africa* (Byron 1980–93, VII, 103, 160).
10. Precisely, it is a long note to l. 269.
11. Hobhouse commented that 'either the memory or the morality of the poet must have failed him, when he forgot or was guilty of this *slip*' (Byron 1980–93, II, 229).

12. Byron 1980–93, II, 230.
13. Hobhouse's notes to his commentary give the titles of Sade's and Tytler's works (Byron 1980–93, II, 322–3). He also cites the imperfect Italian translation of Tytler's essay contained in the 1811 London imprint of Petrarch's poems, that is, Romualdo Zotti's mediocre edition (see Chapter 1 in this volume). For example, Zotti rendered Sade's 'femme tendre et sage' as 'raffinata civetta', a 'refined coquette'. Hobhouse also mentions Tiraboschi and Gibbon (Byron 1980–93, II, 322–3).
14. *Don Juan*, III, 8 (Byron 1980–93, V, 163). Byron adds, a few lines below, that 'Dante's Beatrice and Milton's Eve / Were not drawn from their spouses, you conceive' (*Don Juan*, III, 10). The passage is followed by the story of Haidée and Juan. Andrew Rutherford has suggested that the Laura of *Beppo* was meant as a parody of Petrarch's Laura (Rutherford 1961, 119 n.; see also Beaty 1985, 100–1).
15. The aphorism is recorded in Hunt 1948, 42.
16. See his famous letter to John Murray (21 Feb. 1820) on the character of Italians, *BLJ* VII, 43.
17. On Gifford and the Della Cruscans, see Hargreaves-Mawdsley 1967, 243–51; Gamer 2003, especially 37–41, 48.
18. Gifford 1797, 123–4 (*Mæviad*, ll. 271–3). These lines are the subject of the only illustration of the volume, an engraving by Stothard which shows a man throwing sheets of paper into the fire while two people behind him are about to scatter more paper around. In addition, Gifford says in a note that he has collected several sonnets which he meant 'to prefix to some future edition of the Maeviad, under the true classic head of 'INSIGNIUM VIRORUM / ALIQUOT TESTIMONIA / QUI / BAV: ET MAEV: INCLYTISS: AUCTORIS / MEMINERUNT' (Gifford 1797, 124).
19. Gifford 1797, title page of *Baviad*. The motto means, 'With impunity, then, that one recited to me bad sonnets, this one elegies.' 'Elegos' is an even stranger word. I have not found it elsewhere, but, like 'sonettas', it is probably meant as a derogatory form of *elegias* ('elegies'). I owe this information to Uberto Motta.
20. Sonneteers are 'moon-stricken' and write lame lines on melancholy. 'Imitation. Dactylics. *Being the quintessence of all the Dactylics that ever were, or ever will be written*' (*Anti-Jacobin*, 22–3). The poem was written by Canning and Gifford. For Polwhele's better opinion of sonneteers, see Polwhele 1974, 16 ff.
21. The *Anti-Jacobin* includes many parodies of radical arguments against marriage and traditional morality, such as 'The Progress of Man', 'Loves of Triangles', 'The Rovers' (a parody of German plays), and 'New Morality', which summarises their ideas. After a section on the Universal Man, there is a section on Sensibility, 'Sweet child of sickly Fancy' (l. 125). She drove Rousseau out in the country and on the mountains, where he poured forth his discontent about the world. Her followers are sorts of decadent figures who complain about incurable pains and suffer for every little being, but they praise the massacres in France as inevitable steps towards a better future. This is followed by a section on Justice, where Sensibility is the interface between the Universal Man and the Justice to which he aspires (*Anti-Jacobin*, 224–6). The conclusion is that Britain will certainly defeat France. However, if French ideas and morality creep into British minds, Britain will be lost. Therefore, the intellectual battle is more decisive than war for the future of Britain (*Anti-Jacobin*, 240).
22. In *English Bards and Scotch Reviewers*, Byron defined Bowles as 'The maudlin prince of mournful sonneteers' (l. 330, and Byron's note; Byron 1980–93, I, 405–6). He jibed at Mary Robinson and the Della Cruscans, and he ridiculed

Lofft's patronage of lower-class poets (Byron 1980–93, I, 253, ll.759 ff.; but see the variant to ll. 759–64). These poets are satirised again in *Hints from Horace*, l. 694 and notes (Byron 1980–93, I, 314, 441–2), and in his letters (on Lofft as a patron who ruins writers, *BLJ* II, 76, 21 Aug. 1811; *BLJ* III, 179, 1 June 1812). In 1817 Byron gave Pindemonte 'as bad an account' as he could of his old friends, the Della Cruscans. Byron told him that they were dead because Gifford had destroyed them. They were 'but a sad set of scribes after all – & no great things in any other way.' Pindemonte found Byron's tale funny (*BLJ* V, 233–4, 4 June 1817).

23. Though Byron wrote *The Blues*, a long satire on women writers, some of the women he was involved with were famous bluestockings: Lady Byron, Lady Caroline Lamb, Lady Oxford, and the Countess of Blessington. His relation with Staël was even more complicated. He had mixed feelings about her, since she was a kind of female Byron and he was jealous of her popularity. The character they interpreted – the histrionic exhibitionist – and the social role they played as intellectuals were the same. At Coppet he came to like her better, but later he portrayed her as the unpleasant Lady Bluebottle in *The Blues*. See Frank 1969; Giddey 1982; Lipking 1988, 36–9; Wilkes 1999. Jealousy also seems to underlie Byron's response to Hemans, which turned sour when she became a popular poet in the 1820s. Only then did he begin to joke on her name, calling her in his letters 'Mrs. Hewoman', who should have 'knit blue stockings instead of wearing them' (*BLJ* VII, 158, 12 Aug. 1820; *BLJ* VII, 182, 28 Sept. 1820). Anna Seward received an even harsher treatment. Scott's edition of her works were '6 tomes of the most disgusting trash [...]. Of all Bitches dead or alive a scribbling woman is the most canine' (*BLJ* II, 132, 17 Nov. 1811). On these topics, see Franklin 1992; McGann 1998, 158, 229; McGann 2002, chs 3 and 8; Elfenbein 2004, 56–73; and the excellent Calder 1983.

24. In fact, Polwhele expressed admiration for Petrarch: 'Petrarch, indeed, I can relish for a considerable time: but Spenser and Milton soon produce somnolence' (Polwhele 1974, 18).

25. *Don Juan*, V, 1 (Byron 1980–93, V, 241). Plato's social role was the same as Petrarch, that is, a go-between for repressed people: 'Oh Plato! Plato! you have paved the way, / With your confounded fantasies, to more / Immoral conduct by the fancied sway / Your system feigns o'er the controlless core / Of human hearts, than all the long array / Of poets and romancers: – You're a bore, / A charlatan, a coxcomb – and have been, / At best, no better than a go-between' (*Don Juan*, I, 116).

26. *Don Juan*, V, 2 (Byron 1980–93, V, 241).

27. At the beginning of *Don Juan*, Byron made fun of the poses of mournful sonneteers who tried to find consolation for their trouble in solitary retreats. Juan tries to forget his developing passion for Julia by wandering alone in the countryside. St. 87 of Canto I is a parody of Petrarch's 'Solo et pensoso' and its innumerable eighteenth-century imitations. Another failed diversion of Juan's anxiety is his reading in Spanish Petrarchism mentioned in Canto I, st. 95. Finally, Richard F. Kennedy argued that stanzas 87 and 95 of *Don Juan*, Canto I, may be a parody of *PC*, 211, which gives the magical date and time when Petrarch first saw Laura (Kennedy 1983).

28. Byron, 'Observations upon Observations' (1821) (Byron 1991, 177–8). It is an essay on the Bowles / Pope controversy.

29. Like them, women wanted 'to retain the illusion of the Sentiment – which constitutes their sole empire. [...] I never knew a woman who did not admire Rousseau'

(*BLJ* VIII, 148, 6 July 1821). Women 'hate everything which strips off the tinsel of *Sentiment* – & they are right – or it would rob them of their weapons' (*BLJ* VII, 202, 12 Oct. 1820).

30. It is a passage from *Vita solitaria*, quoted by Coleridge in *The Friend* (2 Feb. 1809) and used by Wordsworth as a conclusion to *The Convention of Cintra* (1809) (Wordsworth 1974, I, 342–3). Bruce Graver has suggested that Wordsworth read with Isola some of Petrarch's prose works, such as the letters (Graver 1996, entry 'Petrarch'). This is unlikely, because those works were known only to a few erudite readers at that time. It was most probably Coleridge who told him about Petrarch's Latin writings.

31. For the early sonnets in the sentimental style, Wordsworth 1997, 392–6. The translation from *PC*, 12 might belong to the period when he was studying Italian with Isola at Cambridge (about 1790) or to 1795–96, when it was copied in the Racedown Notebook. The octave is a free version of the original, and although it was corrected several times, it does not run smoothly. The sestet works better, though some words in ll. 11–14, which are an expanded version of Petrarch's ll. 12–14, sound like fillers. None the less, Wordsworth sent the poem to *The Morning Post* in 1802 (Wordsworth 1997, 725–7). Lines 3–6 of this version are echoed in *Descriptive Sketches, 1793*, ll. 150–5. A copy of Isola 1784 annotated by Wordsworth is held in the Fitzwilliam Museum, Cambridge.

32. See Wordsworth 1997, 724. Wrangham's translations were published only in 1817. The 'Advertisement' to this elegant quarto volume contains a biographic outline which stresses Petrarch's role as one of the main scholars of the western tradition (Wrangham 1817, 2). Wrangham discusses briefly the question of Petrarch's relationship with Laura. He mentions Dobson's biography and Polidori's 1796 edition of the poems, and he does not believe that Laura was married. Like Wordsworth and Coleridge, he insists on Petrarch the scholar to redeem the image of the quasi-debauched, effeminate love poet (Wrangham 1817, 7–8). In his versions Wrangham tried to be as literal as possible. Though occasionally he achieved pleasant results (e.g., his sonnets XIII and XIV), most of his versions are too strained in syntax and pompous in language for Petrarch's subtle delicacy (e.g., II, VII, XV, and many others).

33. His sister read Milton's sonnets to him and he suddenly 'took fire' and wrote three sonnets (Wordsworth 1946, 417).

34. To W. S. Landor, 20 Apr. 1822 (Wordsworth 1978, Part I, 125). He never ceased to believe, however, that the sonnet was a 'minor' form. In the same letter he said that his sonnet were written when he could not work on longer poems. Coleridge also considered Wordsworth's sonnets as diversions from a more serious task, the composition of *The Recluse*.

35. Wordsworth 1978, Part II, 604–5, to A. Dyce, *c.* 22 April 1833. He liked the Shakespearean form even less and, like many of his contemporaries, he considered it 'merely quatrains with a couplet tacked to the end' (Wordsworth 1978, Part II, 455, to W. R. Hamilton, 22 Nov. 1831). See also Robinson 1938, III, 484 (26 Jan. 1836), and Johnson 1973, 16–18. His judgement on Shakespeare's sonnets wavered between admiration and, more often, dislike (see, e.g., *CM (CC)*, I 41).

36. Wordsworth has been credited, even recently, with the invention of the descriptive-meditative sonnet sequence in *The River Duddon* (see, e.g., Going 1976, 26). Of course, neither the subject-matter nor the form were original. J. A. Wagner has suggested that Wordsworth rearranged his early sonnets into a sequence in his *Miscellaneous Sonnets* to form a sort of autobiographic long poem (Wagner 1996,

39, 43). In so doing, he unwittingly returned to the Petrarchan tradition, where sequences are constructed as series of discontinuous events.

37. Wordsworth rambled in Vaucluse for three hours, wondering whether Petrarch had walked in the same places. Some tourists, especially women, would say so; he doubted it on seeing the beauty of the local landscape, which made him think that Petrarch's inspiration was literary. The patriotic poem he had in mind was probably the *canzone* 'Italia mia'. Wordsworth regretted that his poem did not include some lines on the south of France (Isabella Fenwick's note to 'Memorials of a Tour in Italy, 1837' in Wordsworth 1946, 489–90).

38. Wordsworth 1974, III, 28. The other forms included in this kind of poetry are the epitaph, the inscription, the epistles of poets writing in their own persons, and all loco-descriptive poetry. I cannot understand what the last two forms have to do with the rest.

39. Despite this removal, recent criticism has pointed out how Wordsworth applied some Petrarchan conventions to England, which is addressed as a woman in some of his sonnets (see Page 1994, 60–2). The Petrarchan love-sick youth and his Laura are gently satirised in Sonnet VII of *The River Duddon*, and in 'Extempore Effusion upon the Death of James Hogg' where, immediately before a passage on Hemans, he specifies: 'No more of old romantic sorrows, / For slaughtered Youth or love-lorn Maid!' (ll. 41–2).

40. See Wordsworth 1963, 211 ('The Grasmere Journal', 24 Dec. 1802). On his copy of Smith's sonnets, Hunt 1971, 85.

41. Wordsworth's note to the poem (Wordsworth 1947, 403). It should be noted that the poem is part of one of his sonnet cycles, *Poems Composed or Suggested during a Tour, in the Summer of 1833*.

42. On the subject, Hunt 1971; Raycroft 1998, 368–71; Johnston 1998, 80–1; Zimmerman 1999, 109–11.

43. Wordsworth 1946, III, 20–1.

44. Johnson wrongly believed that the sonnet was written because 'the form was in disrepute', though all the hostile critical remarks he quotes belong to the eighteenth century (Johnson 1973, 40).

45. Meyenberg 2005, 104. On the subject see also Manning 1982. The sources of the concluding couplet of Gray's sonnet is discussed in a letter Wordsworth sent to Landor (Wordsworth 1978, part I 80, 3 Sept. 1821).

46. Smith's sonnets are praised in a note as poems where 'softly-coloured description and touching sentiment are most happily combined' (Dyce 1833, 220). For the eulogy of Wordsworth, Dyce 1833, 222.

47. Wordsworth's sonnets won critical approbation more easily than his other poems. As Johnson recalls, Francis Jeffrey was favourable to them, and Matthew Arnold selected 60 sonnets in the anthology of Wordsworth's poems he edited, which includes 160 texts (Johnson 1973, 172).

48. Campbell 'abominates' the Romantic cult of solitude. Petrarch liked retirement rather than complete isolation, which is inhuman. His invectives against cities are 'as unsubstantial' as Rousseau (Campbell 1843, I, 173 ff.; and II, 342–3). Despite Campbell's attention to learning and politics, he pays only marginal attention to the political implications of Petrarch's role as an intellectual, which many women poets found most intriguing. Campbell describes Petrarch's coronation in Rome seriously, though in a note he points out that the ceremony attracted envious people from all quarters. It seems that some of them threw acid on his hair which made him permanently bald, and an old woman emptied a chamber-pot full of stale urine on his head (Campbell 1843, I 209 ff.).

49. Campbell argued that Laura must have been flattered by the attention of one of the most famous men of her time. However, her behaviour was the only way of preserving her honour – a point made by Laura herself in Petrarch's 'Triumphus Mortis', ll. 90–2. In any case, he 'should like to hear her own explanation' before condemning her (Campbell 1843, I, 58). Petrarch's love was not always platonic (Campbell 1843, I, 58; II, 329–30). Sometimes his obsession was irritating. He would have been 'a more various and masculine, and, upon the whole, *a greater poet*' had he not known Laura (Campbell 1843, I, 167). However, Petrarch's constancy was admirable (Campbell 1843, I, 290; II, 355). His illicit passion for Laura was more acceptable than his coldness to his children (Campbell 1843, I, 169). In general, however, Petrarch's character was loveable.

50. Campbell 1843, II, 319–20. Petrarch's morals, which were not blameless, should have made him more tolerant towards 'the western Babylon' (Campbell 1843, I, 169).

51. His Petrarch was a republican, an enemy of the Roman Church, and 'emphatically an *Italian* patriot'. He was sceptical about astrology and almost anticipated Lord Bacon with his anti-Aristotelianism (Campbell 1843, I, 3–10).

52. He believed that Petrarch, unlike Homer and Dante, had never been translated successfully into English. The English language was 'too robust to adapt itself to the graces of Petrarch's poetry; and, when we spin a Petrarchan sonnet, we find the short-haired wool of our speech very unlike the silky and ductile fleece of that of Italy' (Campbell 1843, I, xvi; II, 346, 360). Campbell's taste for Petrarch's sonnets was Romantic; however, he argued that they were monotonous only at first sight (Campbell 1843, II, 362).

53. Maginn's article 'Remarks on Shelley's Adonais' appeared in the *Edinburgh Review* in December 1821 (Stones and Strachan 1999, II, 317–18).

54. They were Mrs Boinville and her daughter Cornelia, with whom he read Petrarch in 1813–14 (White 1940, I, 310).

55. *A Discourse on the Manners of the Ancients Relative to the Subject of Love. A Fragment* (Shelley 1965, VII, 224). In this passage, Shelley extols Dante and Shakespeare, but he argues that Homer was more various and harmonious than Shakespeare, whereas Dante is unequal and inferior to some Greek poets. On the contrary, Shelley finds no defects in Petrarch, and mentions no Greek poet as superior to him.

56. *A Defence of Poetry* (Shelley 1965, VII, 127–8).

57. Shelley knew at least Hobhouse's notes to *Childe Harold*, Canto IV. See Shelley 1964, II, 89 (23 Mar. 1819). On 'Epipsychidion', which was mainly influenced by Dante, see Weinberg 1991, 142–8, 165–6. Shelley's view was a consequence of his hostility to marriage, which appears, for example, in his note to *Queen Mab*, V, 189, and 'Epipsychidion', ll. 130–89 (Shelley 1988, 806–8, 414–16). His rejection of the concept of adultery did not make Shelley's passion for Emilia less embarrassing for himself and his women.

58. Shelley considered the fourteenth century as the golden age of Italian literature. Even Boccaccio was a poet. He was not equal to 'Dante or Petrarch', but he was 'far superior to Tasso and Ariosto, the children of a later and colder day.' The first three were the sources of a new literature (Shelley 1964, II, 517, 27 Sept. 1819).

59. *A Defence of Poetry* (Shelley 1965, VII, 128). *Vita nuova* and *Paradiso* show that 'Dante understood the secret things of love even more than Petrarch.' Besides Petrarch, Plato and Dante are the writers Shelley liked best for their philosophy of love. Later champions of love were Ariosto, Tasso, Shakespeare, Spenser, Calderón, Rousseau and Shelley's great contemporaries.

60. On the influence of Dante's sonnet 'Guido, i' vorrei', which Shelley translated, see Weinberg 1991, 41–2.
61. Shelley 1988, 556, ll. 200–3, 206–7, 280–4.
62. In the evening Percy read Petrarch's 'Triumph of Death' aloud and Calderón. In the same days he also read Dante and Boccaccio. See Shelley 1987, I, 297 (17 Sept. 1819). Shelley was also fond of Petrarch's political poems like 'Italia mia', which he mentioned frequently.
63. They range from micro-loans (e.g., the suggestive rhyme 'verse' / 'universe') to macro-loans such as images and poetic forms (the Triumph). The rhyme 'verse' / 'universe', used by Shelley in 'Lines Written in the Euganean Hills' (ll. 318–19) and 'Ode to the West Wind' (ll. 63, 65), appears in Petrarch's 'Triumphus Mortis' (ll. 71, 75). Petrarchan echoes have been found in 'Adonais' and 'Ode to the West Wind', whose stanzas are perhaps based on the sonnet form. The ode was written a month after reading the 'Triumphus Mortis' (see Jost 1982; White 1940, II 294; Wagner 1996, ch. 2). Shelley's combination of the sonnet with the grandeur of the *terza rima* and the ode, anticipated by Lofft and others, has been read as a way of 'rescuing' the sonnet from its association with women and effeminate poets (see, e.g., Wagner 1996, 76–7).
64. See 'What Dante Means to Me' (Eliot 1965, 130). Eliot's pronouncement was a reflection of his interests more than a unbiased judgement on Shelley. The vague, ghastly images of 'The Triumph of Life' are remote from the graphic clarity of Dante's writing; and the same can be said of Shelley's *terza rima*, whose syntax is tortuous and blurred in comparison to the sculptural quality of Dante's. Stuart Curran has argued that Shelley's interest in Dante was mainly due to his allegoric method. Allegory allowed Shelley to question appearances and concentrate on the way reality is constructed in our minds (Curran 1998, 47). Ralph Pite points out that the recent view of Shelley's reading of Dante as displacing depends on the assumption of Dante's canonicity. This was true in Eliot's time, whereas it wasn't in Shelley's. Shelley could hardly displace an author who had not yet been given a firm place in the tradition (Pite 1994, 163–7).
65. Vassallo 1991, 104. He points out that Rousseau is portrayed as a character of Dante's *Inferno*, mixing up Pier de le Vigne, Farinata degli Uberti and Brunetto Latini (Vassallo 1991, 105). Shelley's 'shape all light', the focal point of the poem, is based on Dante's Matelda, whose episode in *Purgatorio* was translated by Shelley (Vassallo 1991, 107).
66. See Bradley 1914; Stawell 1914; Roe 1953, Robinson 1976, 221–2, 225–31; 196–212; Folliot 1979 gives a detailed list of echoes and borrowings; Schulze 1988; Weinberg 1991, 206–11, 215–18, 227–8. Another work linked to Petrarch's *Triumphs* is *Una favola* (1820), Shelley's Italian prose parable written for Teresa Viviani, the Emilia of 'Epipsychidion'. In *Una favola* a youth is in love with two mistresses, Life and Death, who try to seduce him. Life is more attractive, but his true love is Death, who is the only gateway to Eternity.
67. The memorable opening of 'The Triumph of Life' is a palimpsest of the beginning of 'Triumphus Temporis', ll. 1–36, whereas the beginning of Shelley's dream in the Apennines (ll. 24 ff.) is based on the Vaucluse of Petrarch's vision in 'Triumphus Cupidinis' (ll. 1 ff.). As Vassallo points out, the landscape of Shelley's dreamer merges Petrarch's allegory with Dantean reminiscences (Vassallo 1991, 104).
68. Robinson 1976, 222; Vassallo 1991, 104, 108–9; Pite 1994, 167, 194–5.
69. The sonnet dates from October or early November 1816 (Keats 1988, 571).
70. 'Sleep and Poetry', ll. 389–95 (on Petrarch); ll. 381–4 (on Sappho).
71. Hunt 1867, I, 1–91.

72. Hunt 1867, I, 3–4. The selection starts with Wyatt, Surrey, and other Renaissance sonneteers (170 pp.), followed by Gray, Warton, and other eighteenth-century poets, including Smith, Seward, Robinson, Bowles, Coleridge (12 pp., more than Shakespeare's 11), Lloyd, Wordsworth (17 pp., more than anyone else), Southey, Lamb, Byron, Shelley, Keats (10 pp.), Hunt (6 pp.), Hemans (6 pp.), and Hood. Vol. II includes Victorian and American poets, and a final section of women sonneteers. The Victorians include the Tennysons, De Vere, Barrett Browning (15 pp.), and other minor figures. The Rossettis are not included.

73. Hunt 1867, I, 5. The conclusion of this section argues that any subject can be treated in a sonnet. Hunt mentions examples by Petrarch ('Voi ch'ascoltate'), Dante, Filicaia, Petrarch and Alfieri against the Roman church, Berni, and Casti (Hunt 1867, I, 6).

74. Besides Quadrio and Ceva, Hunt drew on Lofft for this section (Hunt 1867, I, 9–10). Hunt took up the subject again on p. 22, where he cites an anecdote on Petrarch from Foscolo's essay, relating to the fact that Petrarch sang his sonnets to his lute.

75. Hunt 1867, I, 14–15.

76. Hunt mentions Alfieri, Foscolo, and Mme Genlis as admirers of Petrarch (Hunt 1867, I, 19).

77. Hunt 1867, I, 17–20.

78. Before Section VI, Section IV deals with the other main Italian sonneteers. Giusto de' Conti and the early mannerists are ridiculous (Hunt 1867, I, 29). Hunt thinks their ladies did not take them seriously. Alfieri, Foscolo, Monti and Pindemonte prevented the appearance in Italy of a new school of marinists, as in England the Della Cruscans, who were 'English idlers in Florence' (Hunt 1867, I, 51). Section V discusses other legitimate though obsolete forms of sonnets, such as the comic sonnet, which he considered extravagant even though Milton wrote one of them.

79. Hunt 1867, I, 68–9.

80. There are only a couple of pages where Hunt notes that they are not on the Italian model. Before them he discusses Spenser's (Hunt 1867, I, 71–4).

81. Hunt finds Wordsworth's criticism of Gray's sonnet unjust, and he also criticises Coleridge's strictures on Gray (Hunt 1867, I, 84–5).

82. Hunt 1867, I, 88. Hunt's essay is followed by Adams Lee's introduction to American sonnets and sonneteers. In the anthology, Hunt translated a few Italian sonnets, though none by Petrarch.

83. On Hunt's theory of the sonnet and Keats, see also Zillman 1939, 50–63.

84. Hunt 1923, 440–1, where the title is 'Petrarch's Contemplation of Death in the Bower of Laura' (for the original title, Hunt 1923, 742). It is a relatively literal translation, even though Hunt amplified part of the original, especially the final lines of each stanza. He did not add much; he paraphrased the Italian text, expanding the original images and concepts, and he omitted the last three lines of the poem. It is a good translation, which, unlike other versions, gives an idea of the intricate metrical pattern of the *canzone*.

85. Havens 1922, 540–1; Bate 1958, 8–10; Hargreaves-Mawdsley 1967, 59–61.

86. 'O Solitude! if I must with thee dwell', l. 14. Beauty too cannot be relished alone ('To my Brother George', ll. 13–14, Keats 1988, 50, 64). As J. N. Cox notes, many of Hunt's sonnets, unlike Keats's, stem from social commitment (Cox 2003, 62).

87. 'To a Young Lady who Sent Me a Laurel Crown', 'On Receiving a Laurel Crown from Leigh Hunt', 'To the Ladies who Saw Me Crowned' (Keats 1988, 73, 97–8).

The sonnets date from between the late 1816 and the early 1817. On the episode, Bate 1963, 137–40.

88. Keats 1958, I, 292 (10 June 1818). His 'Ode to Apollo' (spring 1817) contains a sort of recantation of the laurel crowning ('like a blank idiot I put on thy wreath, / Thy laurel', ll. 8–9). The two late sonnet 'On Fame' (April 1819) are ironic and even sceptical towards fame. In the first, Keats argues that Fame, like a disdainful lover, is unpredictable (ll. 11–14). In the second sonnet, he wonders why man should spoil his life for fame ('spoil his salvation for a fierce miscreed', l. 14).

89. On Keats's early sonnets, see Bate 1963, 37–9, 41, 63–5, 89, 92–7, 120–2, 133–40, 141–3, 300; Bate 1958, 8–36; 191–7; Zillman 1939, *passim*. The importance of these sonnets for Keats's development cannot be underrated. As Bate wrote, 'the metrical manner in which the sonnet was first treated by Keats [...] is almost a microcosm in which were concentrated the heterogeneous influences of his reading' (Bate 1958, 19).

90. Like most sonneteers of Sensibility, Keats employed a loose Petrarchan form in his 36 early sonnets, written between February 1815 and January 1818. Like Hunt, he varied his caesuras with great liberty and used feminine endings frequently (Bate 1958, 14, 19).

91. Keats 1988, 49–50. Some modern editors print the text as three separate sonnets. The date is also uncertain. Barnard gives December 1815, but other editors indicate *c.* March 1816.

92. Bate specifies that it was the Petrarchan sonnet which was associated with sentimental, effeminate poetry, but the reason for it was that the Shakespearean sonnet was used rarely (Bate 1958, 297–9). Havens records that Keats's praise of Shakespeare's sonnets is the earliest from any sonneteer in the eighteenth and early nineteenth century. Rather than replacing Petrarch with Shakespeare, Keats interfused the characteristics of the Elizabethan sonnet into the ones used by the poets of Sensibility (Havens 1922, 540–1). In any case, Zillman points out that Hunt influenced Keats, even technically, more than any other sonneteer (Zillman 1939, 148, 194, 196).

93. Keats argued that poets sometimes ruin what they are associated with. For example, Wordsworth has spoiled the lakes (Keats 1958, I, 251–2, 21 Mar. 1818).

94. On Keats's sonnets and Wordsworth, Wagner 1996, 85–111; Zillman 1939, 46–8, 147–8. Keats composed few sonnets on places, which were particularly important to Wordsworth. After writing a sonnet in Burns's cottage, Keats talked of 'the flummery of a birth place' as 'Cant! Cant! Cant!', and he specified, 'I cannot write about scenery and visitings' (Keats 1958, I, 324–5, 13 July 1818). Besides the sonnets proper, several embedded sonnets have been found in Keats's longer poems (Wolfson 1997, 282 n. 18).

95. Garrod argued that 'pouncing rhymes' refers to the couplets of the Petrarchan octave. Besides, Keats wanted to avoid the final couplet of the Shakespearean form (Bate 1958, 129). Bate thinks that this uneasiness was also a result of the two thousand couplets of *Endymion* (Bate 1963, 496; see also Bate 1958, 19 ff.).

96. It was probably his dissatisfaction with the final couplet which made him abandon his translation of Ronsard's 'Nature withheld Cassandra in the skies' at l. 12 in September 1818. Keats used the Shakespearean form for Ronsard's Petrarchan original.

97. Keats 1958, II, 108 (3 May 1819). His dissatisfaction with the sonnet and his desire for longer forms may have partly been motivated by gender, given the association of the sonnet with women poets. On this subject, and on Keats's ambivalent

attitude to women writers and readers, see Ross 1988, 156, 170; Homans 1990; Mellor 1993, 178–86.

98. Bate 1958, 118–32; 182–4. Bate points out that whenever Keats 'went back to the lyric, the sonnet stood in his way' (Bate 1963, 495 ff.). After 'If by dull rhymes', Keats wrote only three more sonnets, whose rhyme schemes are extremely irregular. On the conflict between the spontaneity of inspiration and the artificiality of the sonnet, see Lenz 1982, 182–6, 190–3.

99. Bate argues that in the most accomplished odes the stanzas consist of a Shake-spearean quatrain combined with a Petrarchan sestet (Bate 1958, 129–31). By 'Shakespearean quatrain' Bate means an alternate-rhyming quatrain, which is also used in Petrarch's sonnets.

100. See, e.g., Whiting 1963.

101. He wrote to Fanny that his friends were 'spying upon a secret' and he would 'rather die than share it with any body's confidence' (Keats 1958, II, 292–3, June (?) 1820).

102. For this definition of his sonnets, see Keats 1958, II, 104 (30 April 1819).

103. See Keats 1958, I, 370, 22 (?) Sept. 1818; Keats 1958, II, 223, 13 Oct. 1819 (to Fanny).

104. The third sonnet of the series is 'Bright star!' They complain that love is his religion, but he has to fast and pray when 'holinight', the time of love, comes ('The day is gone, and all its sweets are gone!', ll. 9–14). They beg Fanny and heaven that they either respond fully to his craze or free him from it, as he also wrote in several letters in that period. Though Keats had often mentioned the Muse in his poems, he seems to have found the experience of real possession unpleasant and disturbing.

105. Wolfson 1997, 176, and also 170–87. On Keats's sonnet to Fanny, see Bate 1963, 618–20; Homans 1990, 354–5, 365–70.

106. A significant example of his uneasiness with the closeness of the sonnet is a letter dating from 2 January 1819 (Keats 1958, II, 26). He writes that he likes the rondeau because 'you have one idea amplified with greater ease and more delight and freedom' than in the sonnet.

107. Mellor 2000b, 70.

108. See Moers 1976, 179.

109. Staël points out in a note that Corinne was a famous Greek lyric poet, who gave lessons even to Pindar (Staël 1998, 408 n. 29). In 1811 Staël composed a play, *Sapho*, which was published posthumous.

110. Staël 1998, 21. See also a stanza of Corinne's improvised ode to Italian glory and fortune, which also mentions Dante, Tasso, and other Italian artists and writers (Staël 1998, 28 ff.).

111. Staël 1998, 30. Corinne's improvisation was part of the ceremony. The poem is given as a French prose translation of an imaginary Italian original in verse.

112. However, it is noteworthy that Corinne in despair recalls a line of Petrarch on the permanence of suffering. Petrarch the melancholy lover always coexisted with the combative intellectual (Staël 1998, 359). The physical and mental decline of lovelorn Corinne shows that Staël, like Robinson, believed that intense suffering hindered poetic creativity.

113. Staël 1998, 21. Staël added: 'In England he [Oswald] would have judged such a woman very severely, but he did not apply any of the social conventions to Italy' (Staël 1998, 22).

114. See Baiesi 2005, 185.

115. Though Staël warned readers against mixing up Corinne with Corilla Olimpica, she exploited the similarity between their names and the legendary figure of Corilla. See Giuli 1999. As Giuli points out, only three poets in four centuries had received the honour (Petrarch, Tasso, and the *improvvisatore* Perfetti). The conferment of the prize to a woman was scandalous and made Corilla's life difficult.

116. Oswald 'had often seen statesmen borne in triumph by the people, but it was the first time he had witnessed honour done to a woman renowned only for the gifts of genius. Her triumphal chariot had cost no one tears' (Staël 1998, 23). In real life, Corilla Olimpica was the target of violent sexist abuse on the part of the Roman people (Giuli 1999, 173–5).

117. The distance between Italy and England was not unbridgeable. In fact, Corinne was half Italian and half English. The virtues of both cultures coexisted in her personality (see e.g. Staël 1998, 25). Staël used a line of Petrarch to define Corinne's harmonious conversation, which was like 'Il parlar che nell'anima si sente', 'The speech heard in one's soul' (Staël 1998, 26; translation mine).

118. Staël 1998, 231.

119. See Mellor 2000b, 69 ff.

120. Another interesting example is provided by Maria Jewsbury's *History of an Enthusiast* (1830). Julia, the protagonist, is reproached for plunging her spirit 'into an intellectual fountain of emotion, of which Goethe and Schiller, Petrarch and de Staël, and Shelley, and a dozen others, are the presiding spirits,' which 'will be productive of more loss than gain.' Just before this passage, Cecil Percy, the other protagonist of the novel, tells Julia to throw away the 'intense, dreamy, passionate Germans'. She was a realist like him before reading them. Julia replies that they opened up a new world to her, and quotes a passage of Hemans to illustrate the concept. However, he remains of the same opinion (Jewsbury 1830, 65–6). On Jewsbury, see Peel and Sweet 1999, 211–15; Simpson 2003, 360–1.

121. The poem ran through six reprints in a year. Landon's popularity elicited a response from older writers like Coleridge. His *The Improvisatore*, published in *The Amulet for 1828*, is based on Landon, Burns and Thomas Moore, and revolves round love like most of the sonnets Coleridge wrote in the same period. On Staël, Landon and the figure of the *improvvisatrice* see Simpson 2003.

122. The episode was perhaps inspired by *PC*, 238, where Petrarch expresses his envy for a powerful nobleman who kisses Laura during a feast. Another novelty in Landon is her insistence on Petrarch's beauty, which was ignored by most Romantics. She refers to some famous Petrarchan images, such as Laura's 'golden tresses', and celebrates Petrarch's desolate fate and the lasting power of his poems (Landon 1996, 4–7). Like Petrarch, the improvisatrice meets her beloved, Lorenzo, at a 'gorgeous feast' (Landon 1996, 50 ff.). Landon's acquaintance with Petrarch goes back to her school days (Stephenson 1995, 24).

123. Landon 1996, 8. This section ends with a lyric, 'Sappho's Song', i.e., Landon's version of Sappho's last song before her suicide (Landon 1996, 10–11). In the final part of *The Improvisatrice*, the protagonist paints Sappho on the cliffs of Leucadia as a premonition of her own death (Landon 1996, 88–90). Her identification with Sappho is overt in the conclusion, where a posthumous portrait of the improvisatrice shows her as 'a Sappho' (Landon 1996, 103–5).

124. Landon's character seems to be mainly based on Staël's Corinne, who was a 'poetess, writer, and improviser, and one of the most beautiful women in Rome' (Staël

1998, 21). Landon's interest in Staël and Corinne was permanent. It emerged in her first collection, *The Fate of Adelaide, a Swiss Romantic Tale; and Other Poems* (1821), with 'Corinna', her first mask as an *improvvisatrice*, and it continued with the rewriting of Staël's novel in 'The Improvisatrice' (1824) and 'A History of the Lyre' (1829), the translations of the lyrics for Isabel Hill's English version of *Corinne* (1833), and the poem 'Corinne at the Cape of Misena', one of Landon's most successful annual contributions, published in *The Amulet* for 1832. Linda H. Peterson points out that Landon began to dress like Corinne after translating the 'poems' for the English edition of *Corinne*. She encouraged the identification with Staël's heroine and Sappho. Peterson also recalls that Mary Robinson was the archetypal abandoned woman in that period. Robinson's *Memoirs* describe her ability as an *improvvisatrice*. Of course, she was a well-known performer. Peterson 1999, 117, 120.

125.   This is all the more relevant considering that Felicia Hemans excluded Petrarch from her rewritings of Corinne on the Capitol and the other poems on women writers and fame (e.g. 'Corinna', 1827, and its continuation, 'Women and Fame', 1829). Landon deliberately preserved Petrarch's role in the topic, which haunted her as much as Hemans. It should be noted, however, that Hemans wrote a poem on Tasso's missed coronation on the Capitol, 'Tasso's Coronation'.

126.   It is the story of Count Leoni and Catarina Cornaro, the exiled Queen of Cyprus, whose ship is seen by Petrarch as it approaches Venice at sunset: 'One wandered there, whose gazing eye / Deserved to mirror such a sky. / He of the laurel and the lyre, / Whose lip was song, whose heart was fire – / The gentle Petrarch – he whose fame / Was worship of one dearest name, / The myrtle planted on his grave, / Gave all the laurel ever gave; / The life that lives in others' breath – / Love's last sweet triumph over death. / And tell me not of long disdain, / Of hope unblest – of fiery pain, – / Of lute and laurel vowed in vain. / Of such the common cannot deem; / Such love hath an eternal pride! / I'd rather feed on such a dream, / Than win a waking world beside' (Landon 1835, 19–20). Catarina recalls her glorious past, and asks her minstrel, Azalio, to sing a story of yore. He sings 'The Vow of the Peacock'. Landon's narrator says that had Petrarch told Catarina's tale, he would not be telling his. Petrarch is mentioned again in a note ('Divinest Petrarch' for 'Gentle Petrarch', Landon 1835, 112–14). Petrarch took part in a public festival in Venice with tournaments, which he watched seated beside the Doge. Petrarch's 'love of pleasure was satisfied by two days' attendance on the protracted festivity'.

127.   The poem describes the last moments of Sappho's life, which, in this version, were spent with Phaon. The conclusion is dedicated to her grave in the sea, though her suicide is not described (Landon 1835, 115–20).

128.   *The London Literary Gazette and Journal of Belles Lettres, Arts, Sciences, etc.*, 196 (21 Oct. 1820) 685.

129.   Blanchard 1841, II, 197–9. The poem was first published in *The Monthly Magazine*, 47 (1836) 175–6.

130.   Anonymous 1821. The author defines Romantic sonnet-writing and melancholy poses as a new wave of an old disease, which can be cured by 'a full stomach and fat ale'.

131.   See e.g. ll. 19–20 in a sonnet-stanza of *The Restoration of the Works of Art to Italy: A Poem* (1816), and 'Forest Sanctuary', Pt. I, l. 813 and note (Hemans 2000, 19, 292). Hemans was not excited by Petrarch's conceits, and she wondered 'whether the beautiful Laura, or the emblematic Tree, were the real object' of

his affection (*Patriotic Effusions of the Italian Poets*, 1821, in Hemans 2000, 170). Hemans was not indifferent to the themes of Petrarch's poetry, since many of her most characteristic poems describe lovelorn women artists. However, she liked other models better than Petrarch. The most important of them was Staël's *Corinne*, which she cited and rewrote many times, though she also admired tragic figures such as Tasso and Camoens. Hemans 1818 is a personal selection which shows her view of the lyric tradition. Most of the texts are pastoral and amorous sonnets translated from Spanish, Italian, French, Portuguese, and German – languages she mainly learned from her half-Italian mother. Interestingly, Hemans did not translate from Camoens's epic poetry, but from his shorter lyrics, which are Petrarchan like those of some other authors (Metastasio and Bembo). From Petrarch she translated *PC*, 248 (a *blazon* on Laura's beauties) and the Romantic favourite *PC*, 279 (Hemans 1818, 46–7). In comparison to Smith and most eighteenth-century translators, Hemans remained closer to the originals, though she used irregular rhyme schemes, rearranged the order of some lines and omitted some details. Her complex syntax is an attempt at reproducing the sinuosity of the original, though it fails to catch its fluency. This volume of translations marked a significant stage of Hemans's evolution from her early manner to the mature style of the 1820s and 1830s, when she composed several sonnet sequences.

132. Cobbold 1825, 239–41 (the texts have been reprinted recently in Feldman and Robinson 1999, 178–9). Cobbold's book includes English versions of *PC*, 2, 3, 11, 15, 19, 301, 310, 320 (Cobbold 1825, 220–6), whose form is mainly Shakespearean or irregular. Some versions have more than 14 lines, whereas others are translated as little elegies in quatrains in alternating rhymes (e.g., 'Zephiro torna'). The form of the 'Sonnets of Laura' is Shakespearean. The text is cited from the original edition.

133. See Petrarch's 'Triumphus Mortis', ll. 139–47.

134. Tomlinson 1874 (on Laura, 44–9, and Appendix VII, 209–10; on Petrarch's love, 65–6). Tomlinson includes even the story of Giustina Levi-Perotti as a background to his version of 'La gola e 'l somno', though he overlooks the problems raised by her text (Tomlinson 1874, 68). On Wordsworth, Milton, and Bowles, Tomlinson 1874, 77–9; on the English translations, Tomlinson 1874, 97–135. Tomlinson began his translation in 1873, when his wife died. Even an enthusiast like him believed, however, that Dante's Beatrice was more real than Laura as a woman (Tomlinson 1874, 44–8).

135. He selected 60 of Wordsworth's sonnets against 56 of Shakespeare's. Main includes several eighteenth-century sonneteers, but his opinions on them derive from Coleridge and Wordsworth. For example, on the basis of Coleridge's judgement, Bowles is credited a major role in the revival, whereas nothing is said about Smith. Main relates Wordsworth's opinion of her as a definitive critical judgement (Main 1880, 362–3). In his Preface Main writes that he has not followed the principles expounded in Tomlinson's essay. His only rules have been that a sonnet must develop one thought in 14 decasyllabic lines (Main 1880, viii). The authors' names are printed in Gothic type, in order to stress the northern, autonomous character of the English tradition.

136. In particular, 'the love of Petrarch seems to have been love of the kind which breaks no hearts' (Macaulay 1970, 315). The association of Petrarch and Rousseau shows that the interpretation of the poets of Sensibility was still dominant in the 1830s.

137. The relation between Barrett and her Romantic precursors is discussed by Mermin 1989; Stephenson 1989; Stone 1995. On Staël and Barrett, who modelled her Aurora Leigh on Corinne, see Moers 1976, ch. 'Performing Heroinism: The Myth of Corinne'; Kaplan in Barrett 1978, 18–22; Peel and Sweet 1999, 215–20. On Hemans, L.E.L., and Barrett (who wrote some poems on them), see Leighton 1992, 34–6; Peterson 1999.

138. They were extolled as her best work in the nineteenth century, when they were read as a document of her inner life. In the twentieth century, they have been rejected as embarrassing and affected, that is, for being at the same time too confessional, too literary, and self-deprecatory. See e.g. Harrison 1998, 78 ff. An overview of the main critical opinions on the subject can be found in Moore 2000, 164–6, 266–7.

139. After reading Lady Dacre's translations from Petrarch, Barrett wrote: 'I never had an enthusiasm for Petrarch – and the eternal Doubt which hangs around his poetry, as to whether he loved a woman an abstraction or a cloud, seems to me quite enough to convict him of a deficiency in earnestness & intensity. Nevertheless he has written beautifully, if not what is beautiful' (*TBC* III, 246 (mid-May 1837)).

140. Barrett translations from Petrarch are listed in *BC*, 360–1 (entries D1245 to D1255). She translated *PC*, 1 ('Hearers in broken rhyme of echoes old'); *PC*, 61 ('Now blessed be the day & month & year'); *PC*, 72 ('My lovely dame! I see', draft of stanza 1 only); *PC*, 126 ('Pure water, clear & still'); *PC*, 292 ('The eyes I spake such ardent praises on'); *PC*, 359 ('When She, my sweet and faithful consolation', stanza 1 only). Of most of these there are drafts and fair, revised copies. Phillip David Sharp points out that it is surprising that Barrett did not publish her versions from Petrarch. They are finished, titled, and transcribed in a notebook entry entitled 'Sonnets'. Sharp believes that she may well have planned to produce a selected edition of Petrarch. Though she abandoned this project, she wrote 'The Exile's Return' and 'Caterina to Camoens', which deal with the same tradition (Sharp 1977, 98, cited by Stephenson 1989, 36–7). Browning's library held a copy of Penrose's essay on Dante and Petrarch, Petrarch's *De remediis* and *Le rime* (ed. A. Buttura, Paris, 1829), and Tomasini's *Petrarcha redivivus* (1560) (*BC*, 156, 196). There is also a manuscript of Barrett's with 'draft lines on Petrarch and Valclusa', in Pocket Notebook II, *c.* 72 ll. (*BC*, D369, 'I did not think to see except in dreams', unpublished). Barrett also translated from Dante, but she referred to him only occasionally, when she began to correspond with Robert. On their way to Italy, Elizabeth and Robert 'made a pilgrimage' to Vaucluse, where 'the spirit of Petrarch *lives still*'. Her beloved dog, Flush, was baptised in the Sorgue in Petrarch's name. See *TBC* XIV, 45 (19 Nov. 1846), *TBC* XIV, 97 (7 Jan. 1847), *TBC* XIV, 100 (mid-Jan. 1847), *TBC* XIV, 149 (10 Mar. 1847). On Barrett's versions from Petrarch, see also Moore 2000, 170–1, 192–3.

141. Elizabeth was well-read in the Petrarchan tradition. Besides the English sonneteers, she knew Camoëns, who provided the subject for her 'Caterina to Camoëns' and the title of *Sonnets from the Portuguese*, and Vittoria Colonna, who reminded her of Hemans (*TBC* X, 291, 2–3 July 1845). Petrarch appears in some of her poems. In 'Lady's Geraldine's Courtship', Bertram reads Petrarch's and Camoëns's sonnets to her lover while they wander in nature (ll. 161–2). In 'Casa Guidi Windows', Petrarch is mentioned several times, in particular as a poet she loved from her youth (Part I, ll. 1196–7).

142.   Robert Browning's notorious hostility to the sonnet and autobiographic poetry must be added to the obstacles Barrett found on her way. He consented to the publication of *Sonnets from the Portuguese* but he was always uneasy about them. See Going 1976, 69–76; Mermin 1989, 142–3.

143.   This refers in particular to the Italian poems Christina wrote for Charles Cayley.

144.   Stone 1999, 65.

145.   There is no reason to question William Michael Rossetti, who pointed out that Dante was the only Italian poet Dante Gabriel Rossetti 'earnestly loved' (Rossetti 1893, xxvii). On one occasion Rossetti imitated Petrarch. His Italian sonnet for a painting, 'La bella mano', is based on *PC*, 199, a favourite sonnet with the mannerists (Rossetti 1893, 372).

146.   Besides, *The House of Life* was the last nail driven into the coffin of another Romantic and Victorian expectation, that is, love poems which did not hinge on adultery. D. G. Rossetti and Meredith wrote sonnet sequences on marriages, but they turned out to be hells rather than the heavens the public expected.

147.   Waller 1877, III, 656–7, 'Francesco Petrarca'. The entry is accompanied by a full-page plate, the same one as in Tytler's biography. Petrarch's coronation in Rome is described in greater detail than his journeys or his political activity. Christina stresses Petrarch's attempts to bring peace to Italy. She refers to the 1812 edition of Tytler's essay.

148.   Further evidence for this was Simone Memmi's sculpted effigy of her, held in Florence (Waller 1877, III, 657). Mary Arsenau points out that Christina rejected her father's allegorical readings of the figures of Beatrice and Laura. He argued that they did not exist historically. Beatrice stood for the *summum arcanum*, the supreme mystery at the heart of religious worship; Laura was a mere symbol for a Masonic lodge (Arsenau 1999). In a late article on Dante Christina wrote for the *Century* (New York) on the request of Gosse, she interpreted Dante's passion for Beatrice as romantic, unrequited love. On the contrary, she believed that Dante's marriage was unhappy. See Marsh 1994, 509.

149.   Marsh 1994, 212.

150.   Cayley 1879. Cayley's short preface says that Petrarch is the best love poet. His political poems are good, but they do not possess the passionate strength expected from such texts in the nineteenth century. Cayley's was the first complete single-handed translation. He added titles to the *in vita* sonnets, and to a few of those *in morte*. This makes the book look like a novel or a narrative poem, in which each sonnet is a stanza (e.g., Sonnet 3, 'Good Friday, 1327'). In a note to Sonnet 5, Cayley says that Laura is usually believed to be a de Noves who married Hugh de Sade (Cayley 1879, 465).

151.   Marsh 1994, 472–5.

152.   The background to *Monna Innominata* includes other items. The first are the poems Gabriel was adding to *The House of Life*, and the sonnets he was composing on Chatterton, Keats, Shelley and other poets in that period. Besides, in 1877 Christina was asked to trace references to Dante, Petrarch and Boccaccio for Grosart's edition of the *Faerie Queene*. She also read Francis Hueffer's article on Petrarch's friendship with Boccaccio (Marsh 1994, 457, 471). Finally, the library of the Rossetti family held a significant number of collections of sonnets and several editions of Petrarch poems, like Ludovico Dolce (1553), Alessandro Vellutello (1560), and G. Baglioli (1821) (Whitla 1987, 86).

153. The sonnet was later used as a 'Dedicatory Sonnet' to her *Poetical Works* (Rossetti 1904, lxxiii).
154. Rossetti 1997–2000, II, 299 (to D. G. Rossetti, 5 Sept. 1881).
155. Armstrong 1993, 345.
156. Introduction to *Monna Innominata* (Rossetti 1904, 58).
157. One of the sources of *Monna Innominata* is Hueffer 1878, which discusses also women troubadours. In addition, Gabriele Rossetti talks about several troubadours in his essay on Dante.
158. Isobel Armstrong muddles the point, since she erroneously defines the time and place of the troubadours as 'Renaissance Italy' (Armstrong 1993, 345).
159. Rossetti 1904, 58 (Introduction to *Monna Innominata*).
160. Rossetti 1904, 58 (Introduction to *Monna Innominata*).
161. According to Whitla, Christina meant that only unhappiness could lead a writer to speak in the name of a 'monna innominata', that is, to put up the mask of an ancient lady. A happy lover naturally addresses his or her beloved (Whitla 1987, 90–1).
162. Stone 1999, 48–9.
163. Bentley 1987, 72 n. 34.
164. *Goblin Market* was published in 1862, though it circulated even before that date.

Select Bibliography

See also the list of Abbreviations at the beginning of the book. Unless otherwise indicated, quotations are given by author's name, date, and page number.

Primary sources

Anonymous 1763. Trans *PC*, 35 and 132, *The Poetical Calendar*, ed. Francis Fawkes and William Woty, vol. VII (London: Coote) 78–9

Anonymous 1821. 'Sonnettomania', *The New Monthly Magazine, and Literary Journal* (*American Edition*), I:6 652–6

Arnaldi 1964. Arnaldi, Francesco, Lucia Gualdo Rosa and Liliana Monti Sabia (eds), *Poeti latini del Quattrocento* (Milan and Naples: Ricciardi)

Baldacci 1984. Baldacci, Luigi (ed.), *Lirici del Cinquecento* (Milan: Longanesi, 1st edn 1975)

Baretti 1753a. Baretti, Giuseppe, *A Dissertation upon the Italian Poetry, In which are interspersed some Remarks on Mr. Voltaire's Essay on the Epic Poets* (London: Dodsley)

Baretti 1753b. Baretti, Giuseppe, *Remarks on the Italian Language and Writers. In a Letter from M. Joseph Baretti to an English Gentleman in Turin, Written in the Year 1751* (London: Browne)

Baretti 1757. Baretti, Giuseppe, *The Italian Library. Containing An Account of the Lives and Works of the Most Valuable Authors of Italy. With a Preface Exhibiting The Changes of the Tuscan Language, from the barbarous Ages to the present Time* (London: Millar)

Baretti 1776. Baretti, Giuseppe, *Discours sur Shakespeare et sur Monsieur de Voltaire* (London: Nourse; Paris: Durand)

Baretti 1936. Baretti, Giuseppe, *Epistolario*, ed. Luigi Piccioni, 2 vols (Bari: Laterza)

Barrett 1978. Barrett Browning, Elizabeth, *Aurora Leigh and Other Poems*, intro. Cora Kaplan (London: Women's Press)

Barthélemy 1880. Barthélemy, Jean-Jacques, *Voyage du jeune Anacharsis en Grèce vers le milieu du quatrième siècle avant l'ère vulgaire* (1788) (rptd Paris: Firmin-Didot)

Beckford 1970. Beckford, William, *Modern Novel Writing* (1796) and *Azemia* (1797), facsimile reproductions, intro. Herman Mittle Levy Jr, 4 vols in 1 (Gainesville, Florida: Scholars' Facsimiles & Reprints)

Bowles 1978. Bowles, William Lisle, *Fourteen Sonnets; Sonnets Written on Picturesque Spots* [. . .], intro. Donald H. Reiman (New York and London: Garland)

Burney 1958. Burney, Charles, *A General History of Music from the Earliest Ages to 1789*, 3rd edn, 4 vols (London: Becket, Robson and Robinson, 1776–89, rptd Baden Baden: Heitz)

Burney 1988. *Memoirs of Dr. Charles Burney 1726–1769*, ed. Slava Klima, Garry Bowers and Kerry S. Grant (Lincoln and London: University of Nebraska Press)

Burney 1832. Burney, Fanny (ed.), *Memoirs of Doctor Burney Arranged from his own Manuscripts, from Family Papers, and from Personal Recollections*, 3 vols (London: Moxon)

Burney 1904–05. *Diary and Letters of Madame D'Arblay (1778–1840)*, ed. Charlotte Barrett, pref. and notes Austin Dobson, 6 vols (London: Macmillan)

Byron 1980–93. Byron, Lord, *Poetical Works*, ed. Jerome J. McGann, 7 vols (Oxford: Clarendon Press)

Byron 1991. Byron, Lord, *The Complete Miscellaneous Prose*, ed. Andrew Nicholson (Oxford: Clarendon Press)

Campbell 1843. Campbell, Thomas, *Life and Times of Petrarch with Notices of Boccaccio and his Illustrious Contemporaries*, 2nd edn, 2 vols (London: Colburn)

Cayley 1879. Cayley, Charles (ed.), *The Sonnets and Stanzas of Petrarch* (London: Longmans, Green)

Cobbold 1825. Cobbold, Elizabeth, *Poems by Mrs. Elizabeth Cobbold with a Memoir of the Author* (Ipswich: J. Raw)

Coleridge 1949. *The Philosophical Lectures of Samuel Taylor Coleridge*, ed. Kathleen Coburn (London: Pilot Press)

Coleridge 1990. Coleridge, Samuel Taylor, *Sibylline Leaves* 1817 (Oxford and New York: Woodstock)

Collier 1800. Collier, William, *Poems on Various Occasions; with Translations from Authors in Different Languages*, 2 vols (London: Cadell & Davies; and Robson)

Dobson 1784. *Memoirs of Ancient Chivalry, to which are added The Anecdotes of the Times, from the Romance Writers and Historians of those Ages*, trans. from the French of Monsieur De St Palaye (London: Dodsley)

Dobson 1797. Dobson, Susanna, *Petrarch's View of Human Life* (London: Stockdale, 1st edn 1791)

Dobson 1807. *The Literary History of the Troubadours containing their Lives, Extracts from their Works, and many Particulars relative to the Customs, Morals, and History of the Twelfth and Thirteenth Centuries*, collected and abridged from the French [of St Palaye] by Mrs Dobson (London)

Dodsley 1766. Dodsley, Robert (ed.), *A Collection of Poems in Six Volumes. By Several Hands* (London: J. Hughs for J. Dodsley, 1st edn 1747)

Dyce 1833. Dyce, Alexander (ed.), *Specimens of English Sonnets* (London: Pickering)

Fontenelle n.d. Fontenelle, Bernard Le Bovier, sieur de, *Nouveaux dialogues des morts* (Amsterdam: Pierre Mortier)

Fontenelle 1773a. [Fontenelle] 'Whether the Men should court the Women, or the Women the Men? A Dialogue between Sappho and Laura, in the Shades', [trans. Anonymous] *The Macaroni, Scavoir Vivre, and Theatrical Magazine*, (Oct.) 31–2

Fontenelle 1773b. [Fontenelle] 'Whether the Men should court the Women, or the Women the Men? A Dialogue between Sappho and Laura, in the Shades', [trans. Anonymous] *The Macaroni, Scavoir Vivre, and Theatrical Magazine*, (Nov.) 54–5

Foscolo 1953a. Foscolo, Ugo, 'Primo getto dell'articolo su Petrarca', in *Saggi e discorsi critici. Saggi sul Petrarca, Discorso sul testo del Decameron, Scritti minori su poeti italiani e stranieri*, vol. X of *Edizione Nazionale delle Opere di Ugo Foscolo*, ed. C. Foligno (Florence: Le Monnier)

Foscolo 1953b. Foscolo, Ugo, 'Essays on Petrarch', in *Saggi e discorsi critici. Saggi sul Petrarca, Discorso sul testo del Decameron, Scritti minori su poeti italiani e stranieri*, vol. X of *Edizione Nazionale delle Opere di Ugo Foscolo*, ed. C. Foligno (Florence: Le Monnier)

Gibbon 1996. Gibbon, Edward, *The Decline and Fall of the Roman Empire*, 2 vols (Chicago: Encyclopædia Britannica, 1st edn 1952)

Gifford 1797. Gifford, William, *The Baviad, and Mæviad* (London: Wright)

Goethe 1991. Goethe, Johann Wolfgang, *The Sorrows of Werter*, trans. Daniel Malthus 1789 (Oxford and New York: Woodstock)

Gray 1884. Gray, Thomas, *The Works of Thomas Gray. In Prose and Verse*, ed. Edmund Gosse, 3 vols (London: Macmillan)

Gray 1971. *The Correspondence of Thomas Gray*, ed. Paget Toynbee and Leonard Whibley, corrections and additions H. W. Starr, 3 vols (Oxford: Clarendon Press, 1st edn 1935)

Gray 1969. *The Poems of Thomas Gray, William Collins, Oliver Goldsmith*, ed. Roger Lonsdale (London and Harlow: Longmans)

Gray 1985. Gray, Thomas and William Collins, *Poetical Works*, ed. Roger Lonsdale (Oxford and New York: Oxford University Press, 1st edn 1977)

Hallam 1818. Hallam, Henry, *View of the State of Europe during the Middle Ages*, 2 vols (London: Murray)

Hayley 1782. Hayley, William, *An Essay on Epic Poetry* (Dublin: Price, Sleater etc)

Hayley 1789. Hayley, William, *The Young Widow; or, The History of Cornelia Sedley, in a Series of Letters*, 4 vols (London: Robinson)

Hazlitt 1931–34. Hazlitt, William, *The Complete Works of William Hazlitt*, ed. Percival Presland Howe, 21 vols (London: Dent)

Hazlitt 1979. *The Letters of William Hazlitt*, ed. Herschel Moreland Sikes, ass. Willard Hallam Bonner and Gerald Lahey (London and Basingstoke: Macmillan)

Hemans 1818. Hemans, Felicia, *Translations from Camoens and Other Poets, with Original Poetry* (London: Murray; Oxford: Parker)

Hemans 2000. Hemans, Felicia, *Selected Poems, Letters, Reception Materials*, ed. Susan J. Wolfson (Princeton and London: Princeton University Press)

Henderson 1803. Henderson, George (ed.), *Petrarca: A Selection of Sonnets from Various Authors. With an Introductory Dissertation on the Origin and Structure of the Sonnet* (London: Baldwin)

Hueffer 1878. Hueffer, Francis, *The Troubadours. A History of Provençal Life and Literature in the Middle Ages* (London: Chatto & Windus)

Hume 1875. Hume, David, *Essays Moral, Political, and Literary*, ed. T. H. Green and T. H. Grose, 2 vols (London: Longmans, Green)

Hunt 1867. Hunt, Leigh, and S. Adams Lee (eds), *The Book of the Sonnet*, 2 vols (Boston: Roberts Brothers)

Hunt 1923. *The Poetical Works of Leigh Hunt*, ed. H. S. Milford (London: Oxford University Press)

Hunt 1948. Hunt, Leigh, *Table Talk* (New York: George & Helen Macy)

Isola 1784. Isola, Agostino (ed.), *Pieces Selected from the Italian Poets and Translated into English Verse by Some Gentlemen of the University* (Cambridge)

Jewsbury 1830. Jewsbury, Maria J., *The Three Histories. The History of an Enthusiast. The History of a Nonchalant. The History of a Realist* (London: Westley & Davis)

Jones 2002. Jones, Anna Maria, *The Poems of Anna Maria* (Calcutta: Thomson & Ferris, 1793; Women Writers Project electronic edn, Brown University)

Jones 1772. Jones, Sir William, *Poems Consisting Chiefly of Translations from the Asiatick Languages. To Which Are Added Two Essays, I. On the Poetry of the Eastern Nations. II. On the Arts, commonly called Imitative* (Oxford: Clarendon Press)

Jones 1970. *The Letters of Sir William Jones*, ed. Garland Cannon, 2 vols (Oxford: Clarendon Press)

Keats 1958. *The Letters of John Keats 1814–1821*, ed. Hyder Edward Rollins, 2 vols (Cambridge: Cambridge University Press)

Keats 1988. Keats, John, *The Complete Poems* ed. John Barnard (Harmondsworth: Penguin, 1st edn 1973)

Lamb 1975–78. *The Letters of Charles and Mary Lamb (1796–1817)*, ed. Edwin W. Marrs Jr, 3 vols (Ithaca and London: Cornell University Press)

Landon 1835. Landon, Letitia Elizabeth, *The Vow of the Peacock and Other Poems* (London: Saunders & Otley)

Landon 1996. Landon, Letitia Elizabeth, *The Improvisatrice* 1825, ed. Jonathan Wordsworth (Poole and New York: Woodstock)

Langhorne 1770a. Langhorne, John, *Letters to Eleonora*, 2 vols (London: Becket & De Hondt, vol. II, 1771)

Langhorne 1770b. Langhorne, John, *Letters between Theodosius and Constantia*, 2 vols (London: Becket & De Hondt)

Langhorne 1804. Langhorne, John, *The Poetical Works of John Langhorne*, 2 vols (London: Becket & De Hondt, 1766; rptd London: Mawman)

Le Mesurier 1795. [Le Mesurier, Thomas] *Translations Chiefly from the Italian of Petrarch and Metastasio* (Oxford: Cooke)

Lloyd 1977. Lloyd, Charles, *Nugae Canorae: Poems ... Third Edition, with Additions (Including a Sonnet by S. T. Coleridge)*, ed. D. H. Reiman (New York: Garland, rpt of 1819 edn)

Lloyd 1978. Lloyd, Charles, *Poems on Various Subjects*, ed. D. H. Reiman (New York: Garland) (rpt of 1795 edn; bound with *Blank Verse* by Charles Lloyd and Charles Lamb, 1798; *Poetical Essays on the Character of Pope*, 1821, and *Poems* 1823)

Lucia 1774a. Lucia, 'The Completion of Female Beauty and Female Worth; or a Picture of the celebrated Laura, the Mistress of Petrarque', *The Edinburgh Magazine and Review*, (Jan.) 117–18

Lucia 1774b. Lucia, 'Anecdotes of Laura and Petrarque', *The Edinburgh Magazine and Review*, (June) 414–17

Lucia 1774c. Lucia, 'Anecdotes of Laura and Petrarque; concluded from our last †', *The Edinburgh Magazine and Review*, (July) 469–71

Macaulay 1970. Macaulay, Thomas Babington, 'Macaulay on Byron' (Review of T. Moore, *Letters and Journals of Lord Byron: with Notices of his Life*, 1830), in *Lord Byron. The Critical Heritage*, ed. Andrew Rutherford (London: Routledge & K. Paul; New York: Barnes & Noble) 295–316

Main 1880. Main, David (ed.), *A Treasury of English Sonnets* (Edinburgh and London: Blackwood)

Marinda 1716. [Monk, Mary] *Poems and Translations upon Several Occasions* (London: Tonson)

Metastasio 1947. Metastasio, Pietro, *Tutte le opere*, ed. Bruno Brunelli, vol 2 (Milan: Mondadori)

Nott 1775. [Nott, John] *Leonora, An Elegy on the Death of a Young Lady* (London: Davies)

Nott 1777. [Nott, John] *Sonnets and Odes, translated from the Italian of Petrarch; with the original text, and some account of his life* (London: Davies)

Nott 1778. [Nott, John] *Kisses: A Poetical Translation of the Basia of Johannes Secundus Nicolaïus*, 2nd edn (London: Bew)

Nott 1787. [Nott, John] *Selected Odes from the Persian Poet Hafez* (London: Cadell)

Nott 1803. [Nott, John] *Sappho. After a Greek Romance* (London: Cuthell and Martin)

Nott 1808. Nott, John *Petrarch Translated; in a Selection of his Sonnets, and Odes [...]*, by the Translator of Catullus (London: Miller, etc)

Ovid 1991. Ovidio, *Opere*, vol. I, *Amores, Heroides, Medicamina faciei, Ars amatoria, Remedia amoris*, ed. Adriana Della Casa (Turin: UTET, 1st edn 1982)

Parsons 1787. [Parsons, William] *A Poetical Tour in the Years 1784, 1785, and 1786 by a Member of the Arcadian Society at Rome* (London: Robson & Clarke)

Parsons 1798. Parsons, William, *Fidelity, or Love at first Sight. A Tale. With Other Poems* (London)

Parsons 1807. [Parsons, William] *Travelling Recreations*, 2 vols (London: Longman, Hurst, Rees, and Orme)

Penrose 1790. [Penrose, Thomas] *A Sketch of the Lives and Writings of Dante and Petrarch* (London: Stockdale)

Petrarca 1859. *The Sonnets, Triumphs, and Other Poems of Petrarch* (London: Bohn)

Petrarca 1996. Petrarca, Francesco *Trionfi, Rime estravaganti, Codice degli abbozzi*, ed. Vinicio Pacca and Laura Paolino (Milan: Mondadori)

Petrarca 2001. *Petrarch's Lyric Poems. The* Rime sparse *and Other Lyrics*, trans. and ed. Robert M. Durling (Cambridge, MA, and London: Harvard University Press, 1st edn 1976) (refs given by poem number)

Polwhele 1974. Polwhele, Richard *The Unsex'd Females: A Poem*; Mary Ann Radcliffe, *The Female Advocate*, intro. Gina Luria (New York and London: Garland)

Pope 1953–69. Pope, Alexander, *The Twickenham Edition of the Poems of Alexander Pope*, gen. ed. John Butt, 11 vols (London: Methuen)

Potter 1934. Potter, Stephen (ed.), *Minnow among Tritons. Mrs. S. T. Coleridge's Letters to Thomas Poole 1799–1834* (London: Nonesuch Press)

Preston 1781. Preston, William, *Poems on Several Occasions* (Dublin: Halhead)

Preston 1793. Preston, William, *Poetical Works*, 2 vols (Dublin: Graisberry & Campbell)

Preston 1805? Preston, William, *Some Considerations on the History of ancient amatory Writers, and the comparative merits of the three great Roman Elegiac Poets, Ovid, Tibullus and Propertius* (Dublin?)

Robinson 1938. Robinson, Henry Crabb, *Henry Crabb Robinson on Books and Their Writers*, ed. Edith J. Morley, 3 vols (London: Dent)

Robinson 1994a. Robinson, Mary, *Poems, 1791* (Oxford and New York: Woodstock)

Robinson 1994b. *Perdita: The Memoirs of Mary Robinson*, ed. M. J. Levy (London and Chester Springs: Owen; orig. edn *Memoirs of the Late Mrs. Robinson, Written by Herself*, London: Wilks & Taylor, 1801)

Robinson 1996. Robinson, Mary, *The Poetical Works*, intro. Caroline Franklin (London: Routledge/Thoemmes Press)

Robinson 2000a. Robinson, Mary, *Selected Poems*, ed. Judith Pascoe (Peterborough, ONT: Broadview Literary Texts)

Robinson 2005. [Robinson, Mary] *A Letter to the Women of England*, ed. Adriana Craciun, Anne Irmen Close, Megan Musgrave and Orianne Smith (Romantic Circles Electronic Edition, http://www.rc.umd.edu/editions/robinson/mrintro.htm; facsimile of 1st edn, London: Longman & Rees, 1799)

Rossetti 1904. Rossetti, Christina, *The Poetical Works of Christina Georgina Rossetti*, ed. William Michael Rossetti (London and New York: Macmillan)

Rossetti 1997–2000. *The Letters of Christina Rossetti*, ed. Anthony H. Harrison, 3 vols (Charlottesville and London: University Press of Virginia)

Rossetti 1893. Rossetti, Dante Gabriel, *The Poetical Works of Dante Gabriel Rossetti*, ed. William Michael Rossetti (London: Ellis & Elvey)

Rousseau 1989. Rousseau, Jean–Jacques, *Eloisa, or a series of original letters* [1803], trans. William Kenrick, 2 vols (London: Becket & De Hondt, 1764, rptd Oxford: Woodstock)

Seward 1799. Seward, Anna, *Original Sonnets on Various Subjects and Odes Paraphrased from Horace*, 2nd edn (London)

Seward 1810. Seward, Anna, *The Poetical Works of Anna Seward; with extracts from her literary correspondences*, ed. Walter Scott, 3 vols (Edinburgh and London)

Seward 1811. *Letters of Anna Seward: Written between the years 1784 and 1807*, ed. Archibald Constable, 6 vols (Edinburgh and London)

Seward 1936. *The Swan of Lichfield, being a selection of the Correspondence of Anna Seward*, ed. Hesketh Pearson (London: Hamilton)

Shelley 1987. Shelley, Mary, *The Journals of Mary Shelley*, ed. Paula R. Feldman and Diana Scott-Kilvert, 2 vols (Oxford: Clarendon Press)

Shelley 1964. *The Letters of Percy Bysshe Shelley*, ed. Frederick L. Jones, 2 vols (Oxford: Clarendon Press)

Shelley 1965. *The Complete Works of Percy Bysshe Shelley*, ed. Roger Ingpen and Walter E. Peck, 10 vols (New York: Gordian Press, 1st edn 1926–30)

Shelley 1988. Shelley, Percy Bysshe, *Poetical Works*, ed. Thomas Hutchinson, corr. G. M. Matthews (Oxford and New York: Oxford University Press, 1st edn 1970)

Sismondi 1818. Sismondi, Jean-Charles-Léonard Simonde de, *Histoire des républiques italiennes du Moyen Age*, 2nd edn, 16 vols (Paris: Treuttel et Wurtz)

Sismondi 1819. Sismondi, Jean-Charles-Léonard Simonde de, *De la littérature du Midi de l'Europe*, 2nd edn, 4 vols (Paris: Treuttel et Wurtz)

Smith 1993. *The Poems of Charlotte Smith*, ed. Stuart Curran (New York: Oxford University Press)

Smith 2003. *The Collected Letters of Charlotte Smith*, ed. Judith Phillips Stanton (Bloomington and Indianapolis: Indiana University Press)

Smith 2004. Smith, Charlotte, *Celestina*, ed. Loraine Fletcher (Toronto: Broadview)

Staël 1985. Staël, Madame de, *Corinne ou l'Italie*, ed. Simone Balayé (Paris: Gallimard)

Staël 1998. Staël, Madame de, *Corinne, or Italy*, trans. and ed. Sylvia Raphael (Oxford: Oxford University Press)

Thelwall 1792. [Thelwall, John] J.T., 'An Essay on the English Sonnet; Illustrated by a Comparison between the Sonnets of Milton and those of Charlotte Smith', *The Universal Magazine*, (Dec.) 408–14

Tomlinson 1874. Tomlinson, Charles, *The Sonnet. Its Origin, Structure, and Place in Poetry with Original Translations from the Sonnets of Dante, Petrarch, etc. and Remarks on the Art of Translating* (London: Murray)

Toynbee 1909. Toynbee, Paget, *Dante in English Literature from Chaucer to Cary (c. 1380–1844)*, 2 vols (London: Methuen)

Tytler 1784. Tytler, Alexander Fraser, *Essay on the Life and Character of Petrarch. To Which Are Added Seven of His Sonnets Translated from the Italian* (London: Cadell)

Tytler 1810. Tytler, Alexander Fraser, *An Historical and Critical Essay on the Life and Character of Petrarch. With a Translation of a Few of His Sonnets* (Edinburgh: Ballantyne; London: Murray)

Voltaire 1761. *Ancient and Modern History*, vols I–VI of *The Works of M. de Voltaire*, trans. T. Smollet and others (London: Newbery)

Voltaire 1877–85. *Oeuvres complètes de Voltaire*, ed. Louis Moland, 52 vols (Paris: Garnier)

Waller 1877. Waller, John Francis, *Imperial Dictionary of Universal Biography* (London, Glasgow, and Edinburgh: MacKenzie, 1st edn 1857)

Warton 1782. Warton, Joseph *An Essay on the Genius and Writings of Pope*, 2 vols, 4th edn (London: Dodsley)

Warton 1998. *Thomas Warton's History of Poetry*, intro. David Fairer, 4 vols (London: Routledge and Thoemmes Press; 1st edn, *The History of English Poetry from the Eleventh to the Seventeenth Century*, London, 1788)

Wordsworth 1963. *The Journals of Dorothy Wordsworth*, ed. Helen Darbishire (London: Oxford University Press, 1st edn 1958)

Wordsworth 1946. Wordsworth, William, *The Poetical Works*, ed. Ernest De Selincourt and Helen Darbishire (Oxford: Clarendon Press) vol. III

Wordsworth 1947. Wordsworth, William, *The Poetical Works*, ed. Ernest De Selincourt and Helen Darbishire (Oxford: Clarendon Press) vol. IV

Wordsworth 1950. *The Critical Opinions of William Wordsworth*, ed. Markham L. Peacock Jr (Baltimore: Johns Hopkins University Press)

Wordsworth 1974. *The Prose Works of William Wordsworth*, ed. W. J. B. Owen and Jane Worthington Smyser, 3 vols (Oxford: Clarendon Press)

Wordsworth 1978. *The Letters of William and Dorothy Wordsworth*, gen. ed. Ernest de Selincourt, vol. IV, *Later Years*, rev., arr. and ed. Alan G. Hill (Oxford: Clarendon Press)

Wordsworth 1997. Wordsworth, William, *Early Poems and Fragments, 1785–1797*, eds Carol Landon and Jared Curtis (London and Ithaca, NY: Cornell University Press)

Wrangham 1817. Wrangham, Francis, *A Few Sonnets, Attempted from Petrarch in Early Life* (Kent: printed privately at Lee Priory)

Wu 1997. Wu, Duncan (ed.), *Romantic Women Poets. An Anthology* (Oxford: Blackwell)

Secondary Sources

Allen 2002. Allen, Reggie, 'The Sonnets of William Hayley and Gift Exchange', *European Romantic Review*, XIII:4 (Dec.) 383–92

Allen 1996. Allen, Richard C., 'Charles Lloyd, Coleridge, and *Edmund Oliver*', *Studies in Romanticism*, XXXV:2 (Summer) 245–94

Armstrong 1993. Armstrong, Isobel, *Victorian Poetry: Poetry, Poetics, and Politics* (London and New York: Routledge)

Arsenau 1999. Arsenau, Mary, ' "May My Great Love Avail Me": Christina Rossetti and Dante', in *The Culture of Christina Rossetti: Female Poetics and Victorian Contexts*, ed. Mary Arsenau, Anthony H. Harrison, and Lorraine Janzen Kooistra (Athens: Ohio University Press) 22–45

Auerbach 1965. Auerbach, Erich, *Literary Language & Its Public in Late Antiquity and in the Middle Ages*, trans. R. Manheim (London: Routledge & Kegan Paul)

Baiesi 2005. Baiesi, Simona, 'The Influence of the Italian *Improvvisatrici* on British Romantic Women Writers: Letitia Elizabeth Landon's Response', in *British Romanticism and Italian Literature. Translating, Reviewing, Rewriting*, ed. Laura Bandiera and Diego Saglia (Amsterdam and New York: Rodopi) 180–91

Baker 1962. Baker, Herschel, *William Hazlitt* (Cambridge, MA: Harvard University Press)

Barberi 1968. Barberi Squarotti, Giorgio, 'Le poetiche del Trecento in Italia', in *Momenti e problemi di storia dell'estetica* (Milan: Marzorati) vol. I, 255–324

Barth 1985. Barth, Robert J., 'Coleridge's Ideal of Love', *Studies in Romanticism*, XXIV, 113–39

Bate 1958. Bate, Walter Jackson, *The Stylistic Development of Keats* (London: Routledge & Kegan Paul, 1st edn 1945)

Bate 1963. Bate, Walter Jackson, *John Keats* (Harvard: Harvard University Press)

Beaty 1985. Beaty, Frederick L., *Byron the Satirist* (Dekalb: Northern Illinois University Press)

Bentley 1987. Bentley, D. M. R., 'The Meretricious and the Meritorious in *Goblin Market*: A Conjecture and an Analysis', in *The Achievement of Christina Rossetti*, ed. David A. Kent (Ithaca and London: Cornell University Press) 57–81

Billanovich 1947. Billanovich, Giuseppe, *Petrarca letterato: I. Lo scrittoio del Petrarca* (Rome: Edizioni di Storia e Letteratura)

Billanovich 2001. Billanovich, Giuseppe, 'Biografia e opere del Petrarca tra fiaba e realtà', in *L'Italia letteraria e l'Europa. I: Dalle origini al Rinascimento*, Atti del Convegno Internazionale di Aosta, 20–23 ottobre 1997, ed. Nino Borsellino and Bruno Germano (Rome: Salerno Editrice) 75–82

Bitton 1999. Bitton, Michèle, *Poétesses et lettrées juives: Une mémoire eclipsée* (Paris: Editions Publisud)

Blanchard 1841. Blanchard, Laman, *Life and Literary Remains of L.E.L.*, 2 vols (London: Colburn)

Bostetter 1956. Bostetter, Edward B., 'The Original Della Cruscans and the Florence Miscellany', *Huntington Library Quarterly*, XIX, 277–300

Bradley 1914. Bradley, A. C., 'Notes on Shelley's *The Triumph of Life*', *Modern Language Review*, IX, 441–56

Brooks 1992. Brooks, Stella, 'The Sonnets of Charlotte Smith', *Critical Survey*, IV:1, 9–21

Butler 1984. Butler, Marilyn, 'Satire and the Images of Self in the Romantic Period: The Long Tradition of Hazlitt's *Liber Amoris*', in *English Satire and the Satiric Tradition*, ed. Claude Rawson (Oxford and New York: Blackwell) 209–25

Calder 1983. Calder, Jenni, 'The Hero as Lover: Byron and Women', in *Byron: Wrath and Rhyme*, ed. Alan Bold (London and Totowa: Vision Press and Barnes & Noble) 103–24

Castorina 1978. Castorina, Giuseppe G., *Le forme della malinconia. Ricerche sul sonetto in Inghilterra (1748–1800)* (Bologna: Pàtron)

Coffman 1987. Coffman, Ralph J., *Coleridge's Library: A Bibliography of Books Owned or Read by Samuel Taylor Coleridge* (Boston, MA: Hall)

Cox 2003. Cox, Jeffrey N., 'Leigh Hunt's *Foliage*: A Cockney manifesto', in *Leigh Hunt. Life, Poetics, Politics*, ed. Nicholas Roe (London and New York: Routledge) 58–77

Curran 1988. Curran, Stuart, 'Romantic Poetry: The I Altered', in *Romanticism and Feminism*, ed. Anne K. Mellor (Bloomington and Indianapolis: Indiana University Press) 185–207

Curran 1994. Curran, Stuart, 'Mary Robinson's *Lyrical Tales* in Context', in *Re-Visioning Romanticism: British Women Writers, 1776–1837*, ed. Carol Shiner Wilson and Joel Haefner (Philadelphia: University of Pennsylvania Press) 17–35

Curran 1998. Curran, Stuart, ' "Figurando il Paradiso": Shelley e Dante', in *Shelley e l'Italia*, ed. Lilla Maria Crisafulli Jones (Naples: Liguori) 43–53

deJean 1989. deJean, Joan, *Fictions of Sappho 1546–1937* (Chicago and London: University of Chicago Press)

Dolan 2003. Dolan, Elizabeth A., 'British Romantic Melancholia: Charlotte Smith's Elegiac Sonnets, Medical Discourse and the Problem of Sensibility', *Journal of European Studies*, XXXIII:3–4 (130–131) (Dec.), 237–53

Donoghue 1993. Donoghue, Emma, *Passions between Women: British Lesbian Culture 1668–1801* (London: Scarlet Press)

Dotti 1987. Dotti, Ugo, *Vita di Petrarca* (Bari: Laterza)

Dowling 1991. Dowling, William C., *The Epistolary Moment: The Poetics of the Eighteenth-Century Verse Epistle* (Princeton: Princeton University Press)

Elfenbein 2004. Elfenbein, Andrew, 'Byron: Gender and Sexuality', in *The Cambridge Companion to Byron*, ed. Drummond Bone (Cambridge: Cambridge University Press) 56–73

Eliot 1965. Eliot, Thomas Stearns, *To Criticize the Critic* (London: Faber & Faber)

Erdman 1958. Erdman, David V., 'Coleridge as Nehemiah Higginbottom', *Modern Language Notes*, LXXIII (Dec.), 569–80

Fairer 1991. Fairer, David, 'Baby Language and Revolution: The Early Poetry of Charles Lloyd and Charles Lamb', *Charles Lamb Bulletin*, LXXIV (Apr.), 33–52

Fairer 2002. Fairer, David, 'Coleridge's Sonnets from Various Authors (1796): A Lost Conversation Poem?', *Studies in Romanticism*, XLI:4 (Winter), 585–604

Feldman and Robinson 1999. Feldman, Paula R., and Daniel Robinson (eds), *A Century of Sonnets: The Romantic-Era Revival 1750–1850* (New York and Oxford: Oxford University Press)

Fletcher 1998. Fletcher, Loraine, *Charlotte Smith: A Critical Biography* (Basingstoke: Macmillan – now Palgrave Macmillan; New York: St Martin's)

Folliot 1979. Folliot, Katherine, *Shelley's Italian Sunset* (Richmond: H&B Publications)

France 2000. France, Peter (ed.), *The Oxford Guide to Literature in English Translation* (Oxford and New York: Oxford University Press)

Frank 1969. Frank, Frederick S., 'The Demon and the Thunderstorm: Byron and Madame de Staël', *Revue de Littérature Comparée*, XLIII:3, 320–43

Franklin 1992. Franklin, Caroline, *Byron's Heroines* (Oxford: Clarendon Press)

Fulford 1999. Fulford, Tim, *Romanticism and Masculinity: Gender, Politics and Poetics in the Writings of Burke, Coleridge, Cobbett, Wordsworth, De Quincey and Hazlitt* (Basingstoke: Macmillan – now Palgrave Macmillan)

Gamer 2003. Gamer, Michael, ' "Bell's Poetics": *The Baviad*, the Della Cruscans, and the Book of *The World*', in *The Satiric Eye: Forms of Satire in the Romantic Period*, ed. Steven E. Jones (New York: Palgrave Macmillan) 31–53

Gardini 2001. Gardini, Nicola, 'Recuperare il corpo: genere e proibizione sessuale nella storia della letteratura italiana', *Trame*, II:2, 19–38

Garin 1965. Garin, Eugenio, *Italian Humanism. Philosophy and Civic Life in the Renaissance*, trans. Peter Munz (Oxford: Blackwell; 1st edn Bern: Franke, 1947)

Garin 1988. Garin, Eugenio (ed.), *L'uomo del Rinascimento* (Bari: Laterza)

Gerosa 1966. Gerosa, Pietro Paolo, *Umanesimo cristiano del Petrarca. Influenza agostiniana, attinenze medievali* (Turin: Bottega d'Erasmo)

Giddey 1982. Giddey, Ernest, 'Byron and Madame de Staël', in *Lord Byron and His Contemporaries: Essays from the Sixth International Byron Seminar*, ed. Charles E. Robinson (Newark: University of Delaware Press; London and Toronto: Associated University Presses) 166–77

Giuli 1999. Giuli, Paola, 'Tracing a Sisterhood: Corilla Olympica as Corinne's Unacknowledged Alter Ego', in *The Novel's Seductions. Staël's* Corinne *in Critical Enquiry*, ed. Karyna Szmurlo (Lewisburg: Bucknell University Press; London: Associated University Presses) 165–84

Gleckner 1997. Gleckner, Robert F., *Gray Agonistes: Thomas Gray and Masculine Friendship* (Baltimore and London: Johns Hopkins University Press)

Going 1976. Going, William T., *Scanty Plot of Ground. Studies in the Victorian Sonnet* (The Hague and Paris: Mouton)

Graver 1996. Graver, Bruce, 'Duncan Wu's *Wordsworth's Reading: 1770–1790*: A Supplementary List with Corrections', *Romanticism on the Net*, I (Feb.)

Greene 1996. Greene, Ellen (ed.), *Re-Reading Sappho: Reception and Transmission* (Berkeley: University of California Press)

Greer 1995. Greer, Germaine, *Slip-Shod Sibyls: Recognition, Rejection and the Woman Poet* (Harmondsworth: Penguin)

Haggerty 1992. Haggerty, George E., ' "The Voice of Nature" in Gray's *Elegy*', in *Homosexuality in Renaissance and Enlightenment England: Literary Representations in Historical Context*, ed. Claude S. Summers (New York, London, Norwood [Australia]: Haworth Press) 199–214

Hagstrum 1974. Hagstrum, Jean H., 'Gray's Sensibility', in *Fearful Joy: Papers from the Thomas Gray Bicentenary Conference at Carleton University*, ed. James Downey and Ben Jones (Montreal and London: McGill-Queen's University Press) 6–19

Hargreaves-Mawdsley 1967. Hargreaves-Mawdsley, W. N., *The English Della Cruscans and Their Time (1783–1828)* (The Hague: Nijhoff)

Harrison 1998. Harrison, Anthony H., *Victorian Poets and the Politics of Culture: Discourse and Ideology* (Charlottesville and London: University Press of Virginia)

Havens 1922. Havens, Raymond Dexter, *The Influence of Milton on English Poetry* (Cambridge, MA: Harvard University Press)

Hawley 1999. Hawley, Judith, 'Charlotte Smith's *Elegiac Sonnets*: Losses and Gains', in *Women's Poetry in the Enlightenment. The Making of a Canon, 1730–1820*, ed. Isobel Armstrong and Virginia Blain (Basingstoke: Macmillan – now Palgrave Macmillan) 184–98

Hayes 2000. Hayes, Julie Candler, 'Petrarch / Sade: Writing the Life', in *Representations of the Self from the Renaissance to Romanticism*, ed. Patrick Coleman, Jayne Lewis and Jill Kowalik (Cambridge: Cambridge University Press) 117–34

Homans 1990. Homans, Margaret, 'Keats Reading Women, Women Reading Keats', *Studies in Romanticism*, XXIX:3, 341–70

Howe 1947. Howe, Percival Presland, *The Life of William Hazlitt*, 2nd edn (London: Hamish Hamilton; 1st edn London: Secker, 1922)

Hunt 1971. Hunt, Bishop C., Jr, 'Wordsworth and Charlotte Smith', *The Wordsworth Circle*, I, 85–103

Hutchings 1995. Hutchings, W., 'Conversation with a Shadow: Thomas Gray's Latin Poems to Richard West', *Studies in Philology*, XCII:1 (Winter), 118–39

Jackson 1993. Jackson, J. R. de J., *Romantic Poetry by Women: A Bibliography, 1770–1835* (Oxford: Clarendon Press)

Johnson 1973. Johnson, Lee M., *Wordsworth and the Sonnet* (Copenhagen: Rosenkilde & Bagger)

Johnston 1998. Johnston, Kenneth R., *The Hidden Wordsworth: Poet, Lover, Rebel, Spy* (New York and London: Norton)

Jones 1984. Jones, Frederic J., 'Further Evidence of the Identity of Laura', *Italian Studies*, XXXIX, 27–46

Jones 1992. Jones, Frederic J., 'I rapporti tra la Laura de Sade e la Laura del Petrarca', *Italianistica*, XXI:2–3, 485–501

Jones 2000. Jones, Kathleen, *A Passionate Sisterhood: The Sisters, Wives and Daughters of the Lake Poets* (New York: St Martin's – now Palgrave Macmillan)

Jost 1982. Jost, François, 'Anatomy of an Ode: Shelley and the Sonnet Tradition', *Comparative Literature*, XXXIV, 223–46

Jung 2000. Jung, Sandro, 'Die Aesthetik homoerotischer Liebe bei Thomas Gray', *Forum Homosexualität und Literatur*, XXXVII, 103–11

Kennedy 1995. Kennedy, Deborah, 'Thorns and Roses: The Sonnets of Charlotte Smith', *Women's Writing*, II:1, 43–53

Kennedy 1983. Kennedy, Richard F., 'Byron and Petrarch', *The Byron Journal*, XI, 52–3

Klibansky 1981. Klibansky, Raymond, *The Continuity of the Platonic Tradition during the Middle Ages, with a new preface and four supplementary chapters*, together with *Plato's Parmenides in the Middle Ages and the Renaissance, with a new introductory preface* (München: Kraus-Thomson; 1st edns London: Warburg Institute, 1939 and 1941)

Kristeller 1965. Kristeller, Paul Oskar, *Eight Philosophers of the Italian Renaissance* (London: Chatto & Windus, 1st edn 1964)

Labbe 1994. Labbe, Jacqueline M., 'Selling One's Sorrows: Charlotte Smith, Mary Robinson, and the Marketing of Poetry', *The Wordsworth Circle*, XXV:2 (Spring), 68–71

Labbe 2000. Labbe, Jacqueline M., *The Romantic Paradox: Love, Violence and the Uses of Romance, 1760–1830* (Basingstoke: Palgrave Macmillan)

Labbe 2003. Labbe, Jacqueline M., *Charlotte Smith: Romanticism, Poetry and Culture of Gender* (Manchester and New York: Manchester University Press)

Leighton 1992. Leighton, Angela, *Victorian Women Poets: Writing against the Heart* (New York: Harvester Wheatsheaf)

Lenz 1982. Lenz, Bernd, ' "Let the Muse Be Free": Tradition and Experiment in the Sonnets of John Keats', *Anglistentag*, 177–96

Lipking 1988. Lipking, Lawrence, *Abandoned Women and Poetic Tradition* (Chicago and London: University of Chicago Press)

Lockridge 1977. Lockridge, Laurence S., *Coleridge the Moralist* (Ithaca and London: Cornell University Press)

Luria and Tayler 1977. Luria, Gina, and Irene Tayler, 'Gender and Genre: Women in British Romantic Literature', in *What Manner of Woman: Essays on English and American Life and Literature*, ed. Marlene Springer (New York: New York University Press) 98–123

Luther 1994. Luther, Susan, 'A Stranger Minstrel: Coleridge's Mrs Robinson', *Studies in Romanticism*, XXXIII, 391–409

Mack 2000. Mack, Robert L., *Thomas Gray: A Life* (New Haven and London: Yale University Press)

Manning 1982. Manning, Peter J., 'Wordsworth and Gray's Sonnet on the Death of West', *Studies in English Literature 1500–1900*, XXII:3 (Summer), 505–18

Marsh 1994. Marsh, Jan, *Christina Rossetti: A Literary Biography* (London: Cape)

Martin 1982. Martin, Philip W., *Byron: A Poet before His Public* (Cambridge: Cambridge University Press)

Mays 1993. Mays, James C. C., 'Coleridge's "Love": "All He Can Manage, More than He Could"', in *Coleridge's Visionary Languages* (Woodbridge: Boydell Press) 49–66

MacCarthy 2002. MacCarthy, Fiona, *Byron: Life and Legend* (London: Murray)

McCarthy 1997. McCarthy, B. Eugene, *Thomas Gray: The Progress of a Poet* (Madison, NJ: Fairleigh Dickinson University Press; London: Associated University Presses)

McGann 1995. McGann, Jerome J., 'Mary Robinson and the Myth of Sappho', *Modern Language Quarterly*, LVI:1, 55–76

McGann 1998. McGann, Jerome J., *The Poetics of Sensibility: A Revolution in Literary Style* (Oxford: Clarendon Press, 1st edn 1996)

McGann 2002. McGann, Jerome J., *Byron and Romanticism*, ed. James Soderholm (Cambridge: Cambridge University Press)

McKillop 1924. McKillop, Alan D., 'Some Details of the Sonnet Revival', *Modern Language Notes*, XXXIX, 438–40

Mell 1968. Mell, Donald C., 'Form as Meaning in Augustan Elegy: a Reading of Thomas Gray's "Sonnet on the Death of Richard West"', *Papers on Language and Literature*, IV:2 (Spring), 131–43

Mellor 1988. Mellor, Anne K. (ed.), *Romanticism and Feminism* (Bloomington and Indianapolis: Indiana University Press)

Mellor 1993. Mellor, Anne K., *Romanticism and Gender* (New York and London: Routledge)

Mellor 2000a. Mellor, Anne K., 'Mary Robinson and the Scripts of Female Sexuality', in *Representations of the Self from the Renaissance to Romanticism*, ed. Patrick Coleman, Jayne Lewis and Jill Kowalik (Cambridge: Cambridge University Press) 230–59

Mellor 2000b. Mellor, Anne K., *Mothers of the Nation: Women's Political Writing in England, 1780–1830* (Bloomington and Indianapolis: Indiana University Press)

Mergenthal 1997. Mergenthal, Silvia, 'Charlotte Smith and the Romantic Sonnet Revival', in *Feminist Contributions to the Literary Canon: Setting Standards of Taste*, ed. Susanne Fendler (Mellen: Lewiston, Queenston and Lampeter) 65–79

Mermin 1989. Mermin, Dorothy, *Elizabeth Barrett Browning* (Chicago and London: University of Chicago Press)

Meyenberg 2005. Meyenberg, Roger, *Capel Lofft and the English Sonnet Tradition 1770–1815* (Tübingen: Francke)

Moers 1976. Moers, Ellen, *Literary Women* (Garden City, NY: Doubleday)

Moore 2000. Moore, Mary B., *Desiring Voices* (Carbondale and Edwardsville: Southern Illinois University Press)

Morici 1889. Morici, Medardo, *Giustina Perotti-Levi e le petrarchiste marchigiane* (Florence: Ufficio della "Rassegna Nazionale")

Morton 1905. Morton, Edward Payson, 'The English Sonnet (1658–1750)', *Modern Language Notes*, XX:4 (Apr.), 97–8

Most 1996. Most, Glenn W., 'Reflecting Sappho', in Greene 1996, 11–35

Mouret 1976. Mouret, François J.-L., *Les traducteurs anglais de Pétrarque 1754–1798* (Paris: Didier)

Mowl 1998. Mowl, Timothy, *William Beckford: Composing for Mozart* (London: Murray)

Myers 2002. Myers, Anne, 'Charlotte Smith's Androgynous Sonnets', *European Romantic Review*, XIII:4 (Dec.), 379–82

Oliver 1932. Oliver, J. M., *The Life of William Beckford* (London: Oxford University Press)

Ong 1962. Ong, Walter, *The Barbarian Within and Other Fugitive Essays and Studies* (New York: Macmillan)

Page 1994. Page, Judith W., *Wordsworth and the Cultivation of Women* (Berkeley: University of California Press)

Pascoe 1995. Pascoe, Judith, 'Mary Robinson and the Literary Marketplace', in *Romantic Women Writers: Voices and Countervoices*, ed. Paula R. Feldman and Theresa M. Kelley (Hanover, NH, and London: University Press of New England) 252–68

Pascoe 1997. Pascoe, Judith, *Romantic Theatricality: Gender, Poetry and Spectatorship* (Ithaca, NY, and London: Cornell University Press)

Peel and Sweet 1999. Peel, Ellen, and Nanora Sweet, '*Corinne* and the Woman as Poet in England: Hemans, Jewsbury, and Barrett Browning', in *The Novel's Seductions: Staël's Corinne in Critical Enquiry*, ed. Karyna Szmurlo (Lewisburg: Bucknell University Press; London: Associated University Presses) 204–20

Perotti 1999. Perotti, Giuseppe, *Memorie storiche dei Perotti, conti dell'Isola Centipera, nobili di Sassoferrato e di Perugia*, ed. Ferruccio Bestini (Sassoferrato: Istituto Internazionale di Studi Piceni)

Peterson 1994. Peterson, Linda H., 'Becoming an Author: Mary Robinson's *Memoirs* and the Origins of the Woman Artist's Autobiography', in *Re-Visioning Romanticism: British Women Writers, 1776–1837*, ed. Carol Shiner Wilson and Joel Haefner (Philadelphia: University of Pennsylvania Press) 36–50

Peterson 1999. Peterson, Linda H., 'Rewriting *A History of the Lyre*: Letitia Landon, Elizabeth Barrett Browning and the (Re)Construction of the Nineteenth-Century Woman Poet', in *Women's Poetry, Late Romantic to Late Victorian: Gender and Genre, 1830–1890*, ed. Isobel Armstrong and Virginia Blain (Basingstoke: Macmillan – now Palgrave Macmillan) 115–32

Pinch 1996. Pinch, Adela, *Strange Fits of Passion: Epistemologies of Emotion, Hume to Austen* (Stanford: Stanford University Press)

Pite 1994. Pite, Ralph, *The Circle of Our Vision: Dante's Presence in English Romantic Poetry* (Oxford: Clarendon Press)

Raycroft 1998. Raycroft, Brent, 'From Charlotte Smith to Nehemiah Higginbottom: Revising the Genealogy of the Early Romantic Sonnet', *European Romantic Review*, IX:3 (Summer), 363–92

Raysor 1929. Raysor, Thomas M., 'Coleridge and "Asra"', *Studies in Philology*, XXVI (July), 305–24

Reesman 2002. Reesman, Linda L., 'Coleridge and the "Learned Ladies"', *The Coleridge Bulletin*, XX (Winter), 122–8

Robinson 1976. Robinson, Charles, *Shelley and Byron: The Snake and Eagle Wreathed in Fight* (Baltimore and London: Johns Hopkins University Press)

Robinson 1995. Robinson, Daniel, 'Reviving the Sonnet: Women Romantic Poets and the Sonnet Claim', *European Romantic Review*, VI:1 (Summer), 98–127

Robinson 2000b. Robinson, Daniel, ' "Work Without Hope": Anxiety and Embarrassment in Coleridge's Sonnets', *Studies in Romanticism*, XXXIX (Spring), 81–110

Robinson 2003. Robinson, Daniel, 'Elegiac Sonnets: Charlotte Smith's Formal Paradoxy', *Papers on Language & Literature*, XXXIX:2 (Spring), n.p.

Roe 1953. Roe, Ivan, *Shelley: The Last Phase* (London: Hutchinson)

Rogers 1994. Rogers, Katharine M., 'Romantic Aspirations, Restricted Possibilities: The Novels of Charlotte Smith', in *Re-Visioning Romanticism: British Women Writers, 1776–1837*, ed. Carol Shiner Wilson and Joel Haefner (Philadelphia: University of Pennsylvania Press) 72–88

Ross 1988. Ross, Marlon B., *The Contours of Masculine Desire: Romanticism and the Rise of Women's Poetry* (New York and Oxford: Oxford University Press)

Rutherford 1961. Rutherford, Andrew, *Byron: A Critical Study* (Edinburgh: Oliver & Boyd)

Schneider 1952. Schneider, Elisabeth, *The Aesthetics of William Hazlitt: A Study of the Philosophical Basis of his Criticism* (Philadelphia: University of Pennsylvania Press, 1st edn 1933)

Schor 1994. Schor, Esther, *Bearing the Dead: The British Culture of Mourning from the Enlightenment to Victoria* (Princeton: Princeton University Press)

Schulz 1964. Schulz, Max E., 'The Wry Vision of Coleridge's Love Poetry', *The Personalist*, XLV, 214–16

Schulze 1988. Schulze, Earl, 'Allegory against Allegory: "The Triumph of Life"', *Studies in Romanticism*, XXVII, 31–62

Sharp 1977. Sharp, Phillip David, *Poetry in Progress: Elizabeth Barrett Browning and the Sonnets Notebook*, PhD Dissertation (Louisiana State University)

Sheats 2002. Sheats, Paul D., 'Young Coleridge and the Idea of Lyric', *The Coleridge Bulletin*, XX (Winter), 14–31

Simpson 2003. Simpson, Erik, ' "The Minstrels of Modern Italy": Improvisation Comes to Britain', *European Romantic Review*, XIV:3 (Sept.), 345–67

Sloan 1986. Sloan, Kim, *Alexander and John Robert Cozens: The Poetry of Landscape* (New Haven and London: Yale University Press)

Spacks 1976. Spacks, Patricia Meyer, *Imagining a Self: Autobiography and Novel in Eighteenth-Century England* (Cambridge: Harvard University Press)

Spitzer 1955. Spitzer, Leo, 'The Problem of Latin Renaissance Poetry', *Studies in the Renaissance*, II, 118–38

Stanton 1987. Stanton, Judith Phillips, 'Charlotte Smith's "Literary Business": Income, Patronage, and Indigence', *The Age of Johnson: A Scholarly Annual*, ed. Paul J. Korshin (New York: AMS Press) 375–401

Stawell 1914. Stawell, F. Melian, 'Shelley's *The Triumph of Life*', *Essays and Studies*, V, 104–31

Stephenson 1989. Stephenson, Glennis, *Elizabeth Barrett Browning and the Poetry of Love* (Ann Arbor and London: UMI Research Press)

Stephenson 1995. Stephenson, Glennis, *Letitia Landon: The Woman behind L.E.L.*, (Manchester and New York: Manchester University Press)

Stone 1995. Stone, Marjorie, *Elizabeth Barrett Browning* (Basingstoke: Macmillan)

Stone 1999. Stone, Marjorie, ' "*Monna Innominata*" and *Sonnets from the Portuguese*. Sonnet Tradition and Spiritual Trajectories', in *The Culture of Christina Rossetti: Female Poetics and Victorian Contexts*, ed. Mary Arsenau, Anthony H. Harrison and Lorraine Janzen Kooistra (Athens: Ohio University Press) 46–74

Stones and Strachan 1999. Stones, Graeme, and John Strachan (eds), *Parodies of the Romantic Age*, 5 vols (London: Pickering & Chatto)

Taussig 2000. Taussig, Gurion, ' "Lavish Promises": Coleridge, Charles Lamb and Charles Lloyd, 1794–1798', *Romanticism*, VI:1, 78–97

Taylor 2000. Taylor, Anya, 'Romantic *Improvvisatori*: Coleridge, L.E.L., and the Difficulties of Loving', *Philological Quarterly*, LXXIX:4 (Fall), 501–22

Tissoni 1993. Tissoni, Roberto, *Il commento ai classici nel Sette e nell'Ottocento (Dante e Petrarca)*, rev. edn (Padova: Antenore)

Tomory 1989. Tomory, Peter, 'The Fortunes of Sappho: 1770–1850', in *Rediscovering Hellenism: The Hellenic Inheritance and the English Imagination*, ed. G. W. Clarke (Cambridge: Cambridge University Press) 121–35

Trinkaus 1979. Trinkaus, Charles, *The Poet as Philosopher: Petrarch and the Formation of Renaissance Consciousness* (New Haven and London: Yale University Press)

Ty 1995. Ty, Eleanor, 'Engendering a Female Subject: Mary Robinson's (Re)Presentations of the Self', *English Studies in Canada*, XXI:4 (Dec.), 407–31

Vargo 1995. Vargo, Lisa, 'The Claims of "Real Life and Manners": Coleridge and Mary Robinson', *The Wordsworth Circle*, XXVI, 134–7

Vasoli 1968. Vasoli, Cesare, *La dialettica e la retorica dell'Umanesimo. 'Invenzione' e 'Metodo' nella cultura del XV e XVI secolo* (Milan: Feltrinelli)

Vassallo 1984. Vassallo, Peter, *Byron: The Italian Literary Influence* (London: Macmillan)

Vassallo 1991. Vassallo, Peter, 'From Petrarch to Dante: The Discourse of Disenchantment in Shelley's *The Triumph of Life*', *Journal of Anglo-Italian Studies*, I, 102–10

Venuti 1995. Venuti, Lawrence, *The Translator's Invisibility: A History of Translation* (London and New York: Routledge)

Wagner 1996. Wagner, Jennifer Ann, *A Moment's Monument: Revisionary Poetics and the Nineteenth-Century English Sonnet* (Cranbury, NJ, and London: Associated University Presses)

Watson 1967. Watson, George, *The English Petrarchans: A Critical Bibliography of the Canzoniere* (London: The Warburg Institute, University of London)

Weinberg 1991. Weinberg, Alan M., *Shelley's Italian Experience* (Basingstoke and London: Macmillan)

Whalley 1950. Whalley, George, *Samuel Taylor Coleridge: Library Cormorant. A Study of Purpose and Pattern in His Reading*, PhD thesis, 2 vols (University of London, King's College)

White 1998. White, Daniel E., 'Autobiography and Elegy: The Early Romantic Poetics of Gray and Charlotte Smith', in *Early Romantics: Perspectives in British Poetry from*

Pope to Wordsworth, ed. Thomas Woodman (Basingstoke: Macmillan; New York: St Martin's) 57–69

White 1940. White, Newman Ivey, *Shelley*, 2 vols (London: Secker & Warburg)

Whiting 1963. Whiting, George W., 'Charlotte Smith, Keats and the Nightingale', *Keats-Shelley Journal*, XII (Winter), 4–8

Whitla 1987. Whitla, William, 'Questioning the Convention: Christina Rossetti's Sonnet Sequence *Monna Innominata*', in *The Achievements of Christina Rossetti*, ed. D. A. Kent (Ithaca, NY: Cornell University Press) 82–131

Wilkes 1999. Wilkes, Joanne, *Lord Byron and Madame de Staël: Born for Opposition* (Aldershot: Ashgate)

Wilkins 1955. Wilkins, Ernest Hatch, *Studies in the Life and Works of Petrarch* (Cambridge, MA: Mediaeval Academy of America)

Wilkins 1985. Wilkins, Ernest Hatch, *Vita del Petrarca e La formazione del 'Canzoniere'* (Milan: Feltrinelli, 1st edn 1964) (orig. edns *Life of Petrarch*, Chicago: University of Chicago Press, 1961; *The Making of the 'Canzoniere'*, Rome: Edizioni di Storia e di Letteratura, 1951)

Wolfson 1997. Wolfson, Susan J., *Formal Charges: The Shaping of Poetry in British Romanticism* (Stanford, CA: Stanford University Press)

Zillman 1939. Zillman, Lawrence John, *John Keats and the Sonnet Tradition: A Critical and Comparative Study* (Los Angeles: Lymanhouse)

Zimmerman 1999. Zimmerman, Sarah M., *Romanticism, Lyricism, and History* (Albany: State University of New York Press)

Zuccato 1996. Zuccato, Edoardo, *Coleridge in Italy* (Cork: Cork University Press)

Index